STOP!

This is the back of the book.
You wouldn't want to spoil a great ending!

This book is printed "manga-style," in the authentic Japanese right-to-left format. Since none of the artwork has been flipped or altered, readers get to experience the story just as the creator intended. You've been asking for it, so TOKYOPOP® delivered: authentic, hot-off-the-press, and far more fun!

DIRECTIONS

If this is your first time reading manga-style, here's a quick guide to help you understand how it works.

It's easy... just start in the top right panel and follow the numbers. Have fun, and look for more 100% authentic manga from TOKYOPOP®!

D1052423

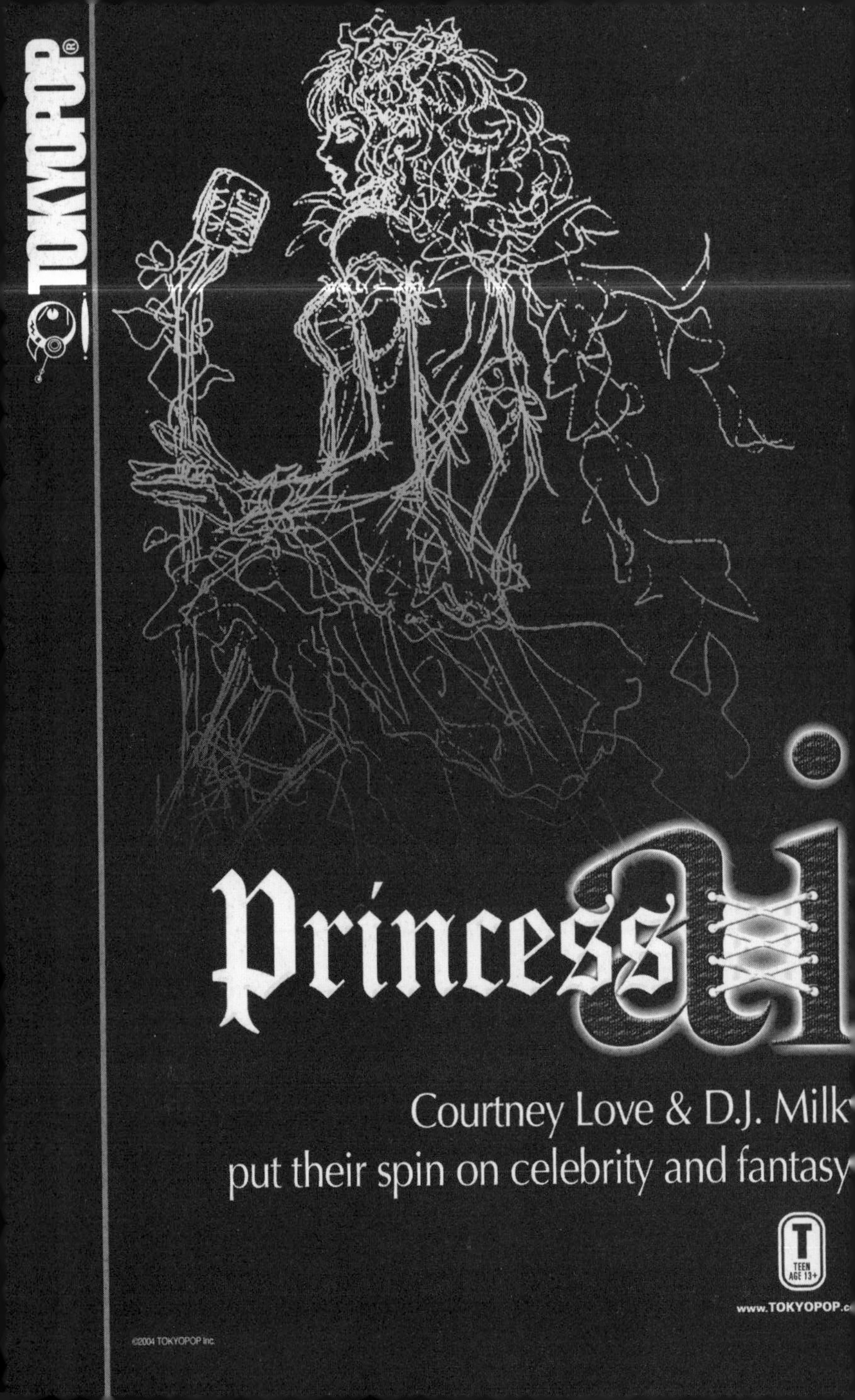
TOKYOPOP®
Princess ai
Courtney Love & D.J. Milk
put their spin on celebrity and fantasy
T
TEEN
AGE 13+
www.TOKYOPOP.c
©2004 TOKYOPOP Inc.

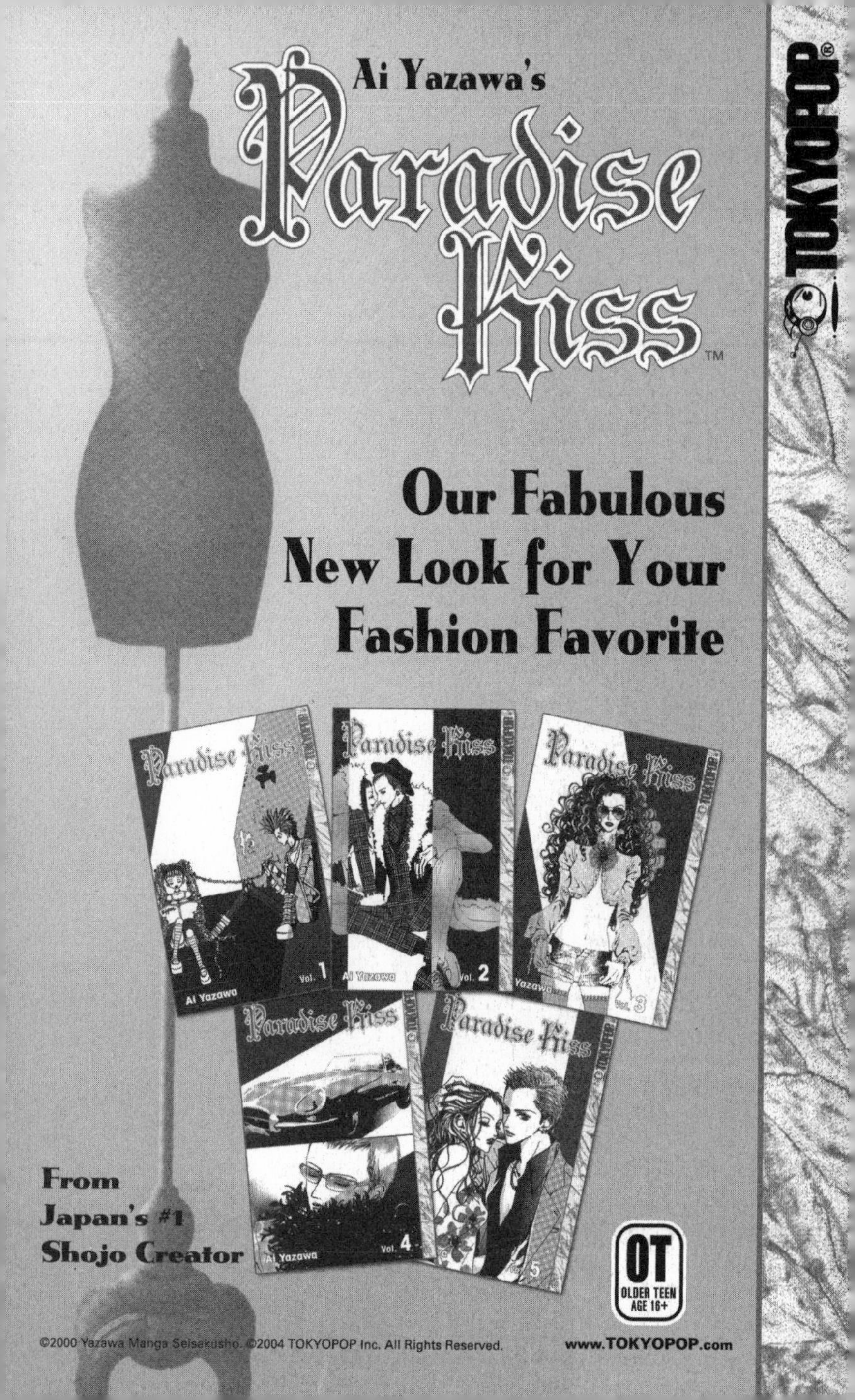
Ai Yazawa's
Paradise Kiss™
Our Fabulous
New Look for Your
Fashion Favorite
From
Japan's #1
Shojo Creator
OT
OLDER TEEN
AGE 16+
©2000 Yazawa Manga Seisakusho. ©2004 TOKYOPOP Inc. All Rights Reserved.
www.TOKYOPOP.com
TOKYOPOP®

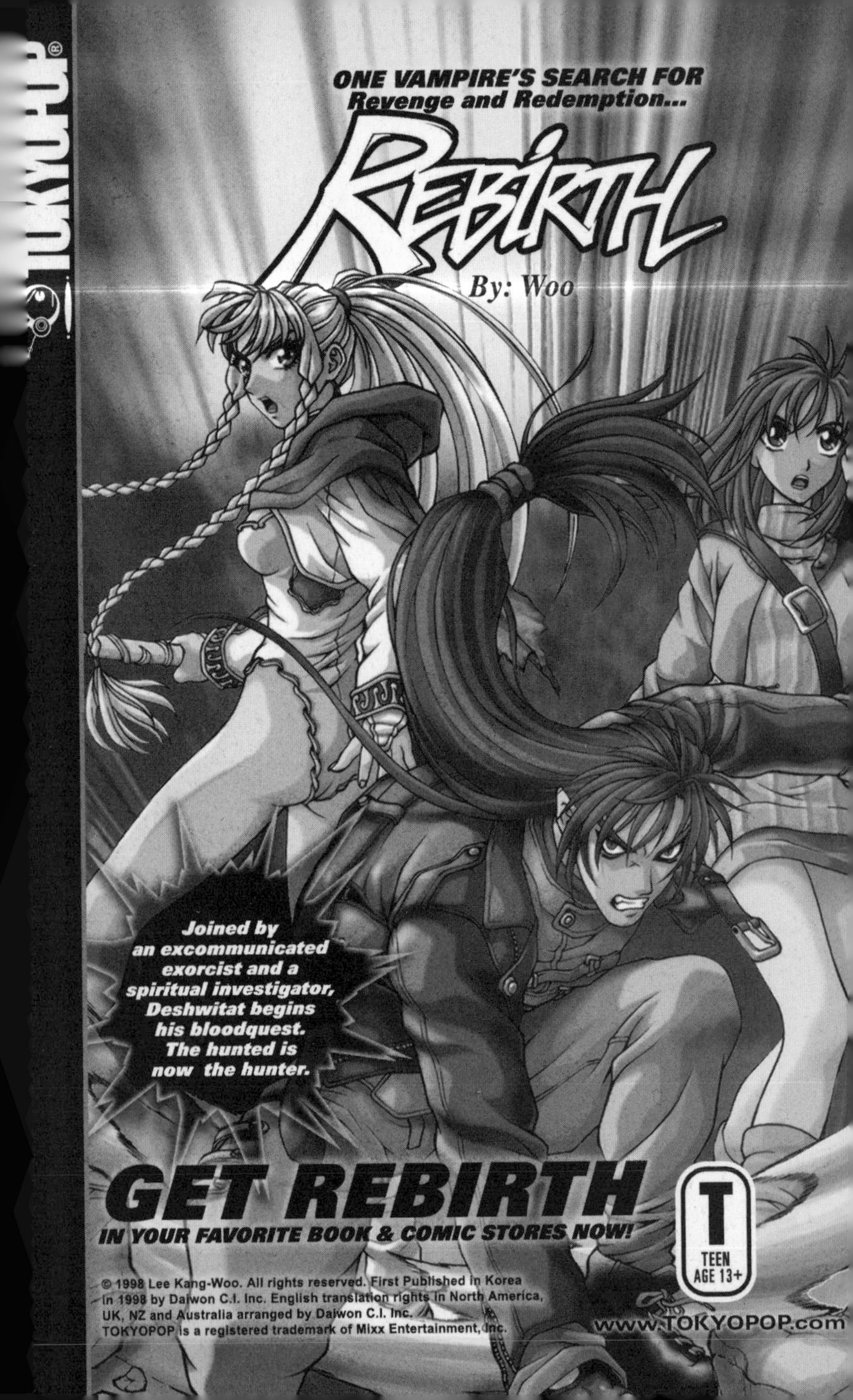
TOKYOPOP
ONE VAMPIRE'S SEARCH FOR
Revenge and Redemption...
REBIRTH
By: Woo
Joined by an excommunicated exorcist and a spiritual investigator, Deshwitat begins his bloodquest. The hunted is now the hunter.
GET REBIRTH
IN YOUR FAVORITE BOOK & COMIC STORES NOW!
T
TEEN
AGE 13+
© 1998 Lee Kang-Woo. All rights reserved. First Published in Korea in 1998 by Daiwon C.I. Inc. English translation rights in North America, UK, NZ and Australia arranged by Daiwon C.I. Inc.
TOKYOPOP is a registered trademark of Mixx Entertainment, Inc.
www.TOKYOPOP.com

THE DEMON

ORORON

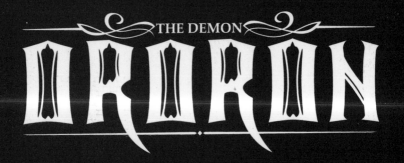

THE DEMON
ORORON

VOLUME 2

BY HAKASE MIZUKI

LOS ANGELES • TOKYO • LONDON • HAMBURG

Translator - Tomoko Kamimoto
English Adaptation - Josh Dysart
Associate Editor - Troy Lewter
Retouch and Lettering - Keiko Okabe
Cover Layout - Ray Makowski

Editor - Luis Reyes
Digital Imaging Manager - Chris Buford
Pre-Press Manager - Antonio DePietro
Production Managers - Jennifer Miller, Mutsumi Miyazaki
Art Director - Matt Alford
Managing Editor - Jill Freshney
VP of Production - Ron Klamert
President & C.O.O. - John Parker
Publisher & C.E.O. - Stuart Levy

E-mail: info@TOKYOPOP.com
Come visit us online at www.TOKYOPOP.com

A  Manga

TOKYOPOP Inc.
5900 Wilshire Blvd. Suite 2000
Los Angeles, CA 90036

The Demon Ororon Vol. 2

ISBN: 1-59182-726-4

First TOKYOPOP printing: June 2004

10 9 8 7 6 5 4 3 2 1

Printed in the USA

THE DEMON ORORON

THE STORY THUS FAR

CHIAKI, THE OFFSPRING OF A MORTAL WOMAN AND A RENEGADE ANGEL, LIVES A HAPPY BUT STRANGE EXISTENCE SHARING A HOUSE WITH A HIP, FORLORN DEMON NAMED ORORON, HIS STYLISH BROTHER OTHELLO, THEIR HELLISH HOUSEKEEPER AND VARIOUS ASSORTED MONSTERS (WHO LOOK A LOT MORE LIKE TEEN SLACKERS THAN CREATURES THAT GO BUMP IN THE NIGHT).

CHIAKI AND ORORON, BOTH DESPERATE FOR LOVE IN A CRUEL UNIVERSE, HAVE PROMISED ETERNAL FRIENDSHIP TO ONE ANOTHER, BUT THEIR PACT IS CONSTANTLY TESTED AS THEY STRUGGLE TO FIND COMMON GROUND BETWEEN CHIAKI'S ANGELIC NATURE AND ORORON'S DEVILISH DISPOSITION.

TO MAKE THINGS WORSE, IT SEEMS ORORON HAS LIED ABOUT HIS HAVING A HUMBLE STATION IN HELL. HE'S NOTHING LESS THAN THE WAYWARD KING OF THE UNDERWORLD, PLAYING ETERNAL HOOKY ON EARTH TO STAY WITH CHIAKI. NOW, AN ENORMOUS BOUNTY HAS BEEN PLACED ON ORORON'S HEAD, SENDING ALL OF HADES INTO A HUNT FOR THE RECREANT KING.

WHEN LAST WE LEFT OUR MISMATCHED TRIBE, A SUPER-NATURAL SOLDIER OF FORTUNE, SYANO, AND HIS TEAM OF ASSASSINS HAD ATTACKED ORORON. CHIAKI GOT CAUGHT UP IN THE BATTLE. AS WE PICK UP OUR NARRATIVE, ORORON HAS SUFFERED A DEVASTATING WOUND AND CHIAKI HAS BEEN CAPTURED.

CAUGHT UP? COOL. LET'S GO!

❧ CONTENTS ❧

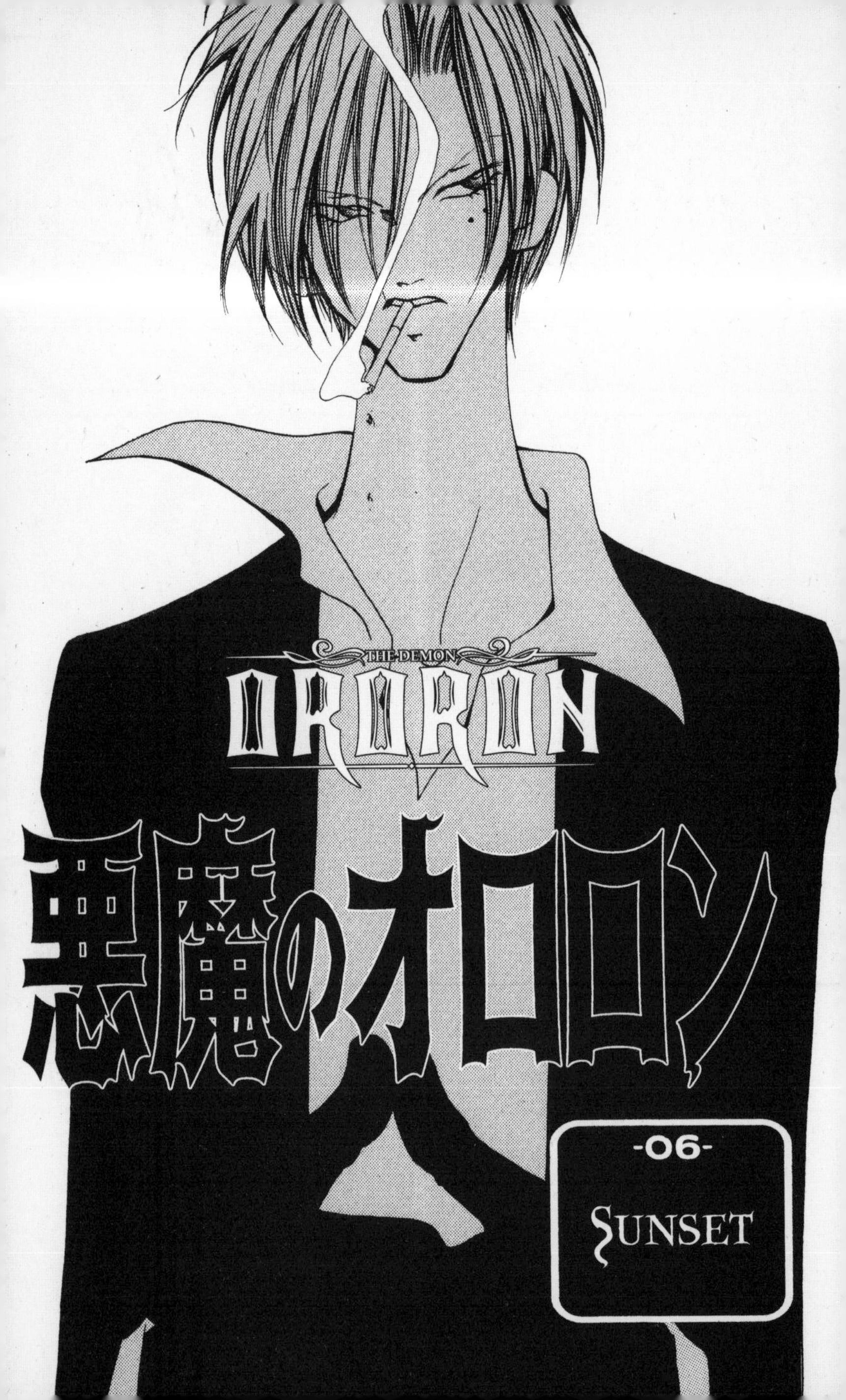
THE DEMON
ORORON
悪魔のオロロン
-06-
SUNSET

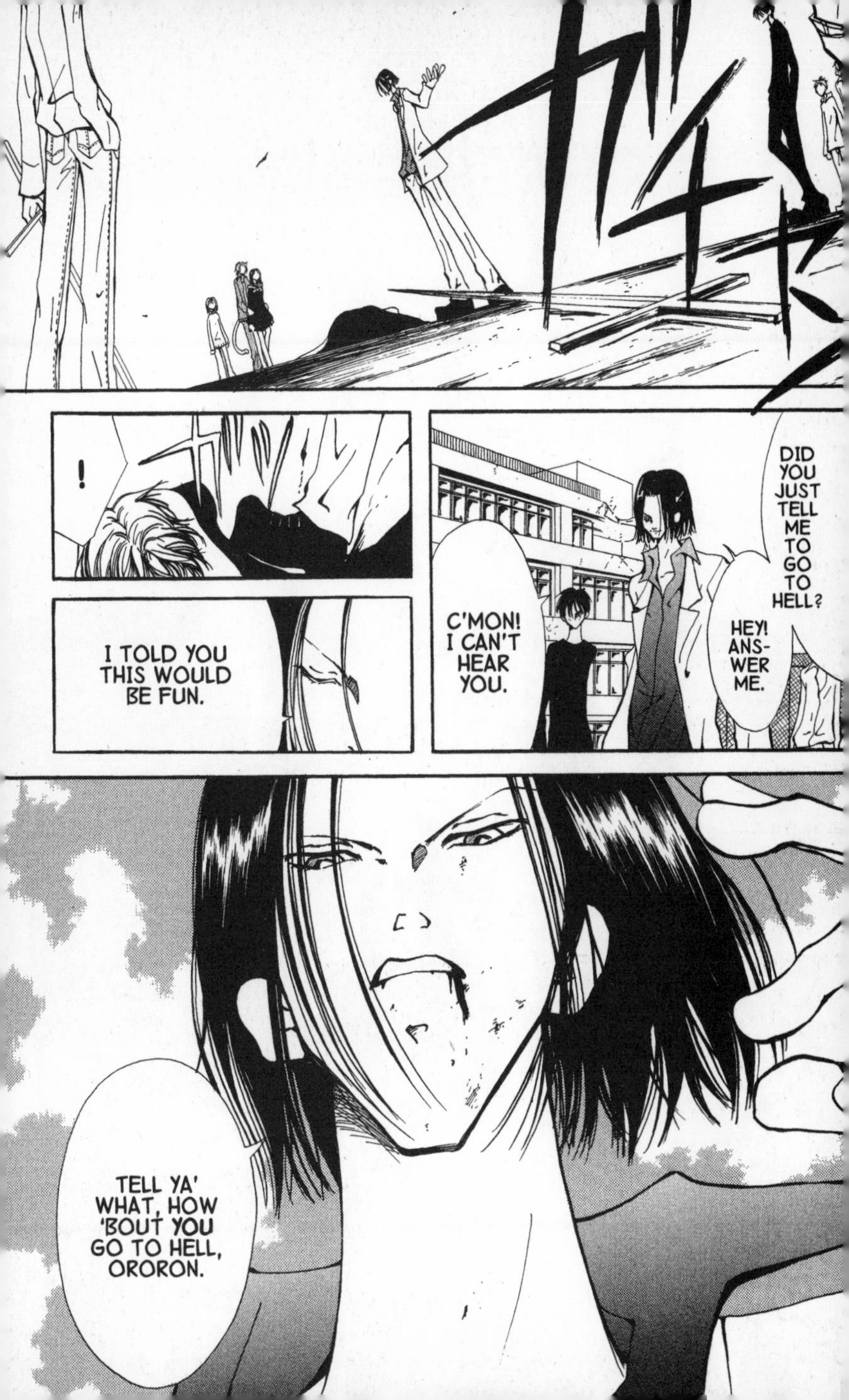
DID YOU JUST TELL ME TO GO TO HELL?
HEY! ANSWER ME.
C'MON! I CAN'T HEAR YOU.
!
I TOLD YOU THIS WOULD BE FUN.
TELL YA' WHAT, HOW 'BOUT YOU GO TO HELL, ORORON.

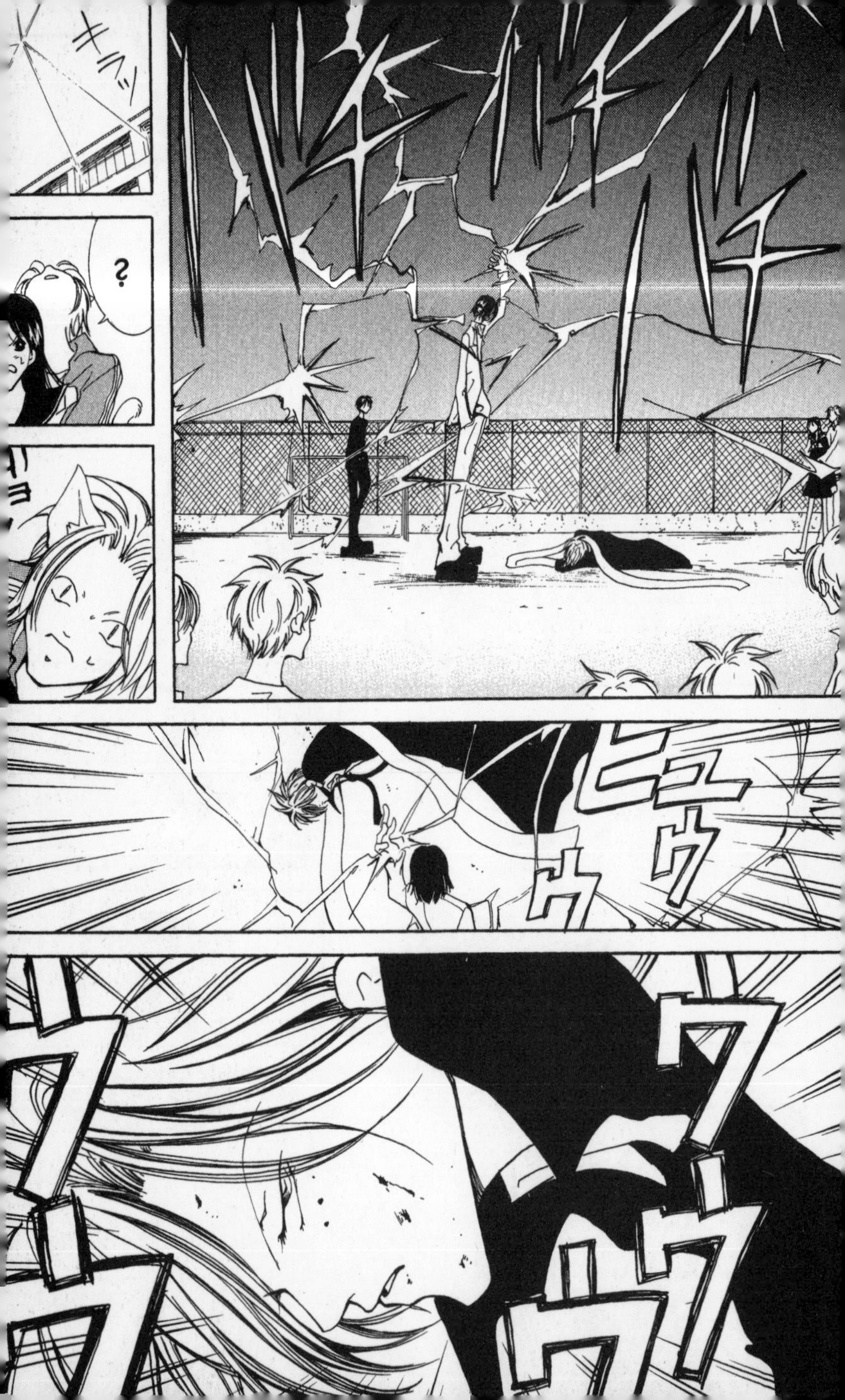
バキバキバキ
キラッ
?
ヒュウゥ
ウウウ

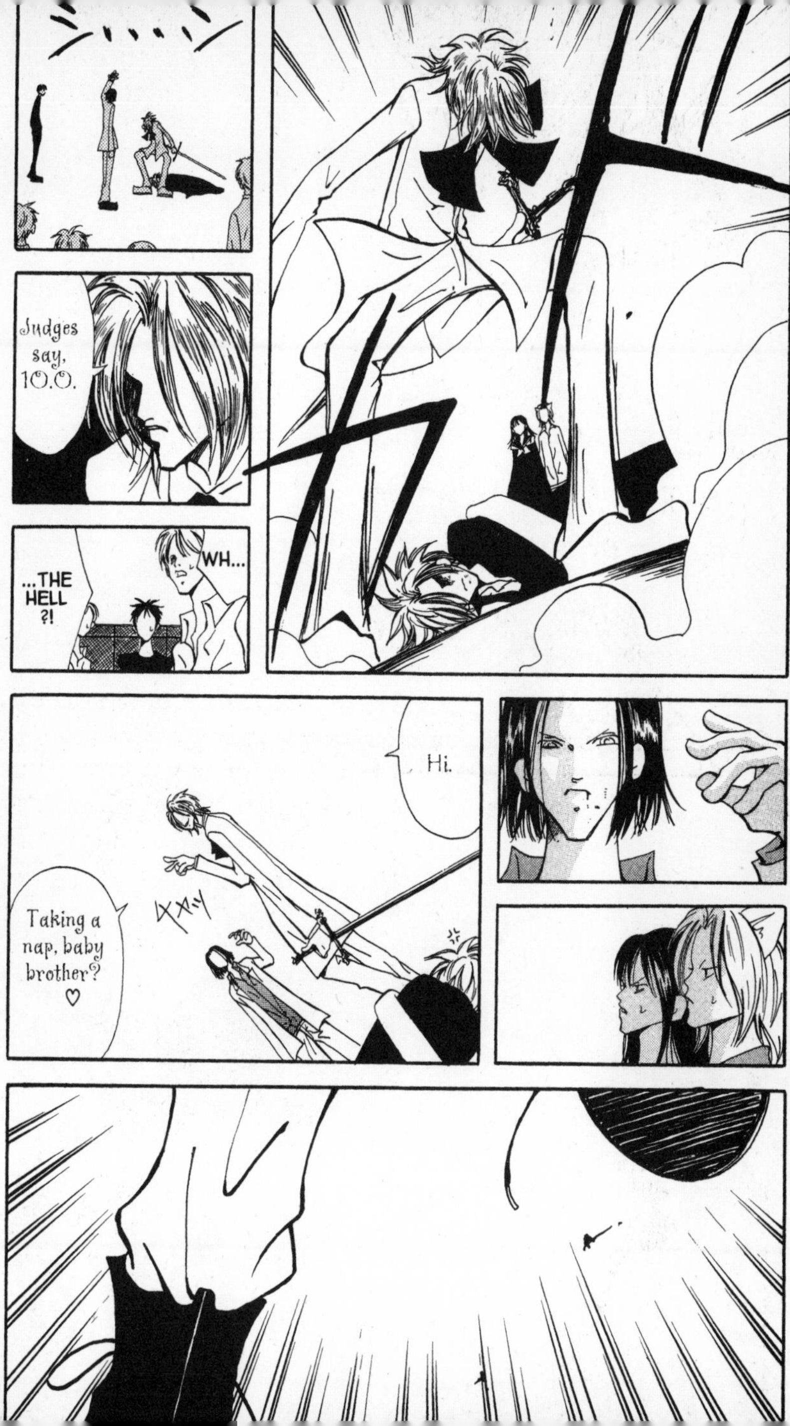
Judges say, 10.0.
WH...
...THE HELL ?!
Hi.
Taking a nap, baby brother? ♡

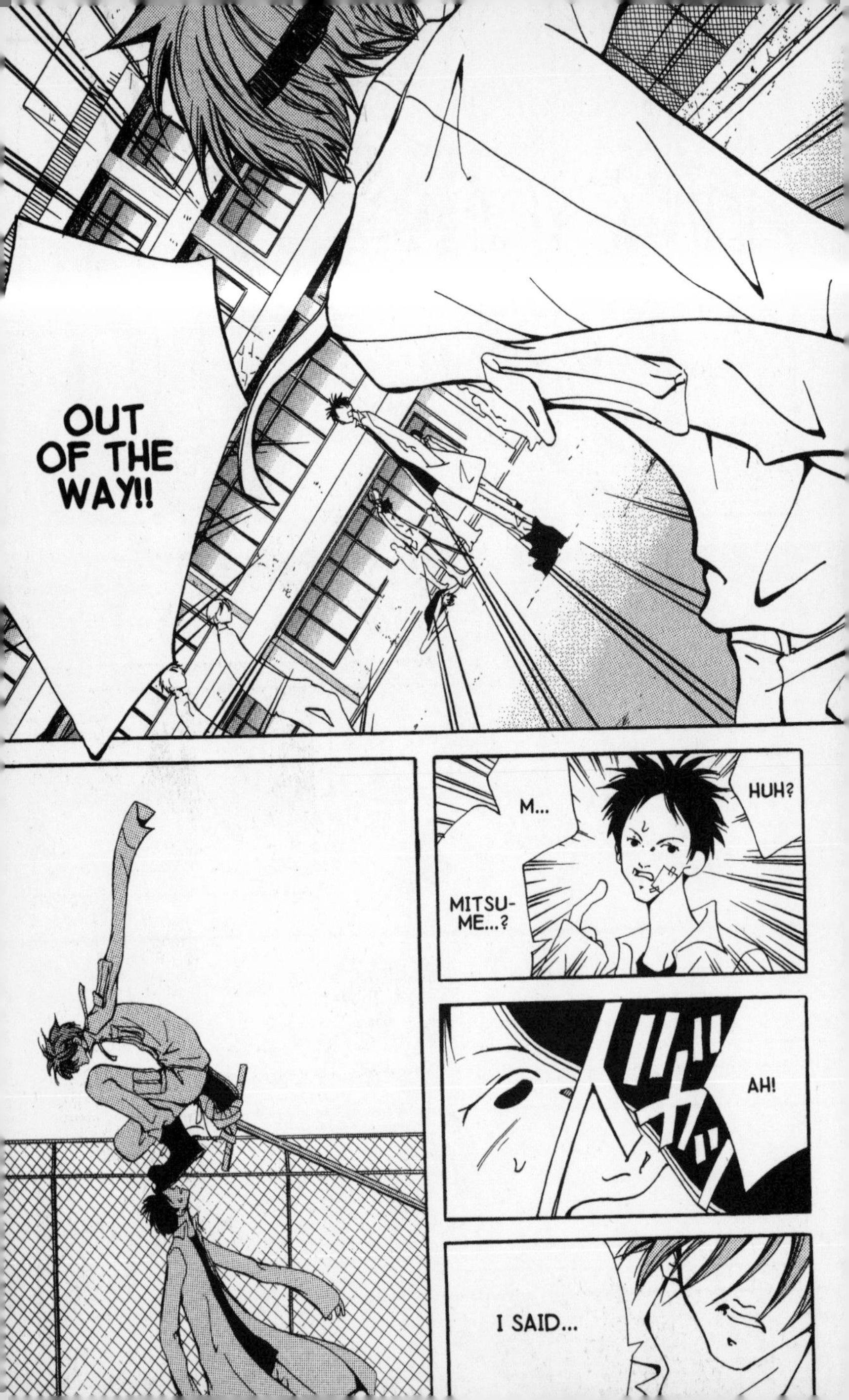
OUT OF THE WAY!!
HUH?
M...
MITSU-ME...?
AH!
I SAID...

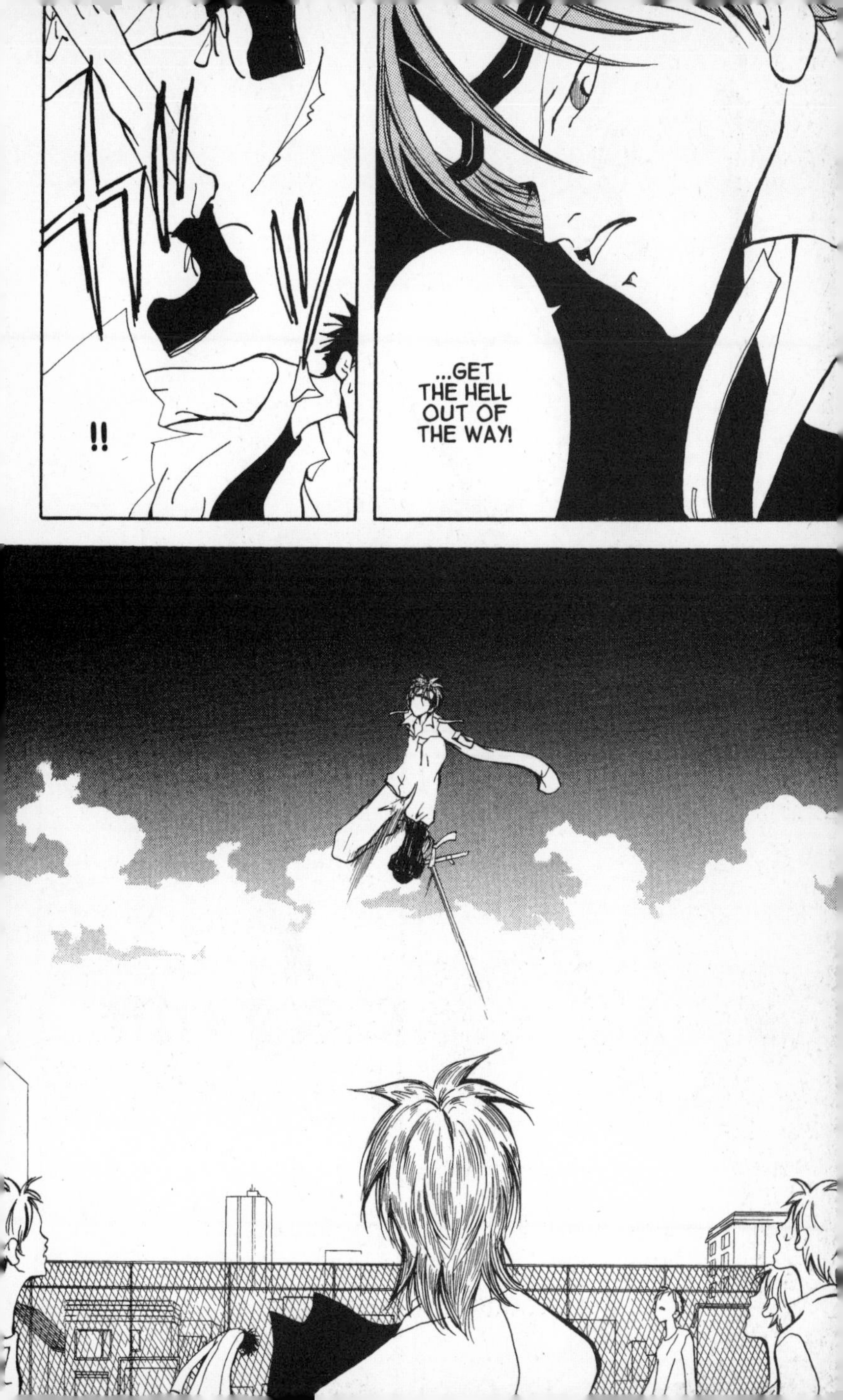
...GET THE HELL OUT OF THE WAY!
!!

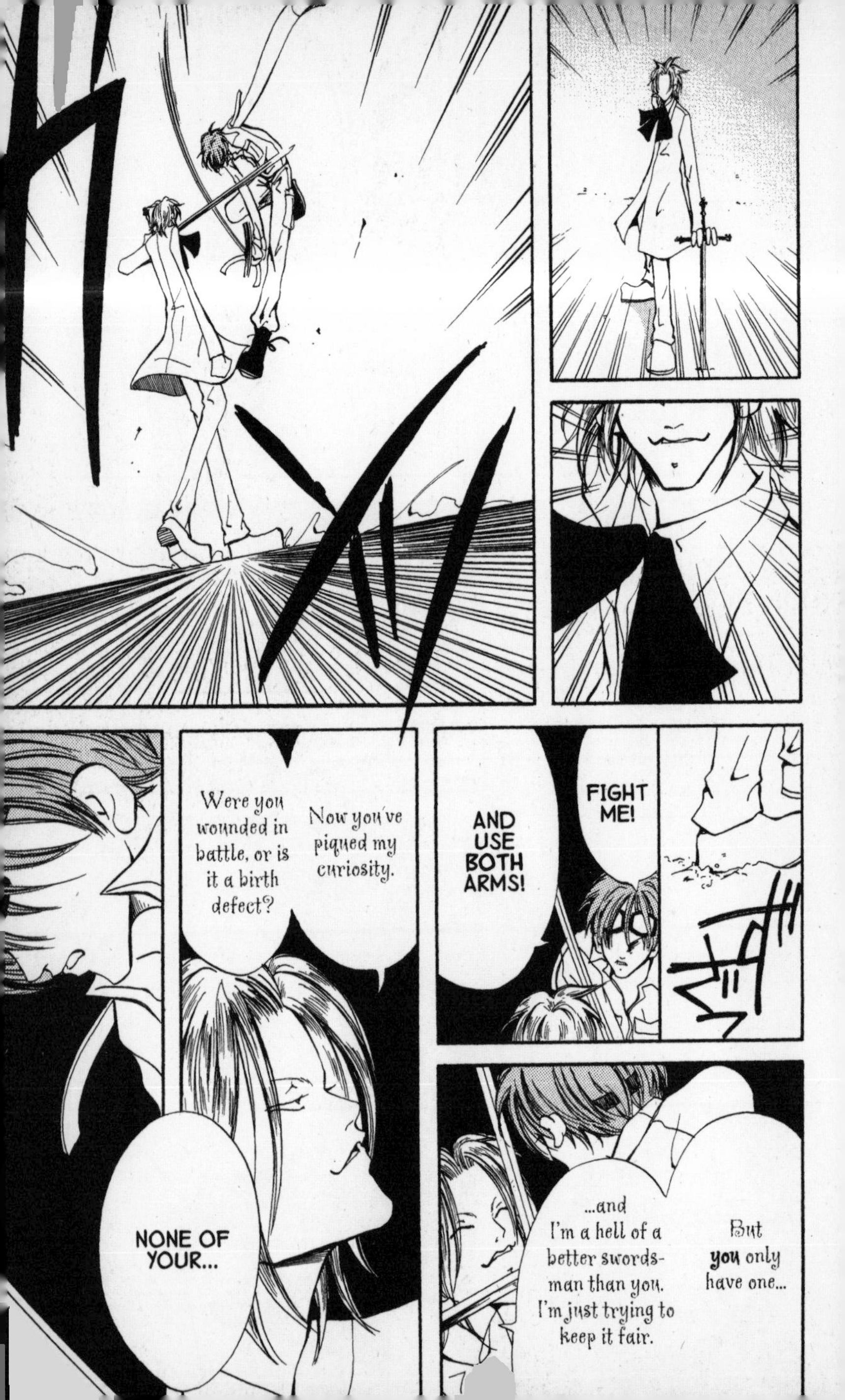
FIGHT ME!
AND USE BOTH ARMS!
But you only have one...
...and I'm a hell of a better swords-man than you. I'm just trying to keep it fair.
Now you've piqued my curiosity.
Were you wounded in battle, or is it a birth defect?
NONE OF YOUR...

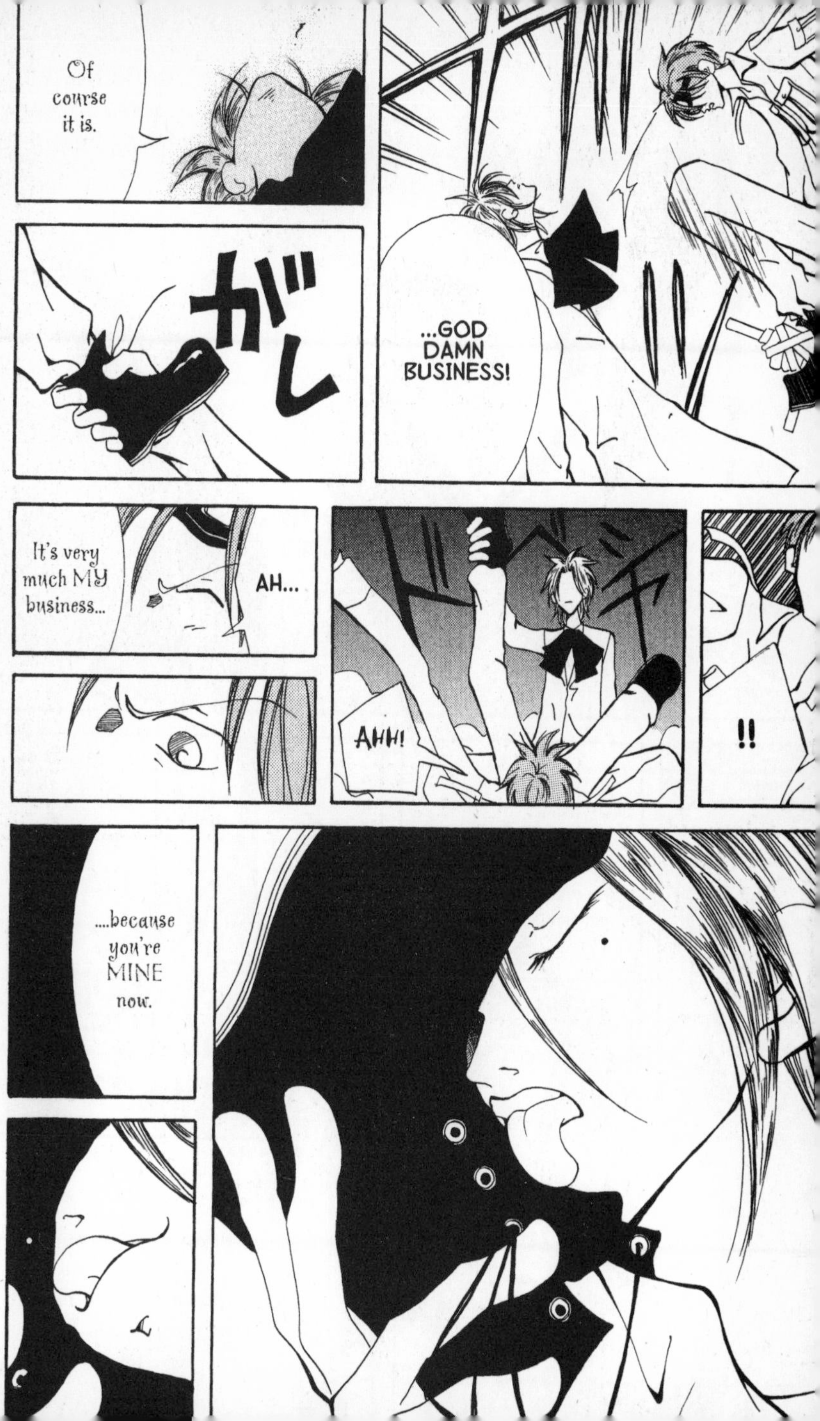
...GOD DAMN BUSINESS!
Of course it is.
がし
!!
AHH!
It's very much MY business...
AH...
...because you're MINE now.

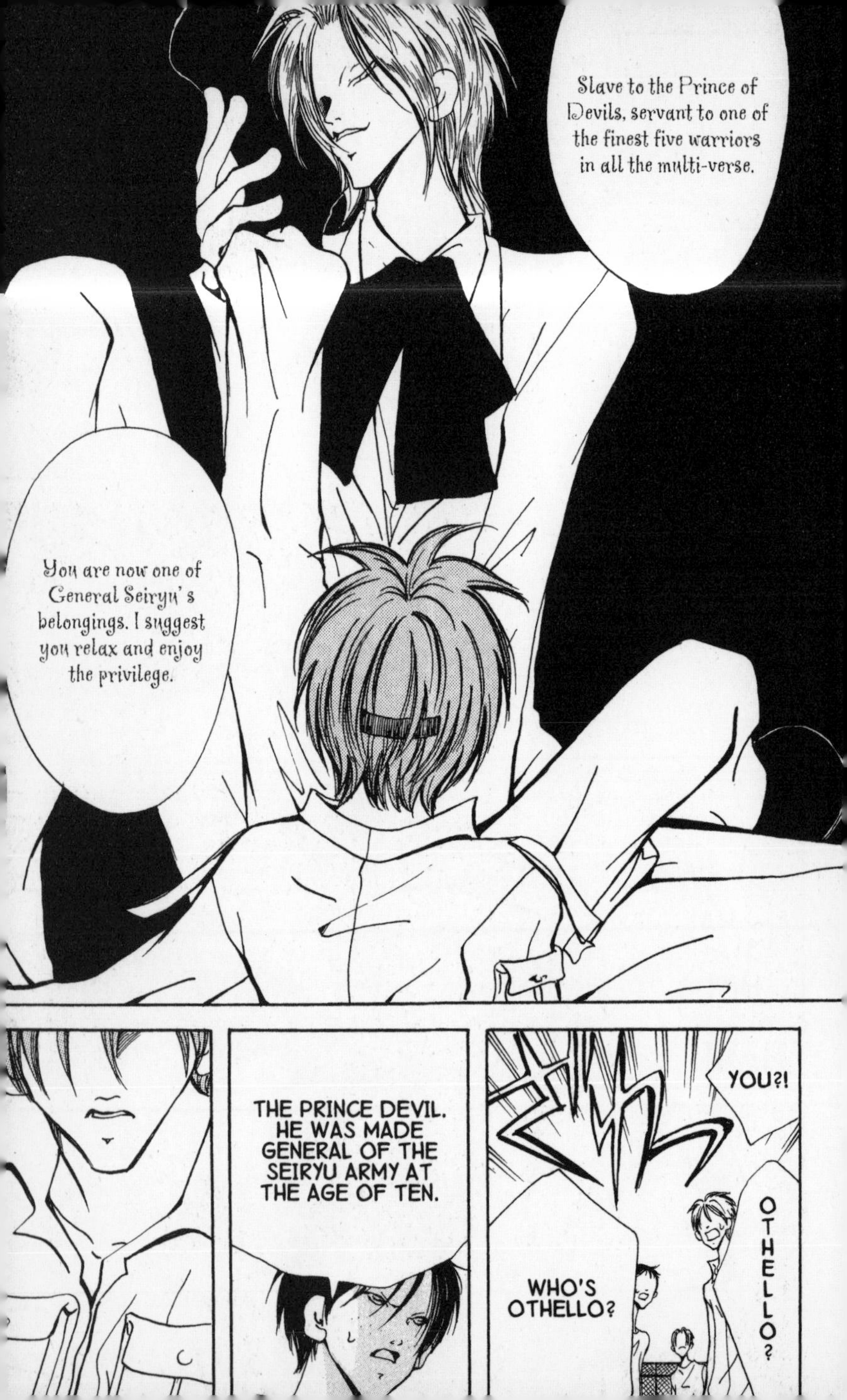
Slave to the Prince of Devils, servant to one of the finest five warriors in all the multi-verse.
You are now one of General Seiryu's belongings. I suggest you relax and enjoy the privilege.
YOU?!
OTHELLO?
WHO'S OTHELLO?
THE PRINCE DEVIL. HE WAS MADE GENERAL OF THE SEIRYU ARMY AT THE AGE OF TEN.

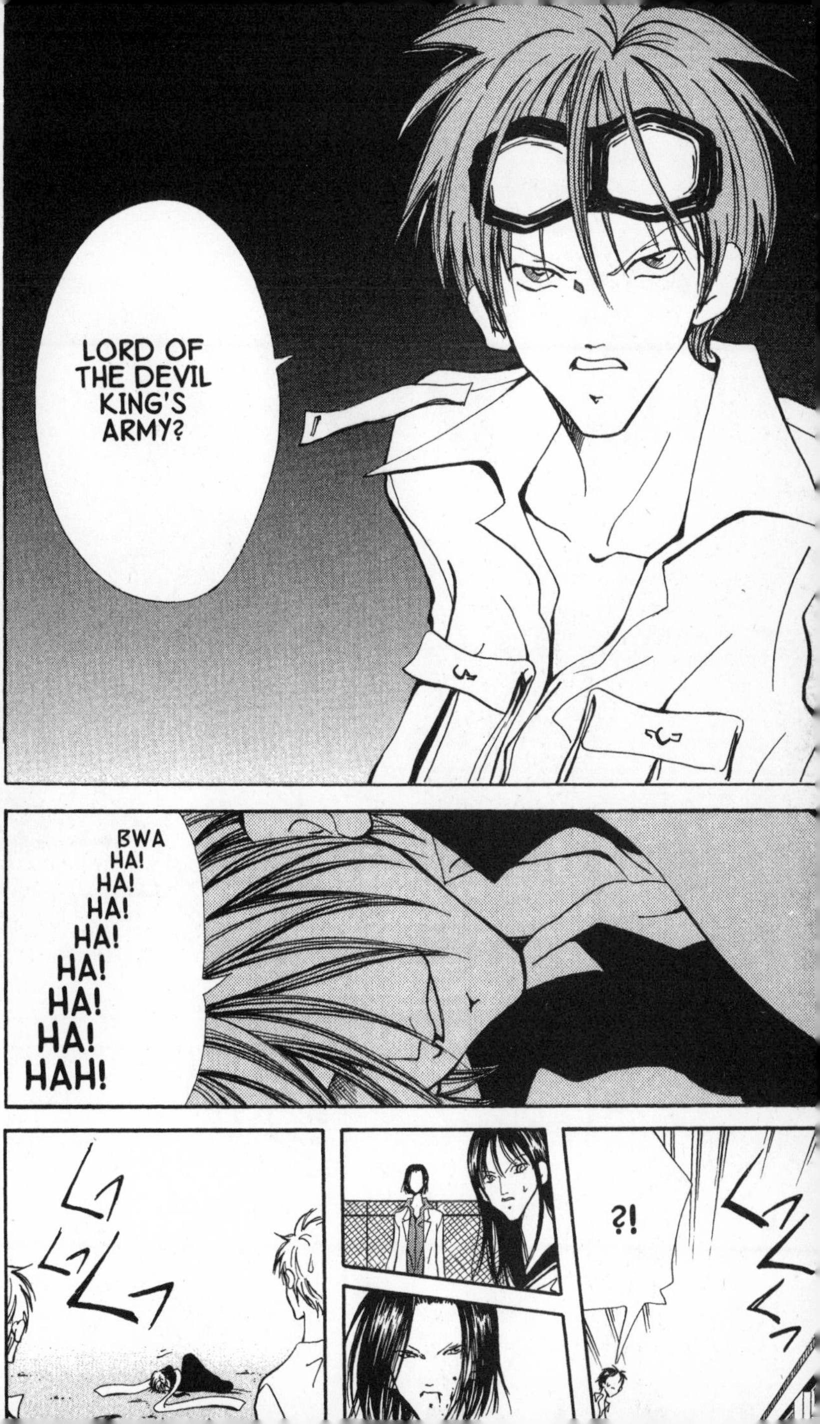
LORD OF THE DEVIL KING'S ARMY?
BWA HA! HA! HA! HA! HA! HA! HA! HAH!
?!

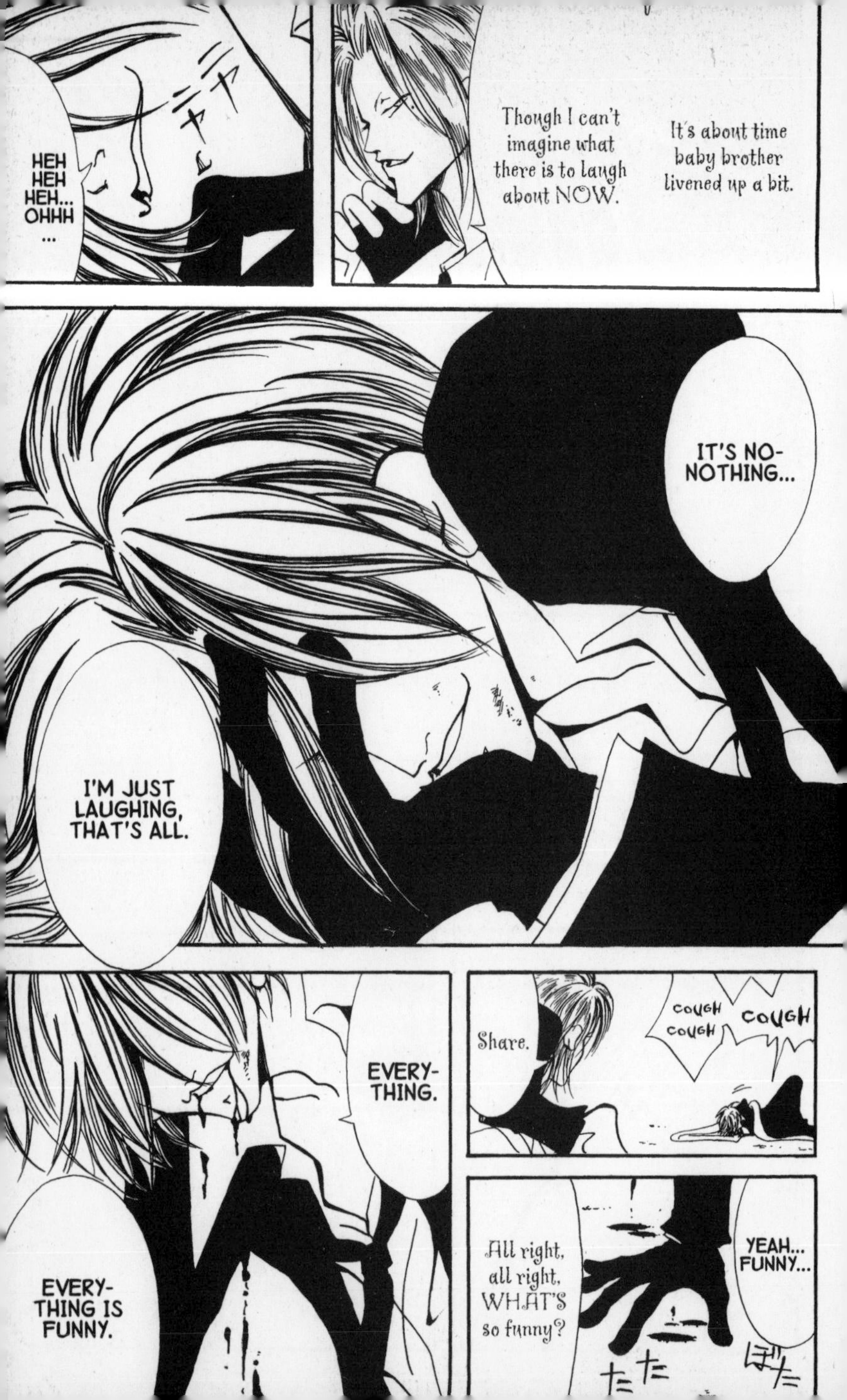
It's about time baby brother livened up a bit.
Though I can't imagine what there is to laugh about NOW.
ニヤ
HEH HEH HEH... OHHH ...
IT'S NO-NOTHING...
I'M JUST LAUGHING, THAT'S ALL.
COUGH
COUGH COUGH
Share.
YEAH... FUNNY...
All right, all right, WHAT'S so funny?
ぱた
たた
EVERY-THING.
EVERY-THING IS FUNNY.

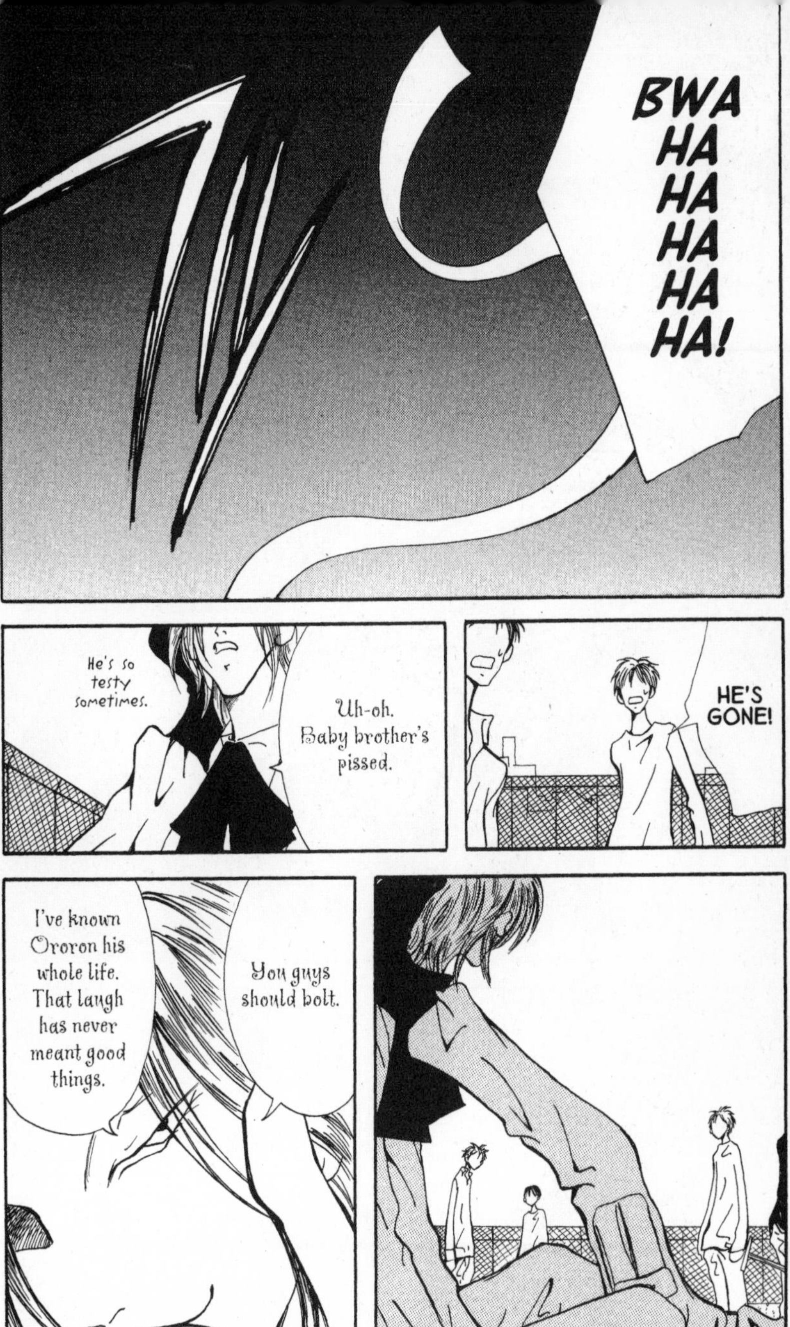
BWA HA HA HA HA HA!
HE'S GONE!
Uh-oh. Baby brother's pissed.
He's so testy sometimes.
You guys should bolt.
I've known Ororon his whole life. That laugh has never meant good things.

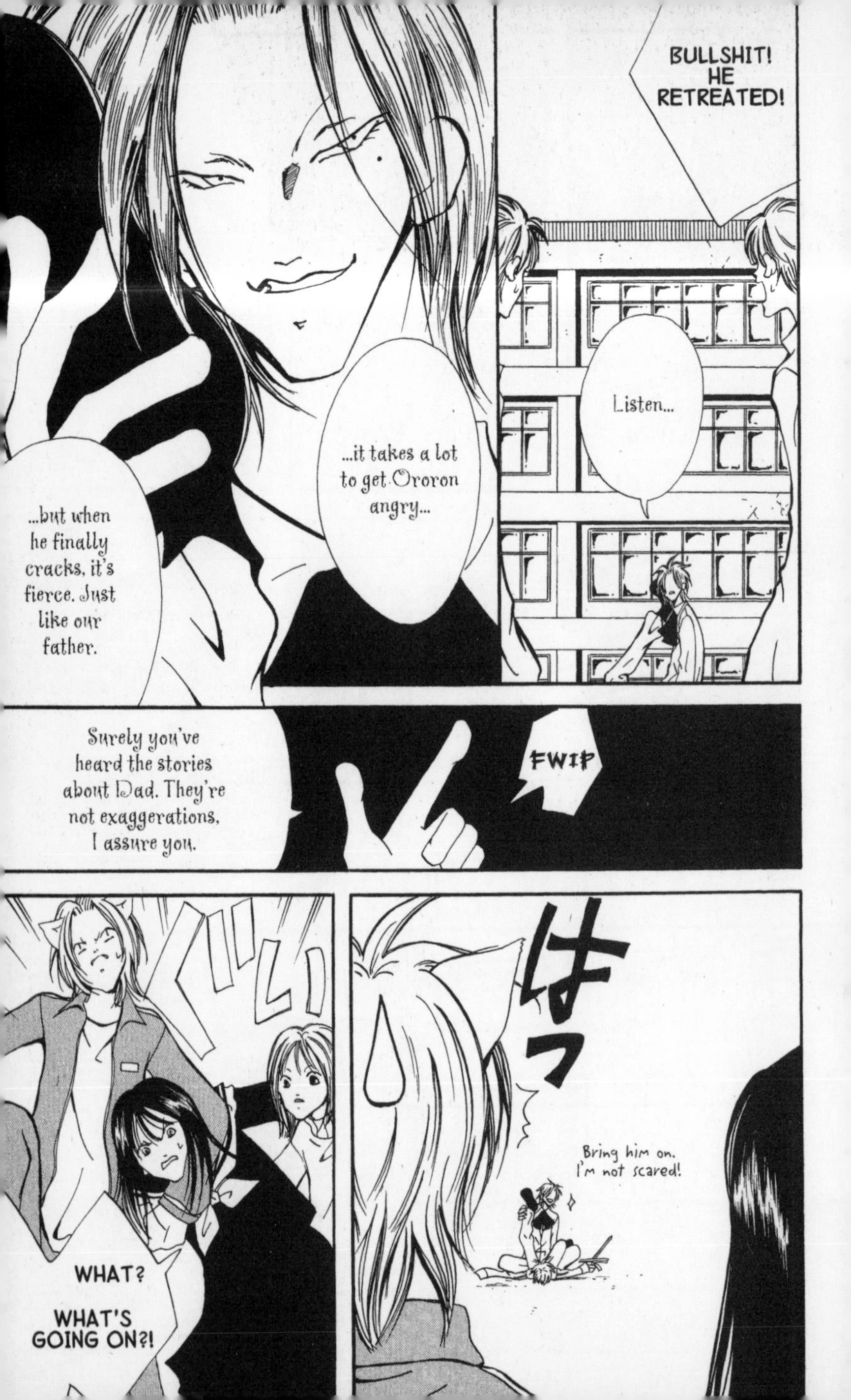
BULLSHIT! HE RETREATED!
Listen...
...it takes a lot to get Ororon angry...
...but when he finally cracks, it's fierce. Just like our father.
FWIP
Surely you've heard the stories about Dad. They're not exaggerations, I assure you.
はっ
Bring him on. I'm not scared!
WHAT?
WHAT'S GOING ON?!

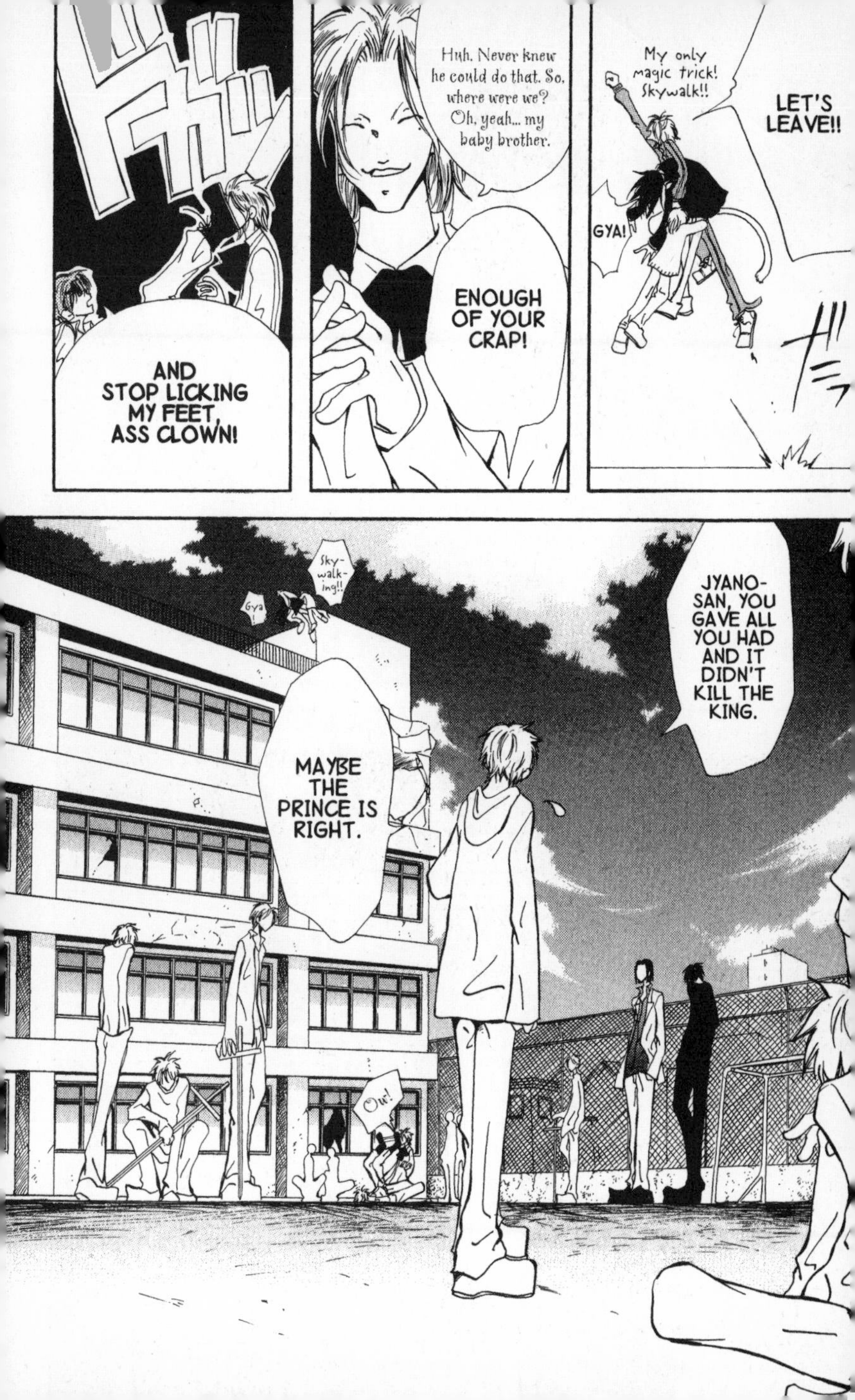
LET'S LEAVE!!
My only magic trick! Skywalk!!
GYA!
Huh. Never knew he could do that. So, where were we? Oh, yeah... my baby brother.
ENOUGH OF YOUR CRAP!
AND STOP LICKING MY FEET, ASS CLOWN!
JYANO-SAN, YOU GAVE ALL YOU HAD AND IT DIDN'T KILL THE KING.
Sky-walking!!
Gya!
MAYBE THE PRINCE IS RIGHT.
Ow!

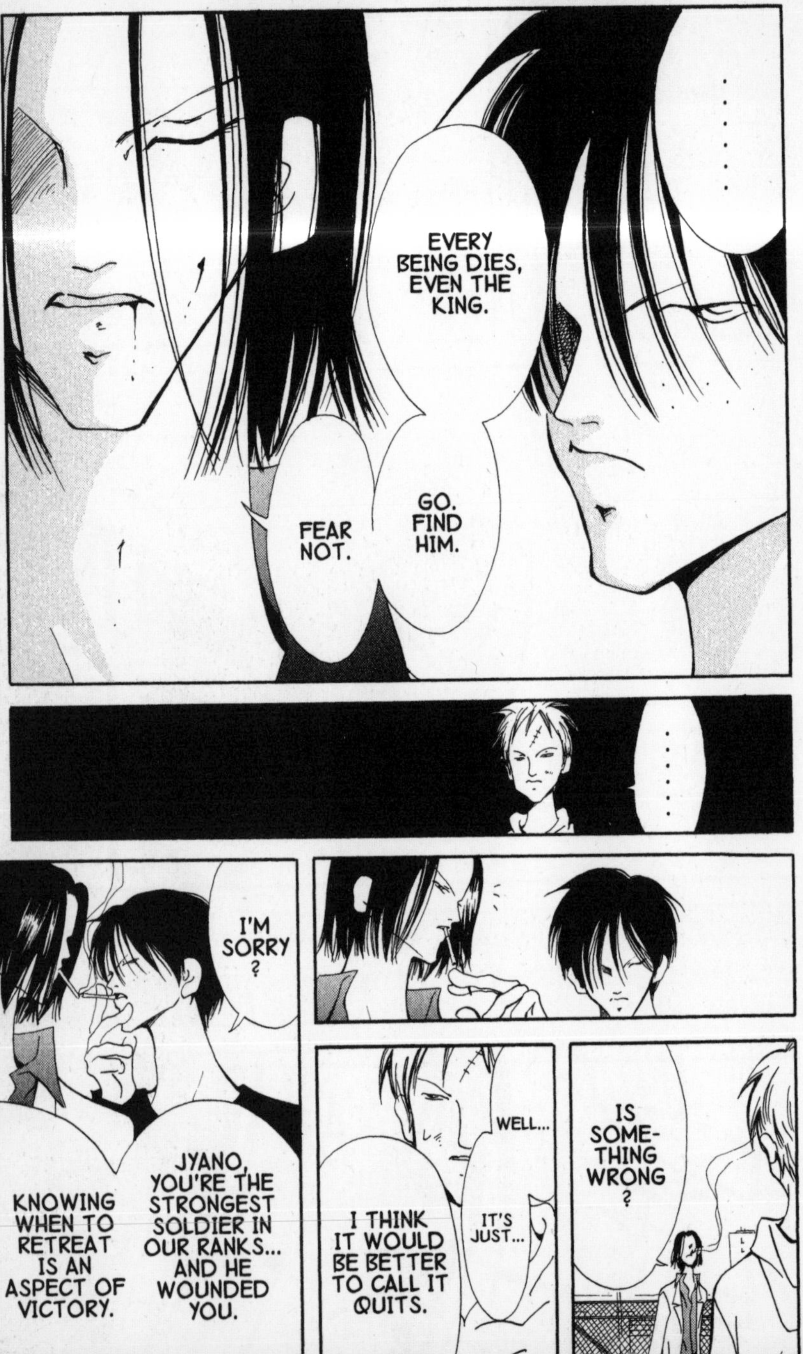
......
EVERY BEING DIES, EVEN THE KING.
GO. FIND HIM.
FEAR NOT.
......
IS SOME-THING WRONG?
WELL...
IT'S JUST...
I THINK IT WOULD BE BETTER TO CALL IT QUITS.
I'M SORRY?
JYANO, YOU'RE THE STRONGEST SOLDIER IN OUR RANKS... AND HE WOUNDED YOU.
KNOWING WHEN TO RETREAT IS AN ASPECT OF VICTORY.

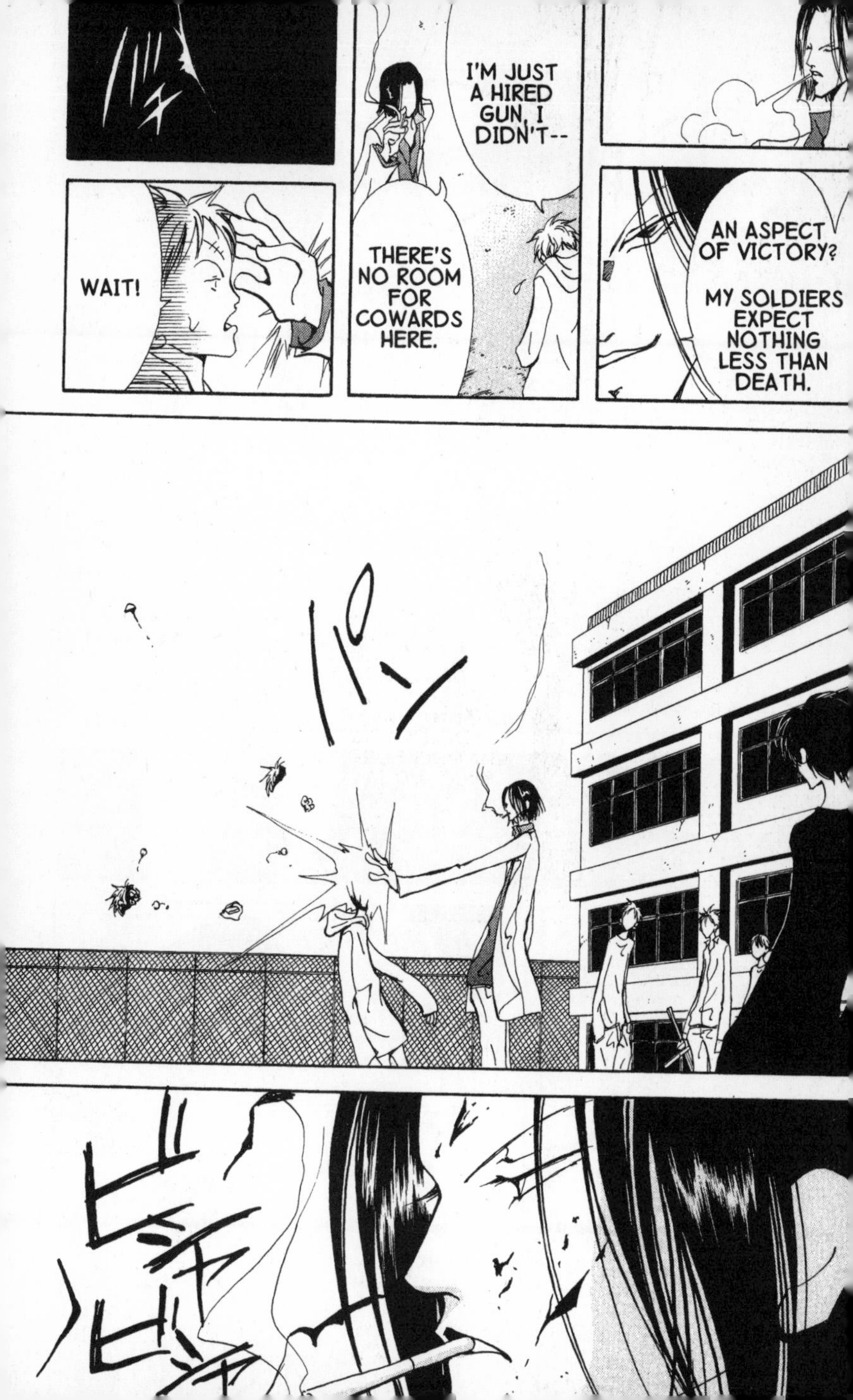
AN ASPECT OF VICTORY?
MY SOLDIERS EXPECT NOTHING LESS THAN DEATH.
I'M JUST A HIRED GUN, I DIDN'T--
THERE'S NO ROOM FOR COWARDS HERE.
WAIT!

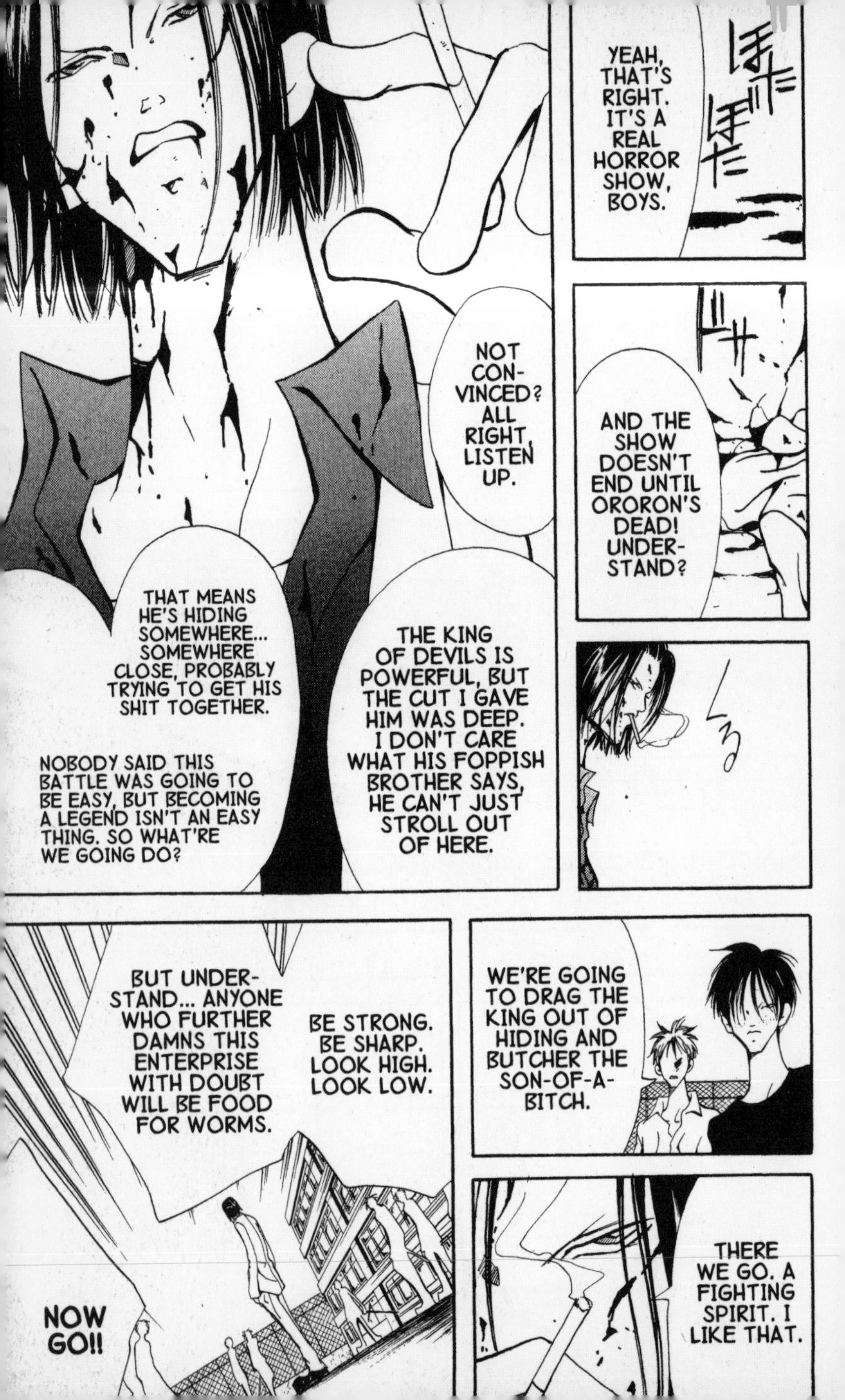
YEAH, THAT'S RIGHT. IT'S A REAL HORROR SHOW, BOYS.
AND THE SHOW DOESN'T END UNTIL ORORON'S DEAD! UNDER-STAND?
NOT CON-VINCED? ALL RIGHT, LISTEN UP.
THE KING OF DEVILS IS POWERFUL, BUT THE CUT I GAVE HIM WAS DEEP. I DON'T CARE WHAT HIS FOPPISH BROTHER SAYS, HE CAN'T JUST STROLL OUT OF HERE.
THAT MEANS HE'S HIDING SOMEWHERE... SOMEWHERE CLOSE, PROBABLY TRYING TO GET HIS SHIT TOGETHER.
NOBODY SAID THIS BATTLE WAS GOING TO BE EASY, BUT BECOMING A LEGEND ISN'T AN EASY THING. SO WHAT'RE WE GOING DO?
WE'RE GOING TO DRAG THE KING OUT OF HIDING AND BUTCHER THE SON-OF-A-BITCH.
THERE WE GO. A FIGHTING SPIRIT. I LIKE THAT.
BUT UNDER-STAND... ANYONE WHO FURTHER DAMNS THIS ENTERPRISE WITH DOUBT WILL BE FOOD FOR WORMS.
BE STRONG. BE SHARP. LOOK HIGH. LOOK LOW.
NOW GO!!

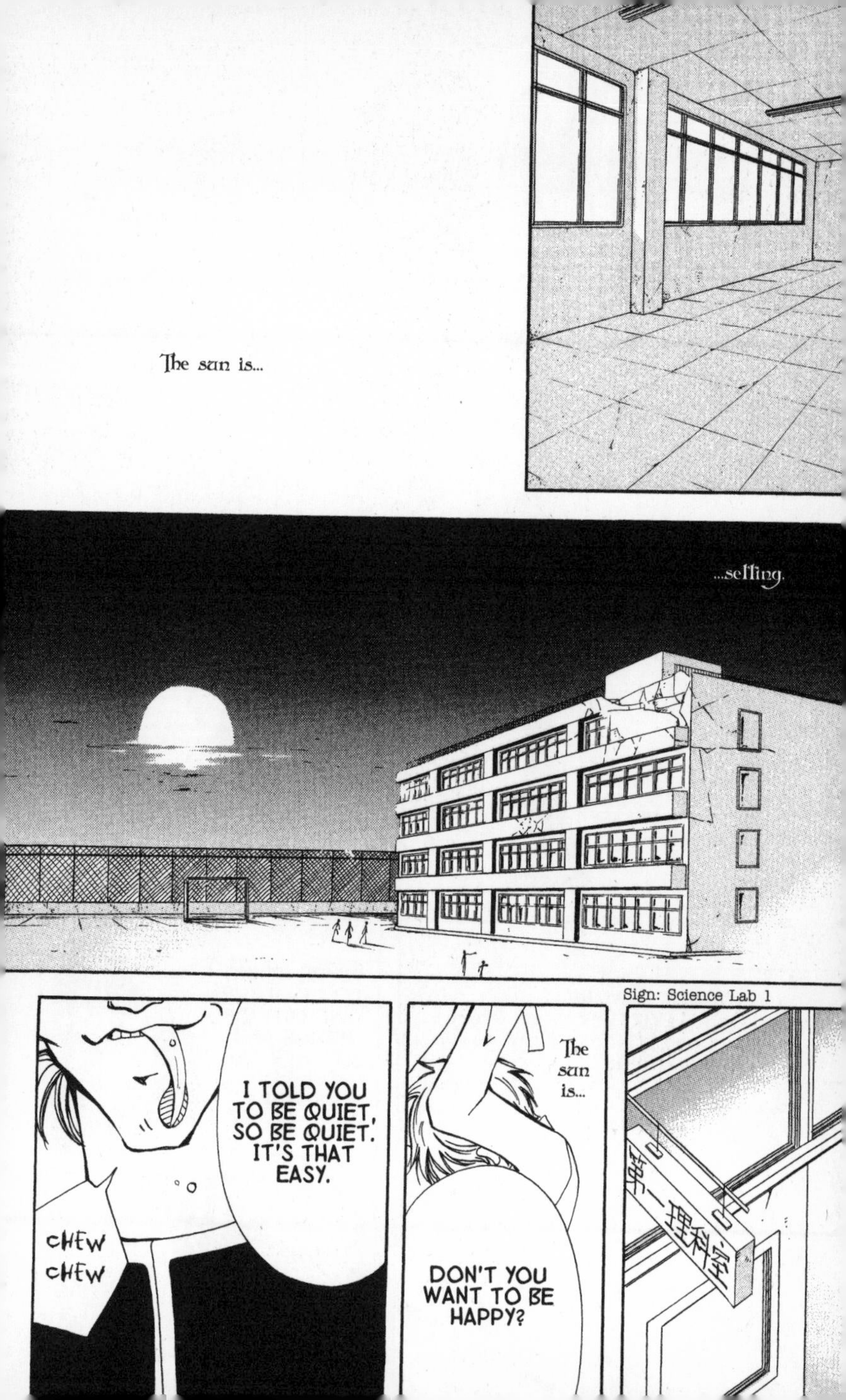
The sun is...
...setting.
Sign: Science Lab 1
第一理科室
The sun is...
DON'T YOU WANT TO BE HAPPY?
I TOLD YOU TO BE QUIET, SO BE QUIET. IT'S THAT EASY.
CHEW CHEW

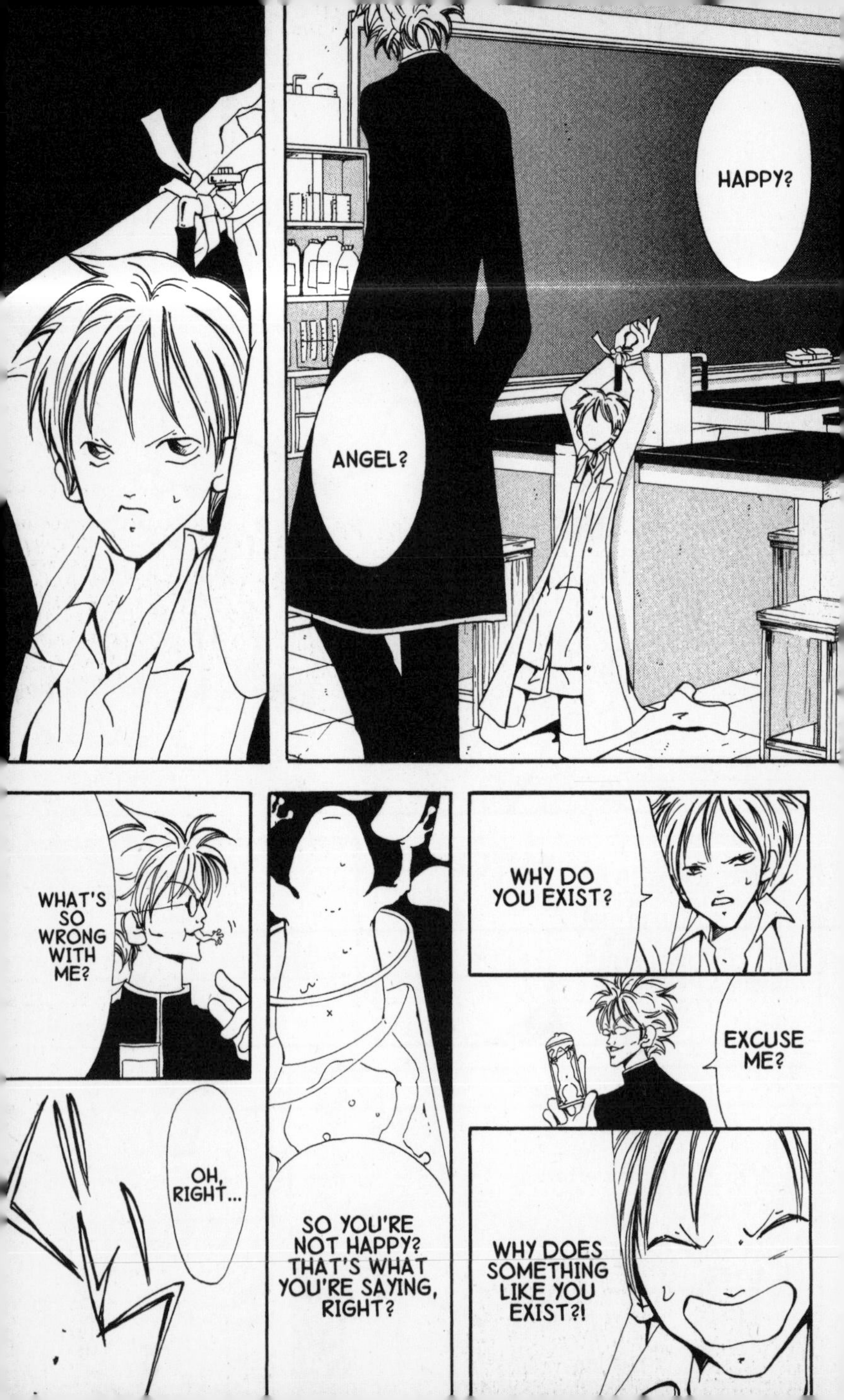
HAPPY?
ANGEL?
WHY DO YOU EXIST?
EXCUSE ME?
WHY DOES SOMETHING LIKE YOU EXIST?!
SO YOU'RE NOT HAPPY? THAT'S WHAT YOU'RE SAYING, RIGHT?
WHAT'S SO WRONG WITH ME?
OH, RIGHT...

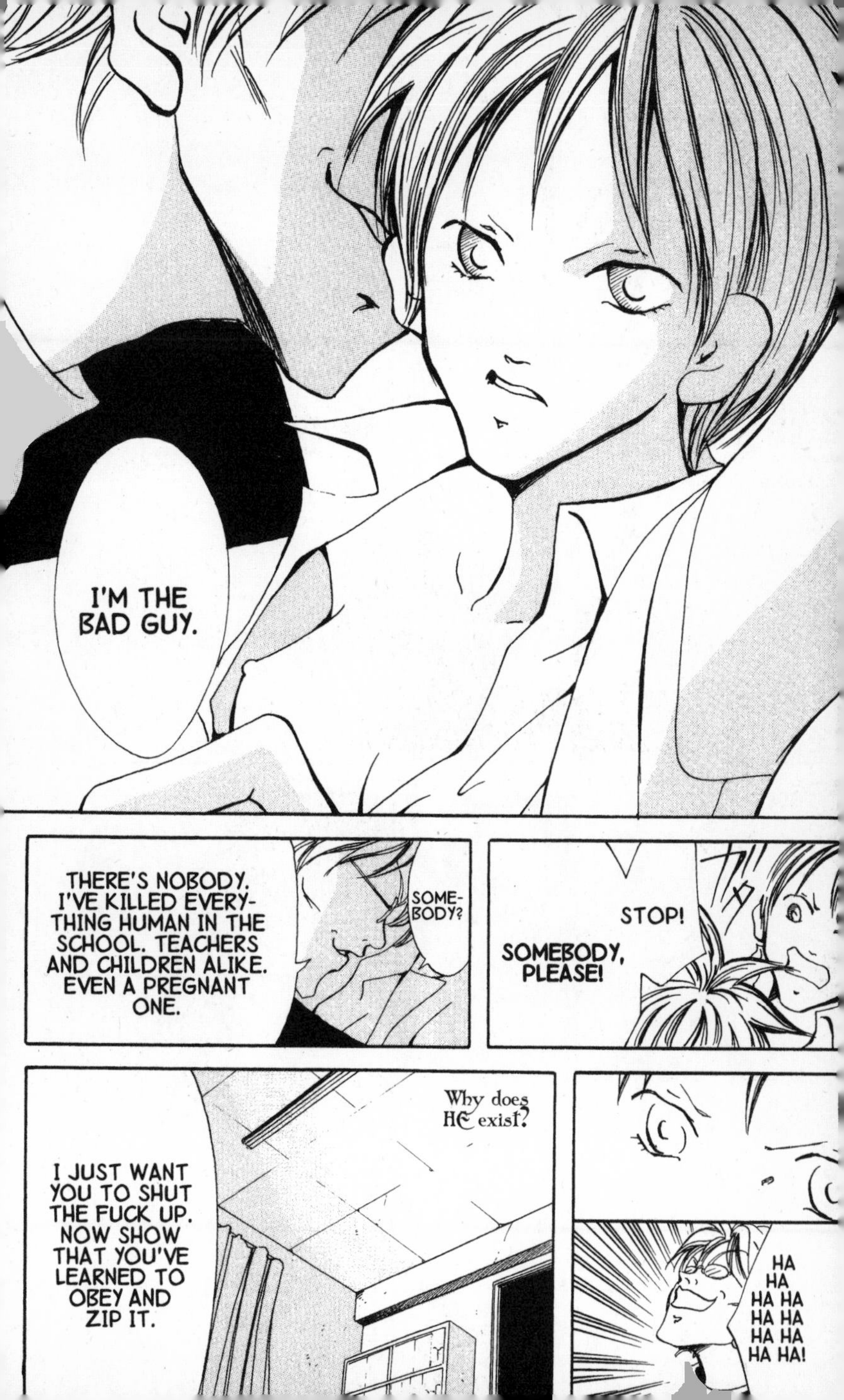
I'M THE BAD GUY.
STOP!
SOMEBODY, PLEASE!
SOME-BODY?
THERE'S NOBODY. I'VE KILLED EVERY-THING HUMAN IN THE SCHOOL. TEACHERS AND CHILDREN ALIKE. EVEN A PREGNANT ONE.
HA HA HA HA HA HA HA HA HA HA!
Why does HE exist?
I JUST WANT YOU TO SHUT THE FUCK UP. NOW SHOW THAT YOU'VE LEARNED TO OBEY AND ZIP IT.

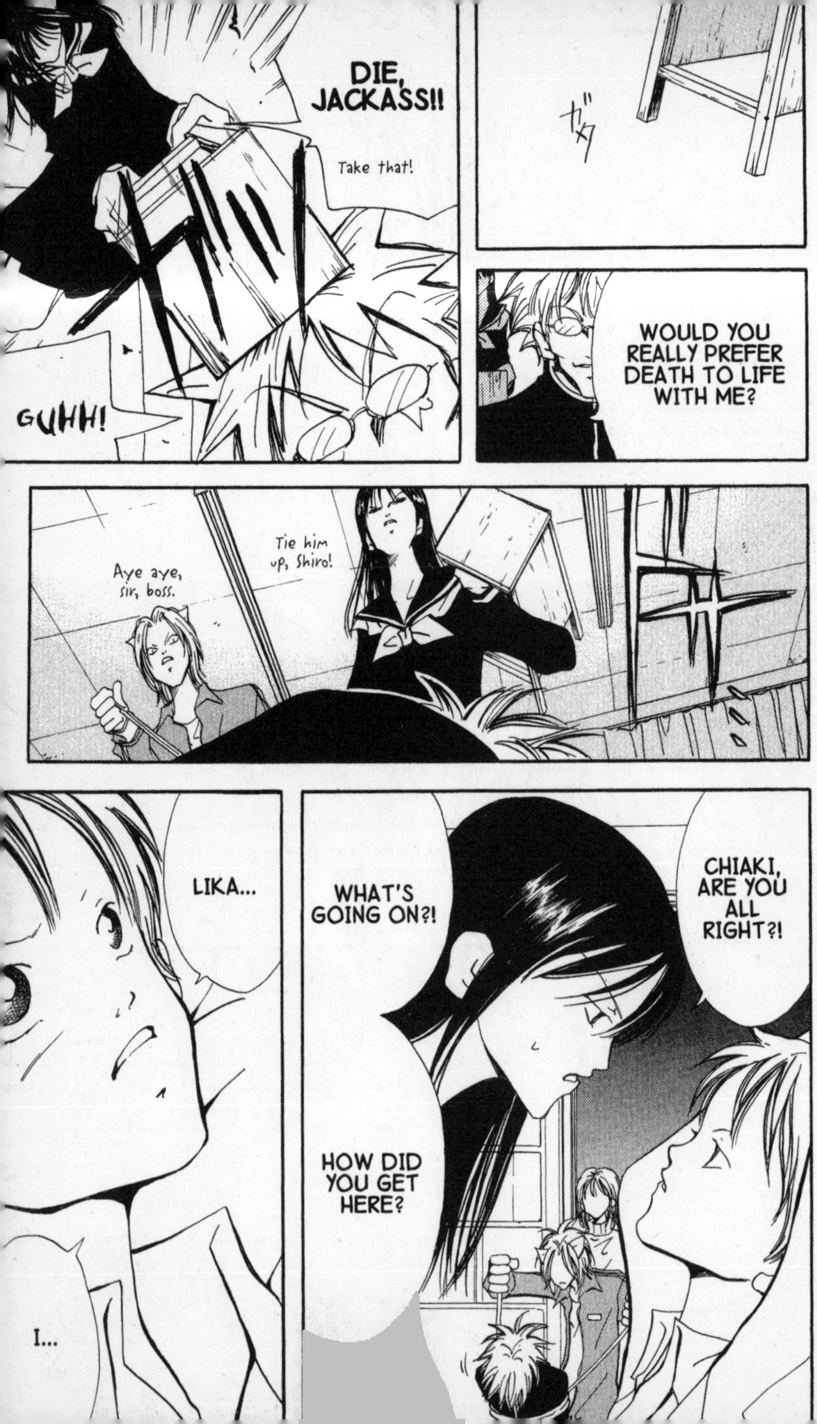
ガタ
WOULD YOU REALLY PREFER DEATH TO LIFE WITH ME?
DIE, JACKASS!!
Take that!
GUHH!
Tie him up, Shiro!
Aye aye, sir, boss.
CHIAKI, ARE YOU ALL RIGHT?!
WHAT'S GOING ON?!
HOW DID YOU GET HERE?
LIKA...
I...

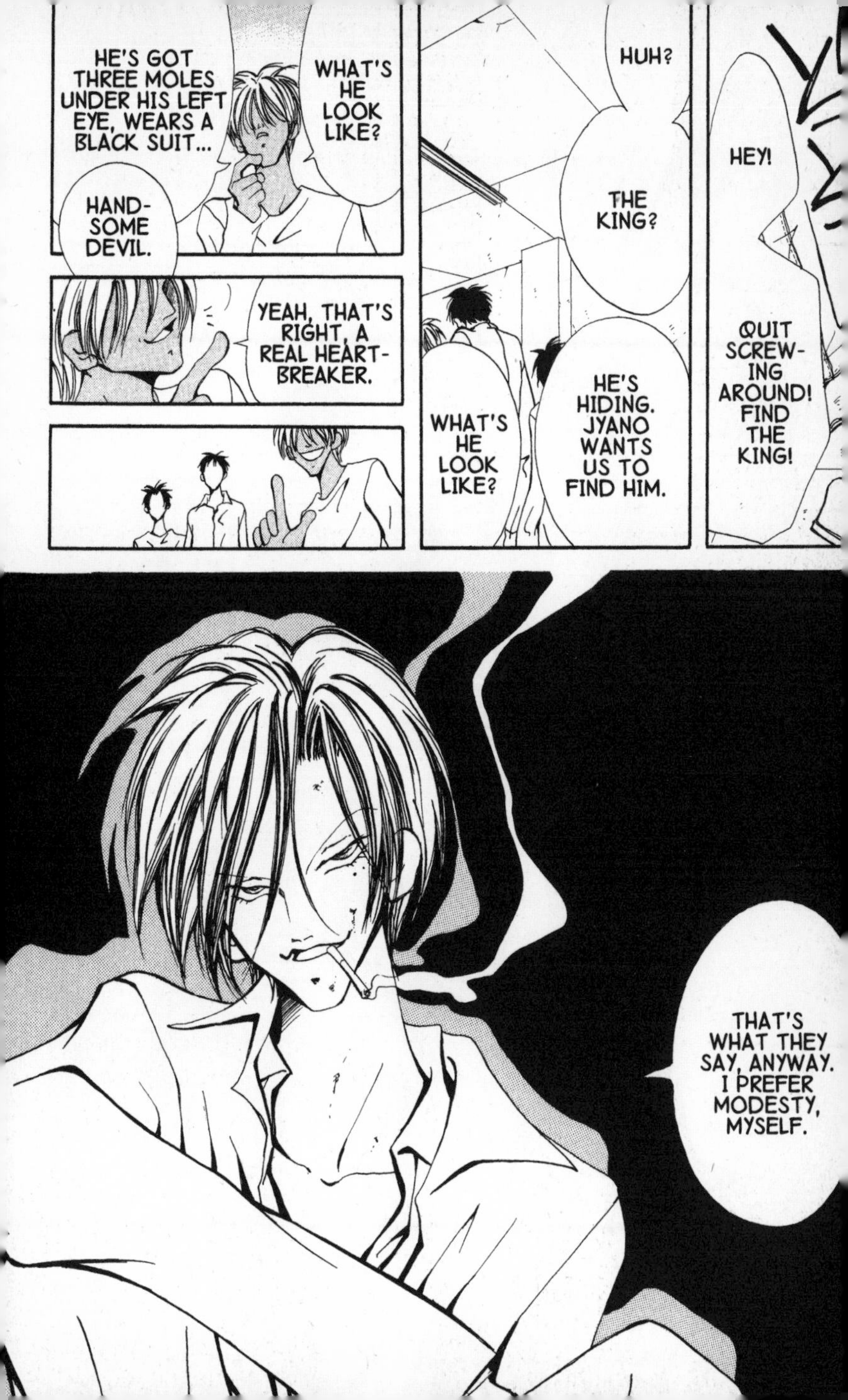
HEY!
QUIT SCREWING AROUND! FIND THE KING!
HUH?
THE KING?
HE'S HIDING. JYANO WANTS US TO FIND HIM.
WHAT'S HE LOOK LIKE?
WHAT'S HE LOOK LIKE?
HE'S GOT THREE MOLES UNDER HIS LEFT EYE, WEARS A BLACK SUIT...
HAND-SOME DEVIL.
YEAH, THAT'S RIGHT, A REAL HEART-BREAKER.
THAT'S WHAT THEY SAY, ANYWAY. I PREFER MODESTY, MYSELF.

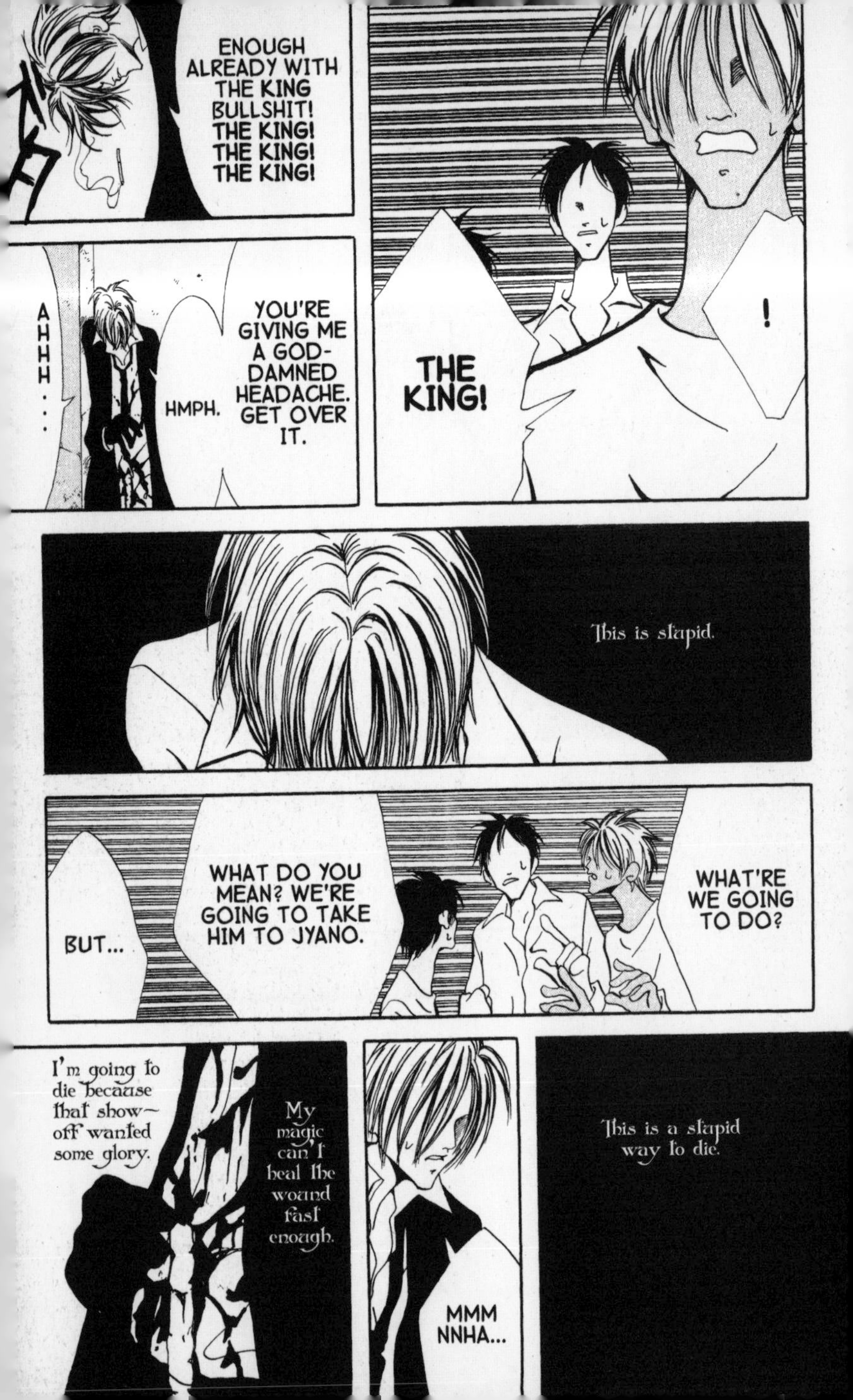
!
THE KING!
ENOUGH ALREADY WITH THE KING BULLSHIT! THE KING! THE KING! THE KING!
YOU'RE GIVING ME A GOD-DAMNED HEADACHE. GET OVER IT.
HMPH.
AHHH...
This is stupid.
WHAT'RE WE GOING TO DO?
WHAT DO YOU MEAN? WE'RE GOING TO TAKE HIM TO JYANO.
BUT...
This is a stupid way to die.
MMM NNHA...
My magic can't heal the wound fast enough.
I'm going to die because that show-off wanted some glory.

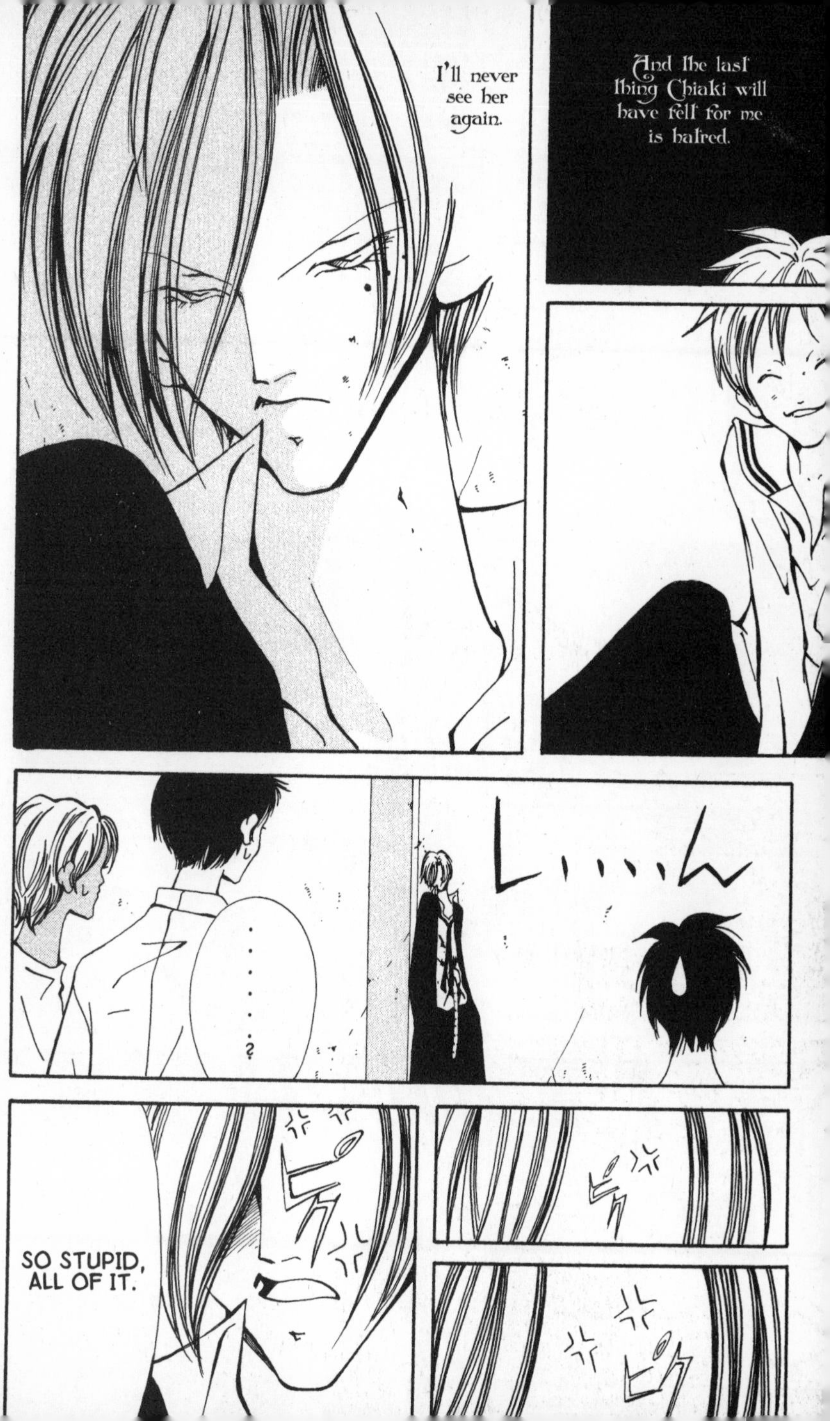
And the last thing Chiaki will have felt for me is hatred.
I'll never see her again.
......?
SO STUPID, ALL OF IT.

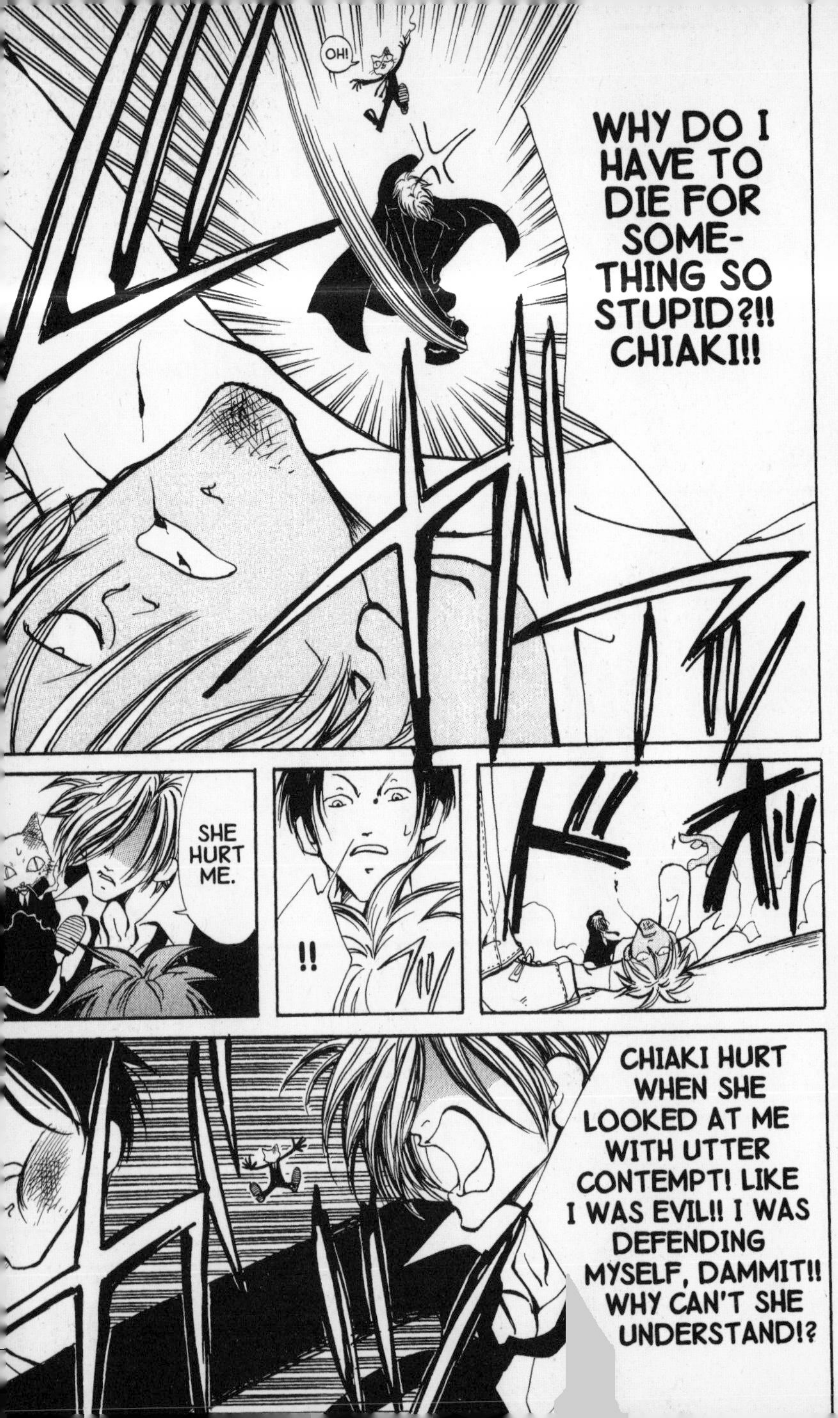
WHY DO I HAVE TO DIE FOR SOME-THING SO STUPID?!! CHIAKI!!
OH!
ドオッ
!!
SHE HURT ME.
CHIAKI HURT WHEN SHE LOOKED AT ME WITH UTTER CONTEMPT! LIKE I WAS EVIL!! I WAS DEFENDING MYSELF, DAMMIT!! WHY CAN'T SHE UNDERSTAND!?

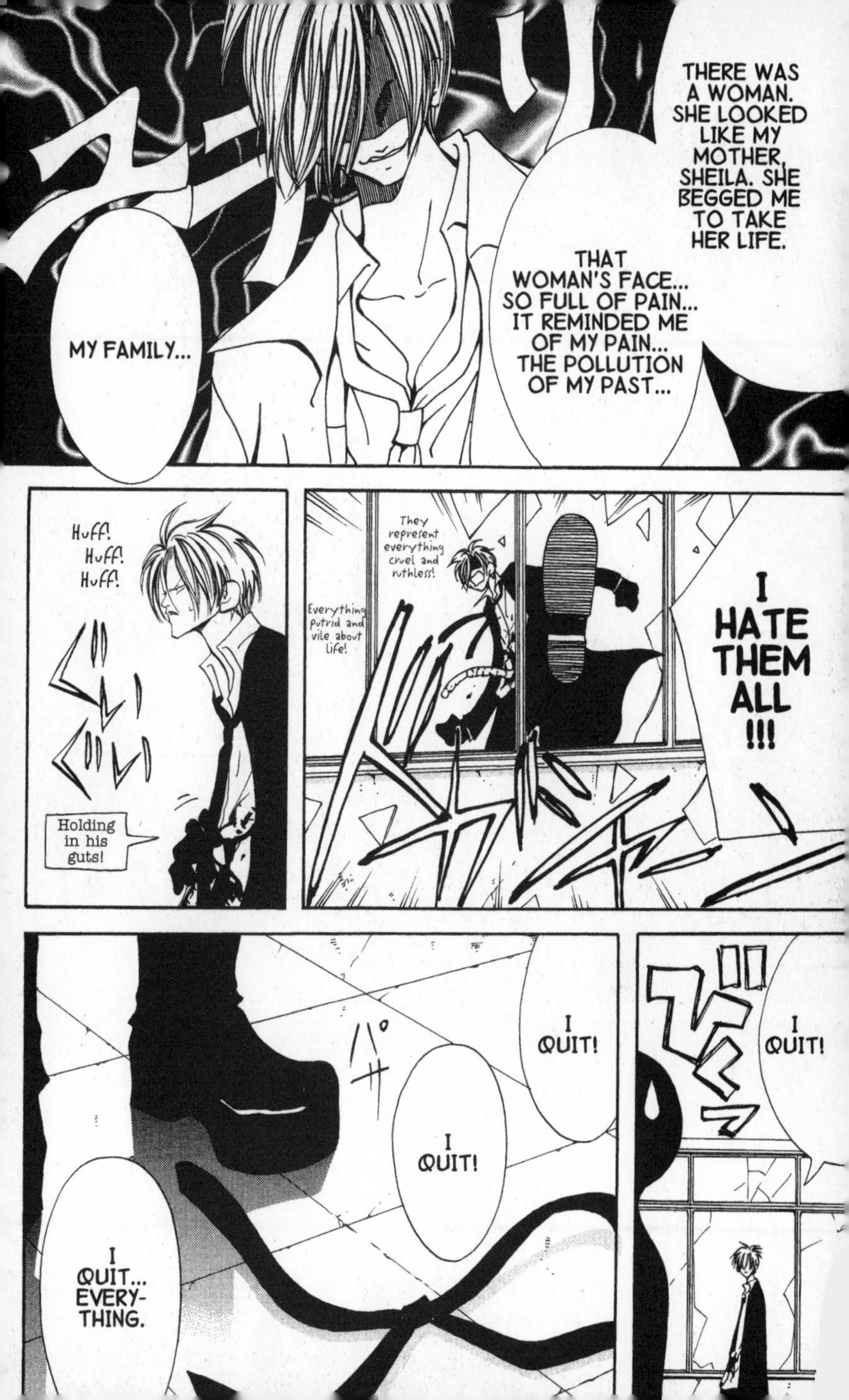
THERE WAS A WOMAN. SHE LOOKED LIKE MY MOTHER, SHEILA. SHE BEGGED ME TO TAKE HER LIFE.
THAT WOMAN'S FACE... SO FULL OF PAIN... IT REMINDED ME OF MY PAIN... THE POLLUTION OF MY PAST...
MY FAMILY...
I HATE THEM ALL!!!
They represent everything cruel and ruthless!
Everything putrid and vile about life!
Huff! Huff! Huff!
Holding in his guts!
I QUIT!
I QUIT!
I QUIT!
I QUIT... EVERY-THING.

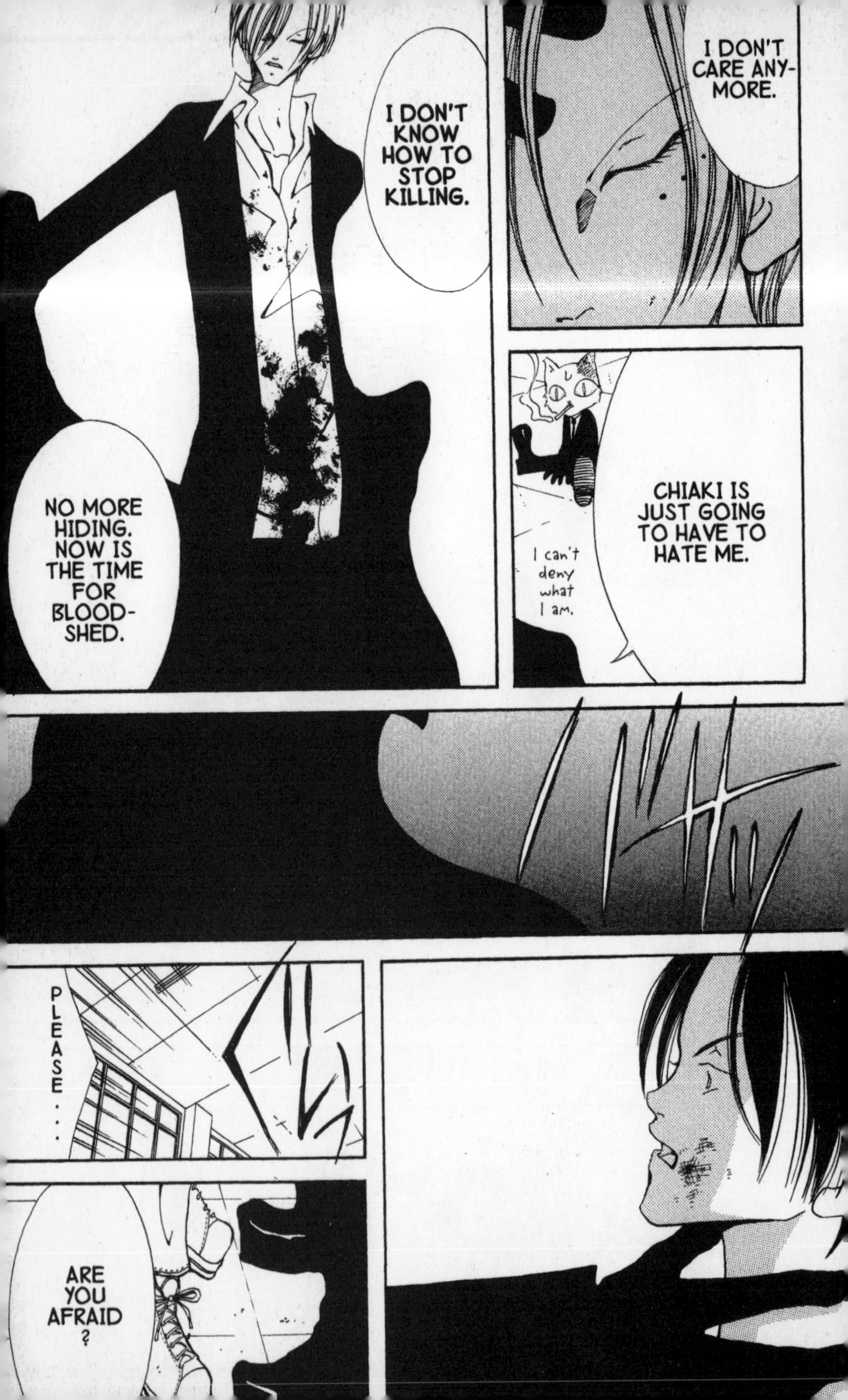
I DON'T CARE ANY-MORE.
CHIAKI IS JUST GOING TO HAVE TO HATE ME.
I can't deny what I am.
I DON'T KNOW HOW TO STOP KILLING.
NO MORE HIDING. NOW IS THE TIME FOR BLOOD-SHED.
PLEASE . . .
ARE YOU AFRAID ?

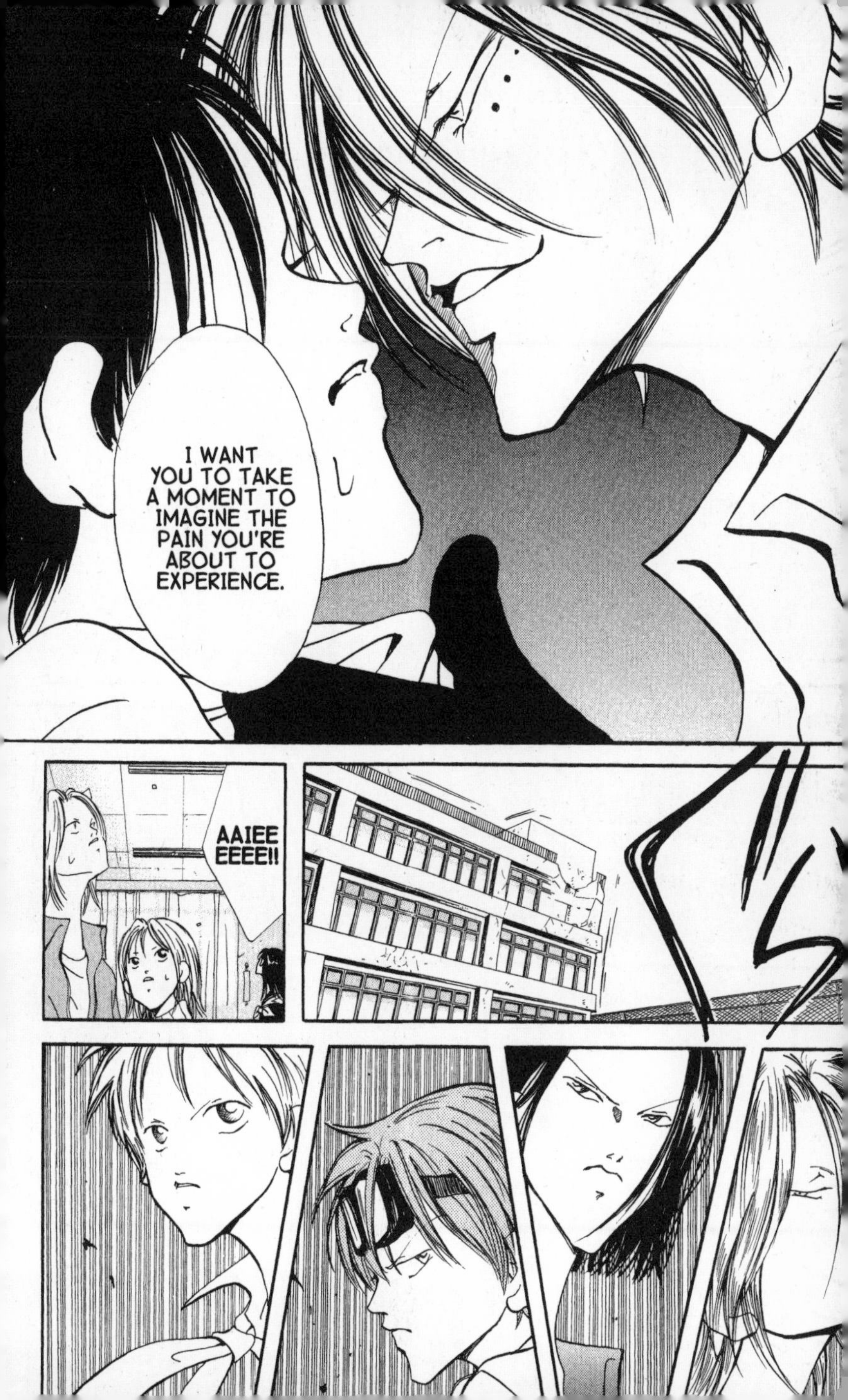
I WANT YOU TO TAKE A MOMENT TO IMAGINE THE PAIN YOU'RE ABOUT TO EXPERIENCE.
AAIEE EEEE!!

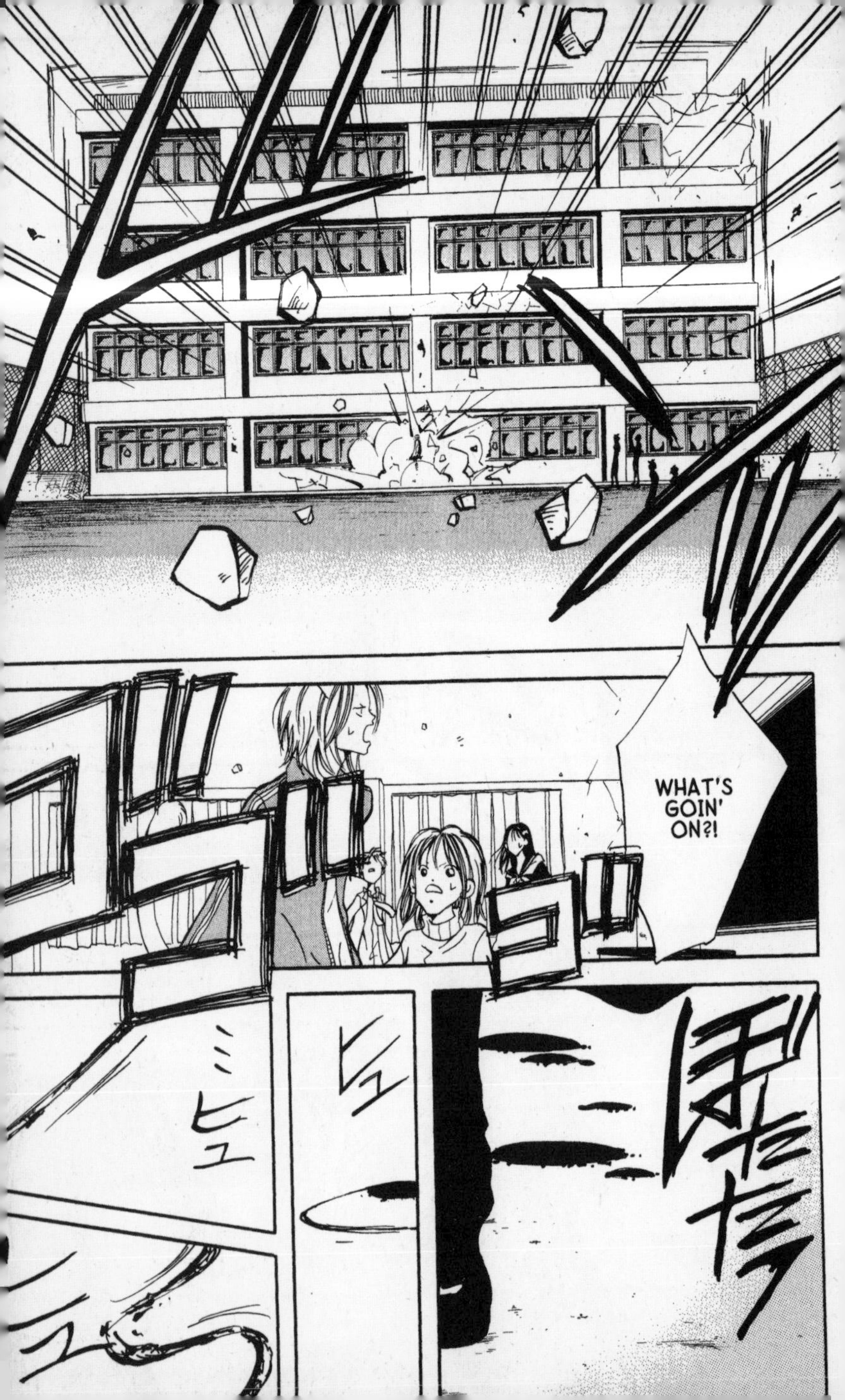
WHAT'S GOIN' ON?!
ヒュ

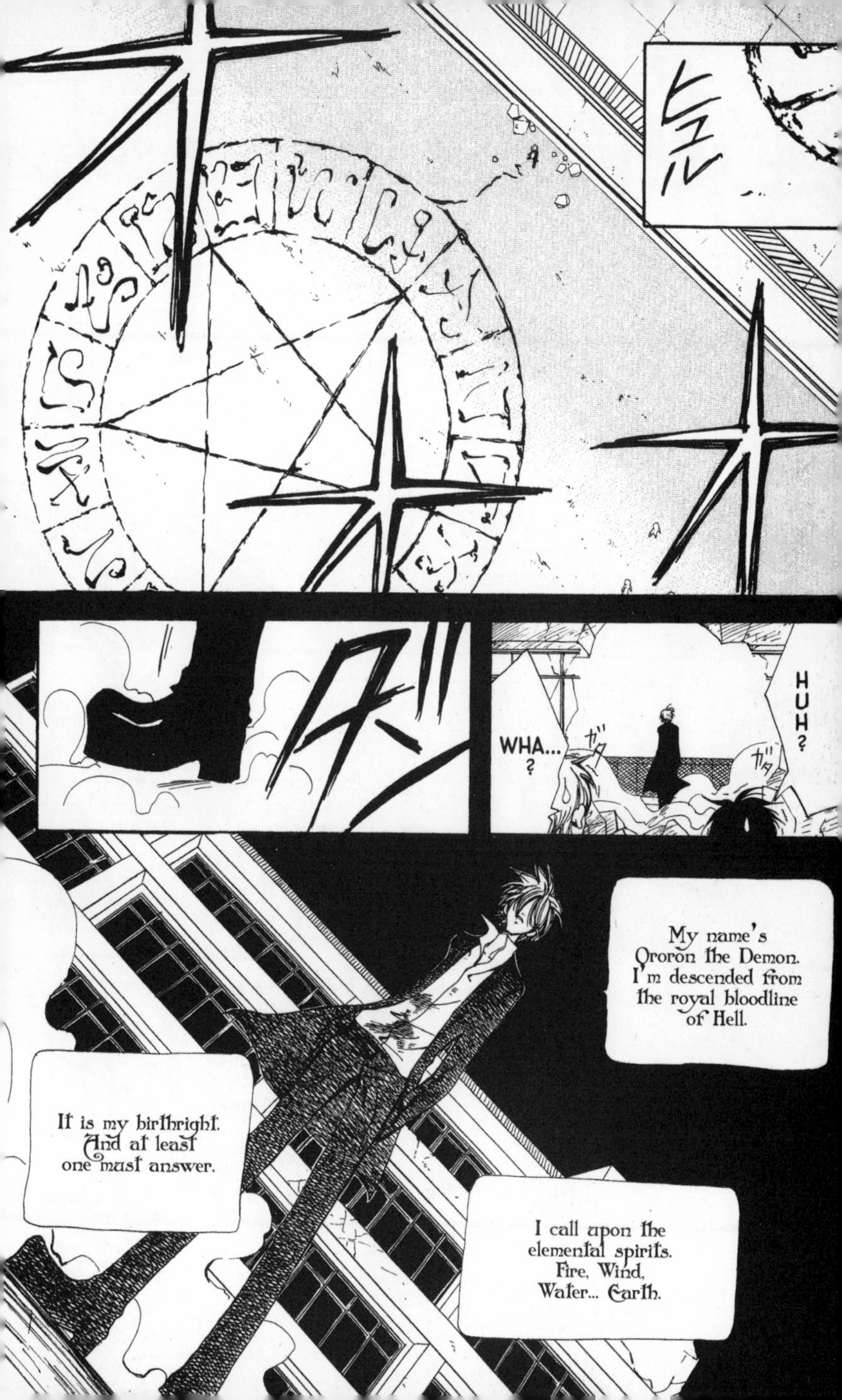

ヒュル
HUH?
WHA...?
ガタ
ガタ
My name's Ororon the Demon. I'm descended from the royal bloodline of Hell.
I call upon the elemental spirits. Fire, Wind, Water... Earth.
It is my birthright. And at least one must answer.

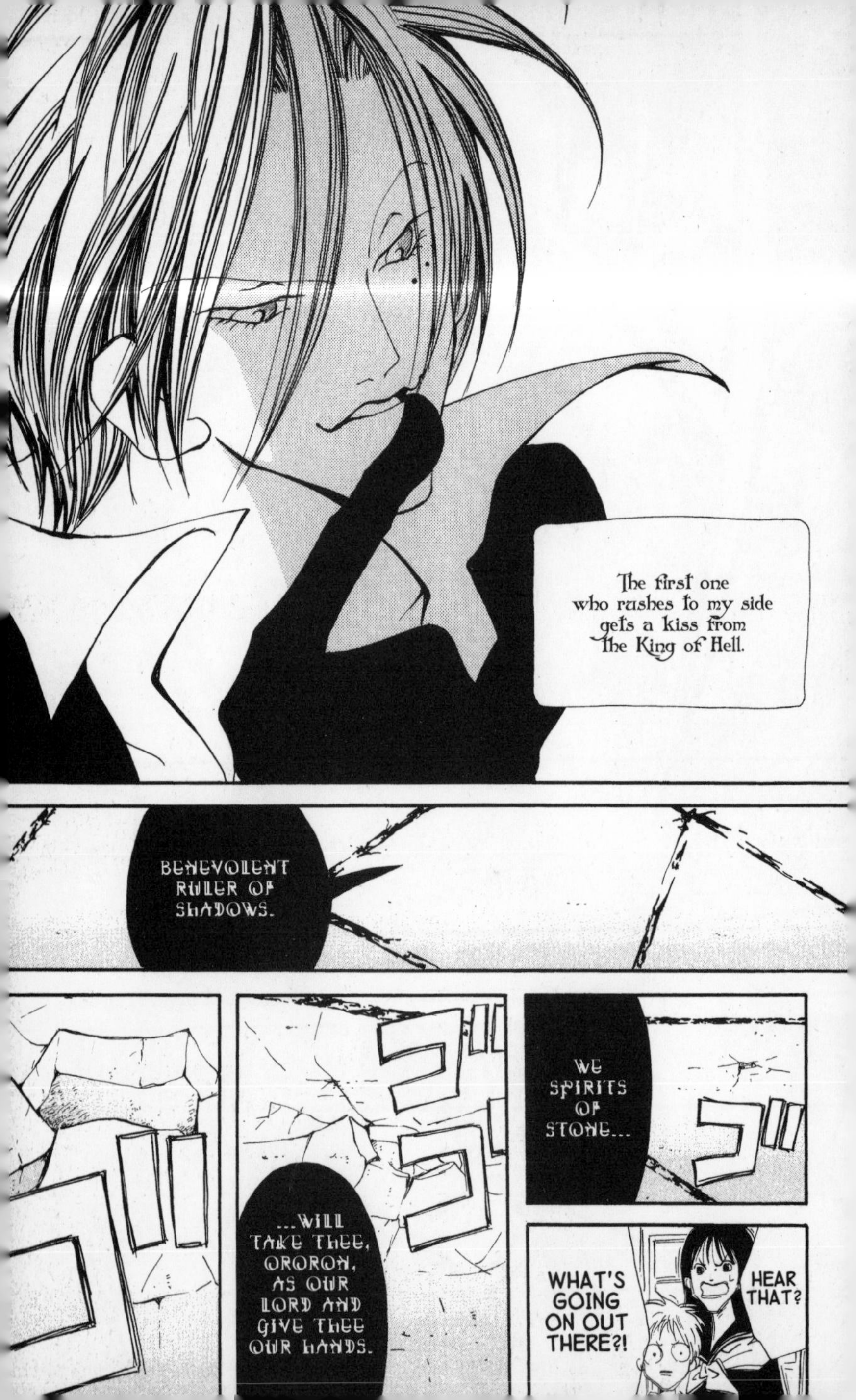

The first one who rushes to my side gets a kiss from the King of Hell.
BENEVOLENT RULER OF SHADOWS.
WE SPIRITS OF STONE...
ゴ
HEAR THAT?
WHAT'S GOING ON OUT THERE?!
ゴゴ
...WILL TAKE THEE, ORORON, AS OUR LORD AND GIVE THEE OUR HANDS.
ゴ

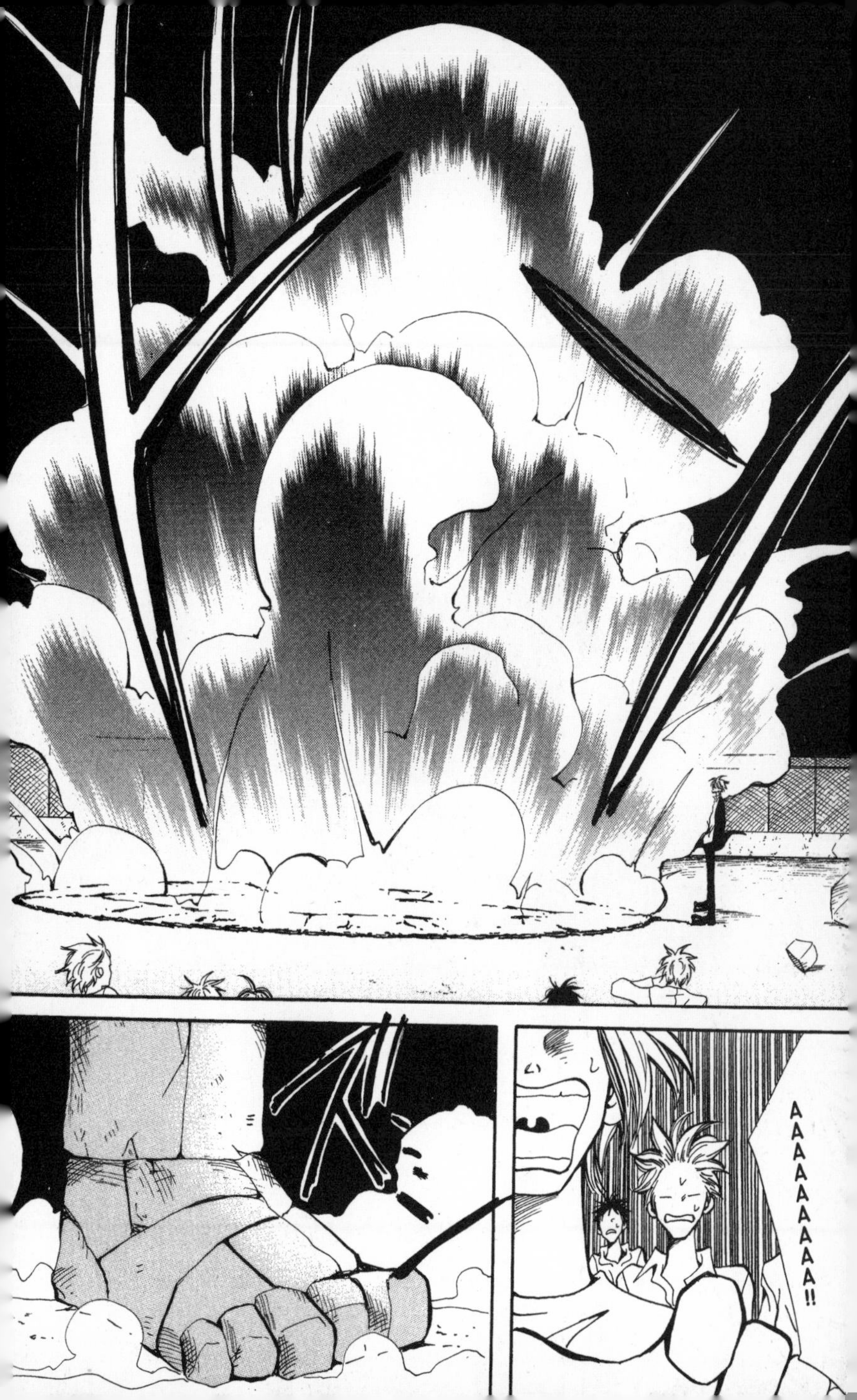
AAAAAAAAAAA!!

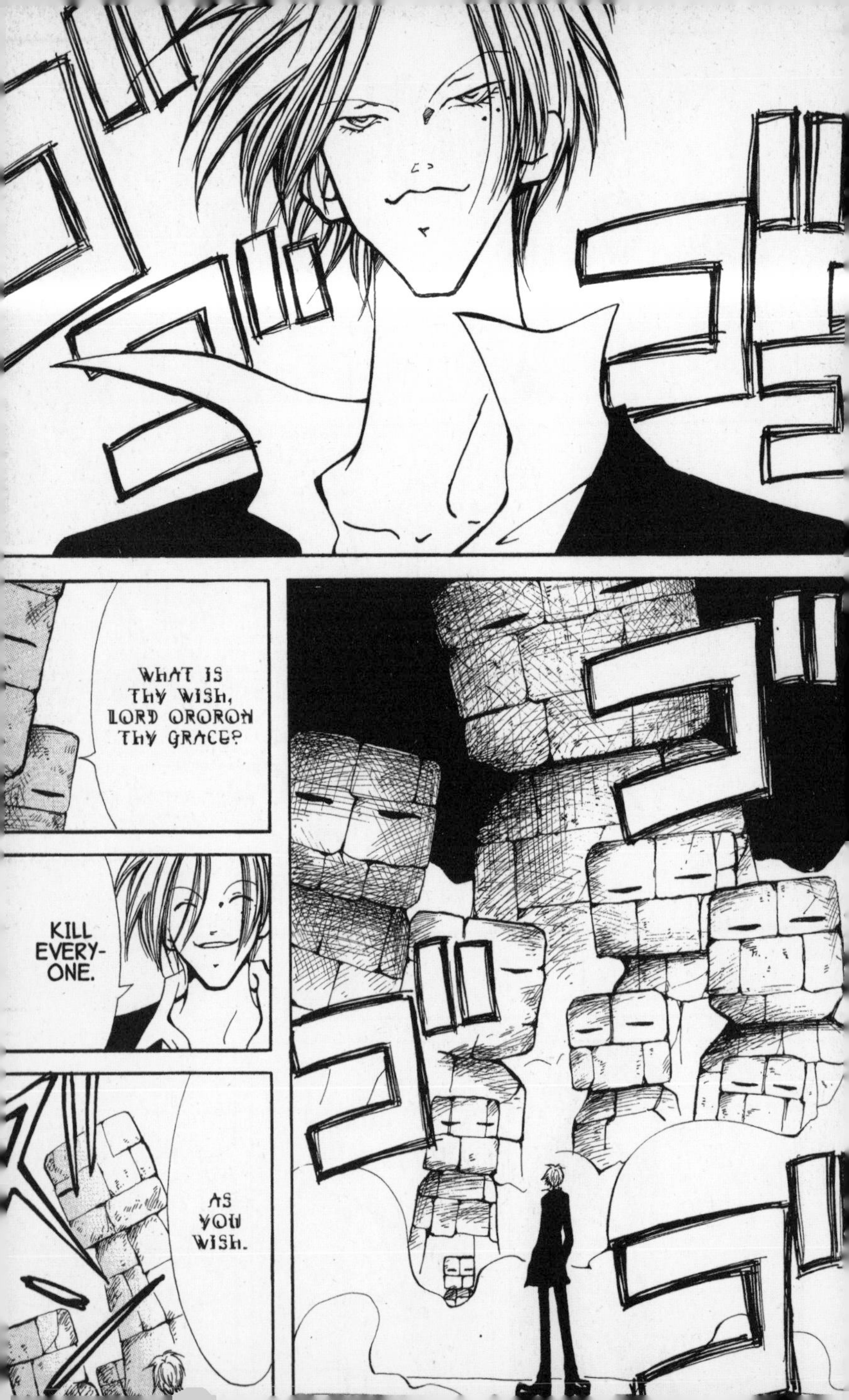
WHAT IS THY WISH, LORD ORORON THY GRACE?
KILL EVERY-ONE.
AS YOU WISH.

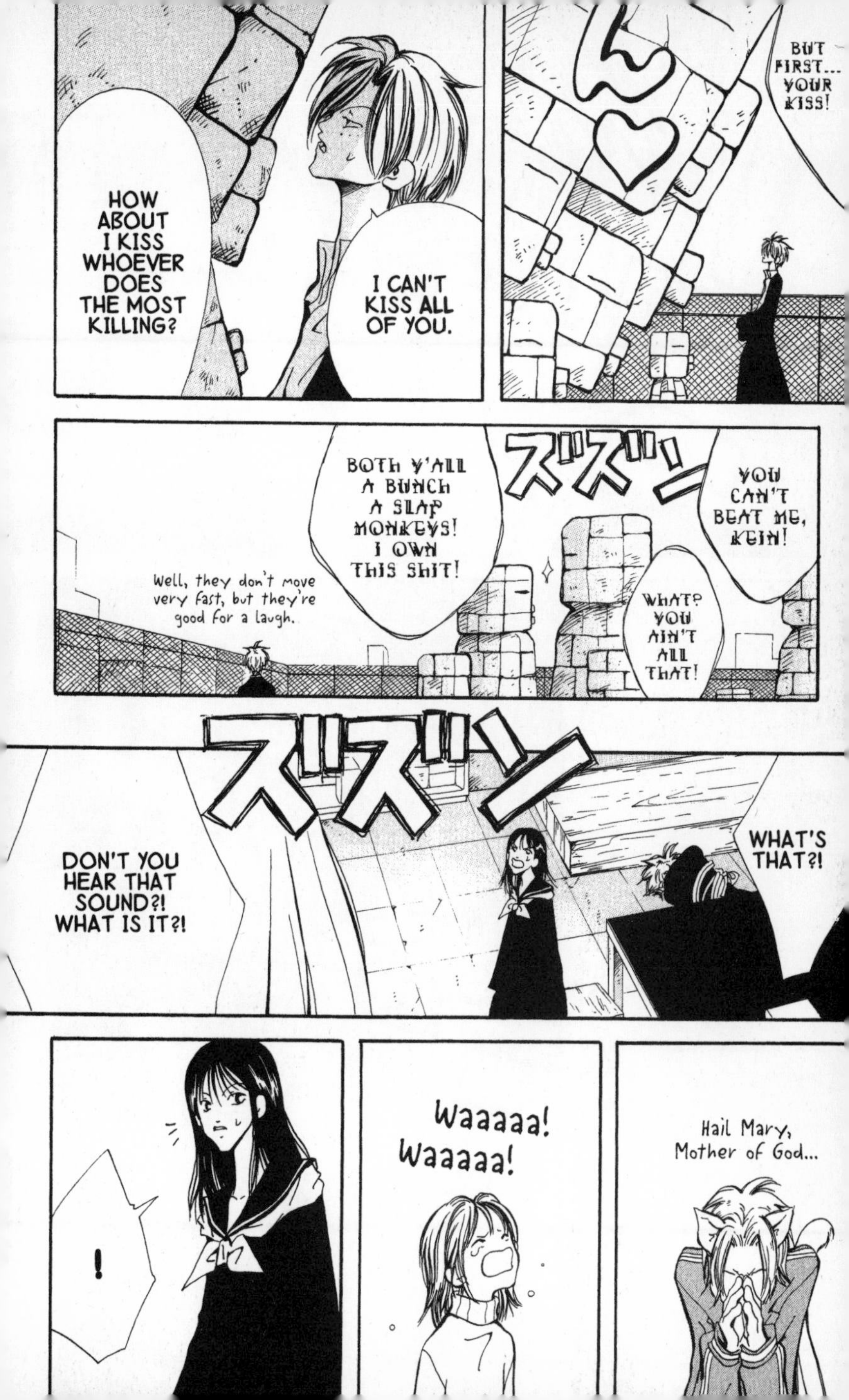
ん♡
BUT FIRST... YOUR KISS!
I CAN'T KISS ALL OF YOU.
HOW ABOUT I KISS WHOEVER DOES THE MOST KILLING?
ズズン
YOU CAN'T BEAT ME, KEIN!
WHAT? YOU AIN'T ALL THAT!
BOTH Y'ALL A BUNCH A SLAP MONKEYS! I OWN THIS SHIT!
Well, they don't move very fast, but they're good for a laugh.
ズズン
WHAT'S THAT?!
DON'T YOU HEAR THAT SOUND?! WHAT IS IT?!
Hail Mary, Mother of God...
Waaaaa! Waaaaa!
!

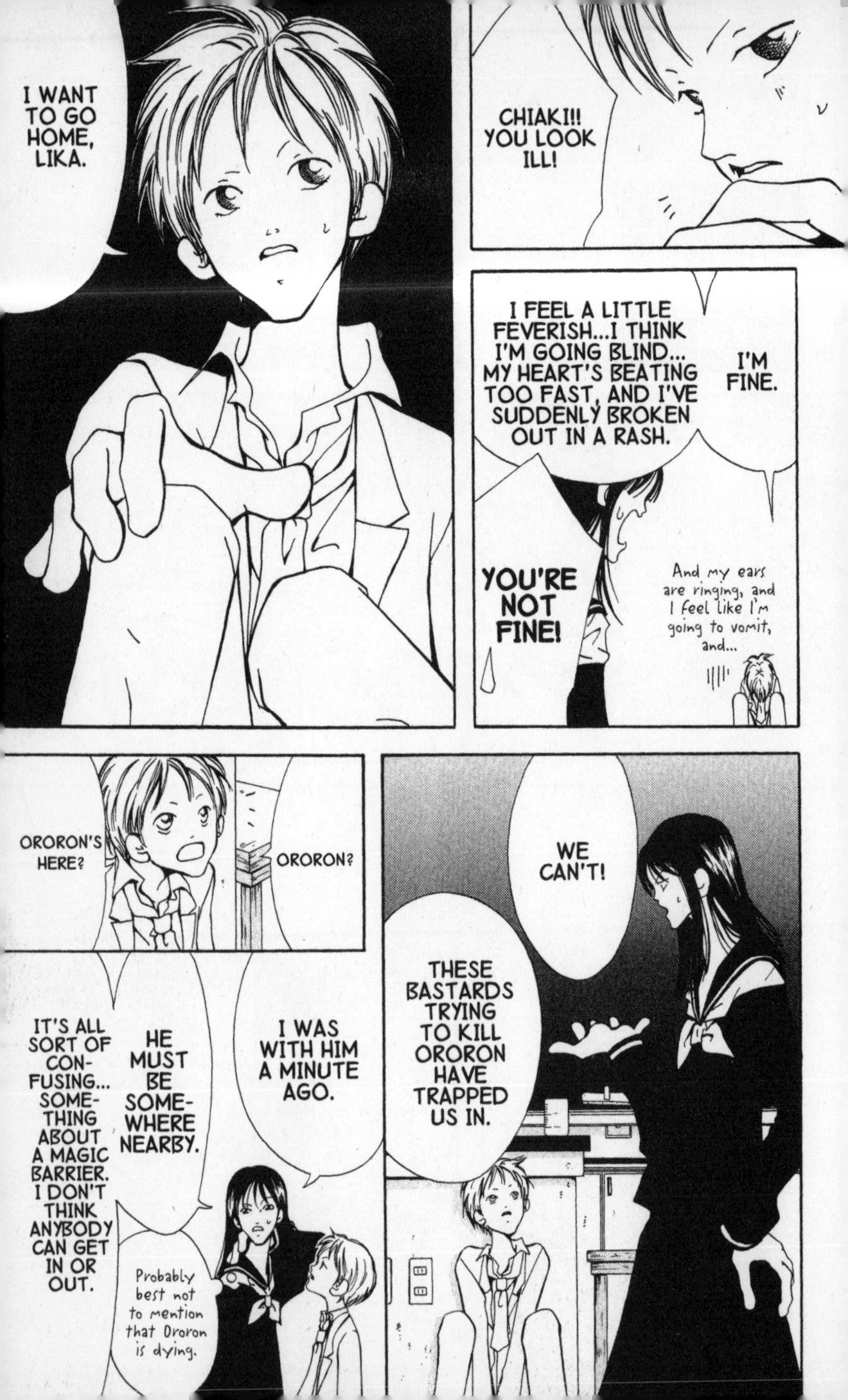
CHIAKI!! YOU LOOK ILL!
I'M FINE.
I FEEL A LITTLE FEVERISH...I THINK I'M GOING BLIND... MY HEART'S BEATING TOO FAST, AND I'VE SUDDENLY BROKEN OUT IN A RASH.
And my ears are ringing, and I feel like I'm going to vomit, and...
YOU'RE NOT FINE!
I WANT TO GO HOME, LIKA.
WE CAN'T!
THESE BASTARDS TRYING TO KILL ORORON HAVE TRAPPED US IN.
ORORON?
ORORON'S HERE?
I WAS WITH HIM A MINUTE AGO.
HE MUST BE SOMEWHERE NEARBY.
IT'S ALL SORT OF CON-FUSING... SOME-THING ABOUT A MAGIC BARRIER. I DON'T THINK ANYBODY CAN GET IN OR OUT.
Probably best not to mention that Ororon is dying.

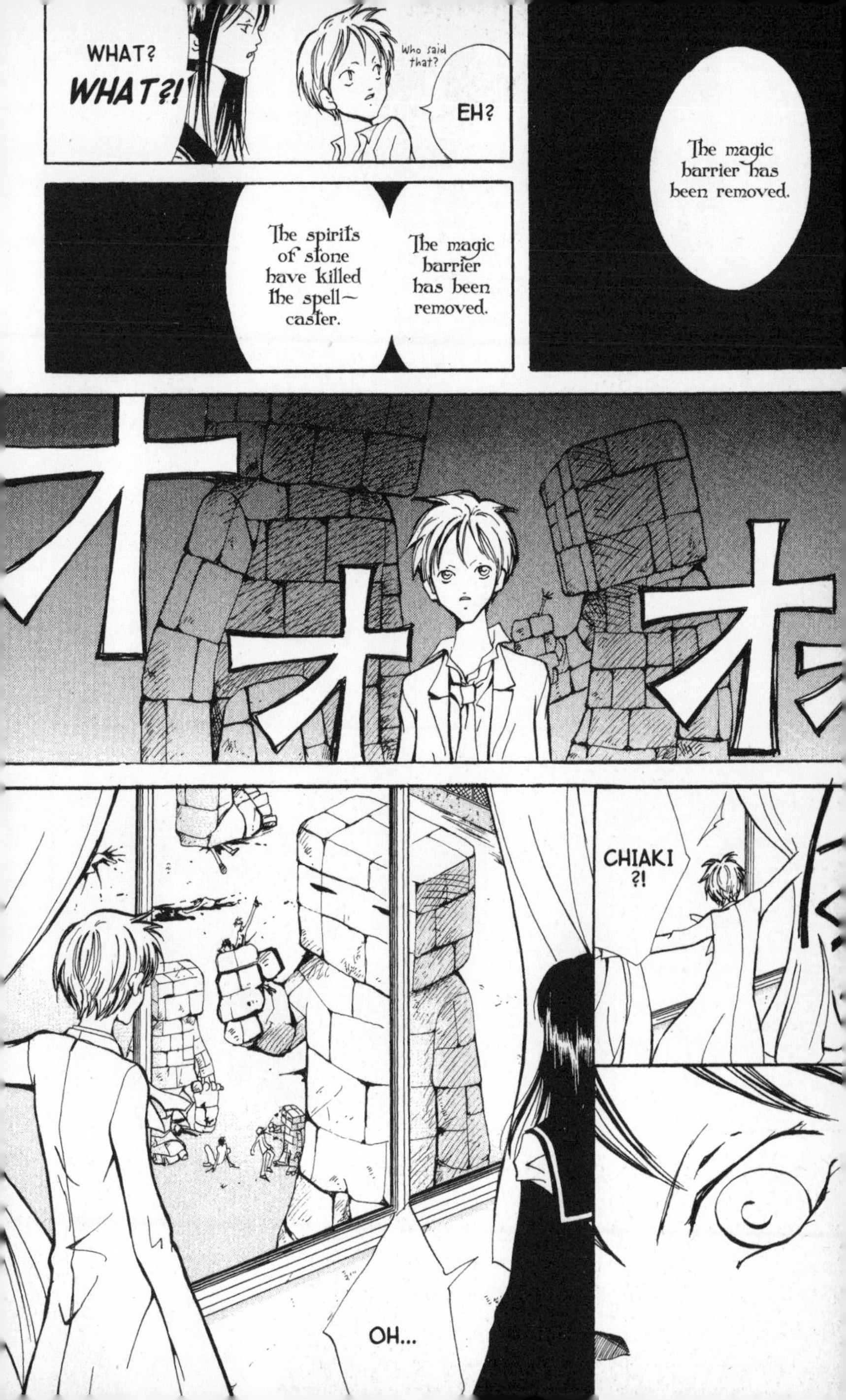

The magic barrier has been removed.
Who said that?
EH?
WHAT? WHAT?!
The magic barrier has been removed.
The spirits of stone have killed the spell-caster.
オ
オ
オ
CHIAKI ?!
OH...

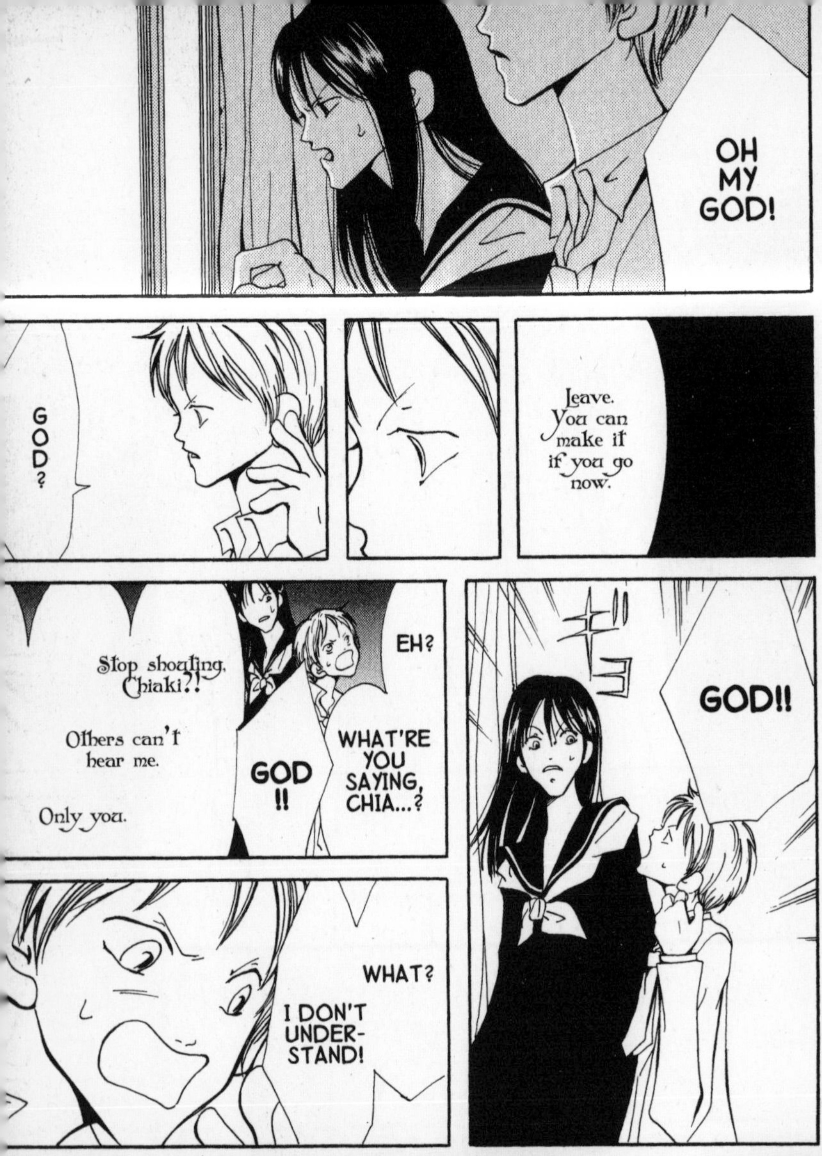
OH MY GOD!
Leave. You can make it if you go now.
GOD?
GOD!!
EH?
WHAT'RE YOU SAYING, CHIA...?
GOD !!
Stop shouting, Chiaki?!
Others can't hear me.
Only you.
WHAT?
I DON'T UNDER-STAND!

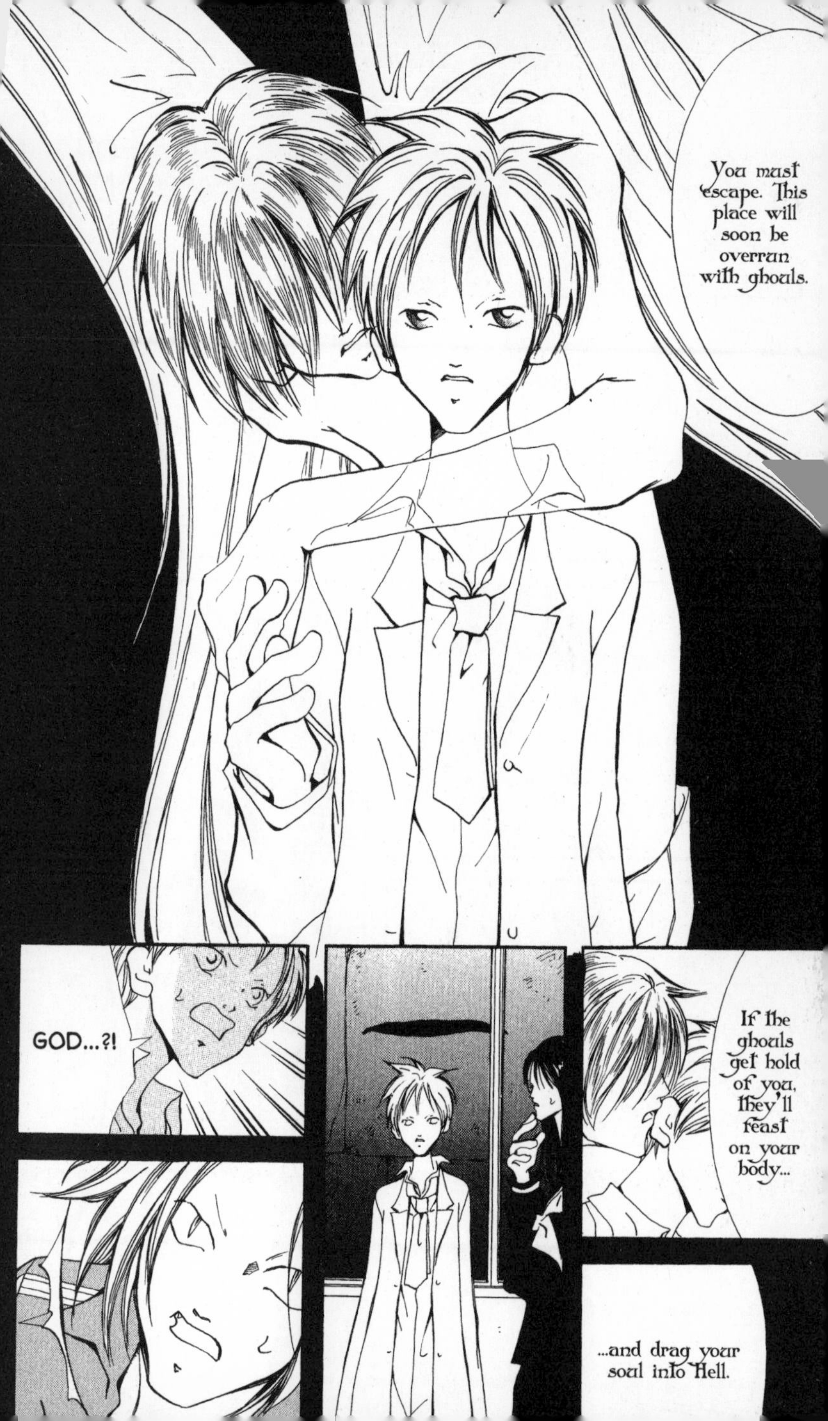
You must escape. This place will soon be overrun with ghouls.
If the ghouls get hold of you, they'll feast on your body...
...and drag your soul into Hell.
GOD...?!

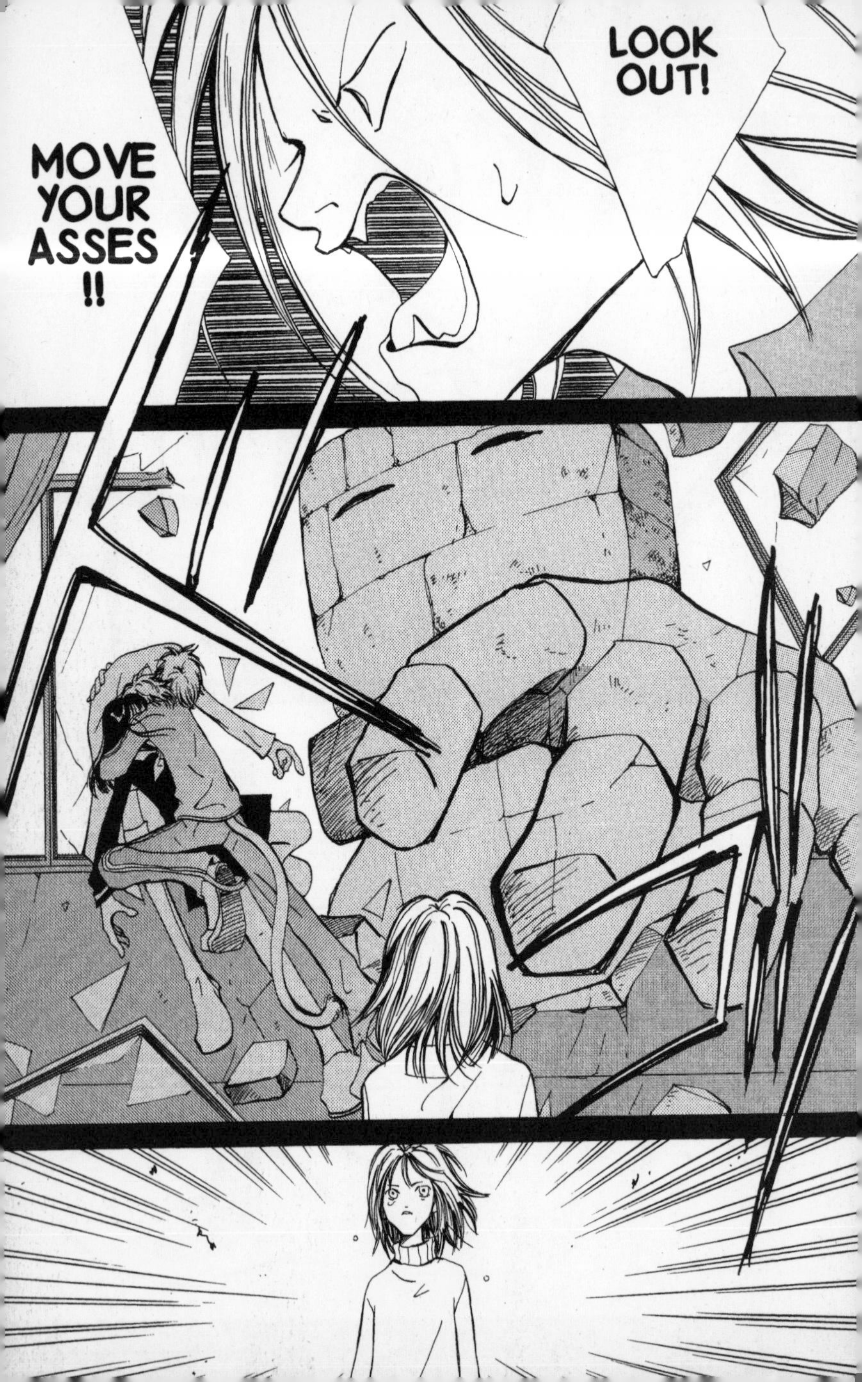
LOOK OUT!
MOVE YOUR ASSES !!

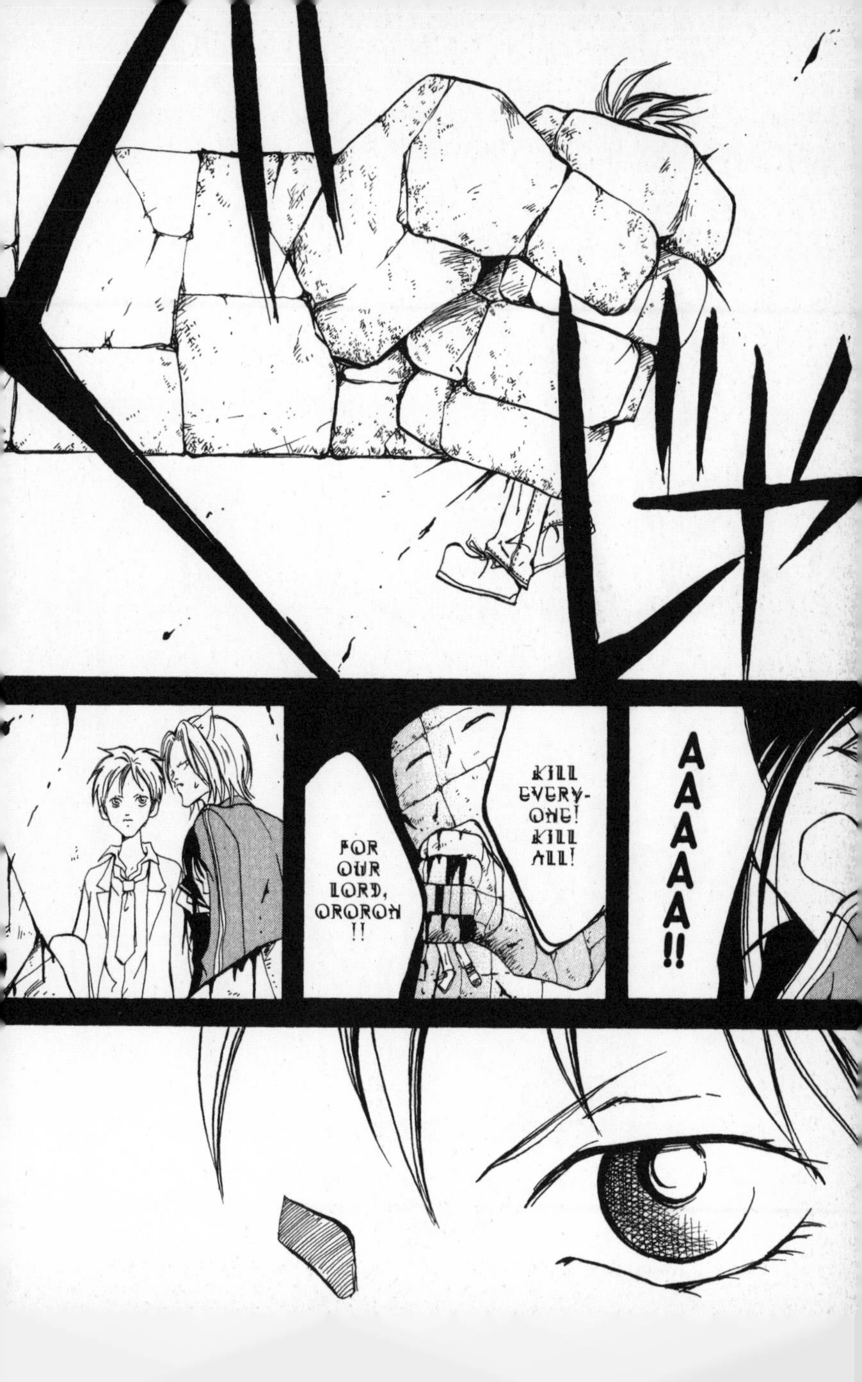
AAAAAA!!
KILL EVERY-ONE! KILL ALL!
FOR OUR LORD, ORORON !!

Our bodies run warm with blood...

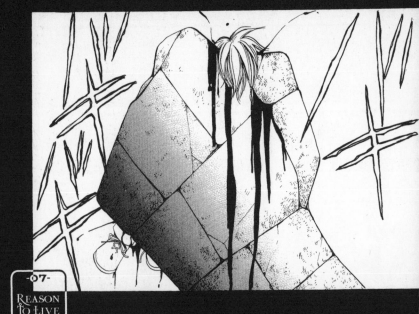

REASON
TO LIVE

We inhale air, devour food.

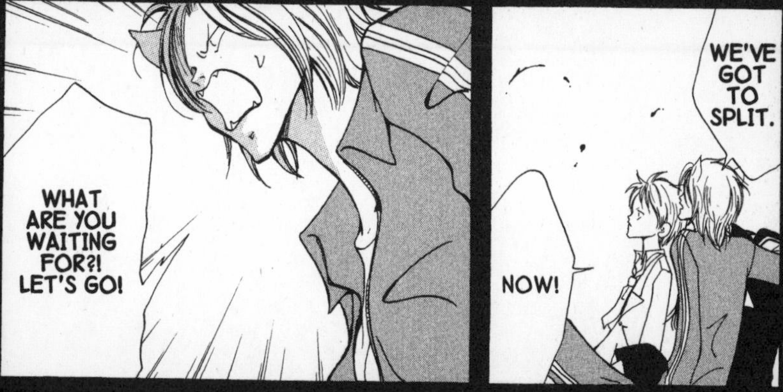
WE'VE GOT TO SPLIT.
NOW!
WHAT ARE YOU WAITING FOR?! LET'S GO!

We're all the same.

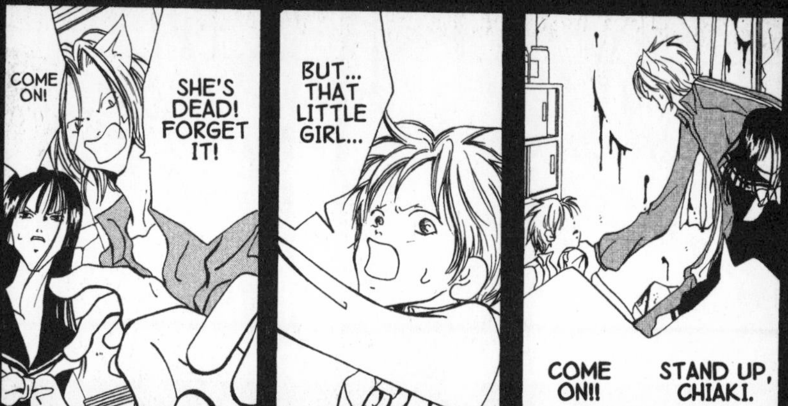
STAND UP, CHIAKI.
COME ON!!
BUT... THAT LITTLE GIRL...
SHE'S DEAD! FORGET IT!
COME ON!

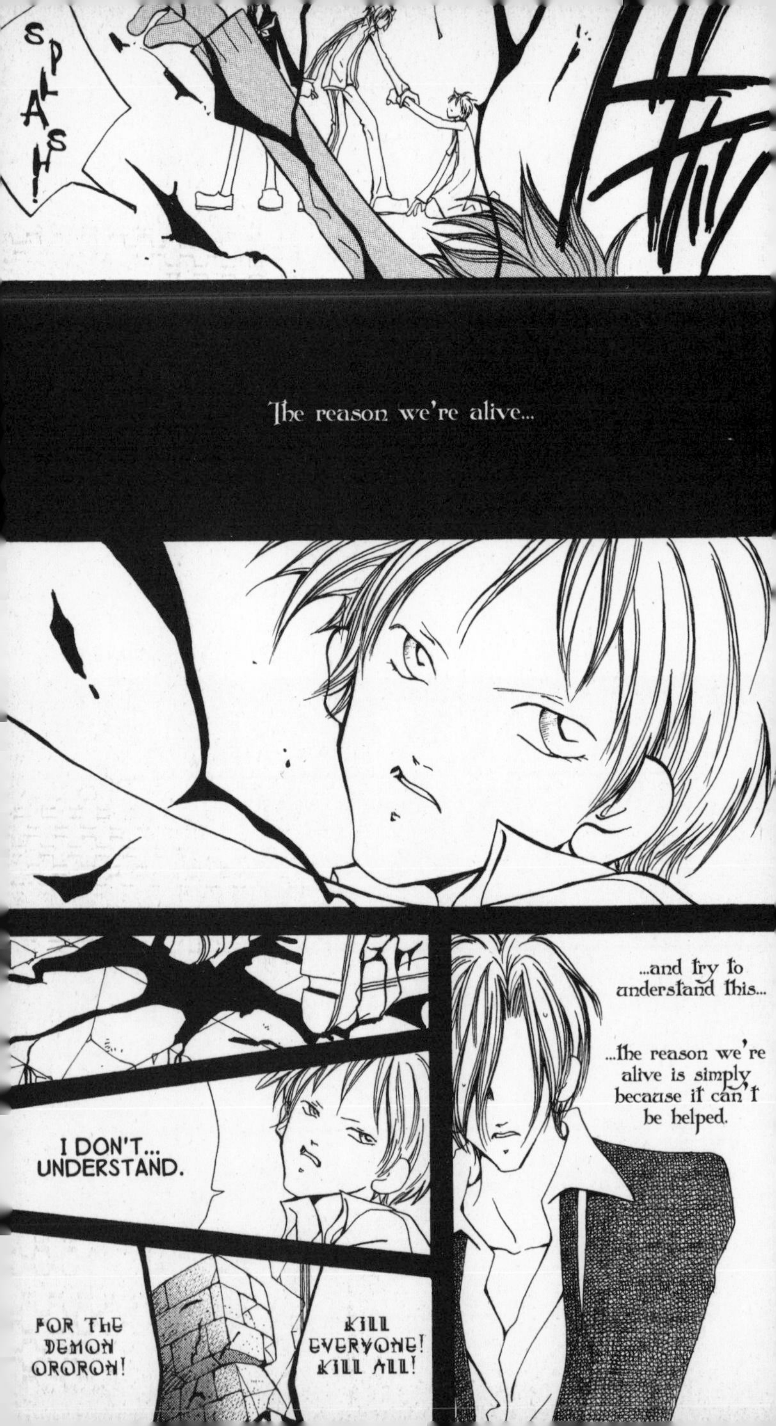
SPLASH!
The reason we're alive...
...and try to understand this...
...the reason we're alive is simply because it can't be helped.
I DON'T... UNDERSTAND.
KILL EVERYONE! KILL ALL!
FOR THE DEMON ORORON!

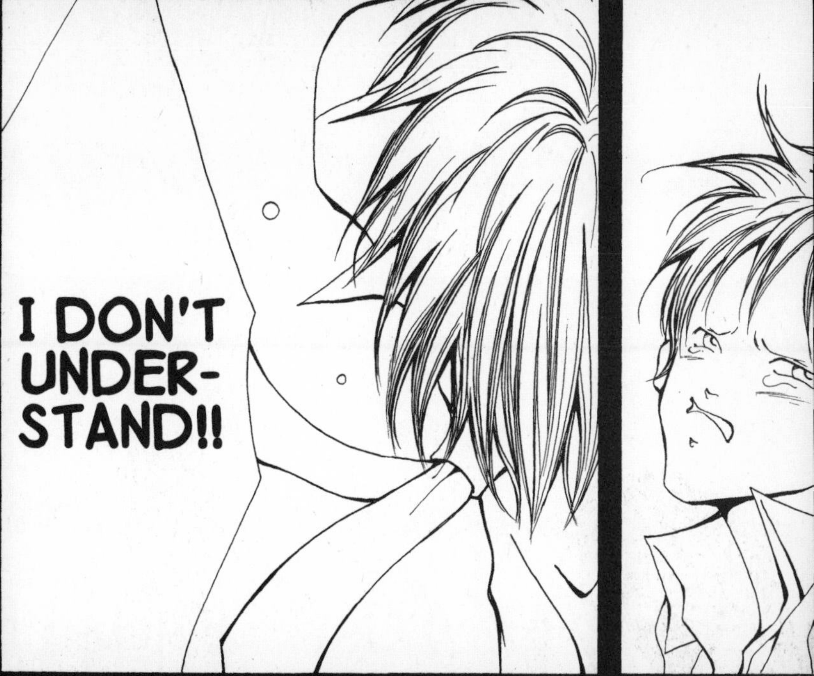
I DON'T UNDER-STAND!!

I don't want to do this anymore... I don't want to live.

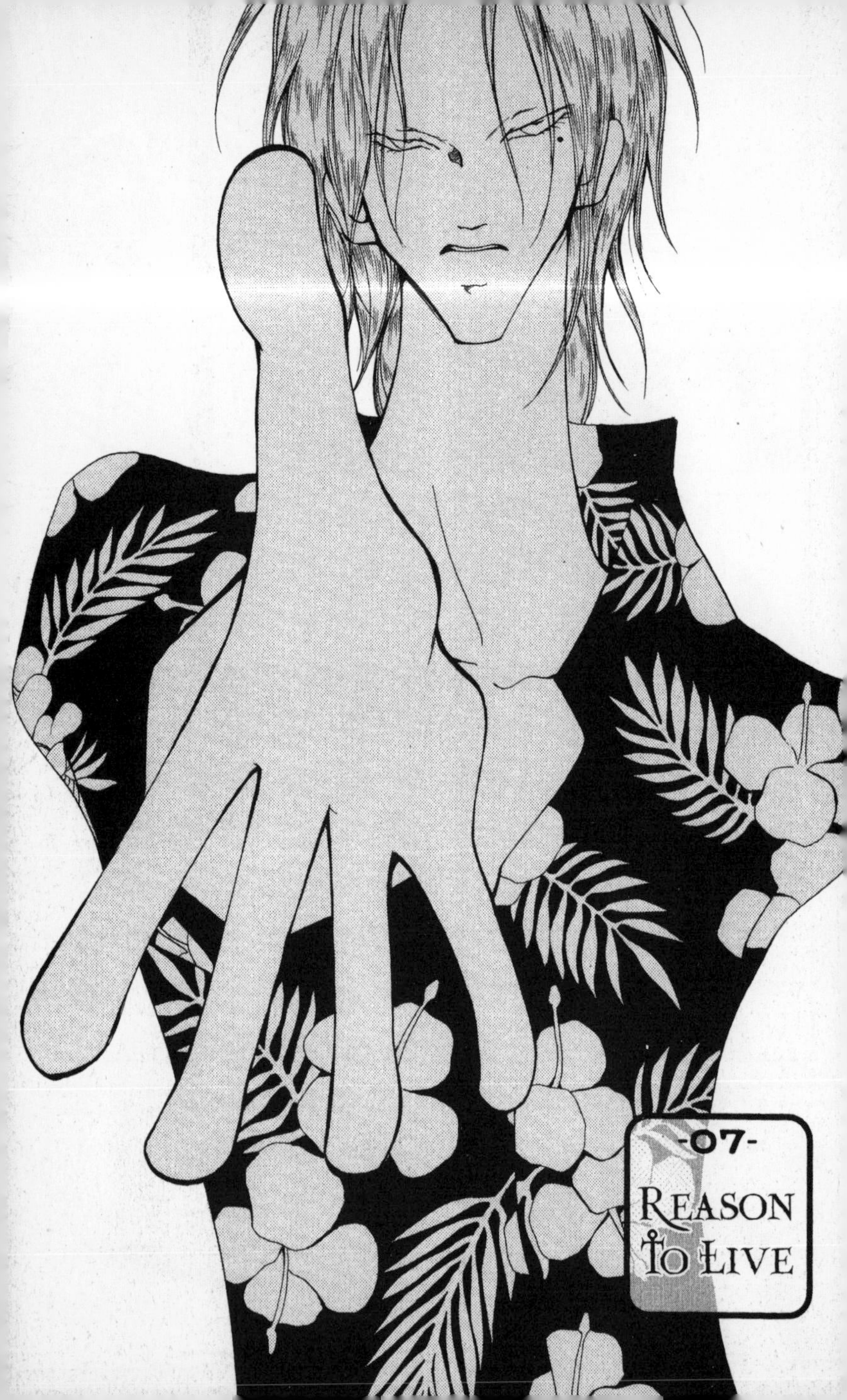
-07-
REASON TO LIVE

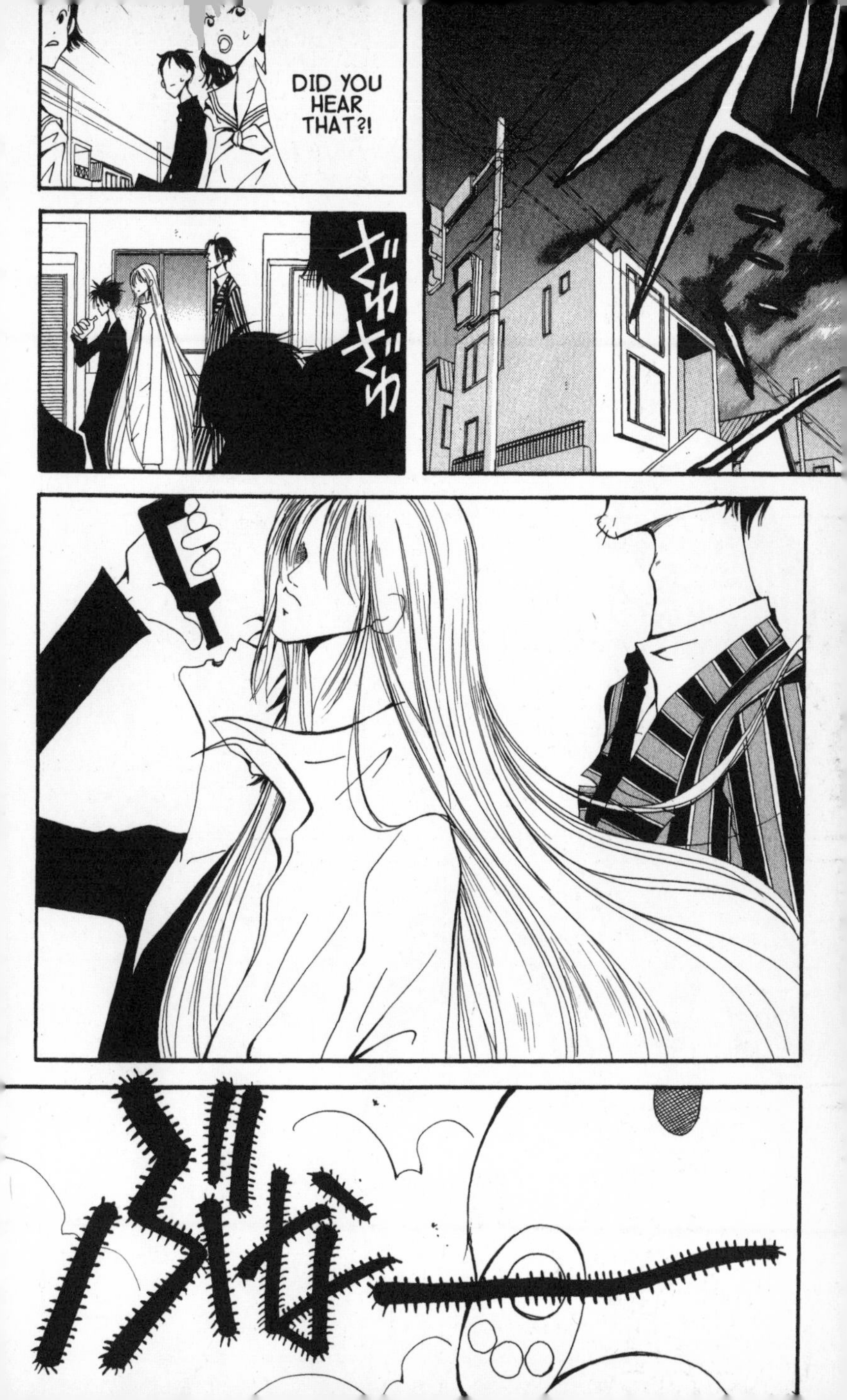
DID YOU HEAR THAT?!
ざわざわ

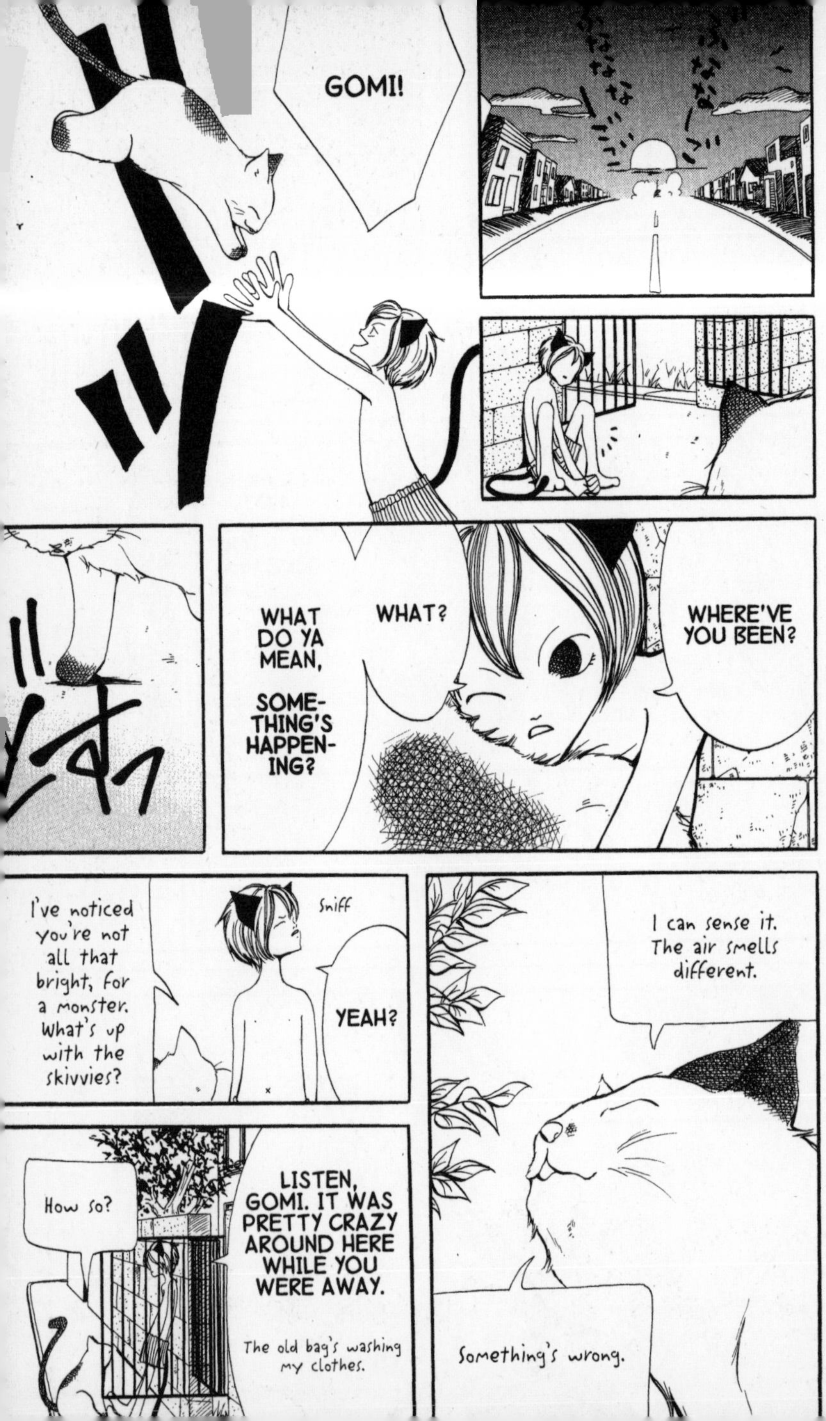
GOMI!
WHERE'VE YOU BEEN?
WHAT?
WHAT DO YA MEAN, SOME-THING'S HAPPEN-ING?
I can sense it. The air smells different.
Something's wrong.
Sniff
YEAH?
I've noticed you're not all that bright, for a monster. What's up with the skivvies?
LISTEN, GOMI. IT WAS PRETTY CRAZY AROUND HERE WHILE YOU WERE AWAY.
The old bag's washing my clothes.
How so?

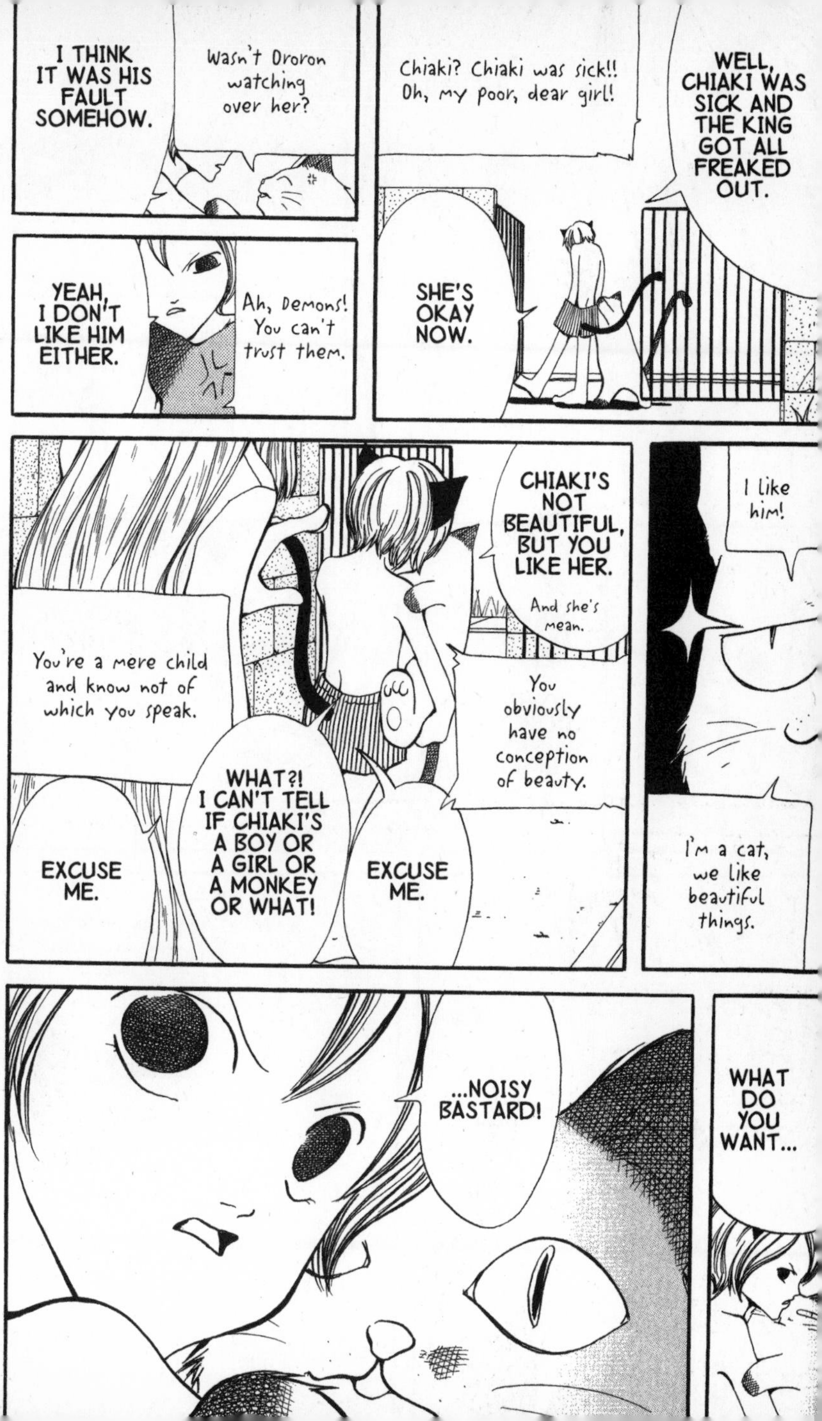

WELL, CHIAKI WAS SICK AND THE KING GOT ALL FREAKED OUT.
Chiaki? Chiaki was sick!! Oh, my poor, dear girl!
SHE'S OKAY NOW.
Wasn't Dororon watching over her?
I THINK IT WAS HIS FAULT SOMEHOW.
Ah, Demons! You can't trust them.
YEAH, I DON'T LIKE HIM EITHER.
I like him!
I'm a cat, we like beautiful things.
CHIAKI'S NOT BEAUTIFUL, BUT YOU LIKE HER.
And she's mean.
You obviously have no conception of beauty.
EXCUSE ME.
WHAT?! I CAN'T TELL IF CHIAKI'S A BOY OR A GIRL OR A MONKEY OR WHAT!
You're a mere child and know not of which you speak.
EXCUSE ME.
WHAT DO YOU WANT...
...NOISY BASTARD!

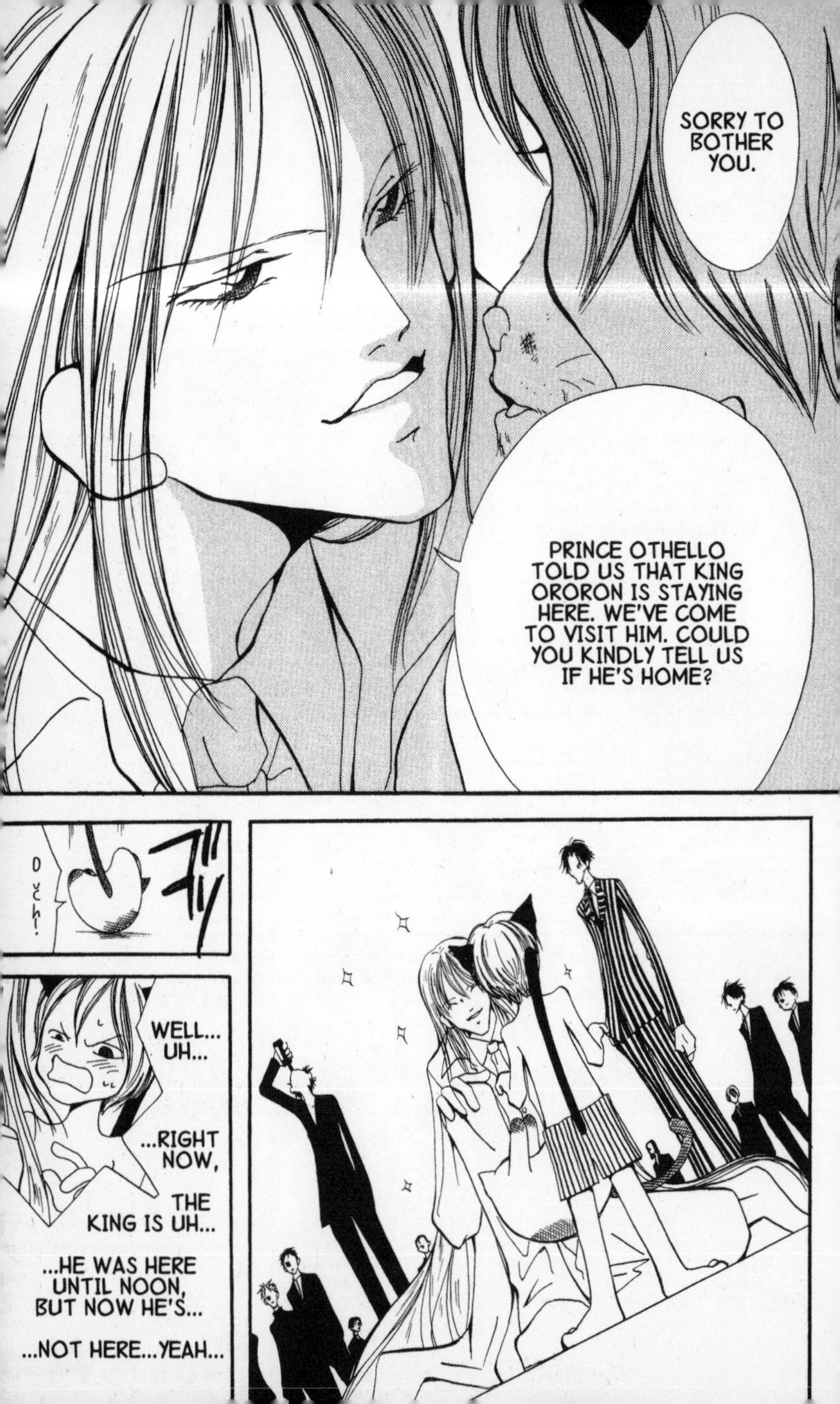
SORRY TO BOTHER YOU.
PRINCE OTHELLO TOLD US THAT KING ORORON IS STAYING HERE. WE'VE COME TO VISIT HIM. COULD YOU KINDLY TELL US IF HE'S HOME?
Ouch!
WELL... UH...
...RIGHT NOW,
THE KING IS UH...
...HE WAS HERE UNTIL NOON, BUT NOW HE'S...
...NOT HERE...YEAH...

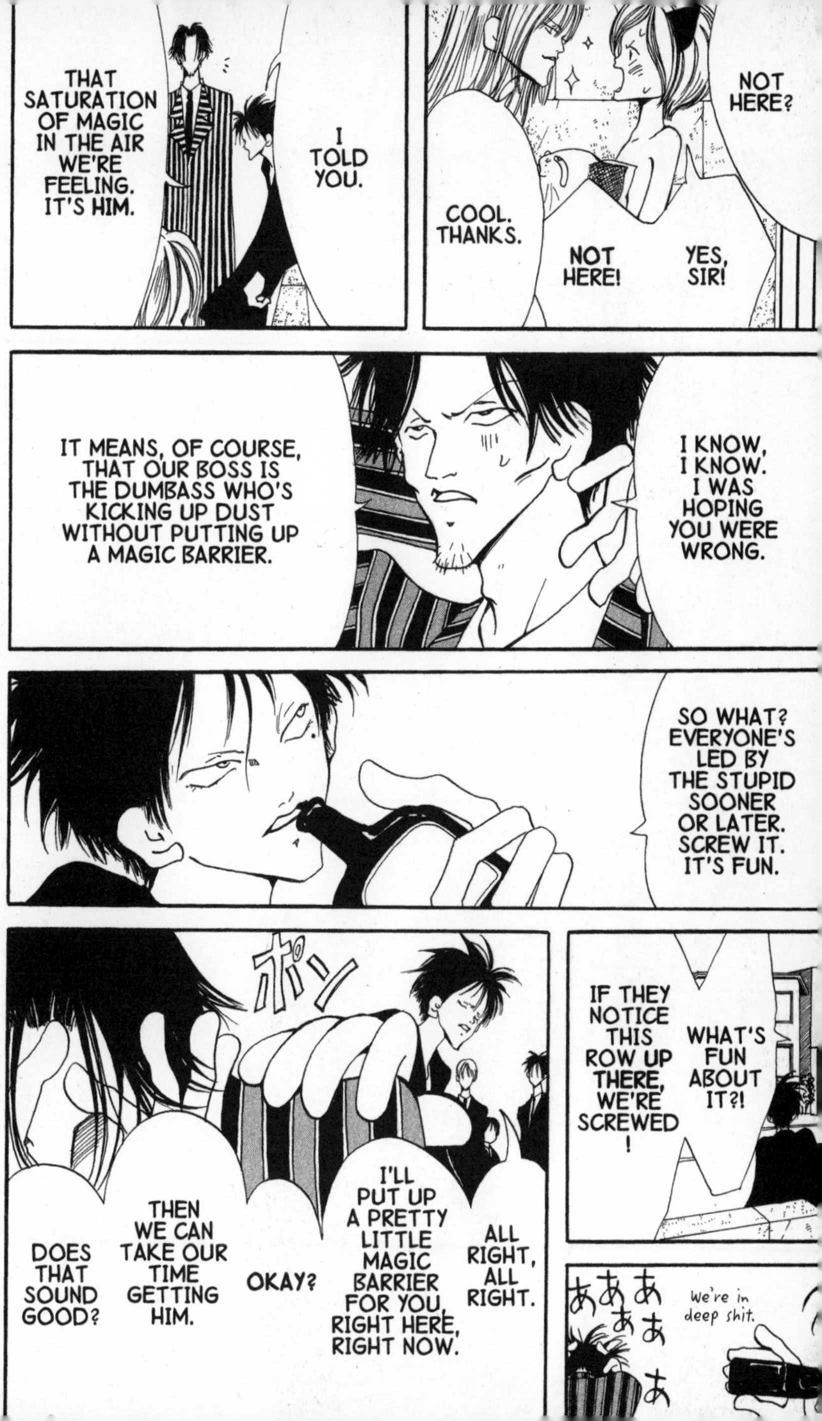
NOT HERE?
YES, SIR!
NOT HERE!
COOL. THANKS.
I TOLD YOU.
THAT SATURATION OF MAGIC IN THE AIR WE'RE FEELING. IT'S HIM.
I KNOW, I KNOW. I WAS HOPING YOU WERE WRONG.
IT MEANS, OF COURSE, THAT OUR BOSS IS THE DUMBASS WHO'S KICKING UP DUST WITHOUT PUTTING UP A MAGIC BARRIER.
SO WHAT? EVERYONE'S LED BY THE STUPID SOONER OR LATER. SCREW IT. IT'S FUN.
WHAT'S FUN ABOUT IT?!
IF THEY NOTICE THIS ROW UP THERE, WE'RE SCREWED!
ああああああ
We're in deep shit.
ポン
ALL RIGHT, ALL RIGHT.
I'LL PUT UP A PRETTY LITTLE MAGIC BARRIER FOR YOU, RIGHT HERE, RIGHT NOW.
OKAY?
THEN WE CAN TAKE OUR TIME GETTING HIM.
DOES THAT SOUND GOOD?

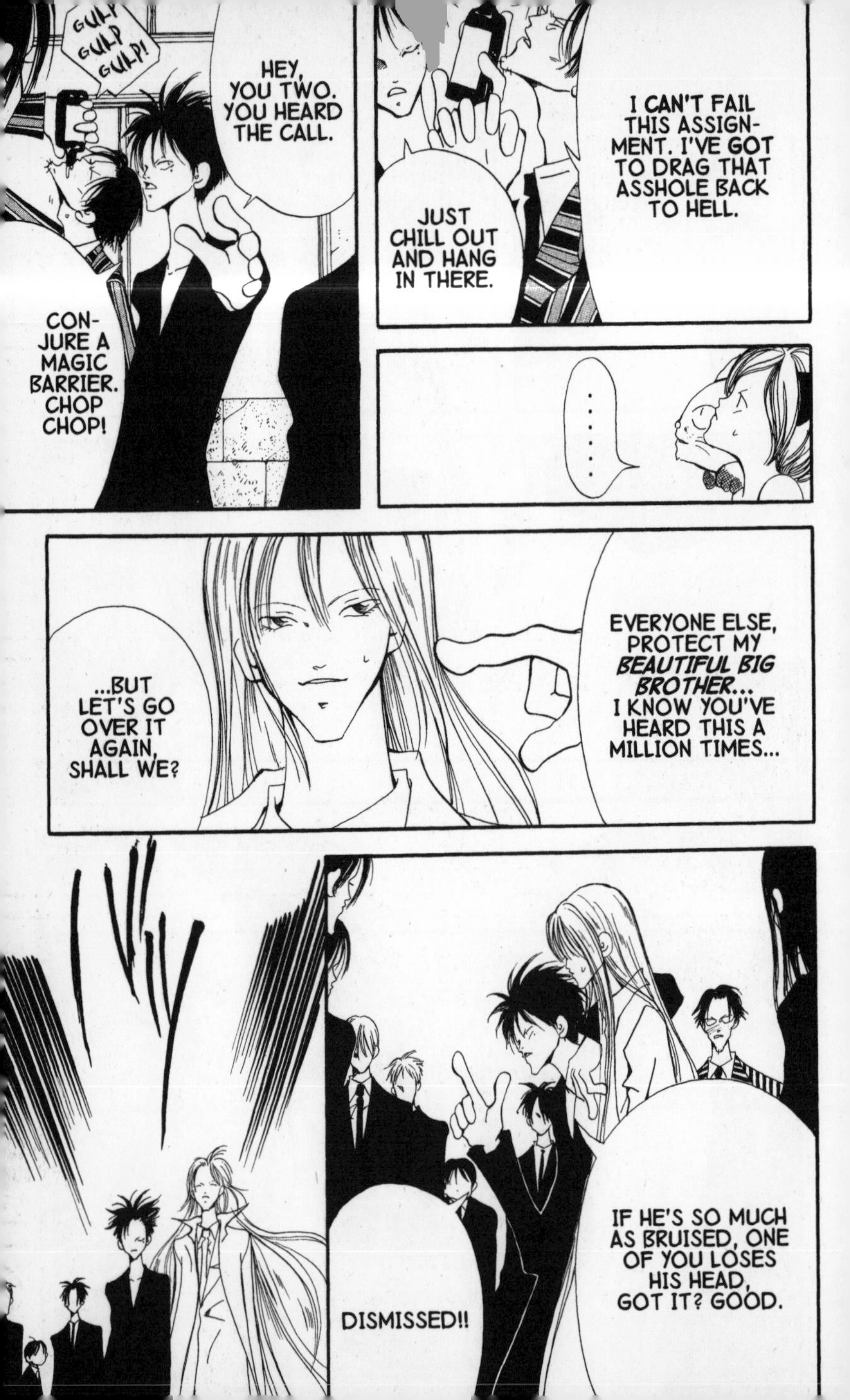

I CAN'T FAIL THIS ASSIGN-MENT. I'VE GOT TO DRAG THAT ASSHOLE BACK TO HELL.
JUST CHILL OUT AND HANG IN THERE.
......
HEY, YOU TWO. YOU HEARD THE CALL.
GULP GULP GULP!
CON-JURE A MAGIC BARRIER. CHOP CHOP!
EVERYONE ELSE, PROTECT MY *BEAUTIFUL BIG BROTHER*... I KNOW YOU'VE HEARD THIS A MILLION TIMES...
...BUT LET'S GO OVER IT AGAIN, SHALL WE?
IF HE'S SO MUCH AS BRUISED, ONE OF YOU LOSES HIS HEAD, GOT IT? GOOD.
DISMISSED!!

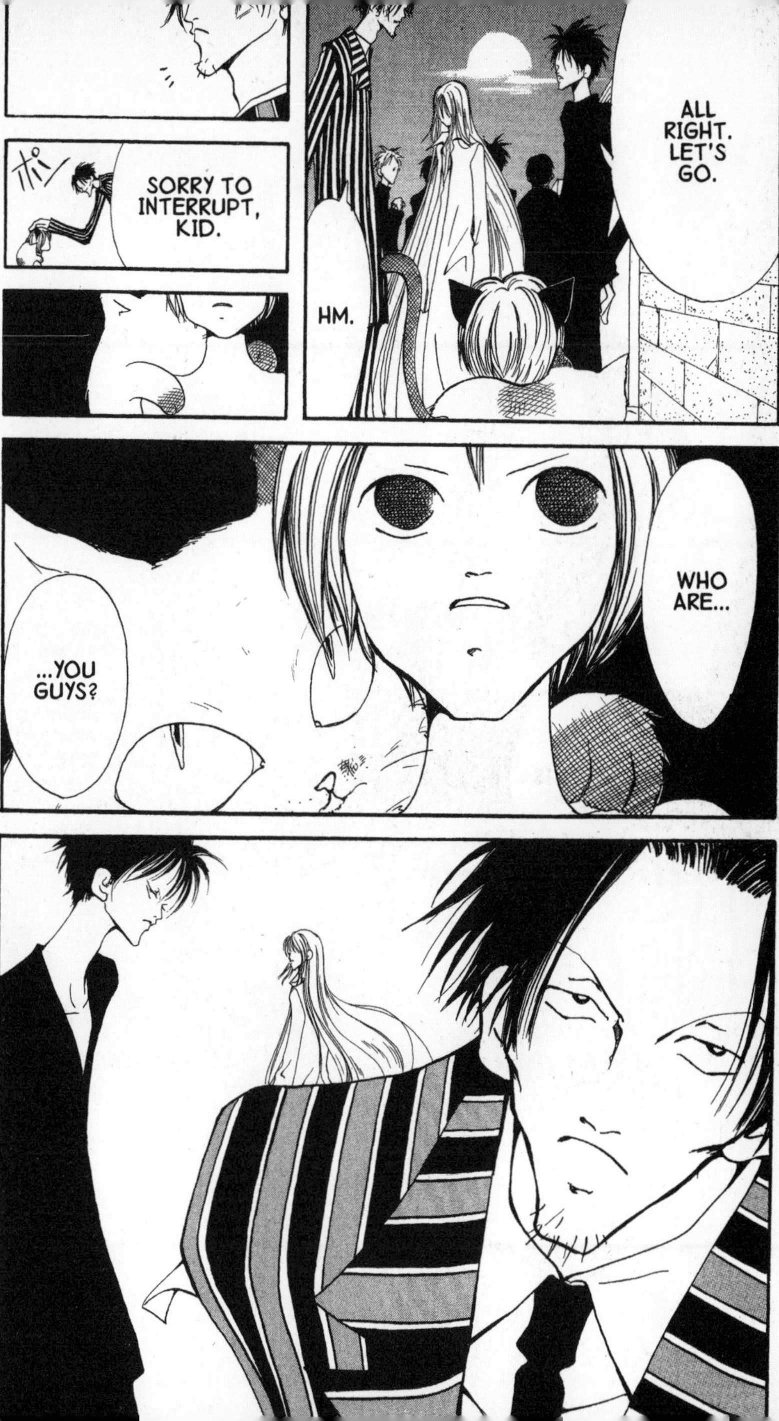
ALL RIGHT. LET'S GO.
HM.
ポン
SORRY TO INTERRUPT, KID.
WHO ARE...
...YOU GUYS?

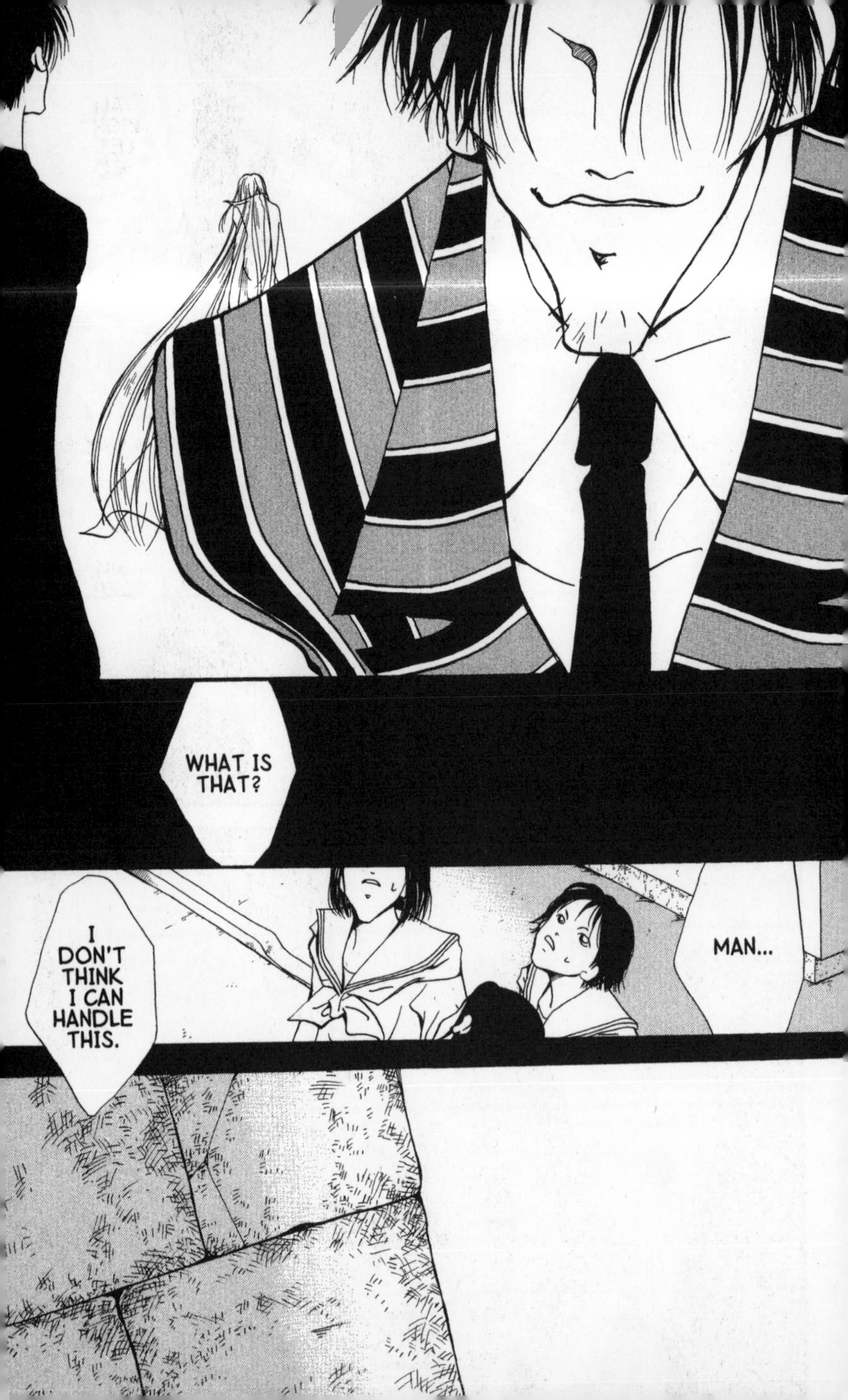

WHAT IS THAT?
MAN...
I DON'T THINK I CAN HANDLE THIS.

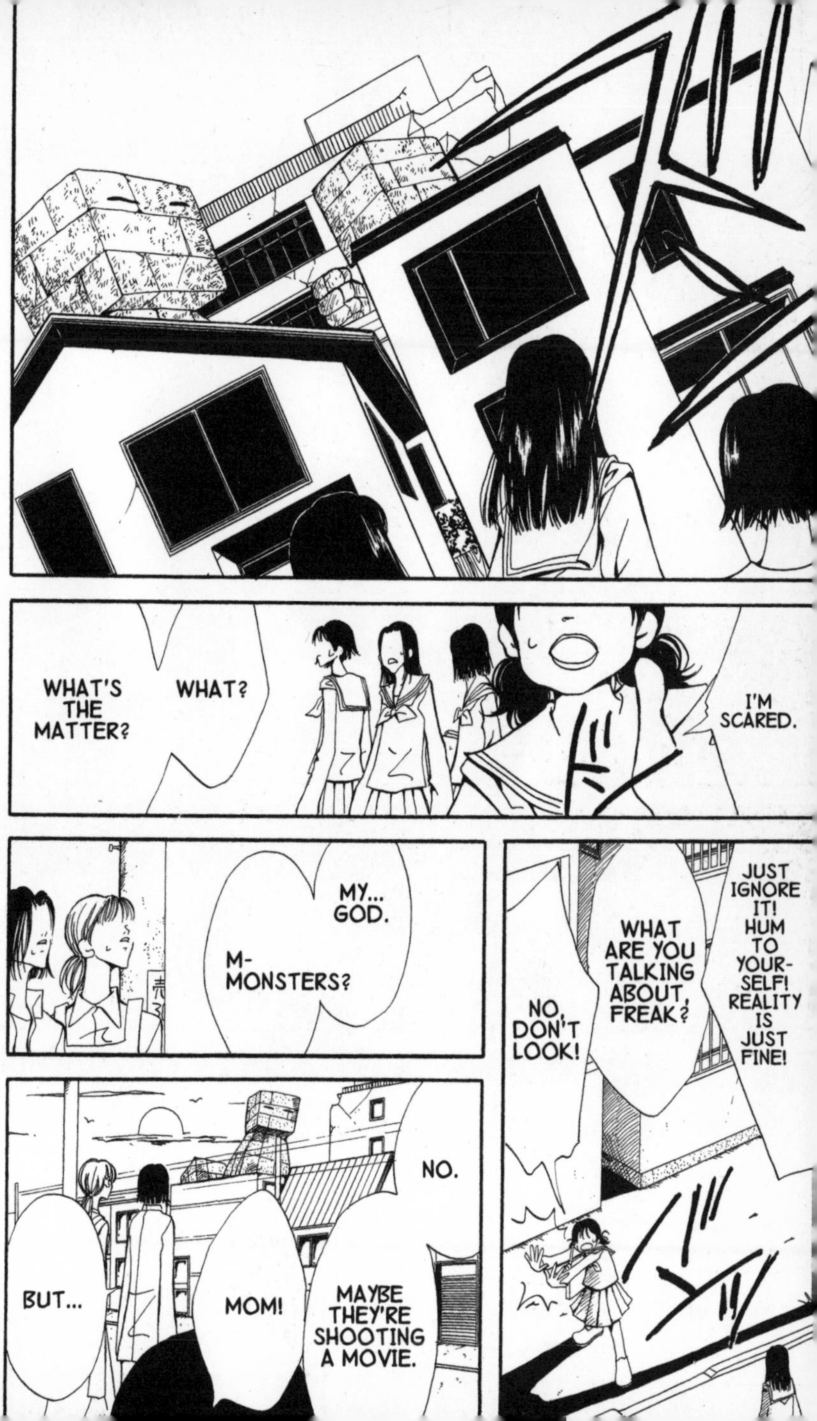
I'M SCARED.
WHAT?
WHAT'S THE MATTER?
JUST IGNORE IT! HUM TO YOURSELF! REALITY IS JUST FINE!
WHAT ARE YOU TALKING ABOUT, FREAK?
NO, DON'T LOOK!
MY... GOD.
M-MONSTERS?
NO.
MAYBE THEY'RE SHOOTING A MOVIE.
MOM!
BUT...

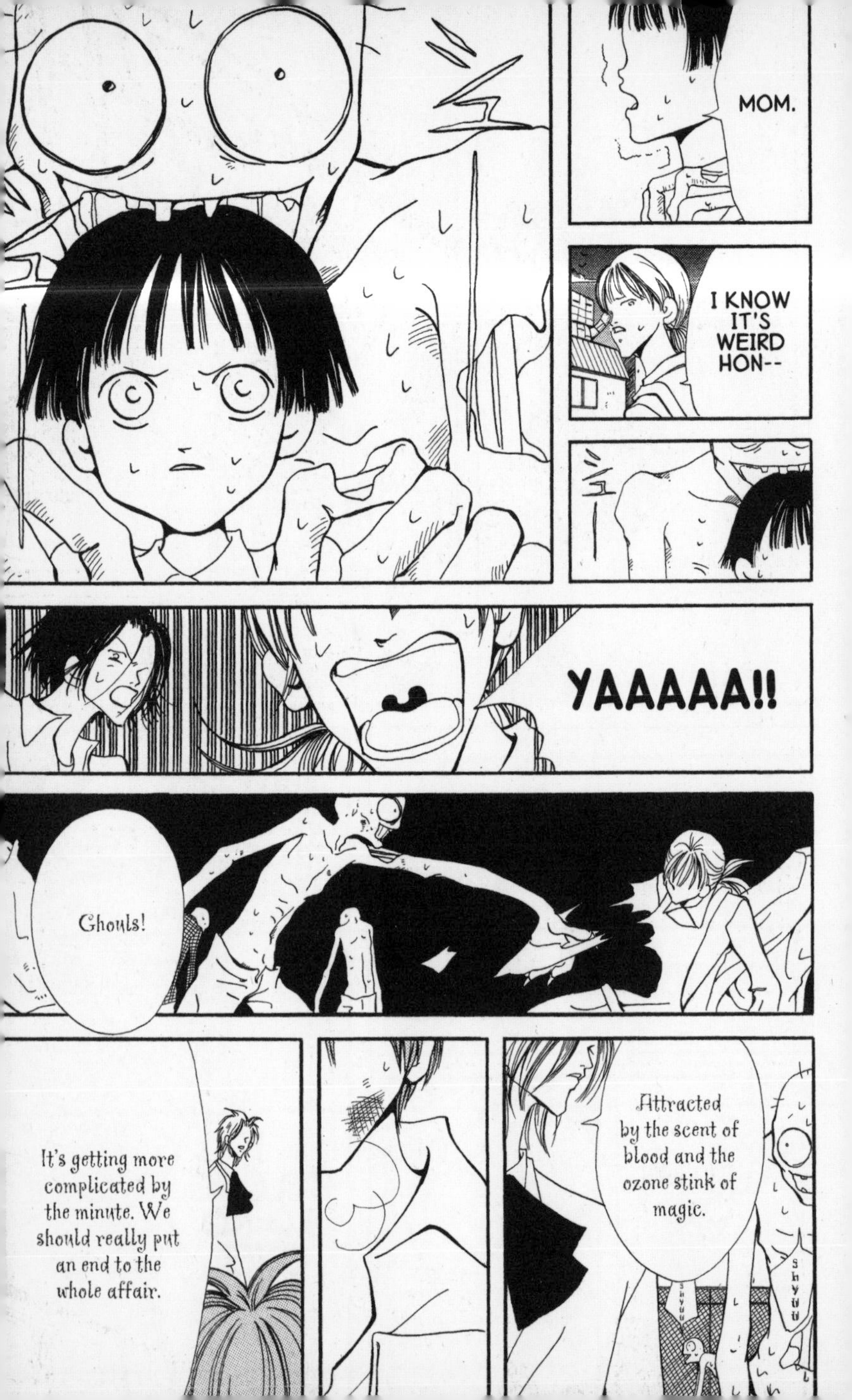
MOM.
I KNOW IT'S WEIRD HON--
YAAAAA!!
Ghouls!
Attracted by the scent of blood and the ozone stink of magic.
Shyuu
Shyuu
It's getting more complicated by the minute. We should really put an end to the whole affair.

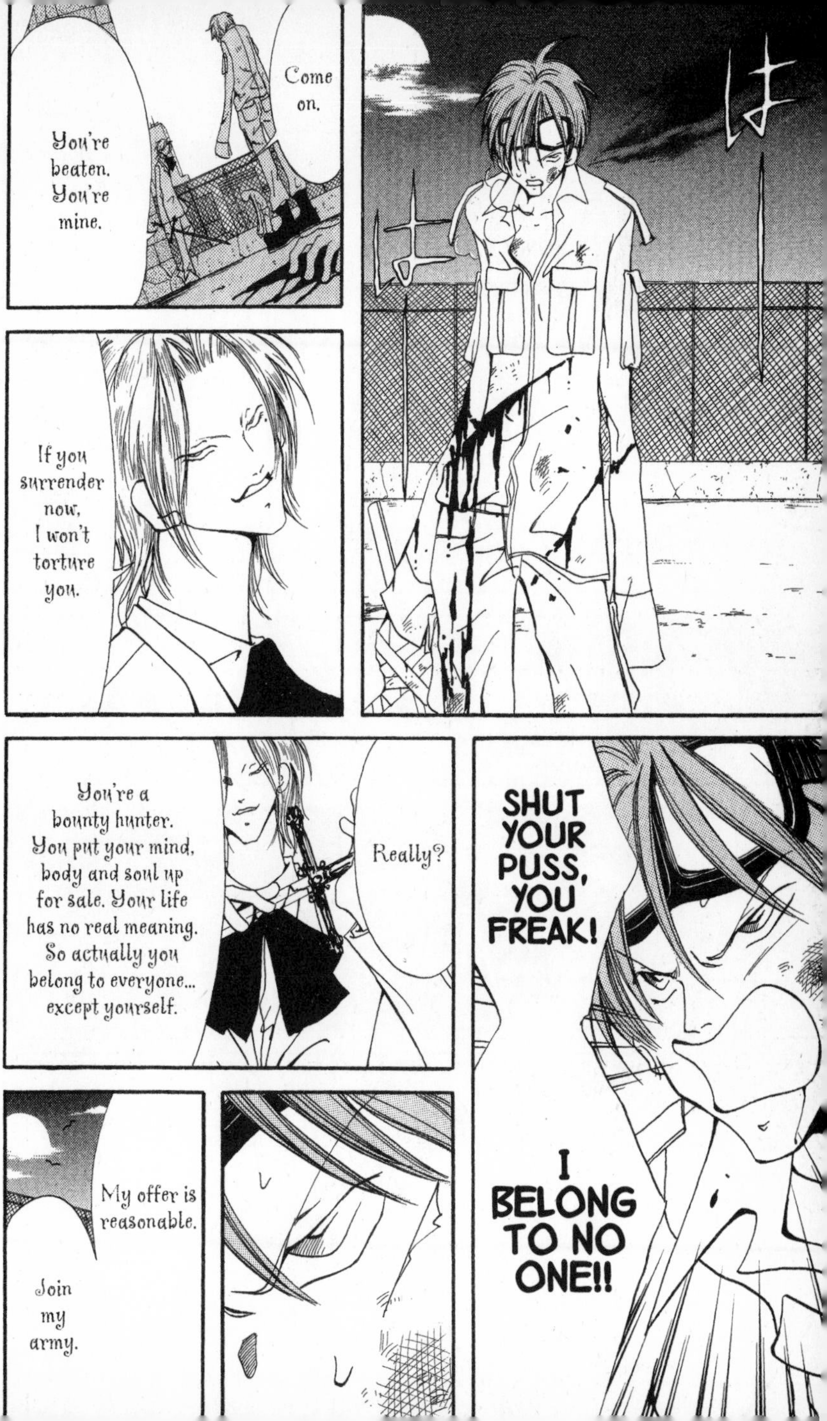

はー
は
Come on.
You're beaten. You're mine.
If you surrender now, I won't torture you.
SHUT YOUR PUSS, YOU FREAK!
I BELONG TO NO ONE!!
Really?
You're a bounty hunter. You put your mind, body and soul up for sale. Your life has no real meaning. So actually you belong to everyone... except yourself.
My offer is reasonable.
Join my army.

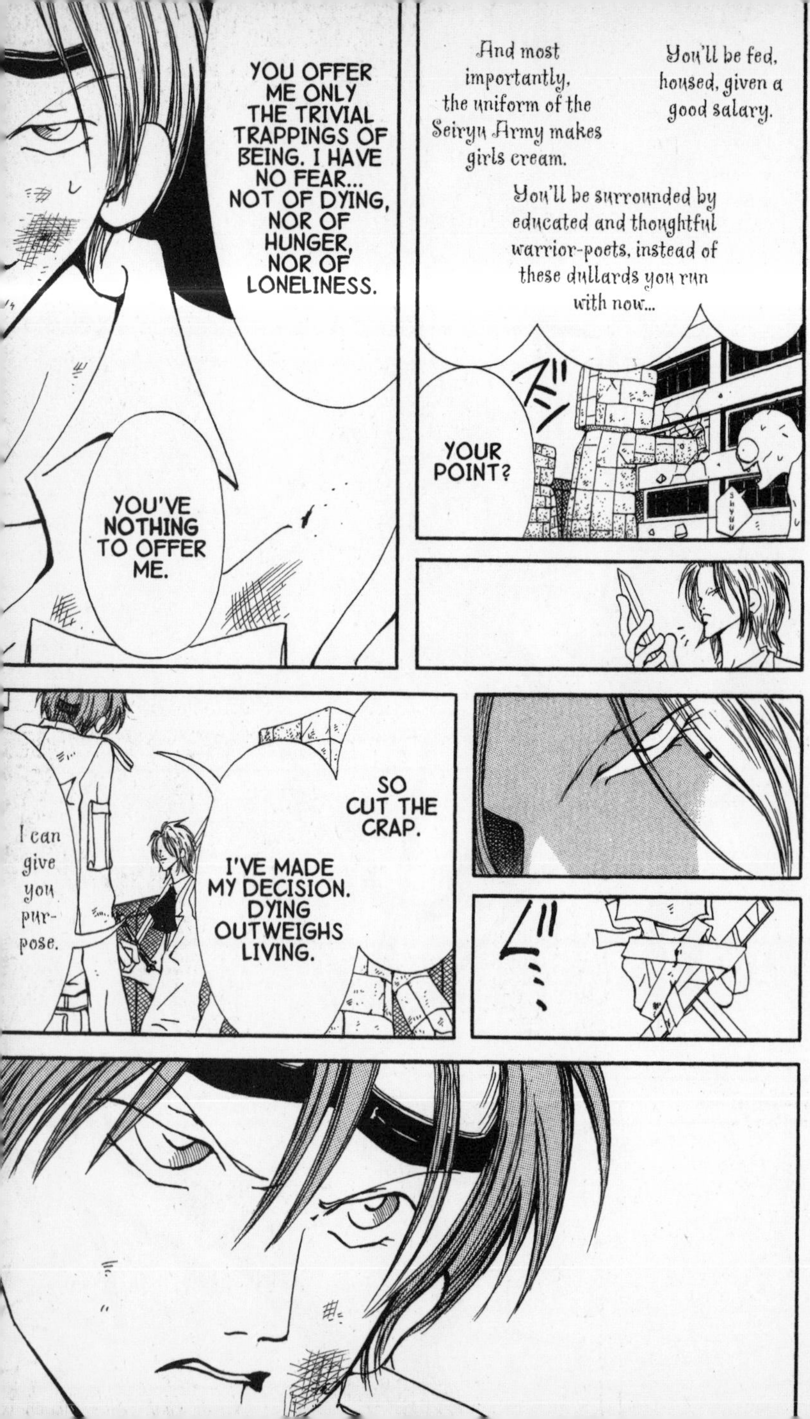
You'll be fed, housed, given a good salary.
And most importantly, the uniform of the Seiryu Army makes girls cream.
You'll be surrounded by educated and thoughtful warrior-poets, instead of these dullards you run with now...
ズン
YOUR POINT?
shyuu
YOU OFFER ME ONLY THE TRIVIAL TRAPPINGS OF BEING. I HAVE NO FEAR... NOT OF DYING, NOR OF HUNGER, NOR OF LONELINESS.
YOU'VE NOTHING TO OFFER ME.
SO CUT THE CRAP.
I'VE MADE MY DECISION. DYING OUTWEIGHS LIVING.
I can give you pur-pose.

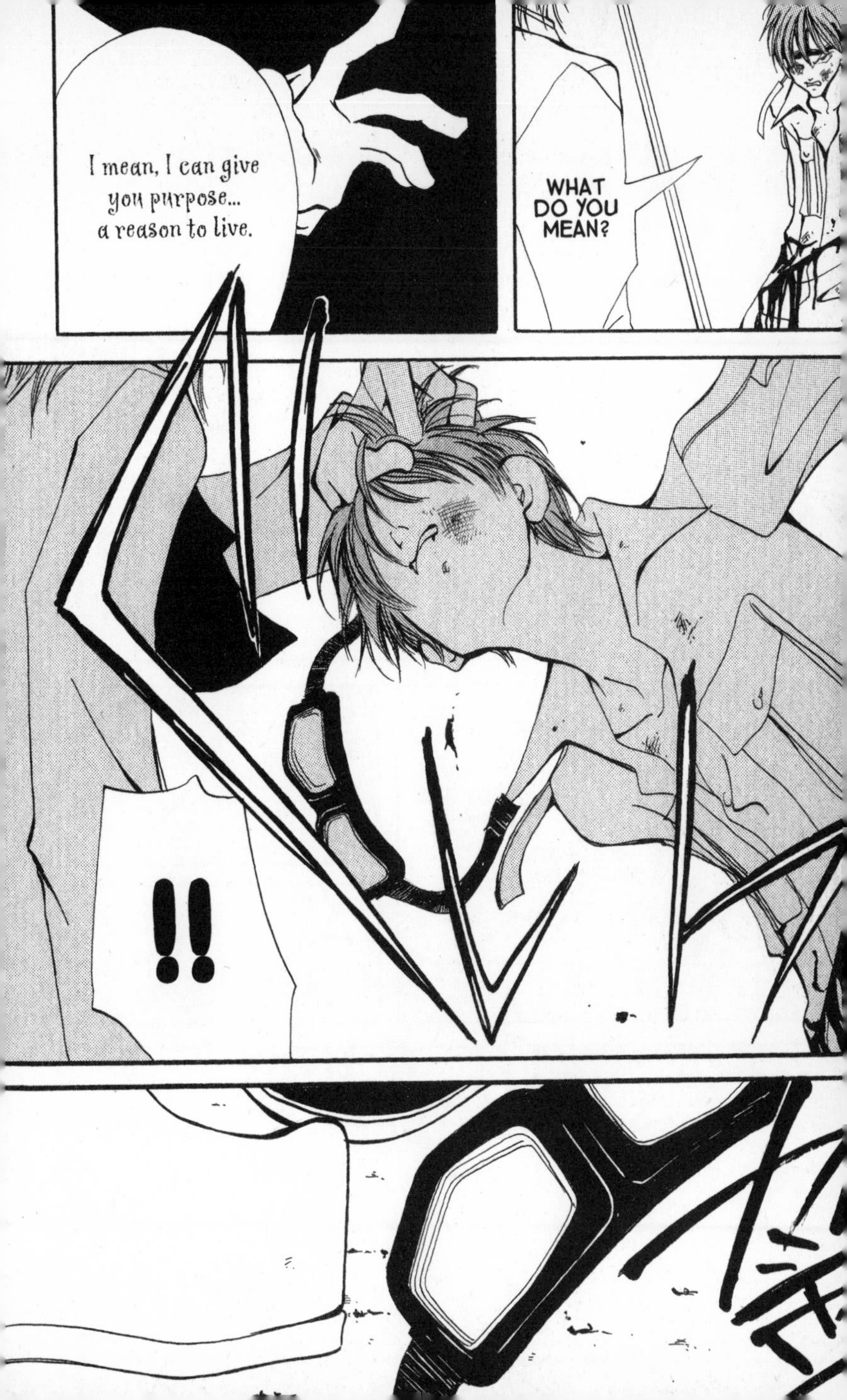
WHAT DO YOU MEAN?
I mean, I can give you purpose... a reason to live.
!!

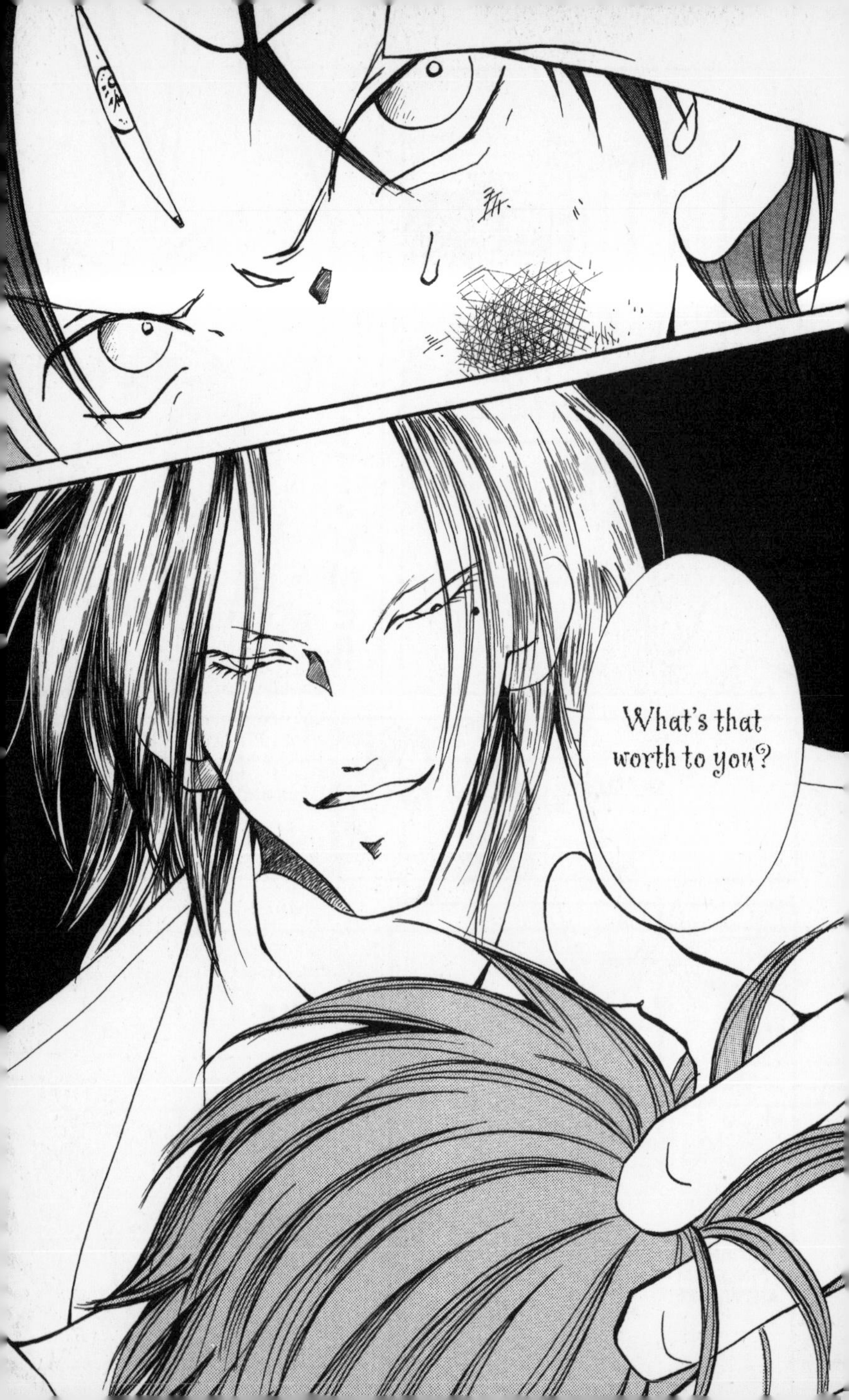
What's that worth to you?

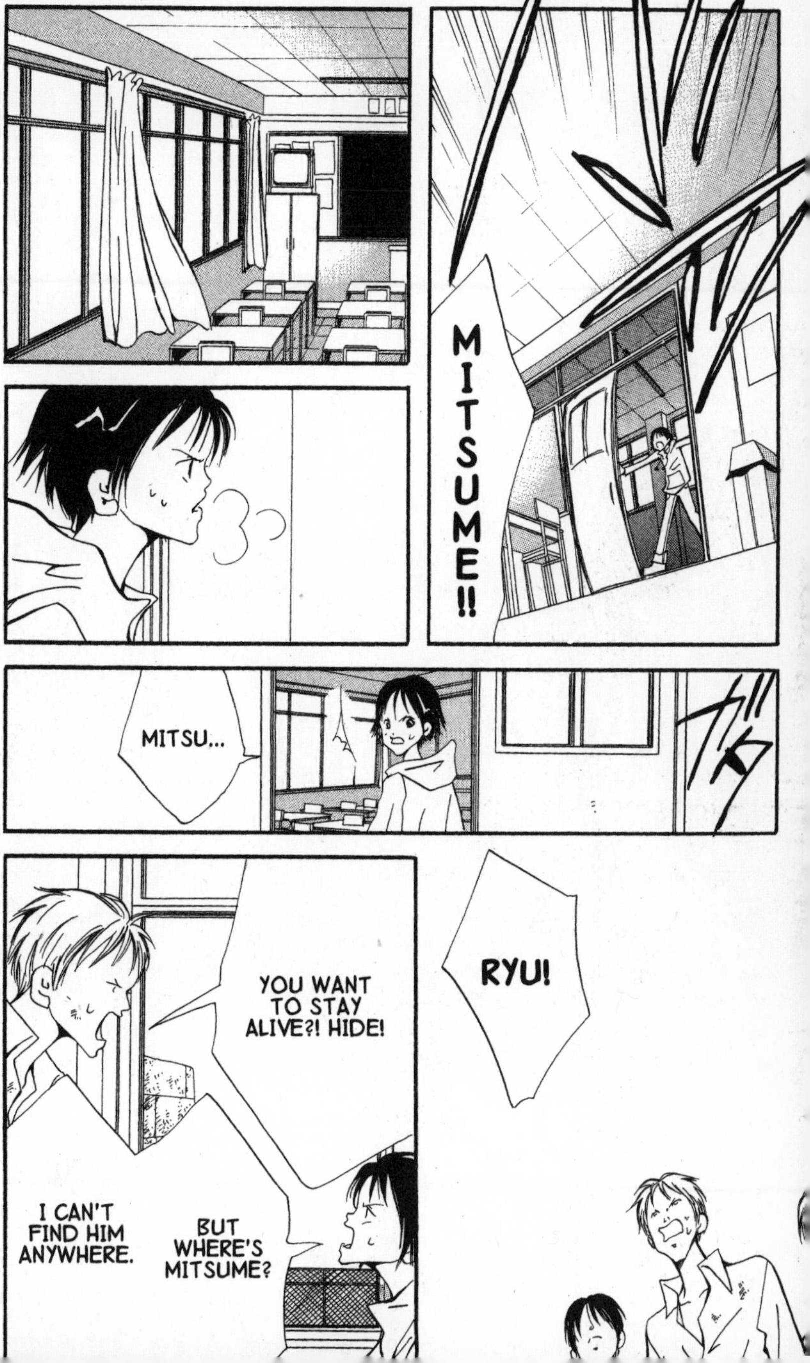
MITSUME!!
MITSU...
RYU!
YOU WANT TO STAY ALIVE?! HIDE!
BUT WHERE'S MITSUME?
I CAN'T FIND HIM ANYWHERE.

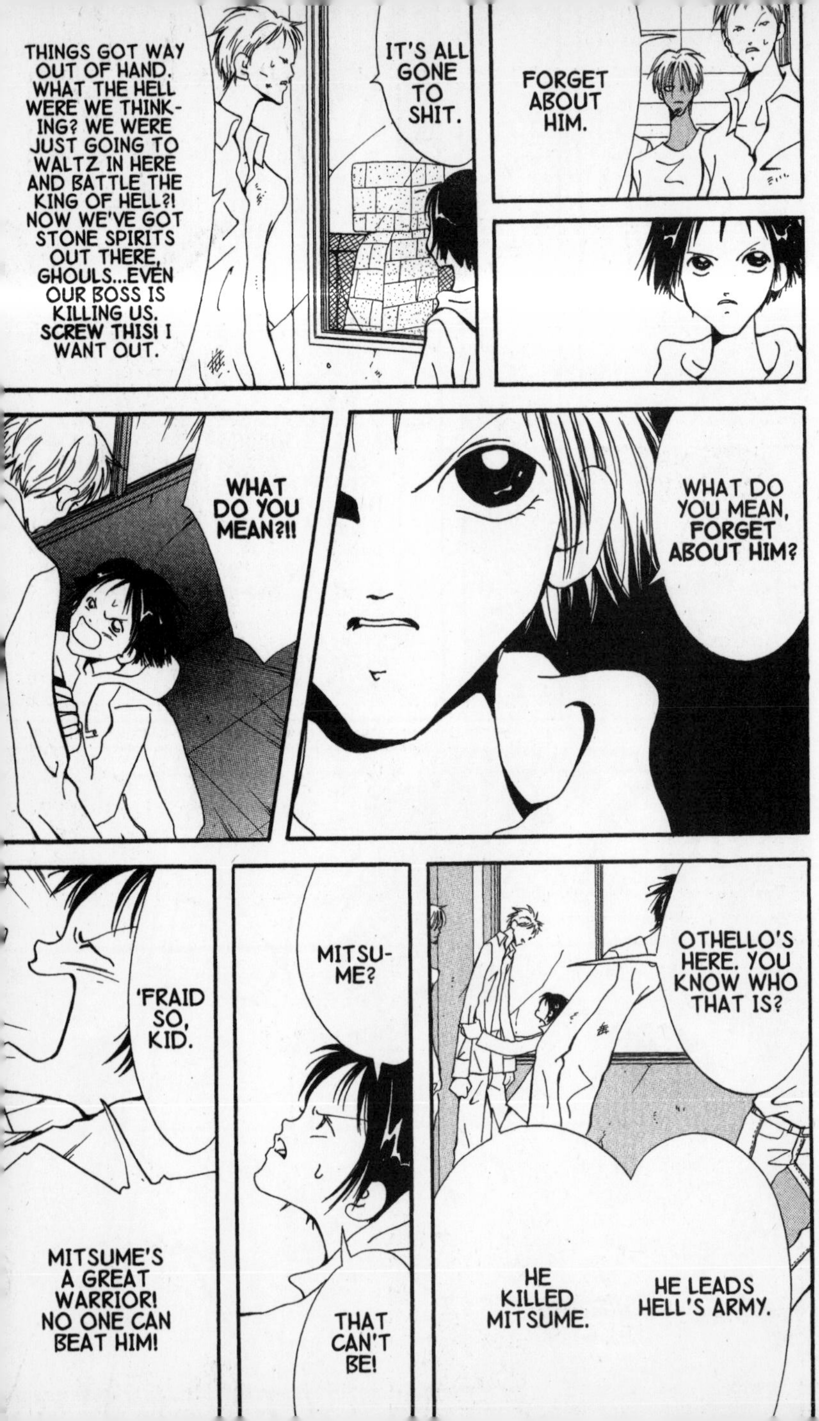
FORGET ABOUT HIM.
IT'S ALL GONE TO SHIT.
THINGS GOT WAY OUT OF HAND. WHAT THE HELL WERE WE THINKING? WE WERE JUST GOING TO WALTZ IN HERE AND BATTLE THE KING OF HELL?! NOW WE'VE GOT STONE SPIRITS OUT THERE, GHOULS...EVEN OUR BOSS IS KILLING US. SCREW THIS! I WANT OUT.
WHAT DO YOU MEAN, FORGET ABOUT HIM?
WHAT DO YOU MEAN?!!
OTHELLO'S HERE. YOU KNOW WHO THAT IS?
HE LEADS HELL'S ARMY.
HE KILLED MITSUME.
MITSUME?
THAT CAN'T BE!
'FRAID SO, KID.
MITSUME'S A GREAT WARRIOR! NO ONE CAN BEAT HIM!

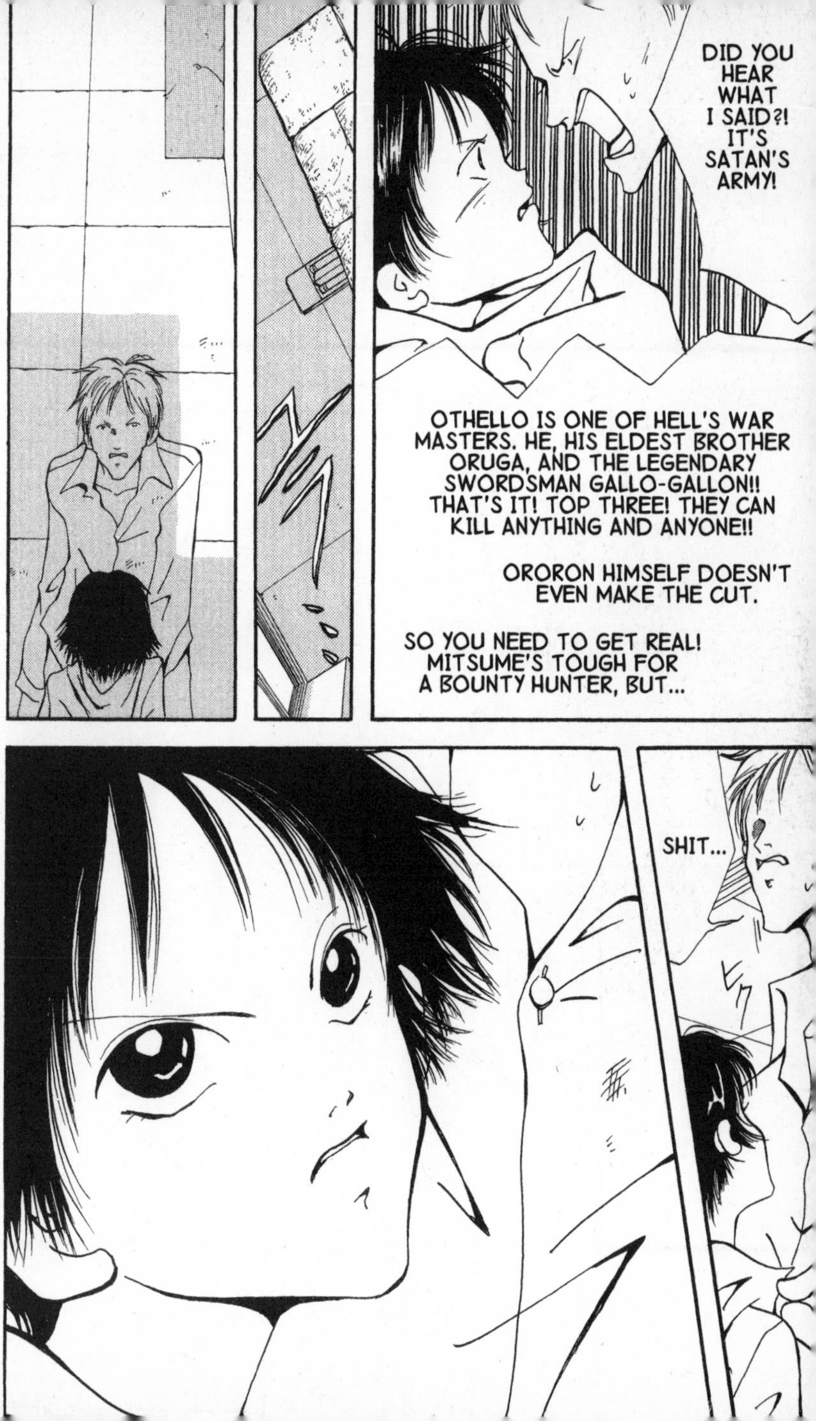
DID YOU HEAR WHAT I SAID?! IT'S SATAN'S ARMY!
OTHELLO IS ONE OF HELL'S WAR MASTERS. HE, HIS ELDEST BROTHER ORUGA, AND THE LEGENDARY SWORDSMAN GALLO-GALLON!! THAT'S IT! TOP THREE! THEY CAN KILL ANYTHING AND ANYONE!!
ORORON HIMSELF DOESN'T EVEN MAKE THE CUT.
SO YOU NEED TO GET REAL! MITSUME'S TOUGH FOR A BOUNTY HUNTER, BUT...
SHIT...

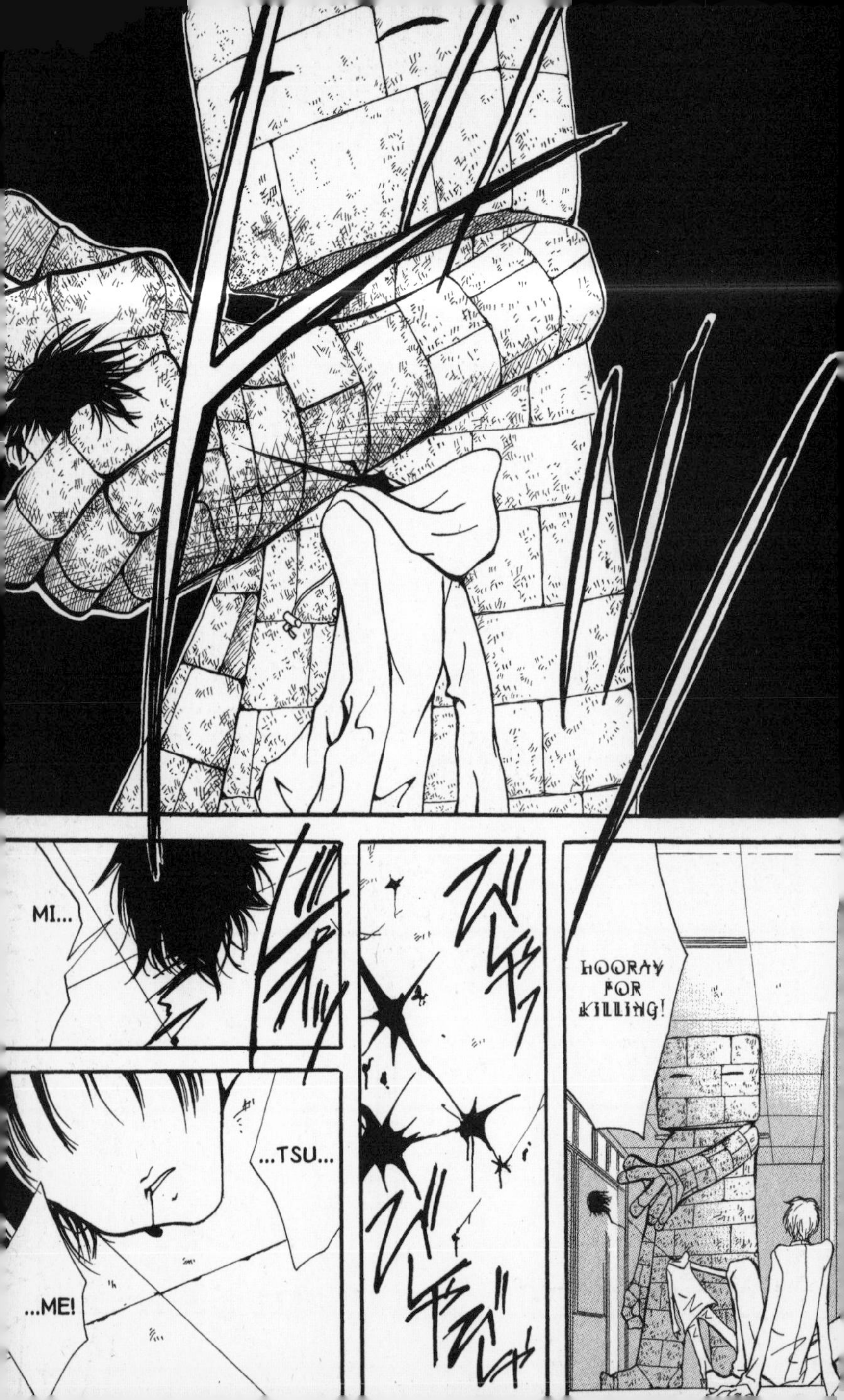
HOORAY FOR KILLING!
MI...
...TSU...
...ME!

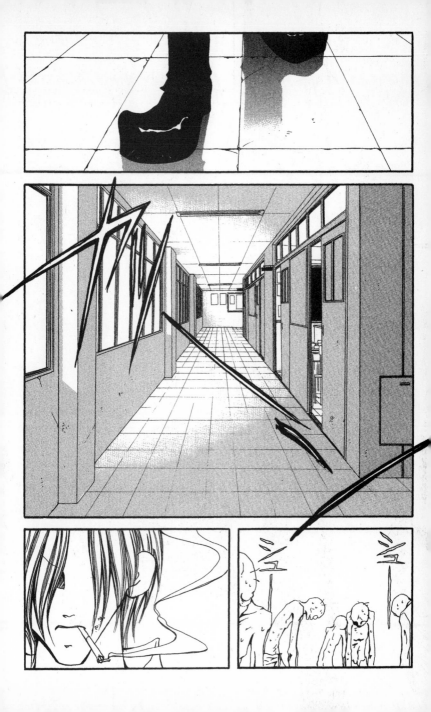

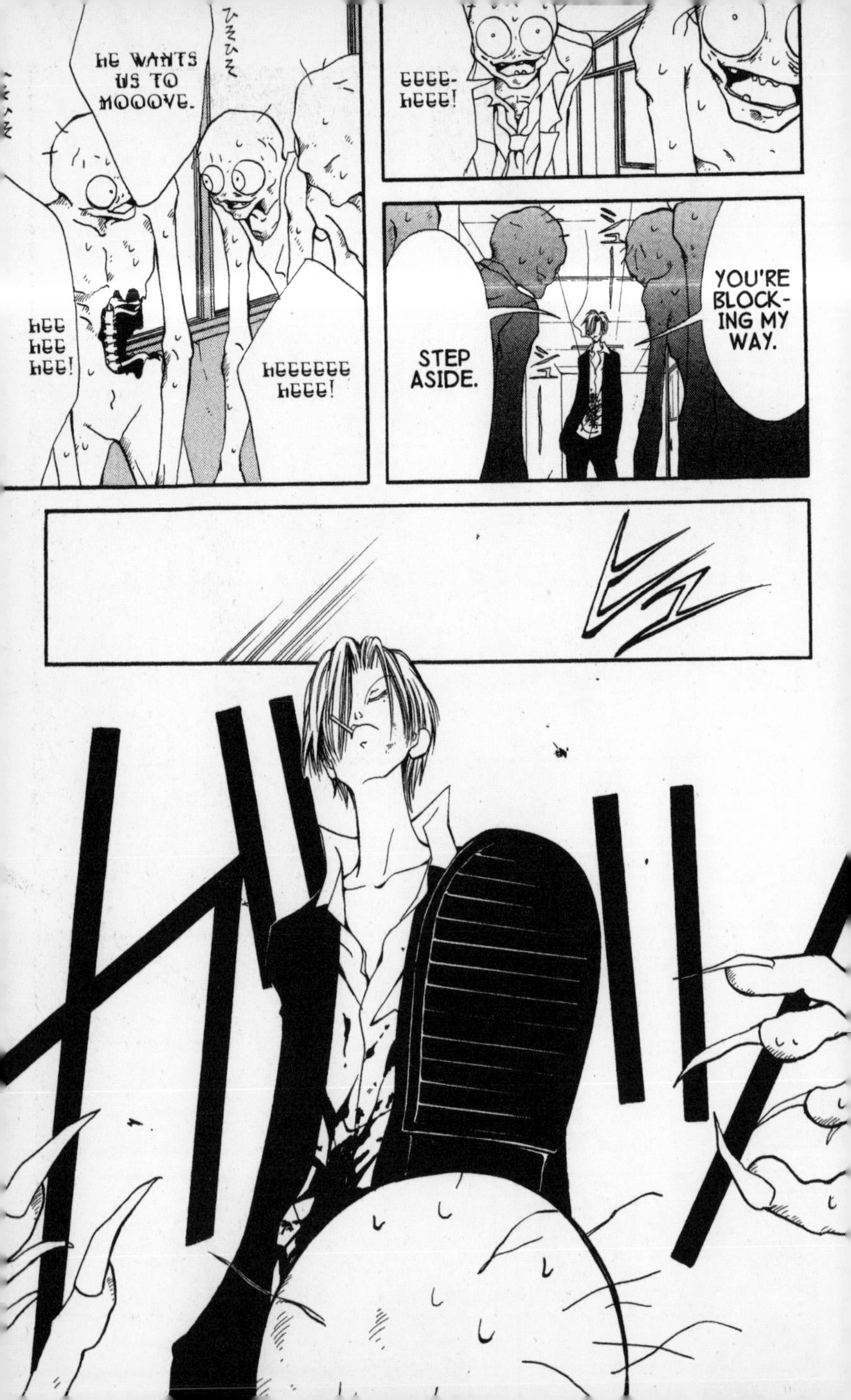
EEEE-
HEEE!
YOU'RE BLOCKING MY WAY.
STEP ASIDE.
HE WANTS US TO MOOOVE.
HEEEEEEE HEEE!
HEE HEE HEE!

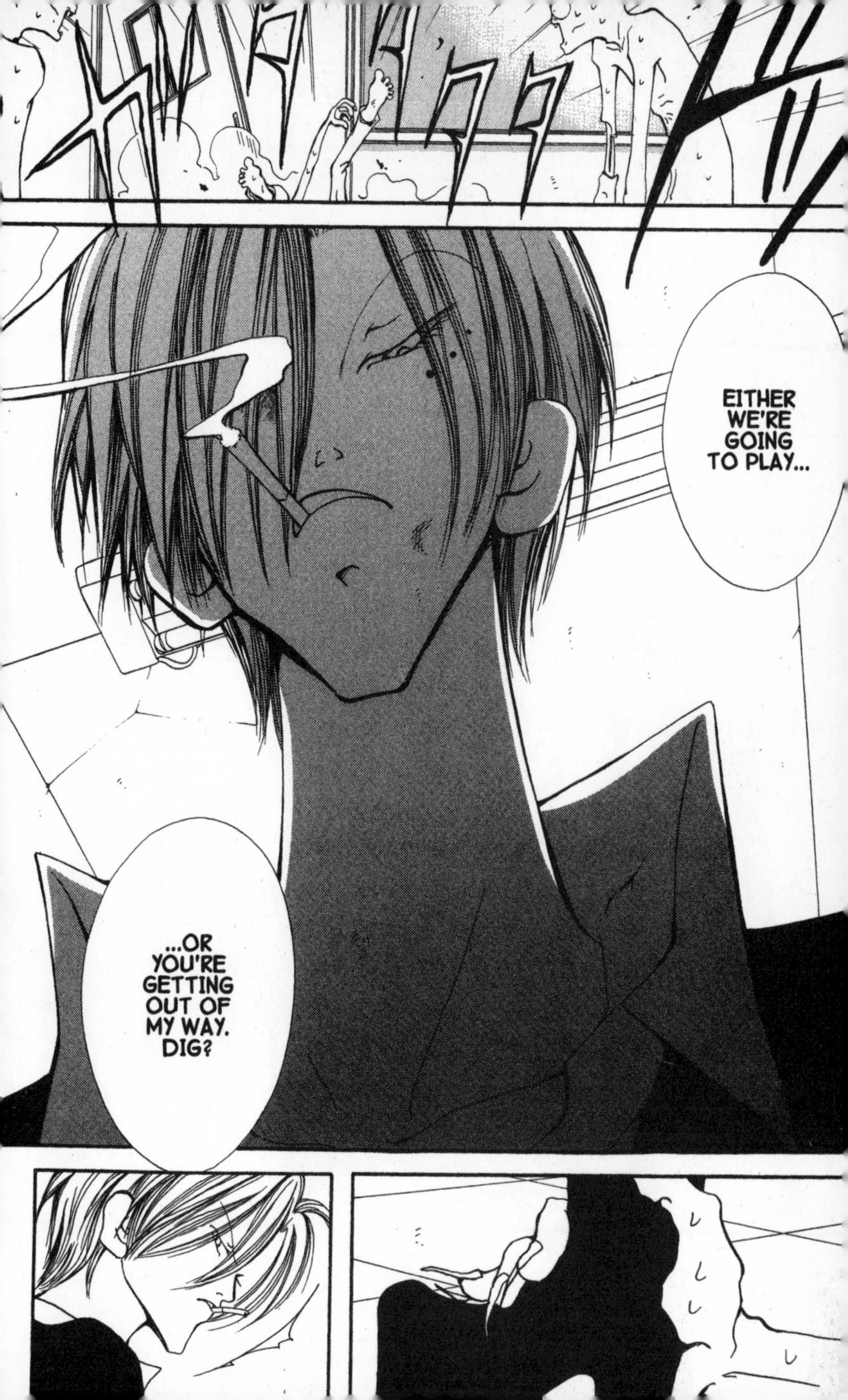
EITHER WE'RE GOING TO PLAY...
...OR YOU'RE GETTING OUT OF MY WAY. DIG?

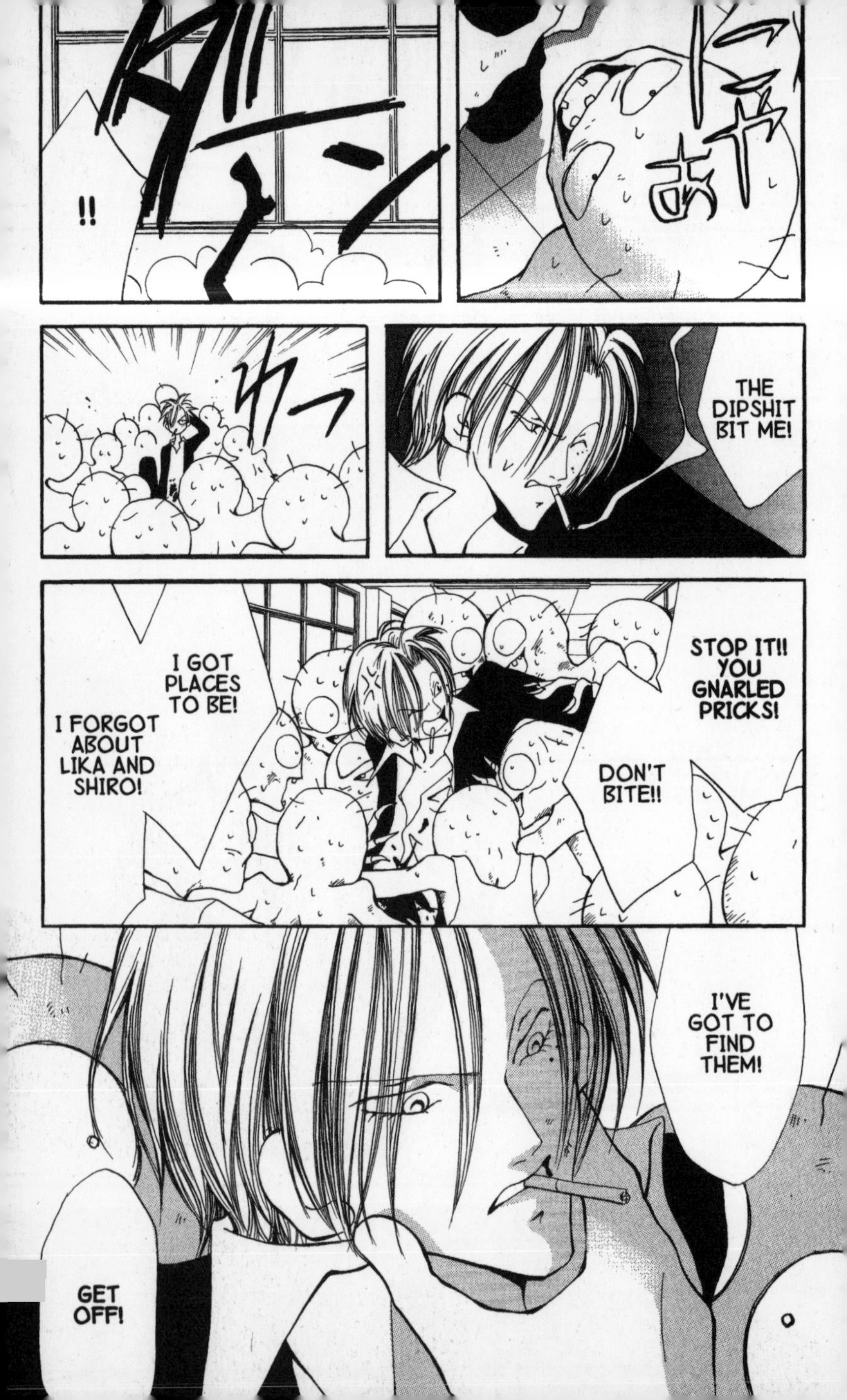
!!
THE DIPSHIT BIT ME!
STOP IT!! YOU GNARLED PRICKS!
DON'T BITE!!
I GOT PLACES TO BE!
I FORGOT ABOUT LIKA AND SHIRO!
I'VE GOT TO FIND THEM!
GET OFF!

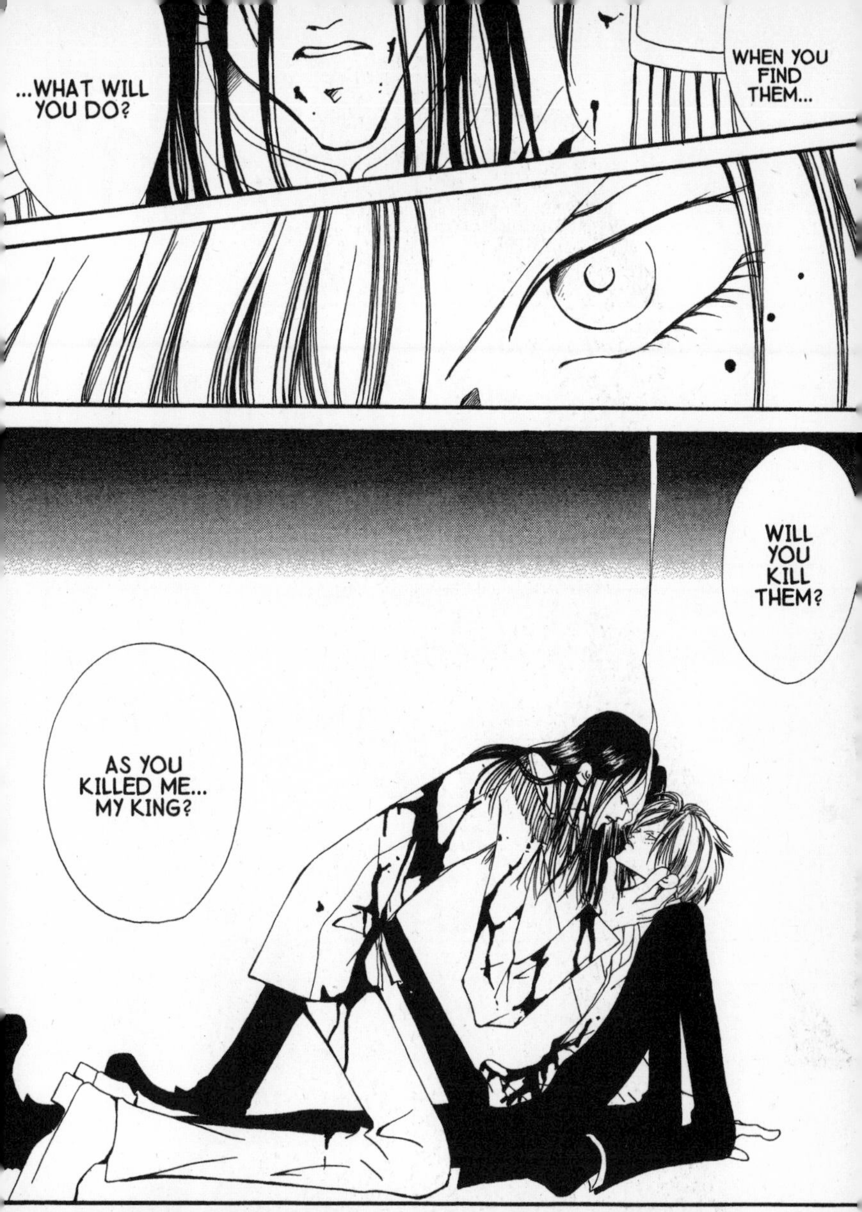
WHEN YOU FIND THEM...
...WHAT WILL YOU DO?
WILL YOU KILL THEM?
AS YOU KILLED ME... MY KING?

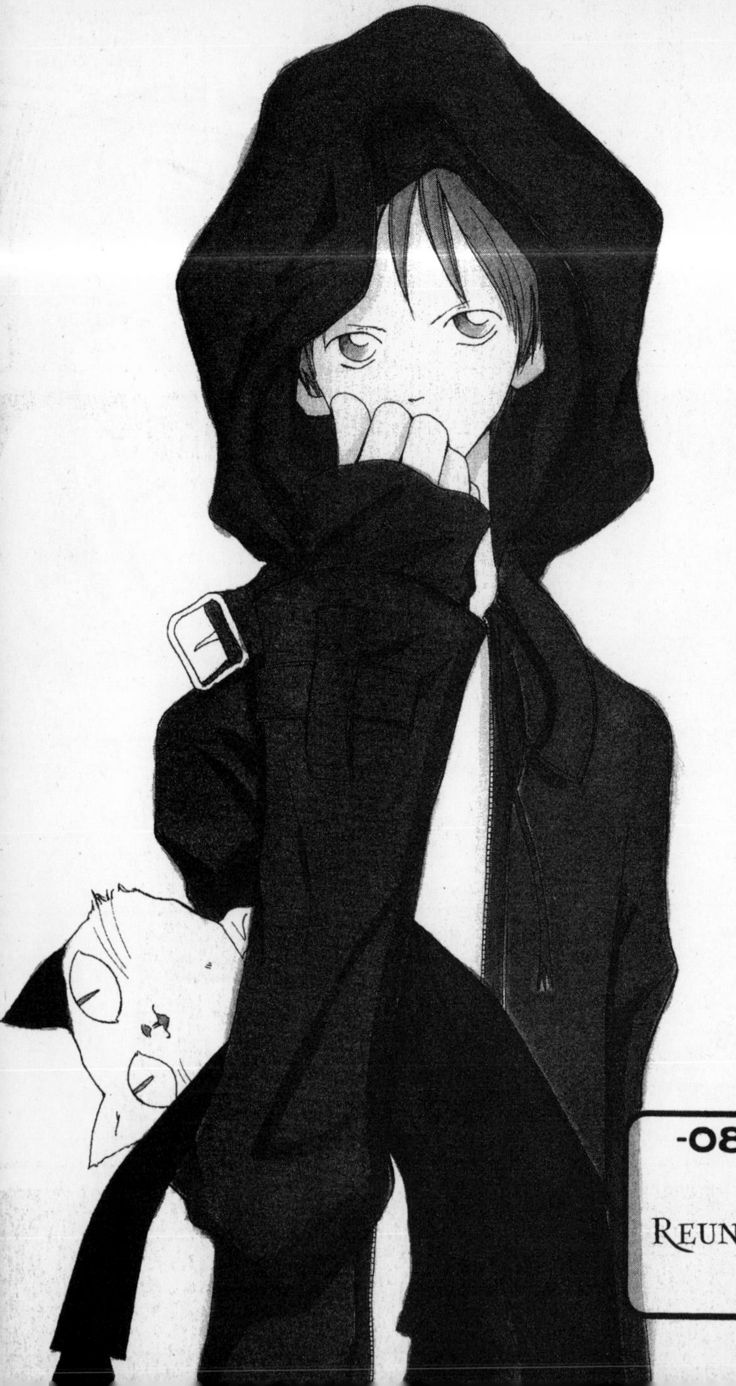

-08-

Reunion

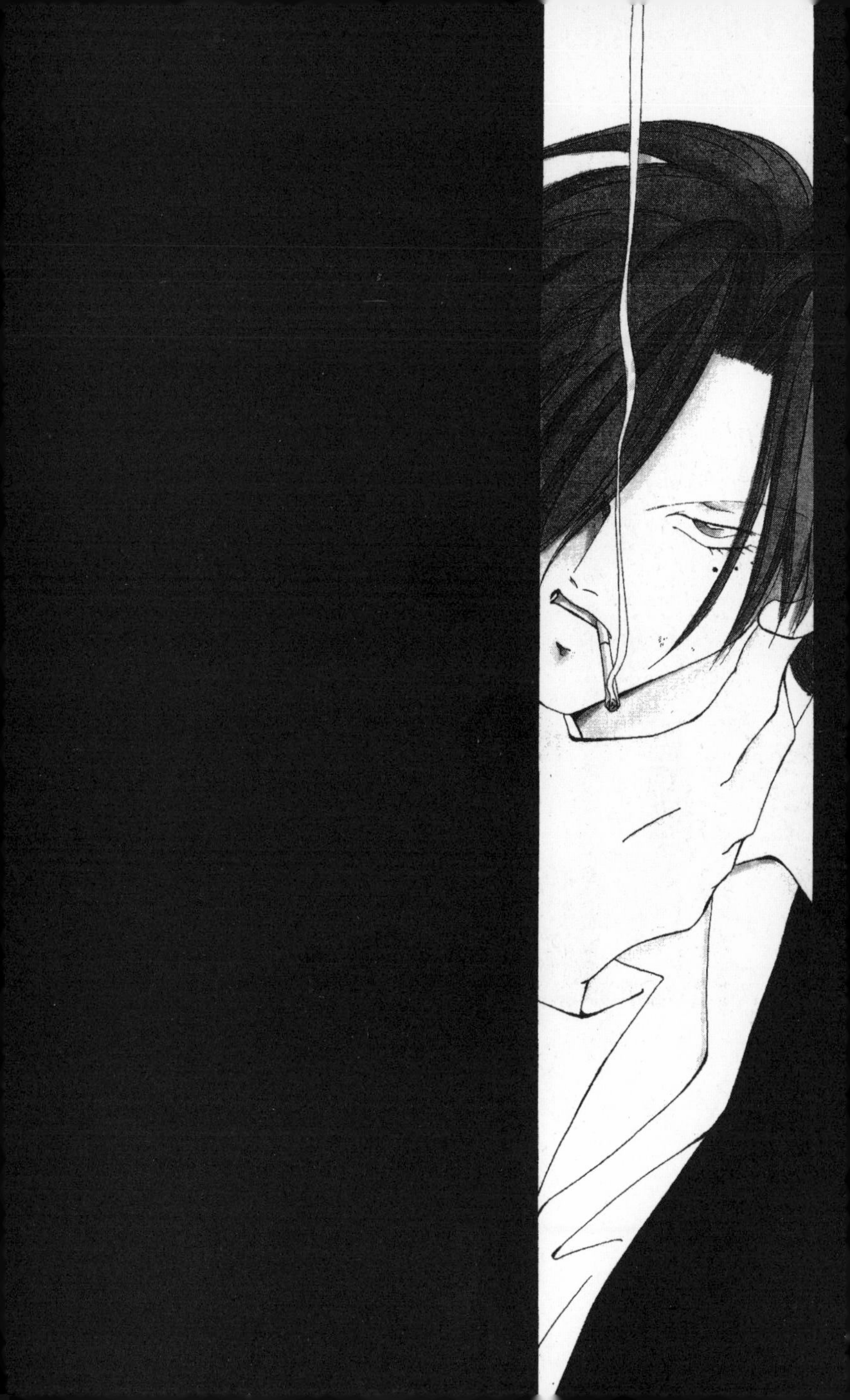

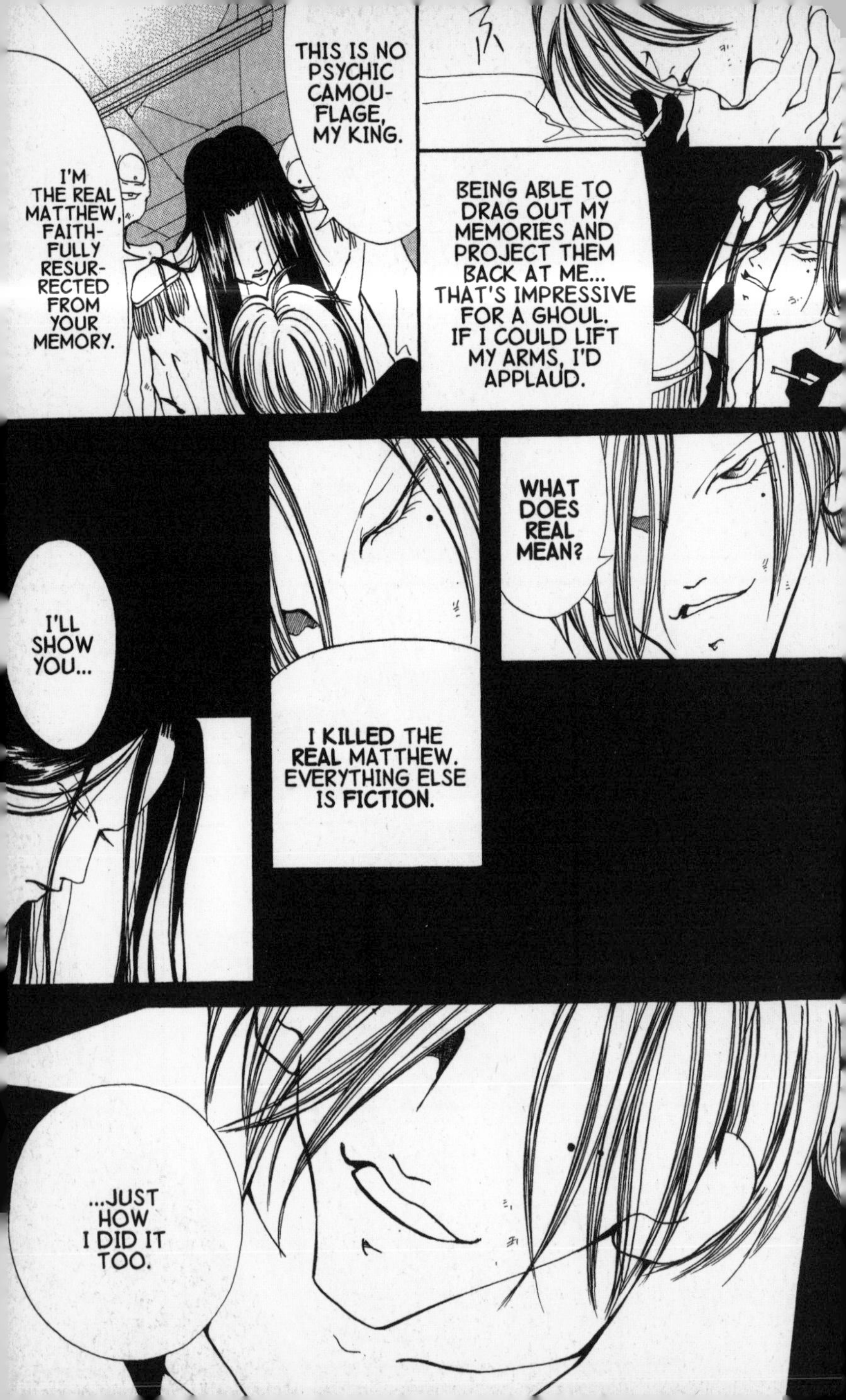
BEING ABLE TO DRAG OUT MY MEMORIES AND PROJECT THEM BACK AT ME... THAT'S IMPRESSIVE FOR A GHOUL. IF I COULD LIFT MY ARMS, I'D APPLAUD.
THIS IS NO PSYCHIC CAMOU-FLAGE, MY KING.
I'M THE REAL MATTHEW, FAITH-FULLY RESUR-RECTED FROM YOUR MEMORY.
WHAT DOES REAL MEAN?
I KILLED THE REAL MATTHEW. EVERYTHING ELSE IS FICTION.
I'LL SHOW YOU...
...JUST HOW I DID IT TOO.

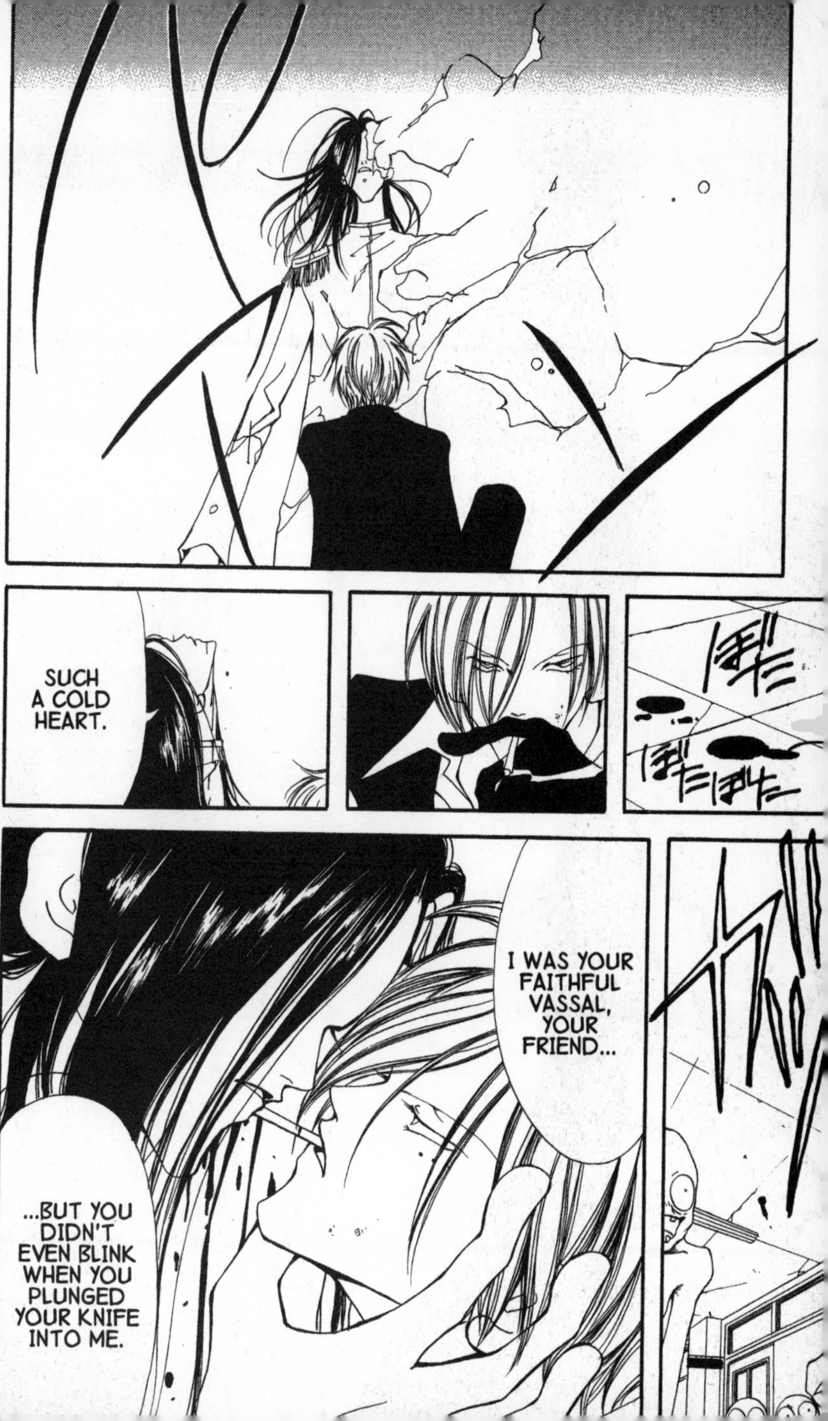
SUCH A COLD HEART.
I WAS YOUR FAITHFUL VASSAL, YOUR FRIEND...
...BUT YOU DIDN'T EVEN BLINK WHEN YOU PLUNGED YOUR KNIFE INTO ME.

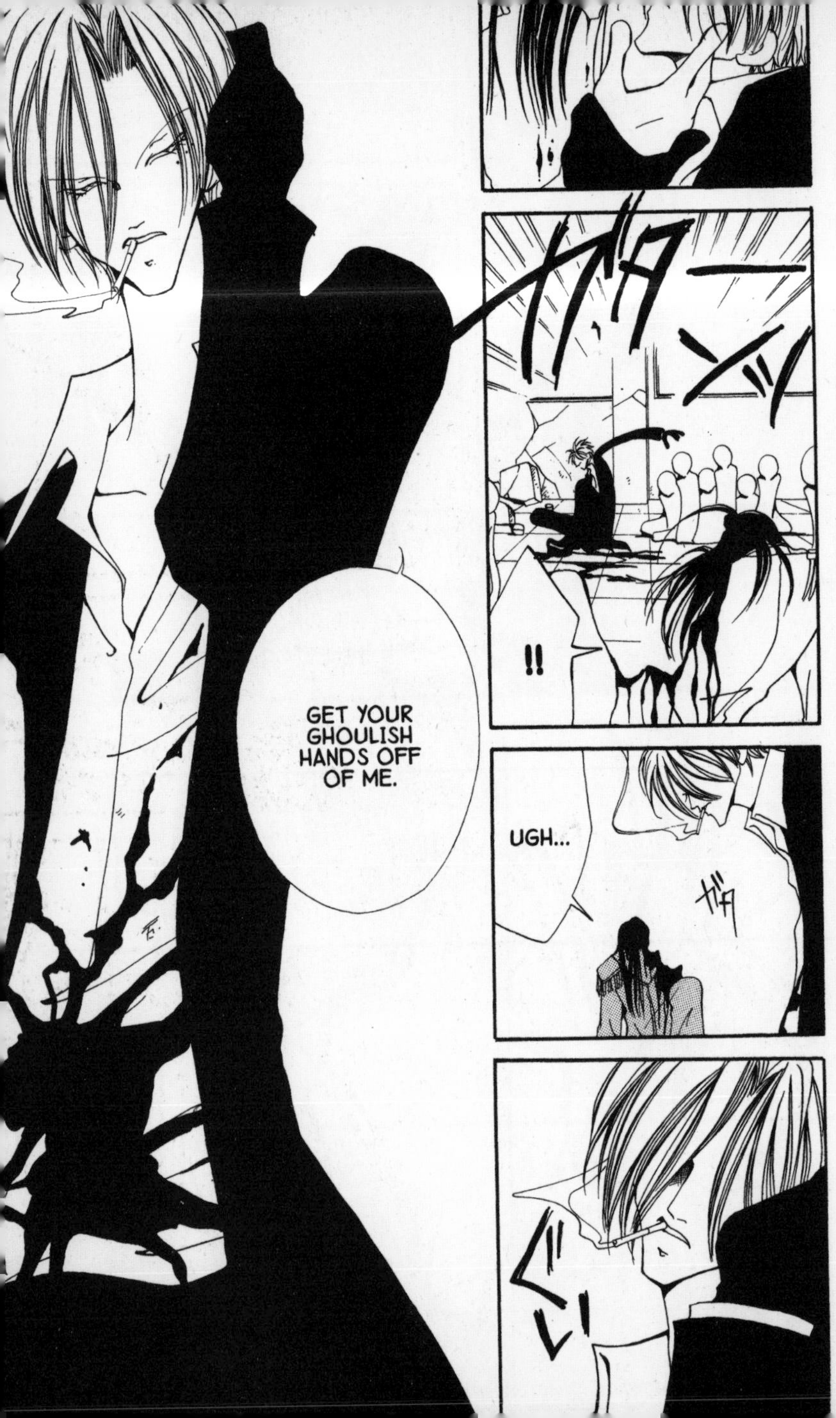
!!
UGH...
GET YOUR GHOULISH HANDS OFF OF ME.

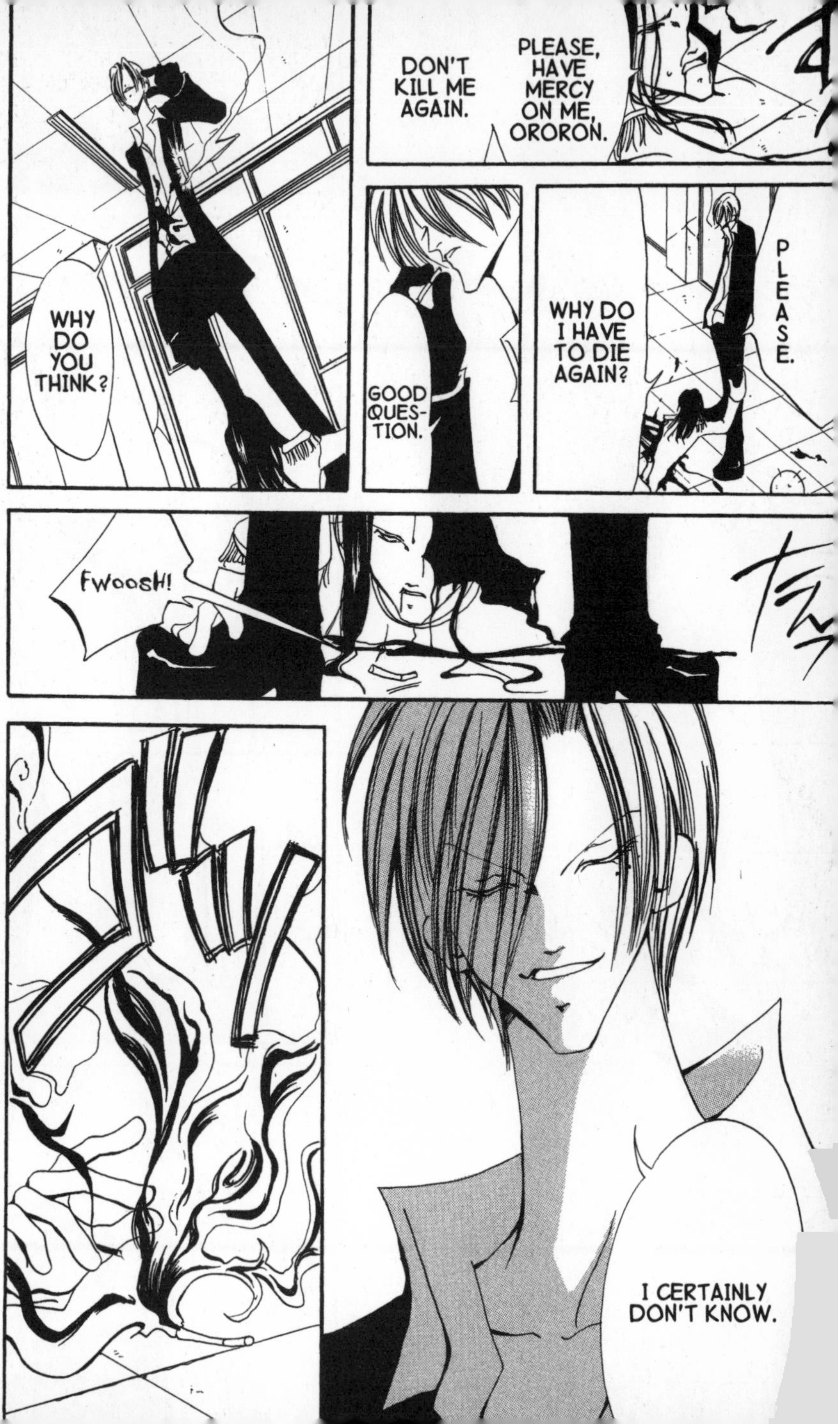
PLEASE, HAVE MERCY ON ME, ORORON.
DON'T KILL ME AGAIN.
PLEASE.
WHY DO I HAVE TO DIE AGAIN?
GOOD QUES-TION.
WHY DO YOU THINK?
FWOOSH!
I CERTAINLY DON'T KNOW.

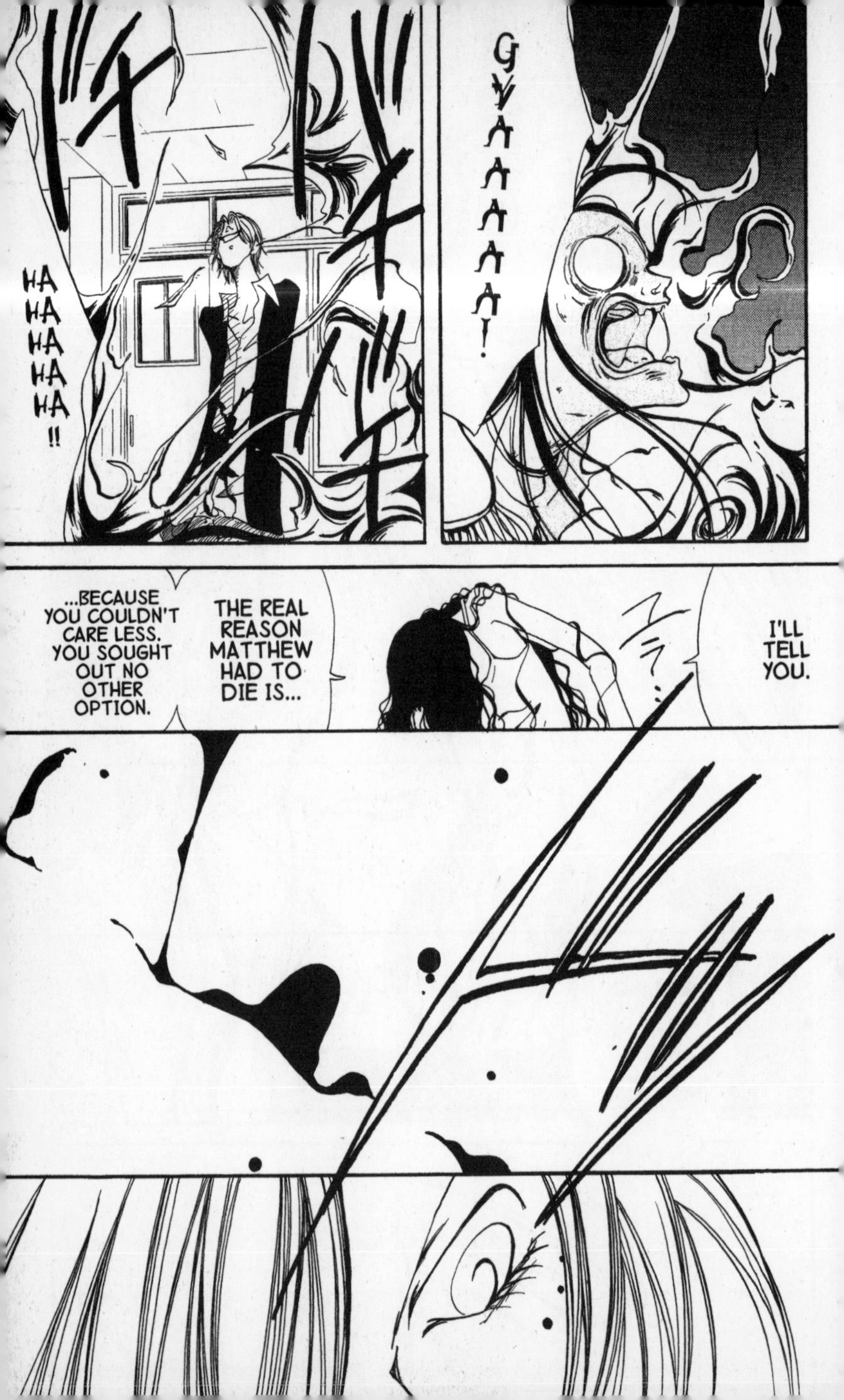
GYAAAAAA!
HA HA HA HA HA!!
I'LL TELL YOU.
THE REAL REASON MATTHEW HAD TO DIE IS...
...BECAUSE YOU COULDN'T CARE LESS. YOU SOUGHT OUT NO OTHER OPTION.

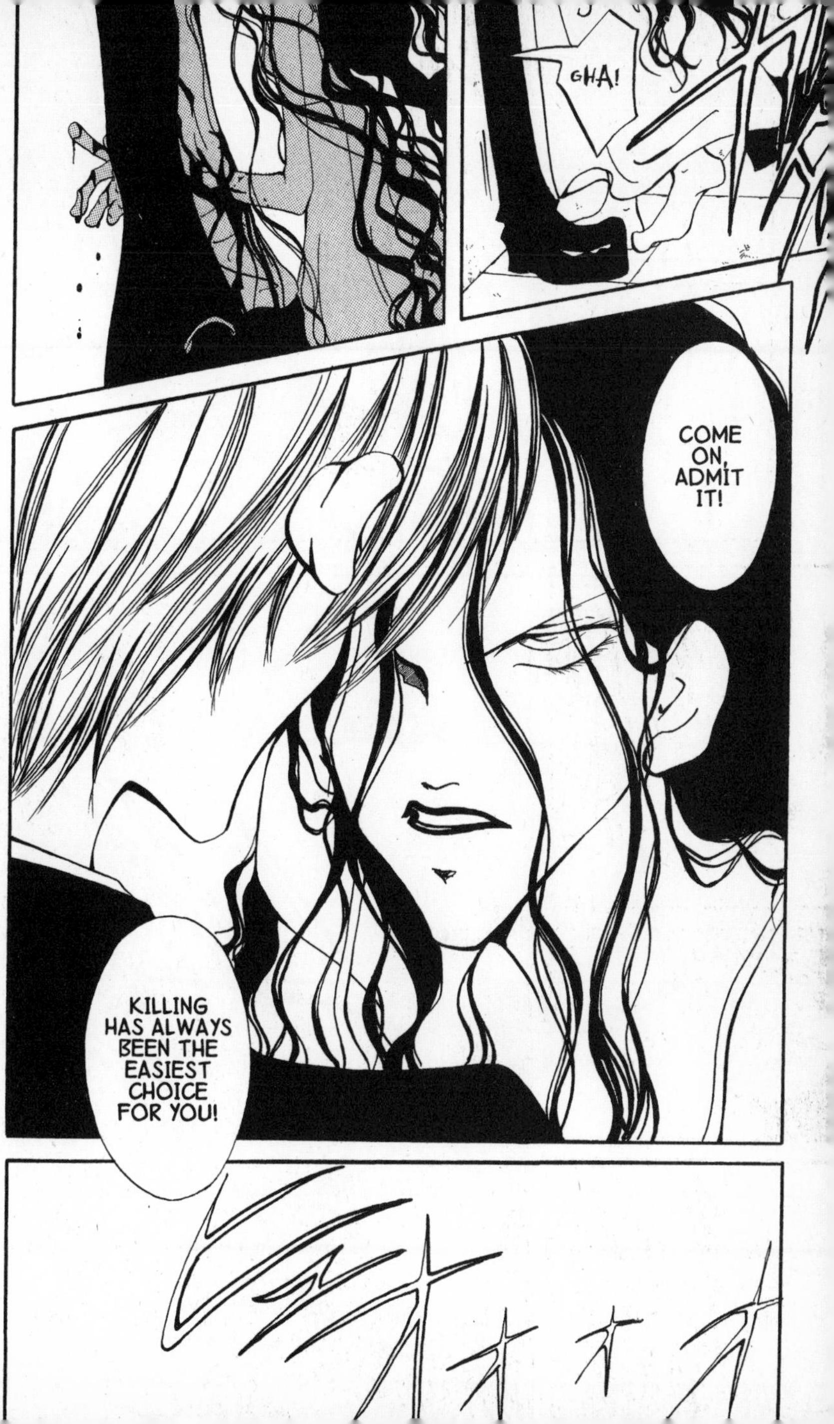
GHA!
COME ON, ADMIT IT!
KILLING HAS ALWAYS BEEN THE EASIEST CHOICE FOR YOU!

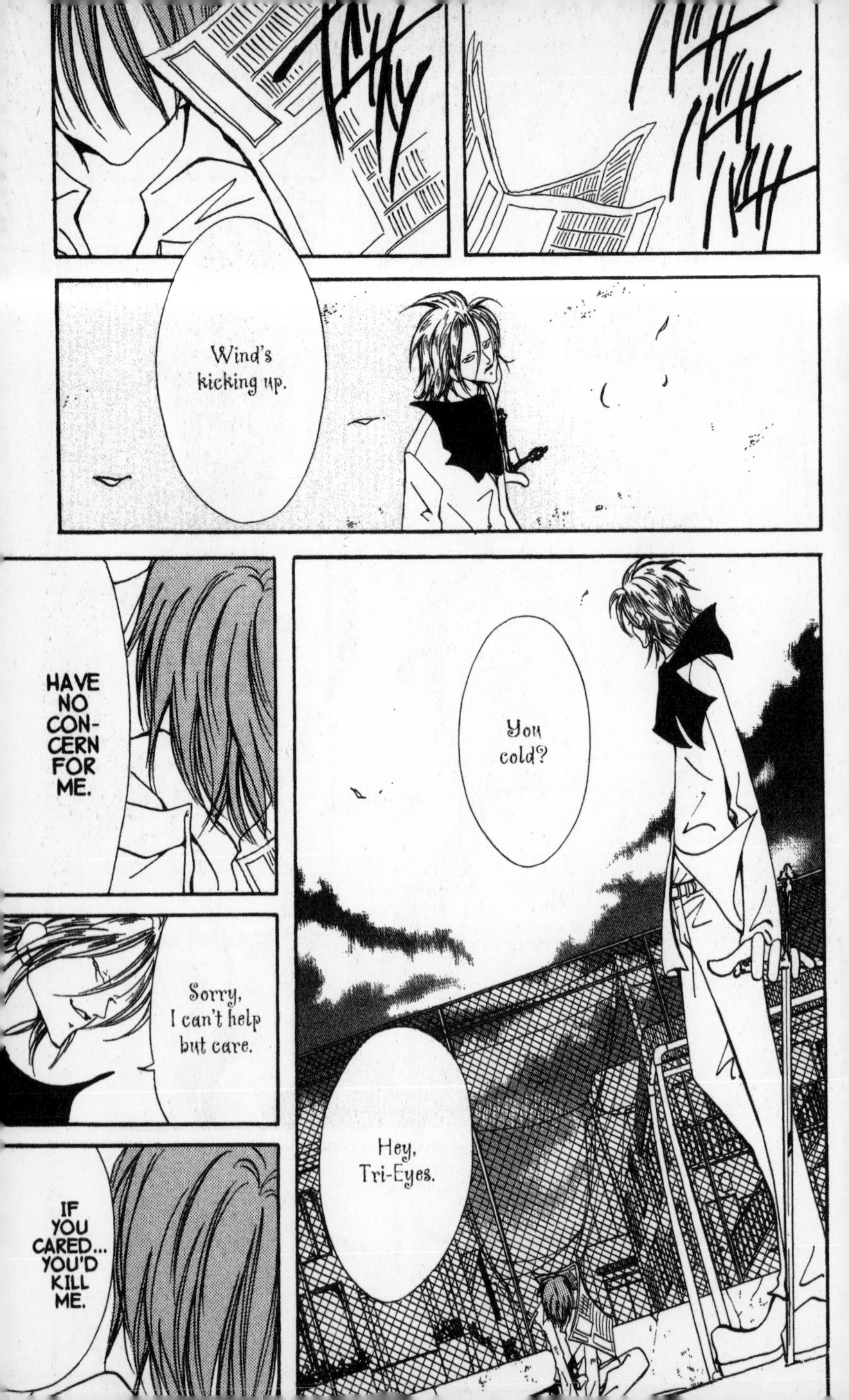
Wind's kicking up.
You cold?
Hey, Tri-Eyes.
HAVE NO CONCERN FOR ME.
Sorry, I can't help but care.
IF YOU CARED... YOU'D KILL ME.

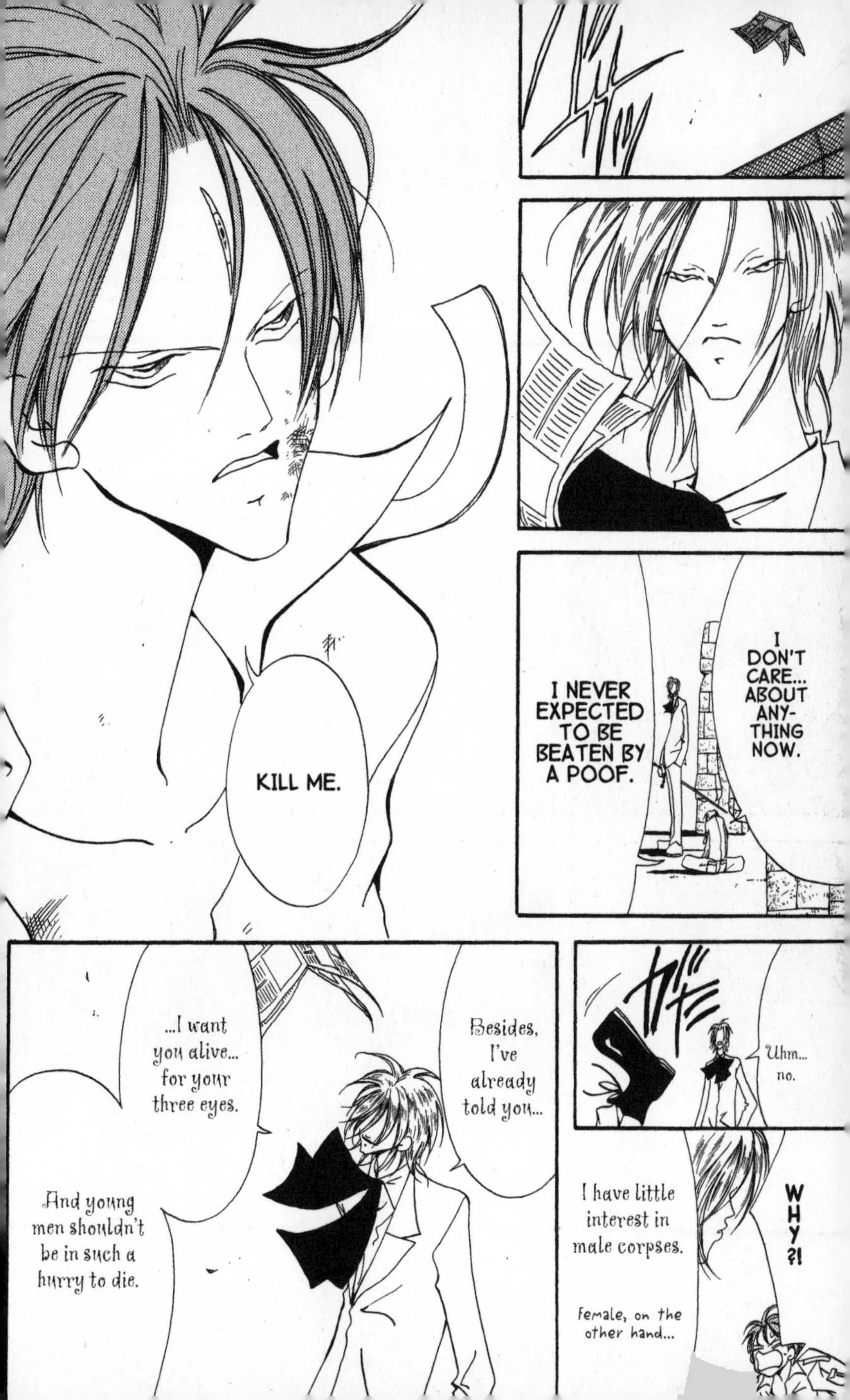
I DON'T CARE... ABOUT ANYTHING NOW.
I NEVER EXPECTED TO BE BEATEN BY A POOF.
KILL ME.
Uhm... no.
WHY?!
I have little interest in male corpses.
Female, on the other hand...
Besides, I've already told you...
...I want you alive... for your three eyes.
And young men shouldn't be in such a hurry to die.

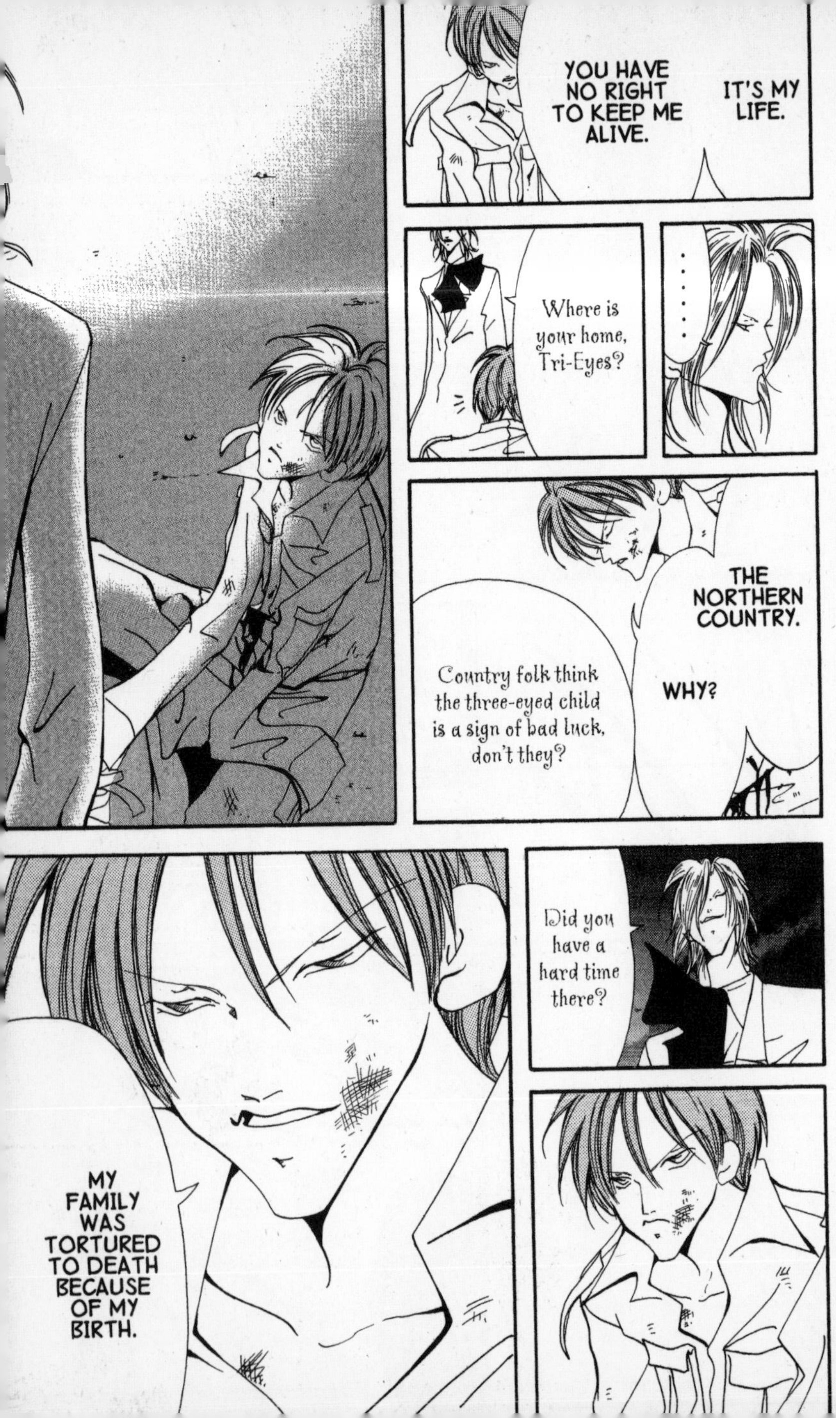
IT'S MY LIFE.
YOU HAVE NO RIGHT TO KEEP ME ALIVE.
......
Where is your home, Tri-Eyes?
THE NORTHERN COUNTRY.
WHY?
Country folk think the three-eyed child is a sign of bad luck, don't they?
Did you have a hard time there?
MY FAMILY WAS TORTURED TO DEATH BECAUSE OF MY BIRTH.

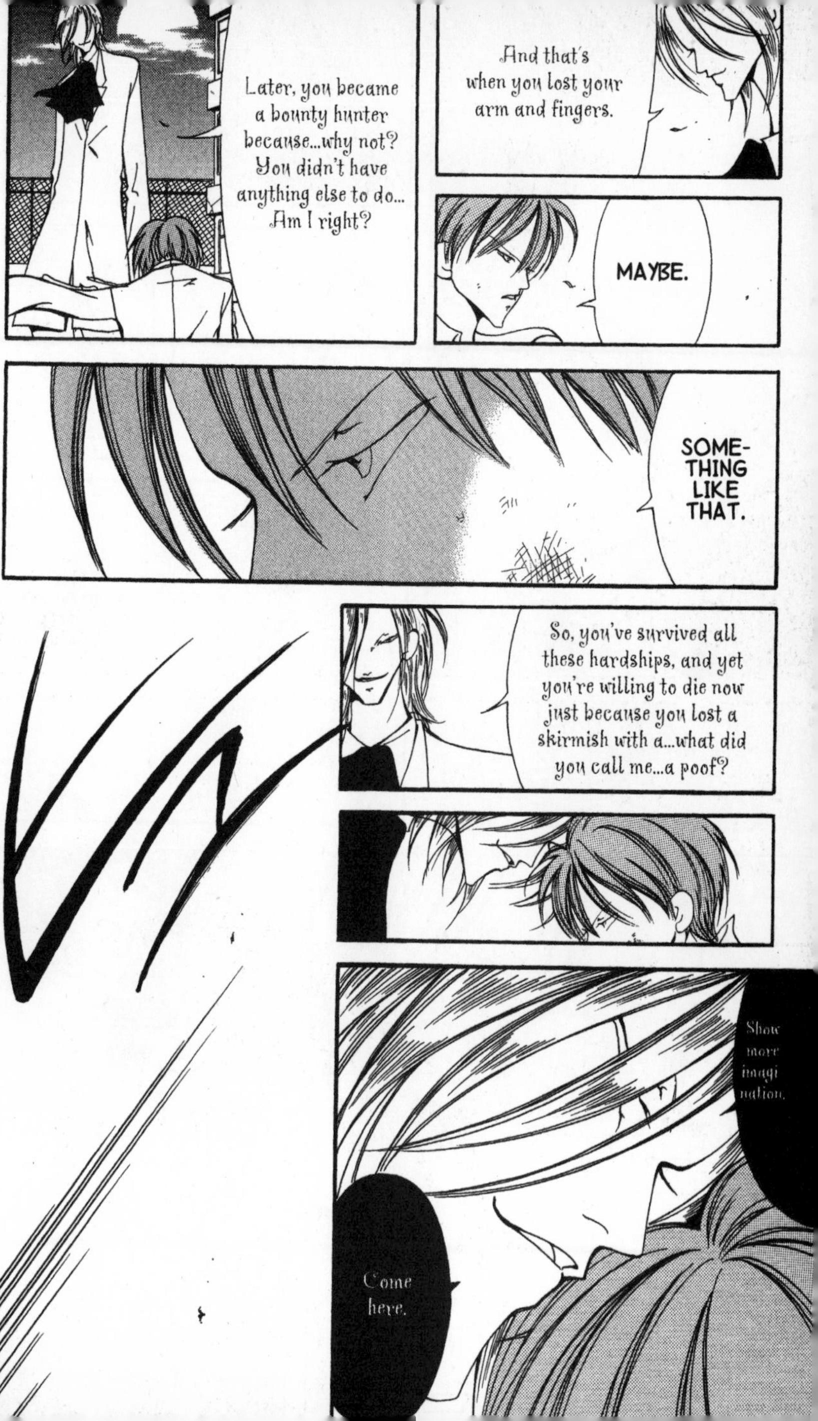
And that's when you lost your arm and fingers.
MAYBE.
Later, you became a bounty hunter because...why not? You didn't have anything else to do... Am I right?
SOMETHING LIKE THAT.
So, you've survived all these hardships, and yet you're willing to die now just because you lost a skirmish with a...what did you call me...a poof?
Show more imagination.
Come here.

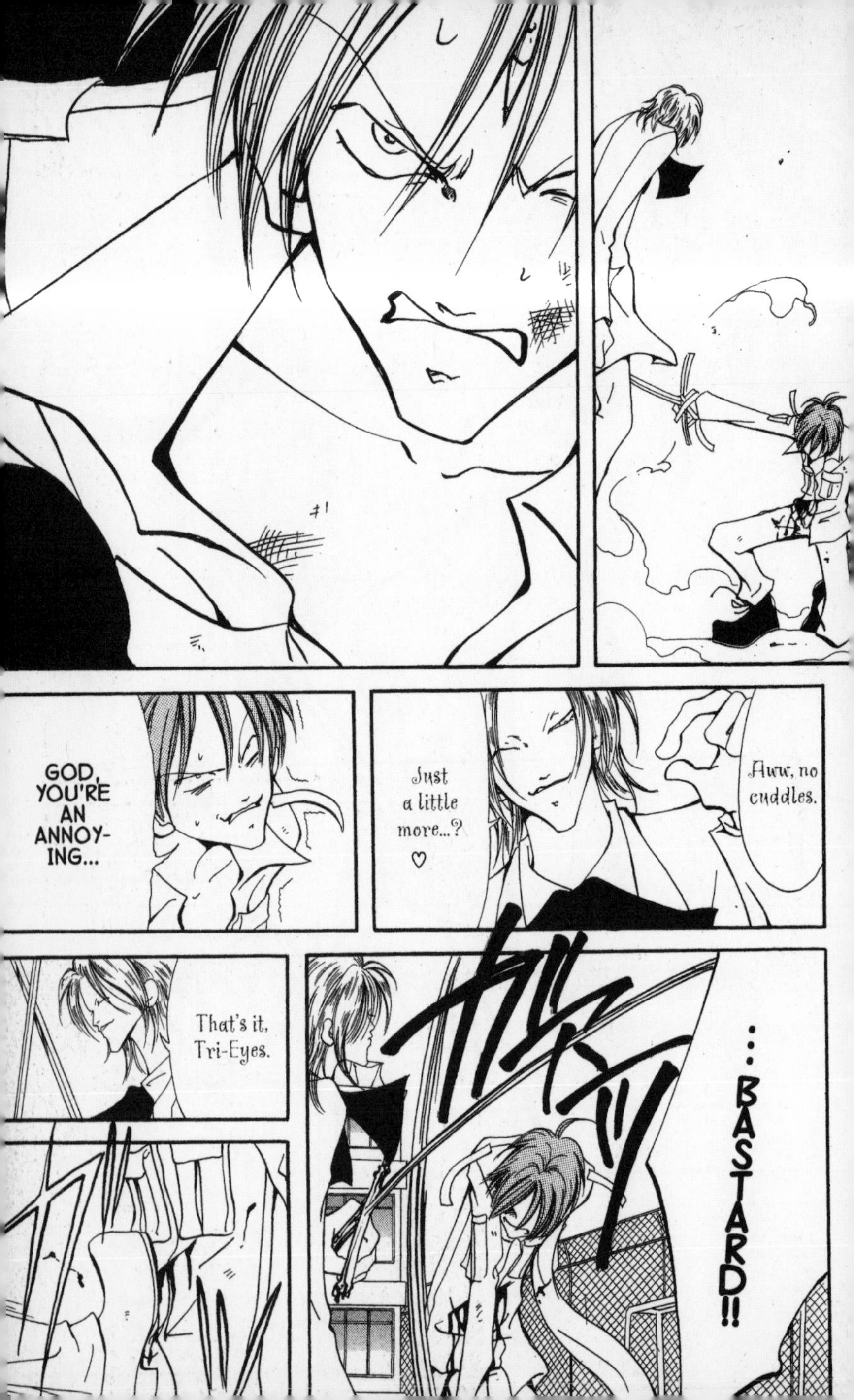
Aww, no cuddles.
Just a little more...? ♡
GOD, YOU'RE AN ANNOY-ING...
...BASTARD!!
That's it, Tri-Eyes.

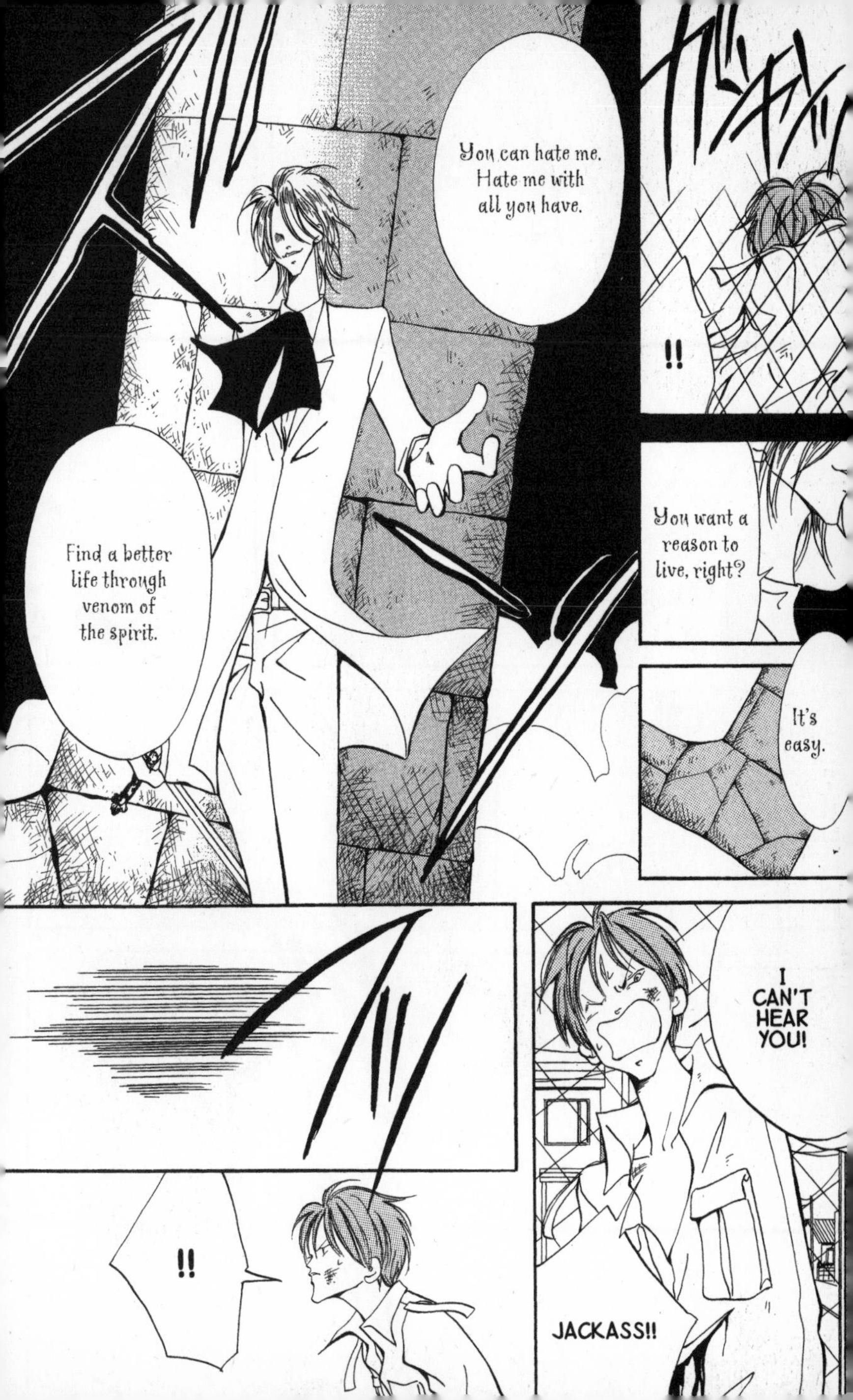
!!
You want a reason to live, right?
It's easy.
You can hate me. Hate me with all you have.
Find a better life through venom of the spirit.
I CAN'T HEAR YOU!
JACKASS!!
!!

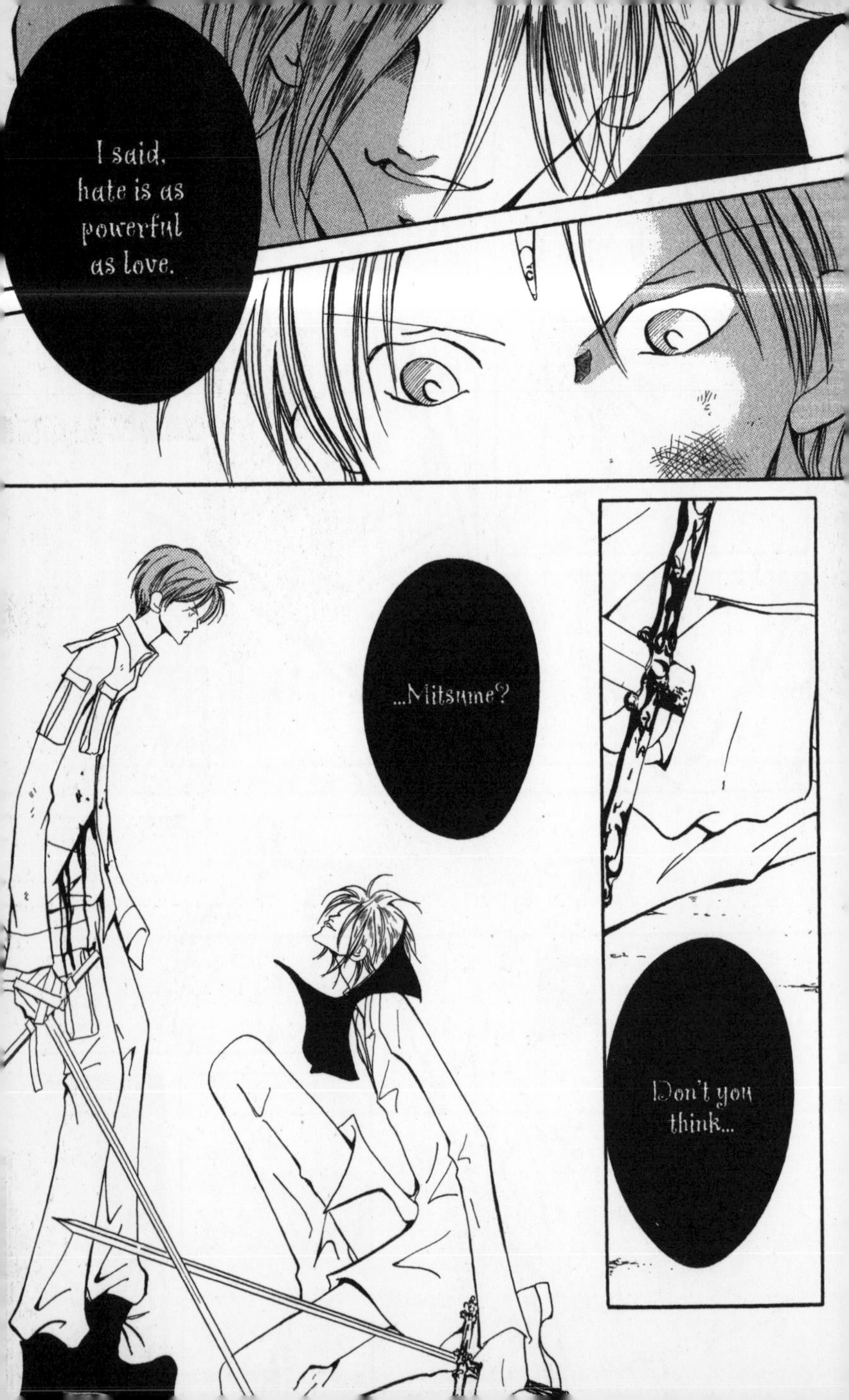
I said, hate is as powerful as love.
Don't you think...
...Mitsume?

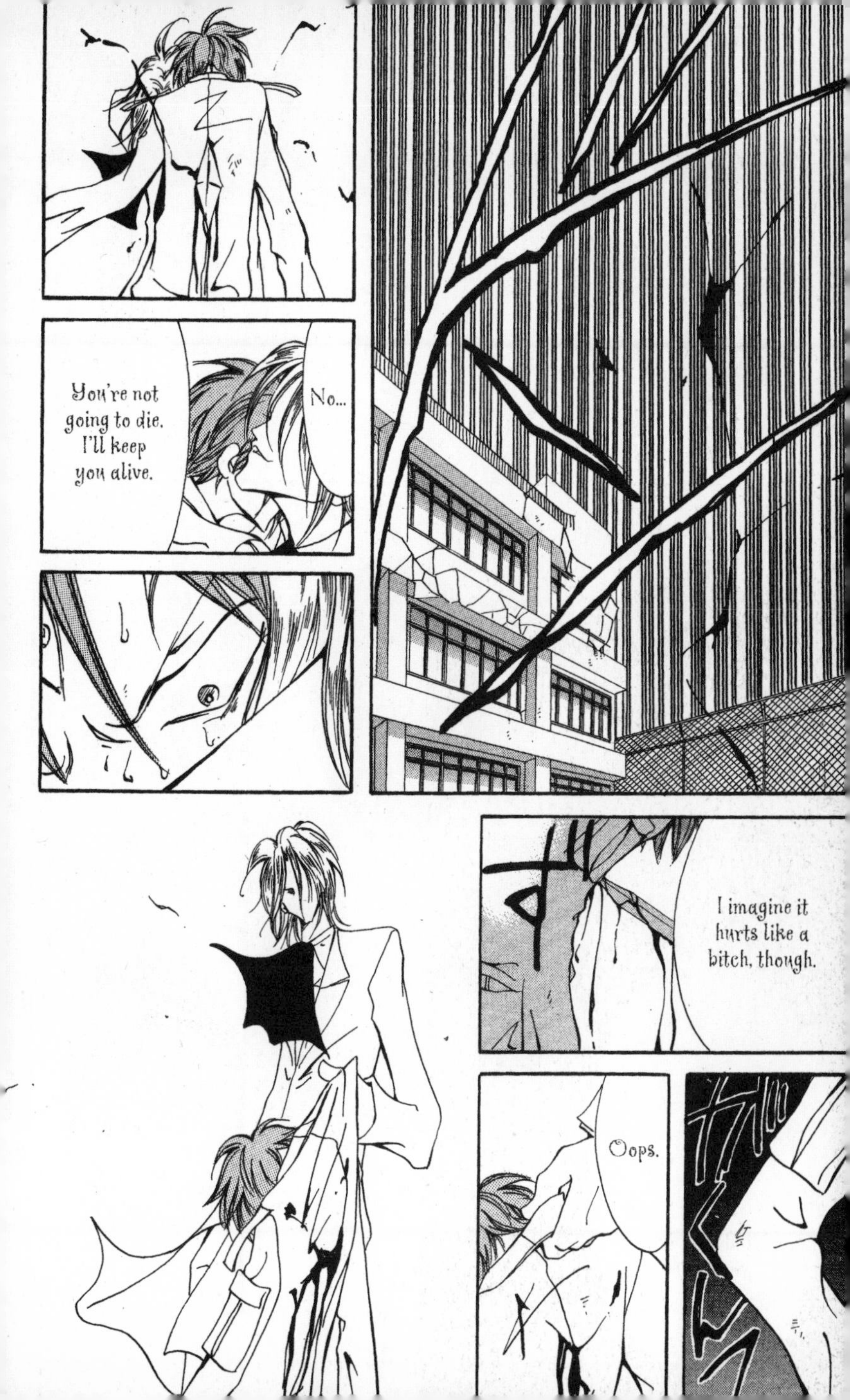
No...
You're not going to die. I'll keep you alive.
I imagine it hurts like a bitch, though.
Oops.

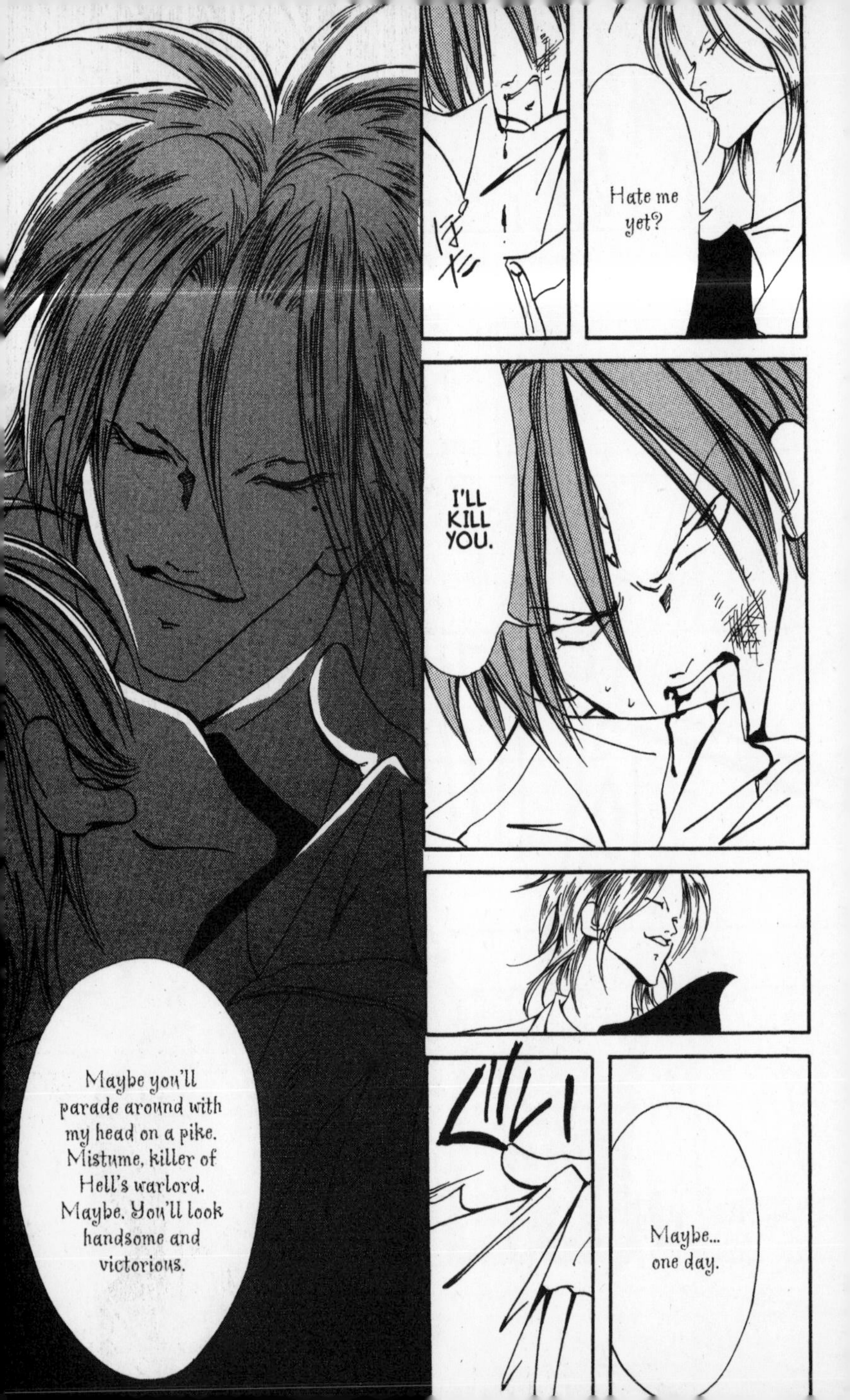
Hate me yet?
ぽた
I'LL KILL YOU.
Maybe... one day.
Maybe you'll parade around with my head on a pike. Mistume, killer of Hell's warlord. Maybe. You'll look handsome and victorious.

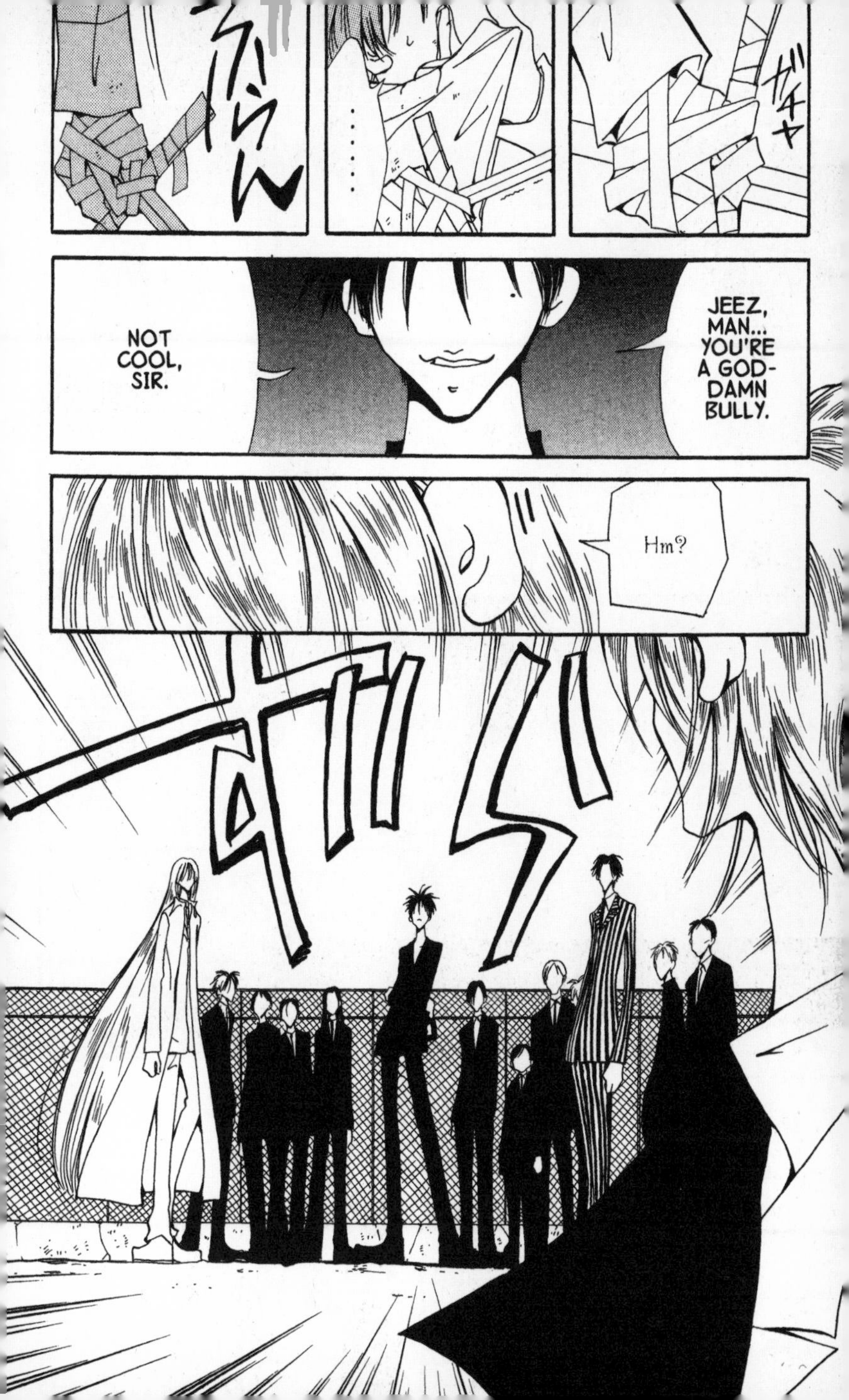

ガチャ
......
ふらん
JEEZ, MAN... YOU'RE A GOD-DAMN BULLY.
NOT COOL, SIR.
Hm?

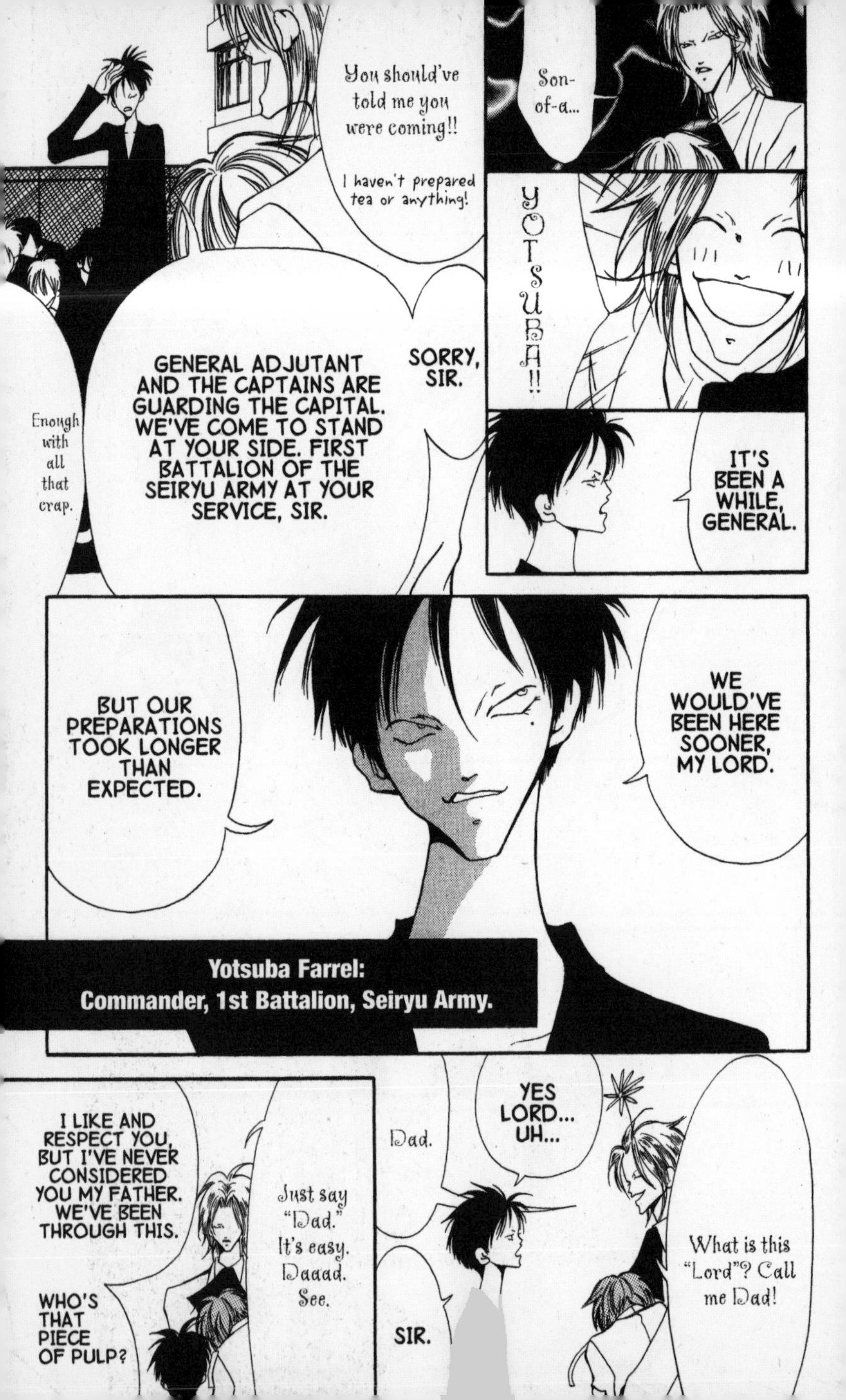
Son-of-a...
YOTSUBA!!
IT'S BEEN A WHILE, GENERAL.
You should've told me you were coming!!
I haven't prepared tea or anything!
SORRY, SIR.
GENERAL ADJUTANT AND THE CAPTAINS ARE GUARDING THE CAPITAL. WE'VE COME TO STAND AT YOUR SIDE. FIRST BATTALION OF THE SEIRYU ARMY AT YOUR SERVICE, SIR.
Enough with all that crap.
WE WOULD'VE BEEN HERE SOONER, MY LORD.
BUT OUR PREPARATIONS TOOK LONGER THAN EXPECTED.
Yotsuba Farrel:
Commander, 1st Battalion, Seiryu Army.
YES LORD... UH...
What is this "Lord"? Call me Dad!
Dad.
SIR.
Just say "Dad." It's easy. Daaad. See.
I LIKE AND RESPECT YOU, BUT I'VE NEVER CONSIDERED YOU MY FATHER. WE'VE BEEN THROUGH THIS.
WHO'S THAT PIECE OF PULP?

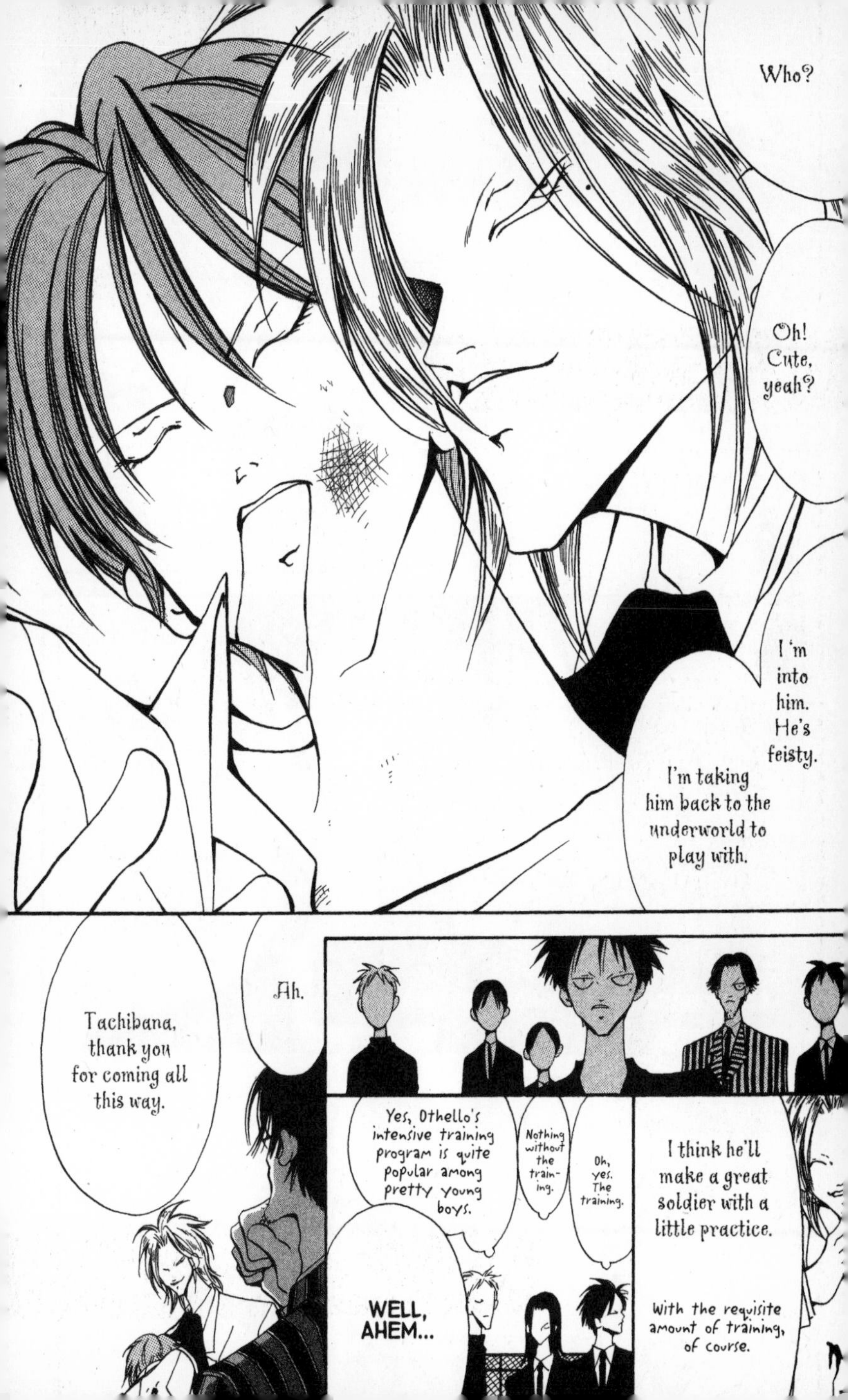
Who?
Oh! Cute, yeah?
I'm into him. He's feisty.
I'm taking him back to the underworld to play with.
I think he'll make a great soldier with a little practice.
With the requisite amount of training, of course.
Oh, yes. The training.
Nothing without the training.
Yes, Othello's intensive training program is quite popular among pretty young boys.
WELL, AHEM...
Ah.
Tachibana, thank you for coming all this way.

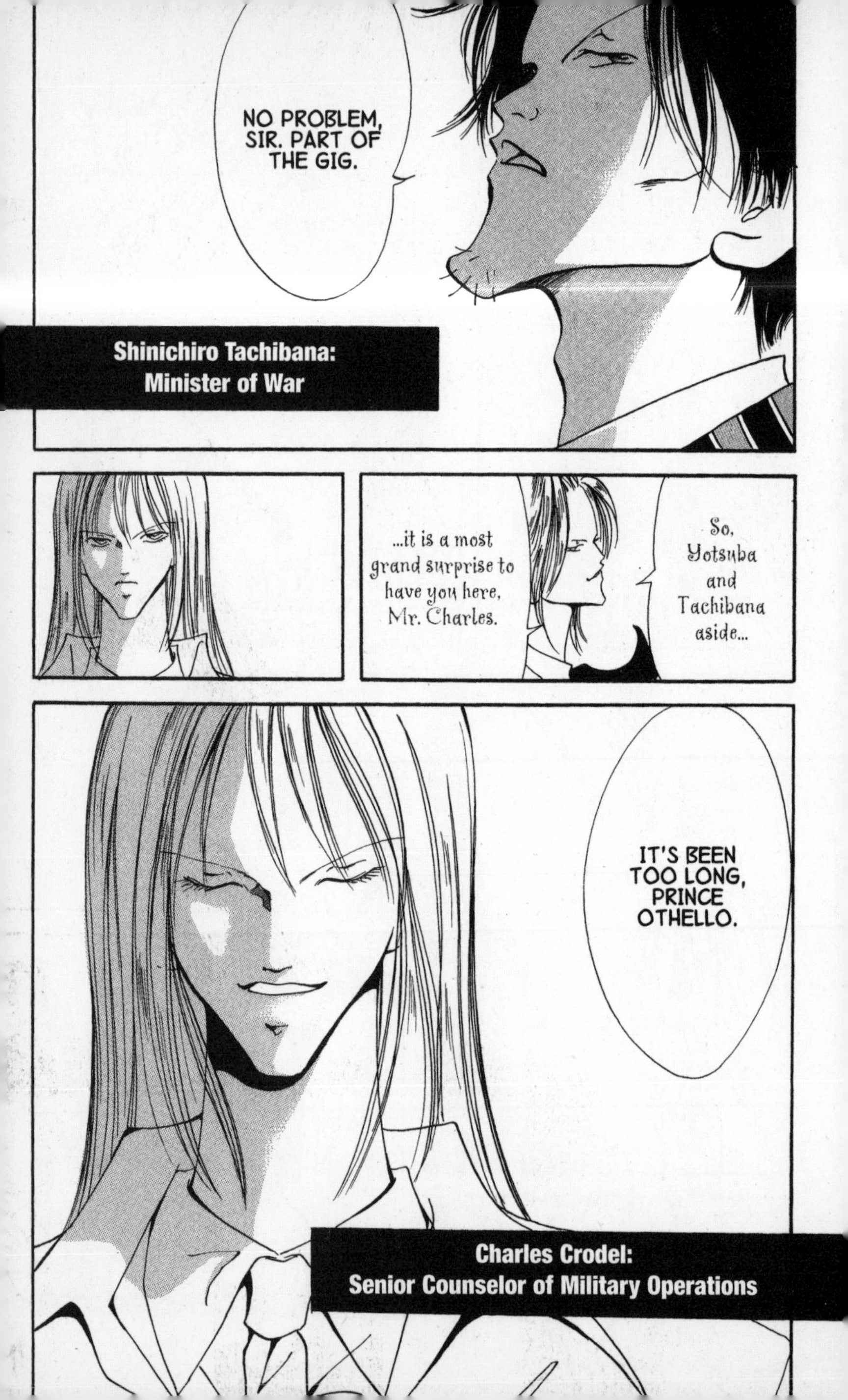

NO PROBLEM, SIR. PART OF THE GIG.
Shinichiro Tachibana: Minister of War
So, Yotsuba and Tachibana aside...
...it is a most grand surprise to have you here, Mr. Charles.
IT'S BEEN TOO LONG, PRINCE OTHELLO.
Charles Crodel: Senior Counselor of Military Operations

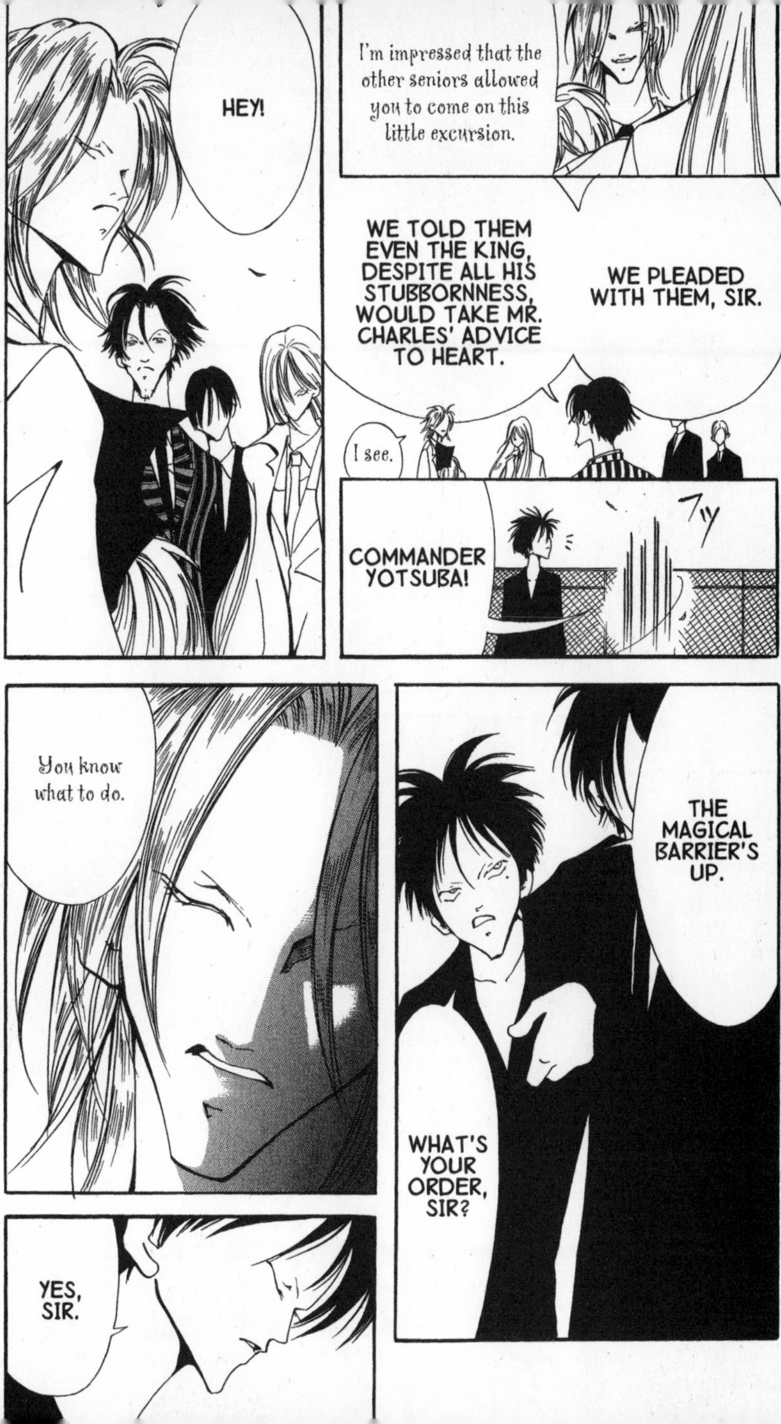
I'm impressed that the other seniors allowed you to come on this little excursion.
WE PLEADED WITH THEM, SIR.
WE TOLD THEM EVEN THE KING, DESPITE ALL HIS STUBBORNNESS, WOULD TAKE MR. CHARLES' ADVICE TO HEART.
I see.
COMMANDER YOTSUBA!
HEY!
THE MAGICAL BARRIER'S UP.
WHAT'S YOUR ORDER, SIR?
You know what to do.
YES, SIR.

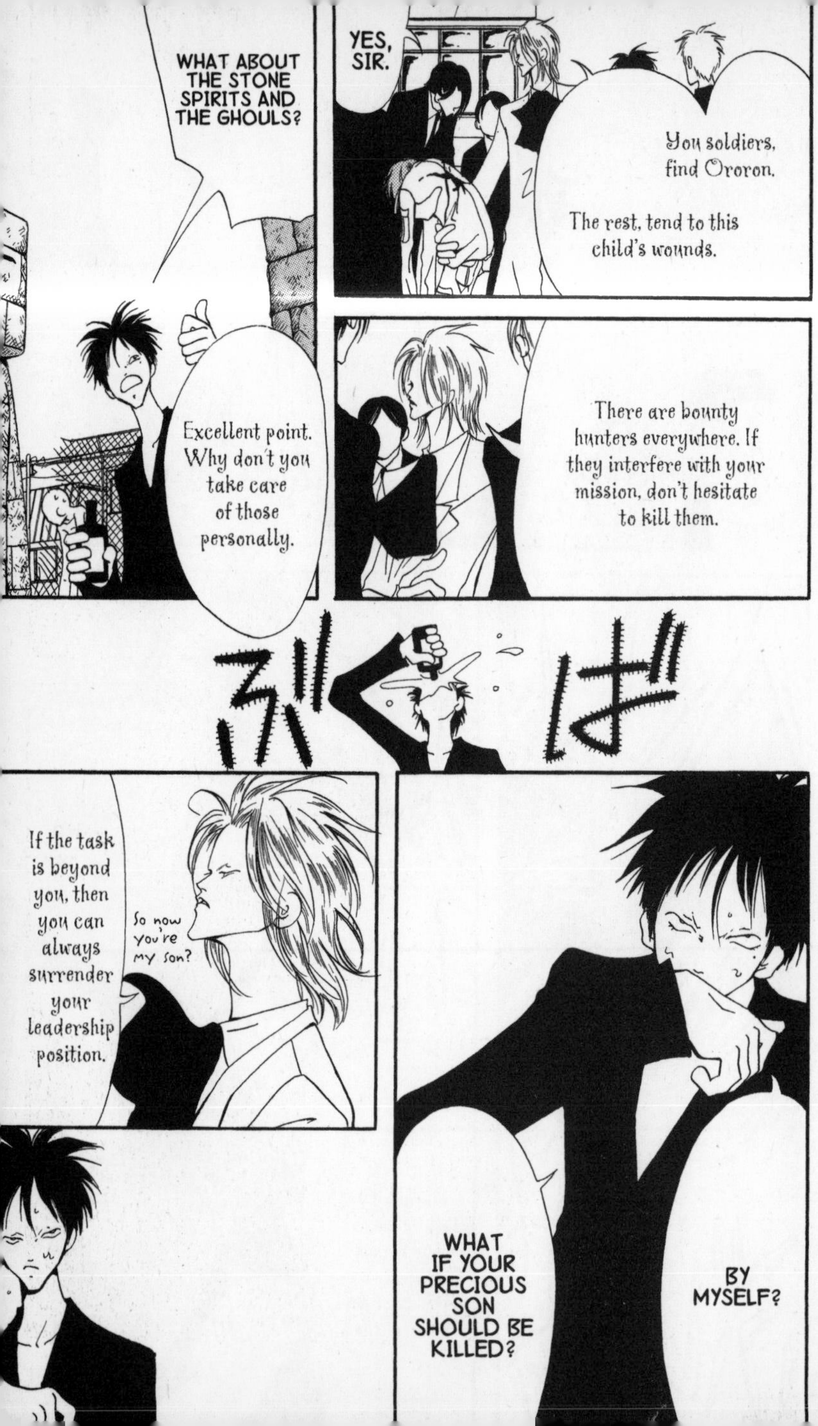
You soldiers, find Ororon.
The rest, tend to this child's wounds.
YES, SIR.
There are bounty hunters everywhere. If they interfere with your mission, don't hesitate to kill them.
WHAT ABOUT THE STONE SPIRITS AND THE GHOULS?
Excellent point. Why don't you take care of those personally.
ぶ ば
BY MYSELF?
WHAT IF YOUR PRECIOUS SON SHOULD BE KILLED?
If the task is beyond you, then you can always surrender your leadership position.
So now you're my son?

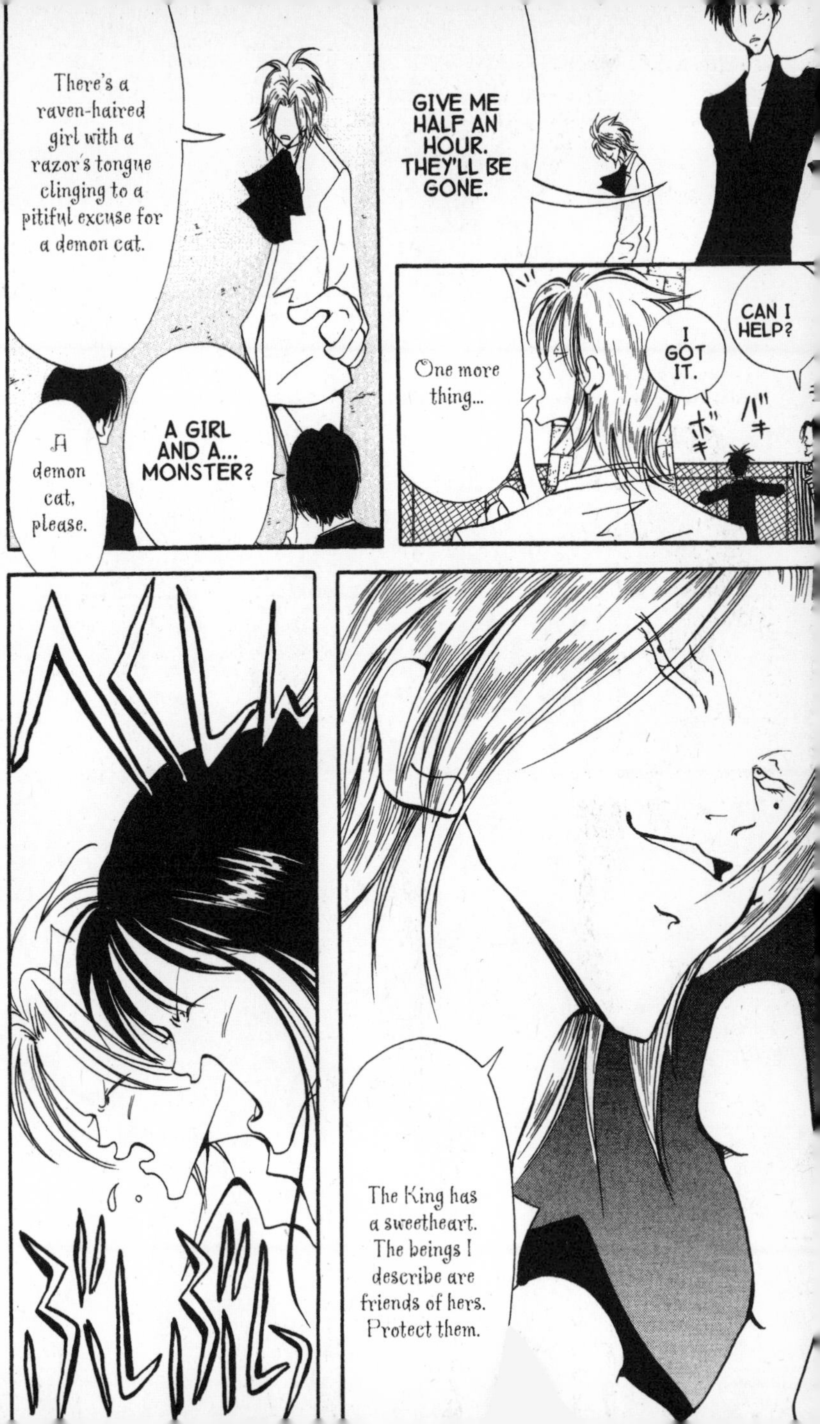
GIVE ME HALF AN HOUR. THEY'LL BE GONE.
CAN I HELP?
I GOT IT.
バキ
ボキ
One more thing...
There's a raven-haired girl with a razor's tongue clinging to a pitiful excuse for a demon cat.
A GIRL AND A... MONSTER?
A demon cat, please.
The King has a sweetheart. The beings I describe are friends of hers. Protect them.

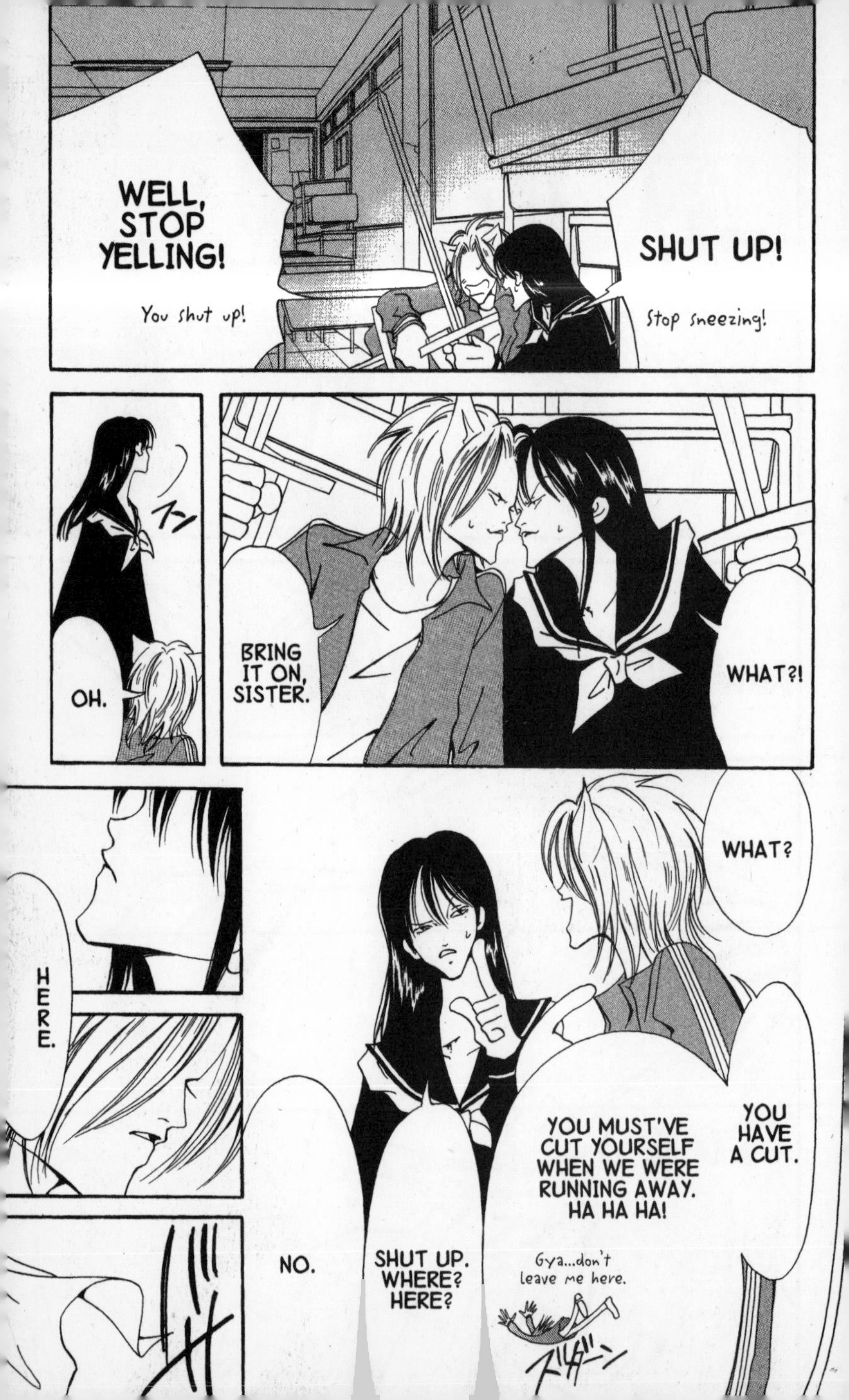
SHUT UP!
Stop sneezing!
WELL, STOP YELLING!
You shut up!
WHAT?!
BRING IT ON, SISTER.
OH.
WHAT?
YOU HAVE A CUT.
YOU MUST'VE CUT YOURSELF WHEN WE WERE RUNNING AWAY. HA HA HA!
Gya...don't leave me here.
SHUT UP. WHERE? HERE?
NO.
HERE.

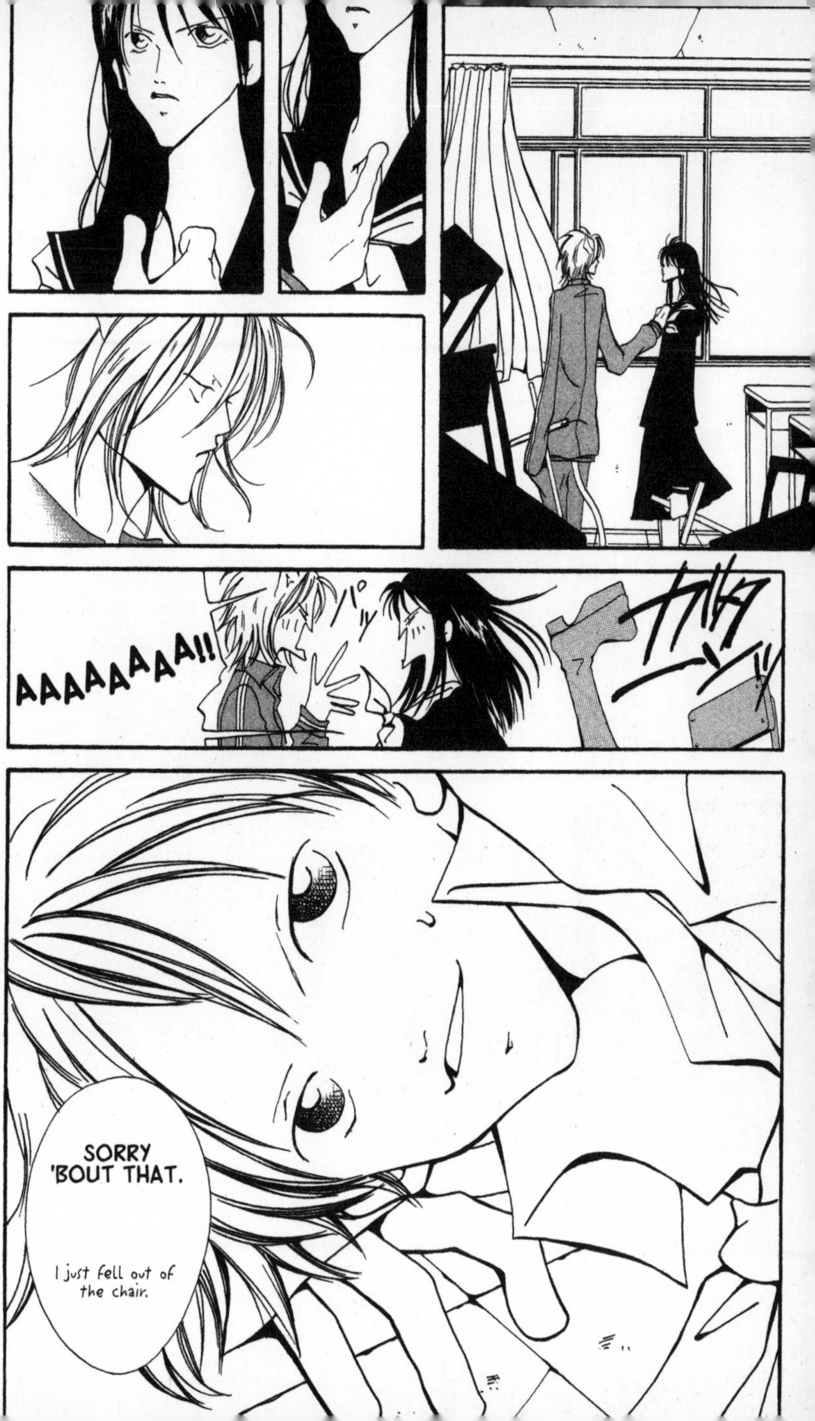

ガタン
パッ
AAAAAAAA!!
SORRY 'BOUT THAT.
I just fell out of the chair.

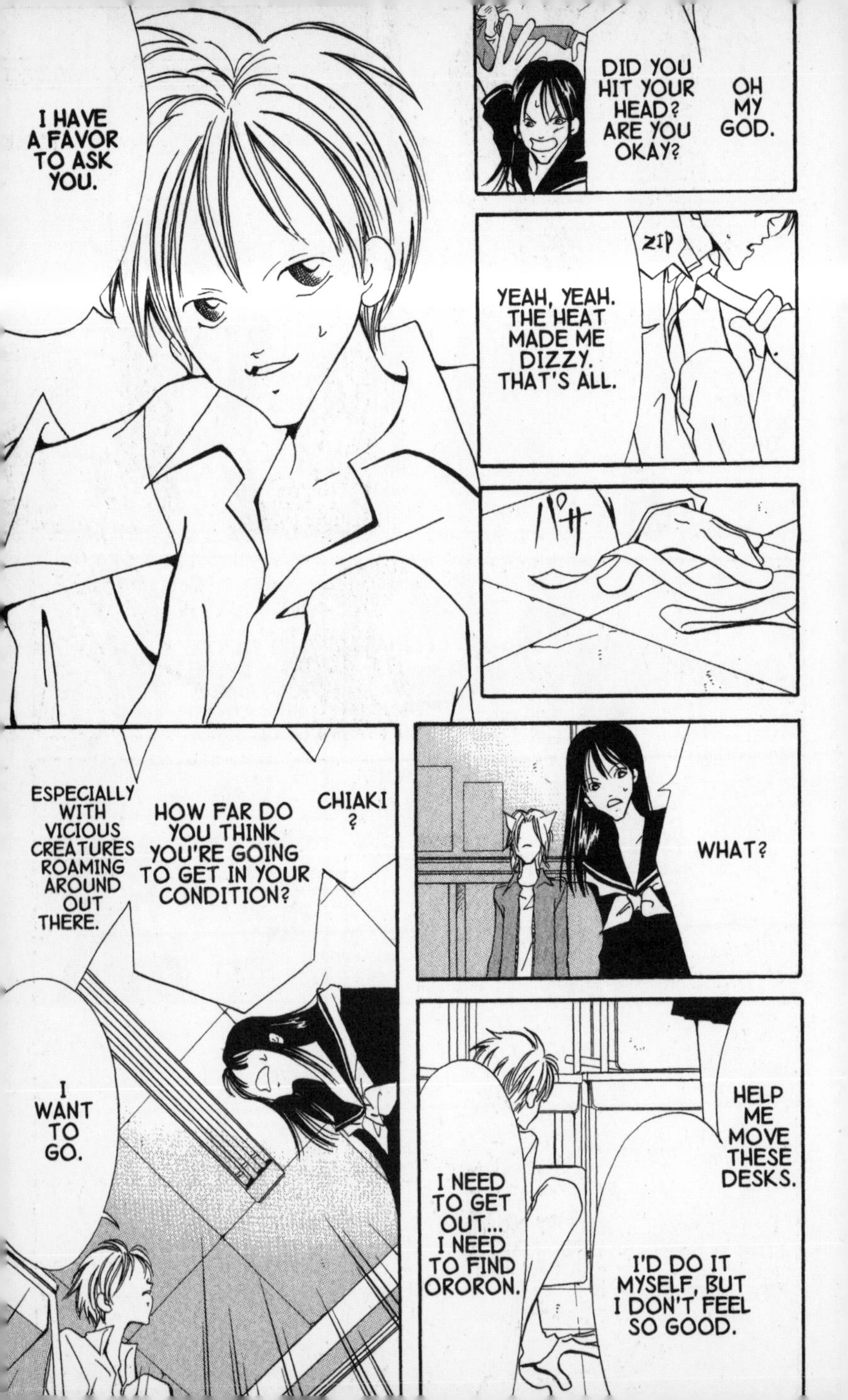
OH MY GOD.
DID YOU HIT YOUR HEAD? ARE YOU OKAY?
ZIP
YEAH, YEAH. THE HEAT MADE ME DIZZY. THAT'S ALL.
パサ
I HAVE A FAVOR TO ASK YOU.
WHAT?
HELP ME MOVE THESE DESKS.
I NEED TO GET OUT... I NEED TO FIND ORORON.
I'D DO IT MYSELF, BUT I DON'T FEEL SO GOOD.
CHIAKI?
HOW FAR DO YOU THINK YOU'RE GOING TO GET IN YOUR CONDITION?
ESPECIALLY WITH VICIOUS CREATURES ROAMING AROUND OUT THERE.
I WANT TO GO.

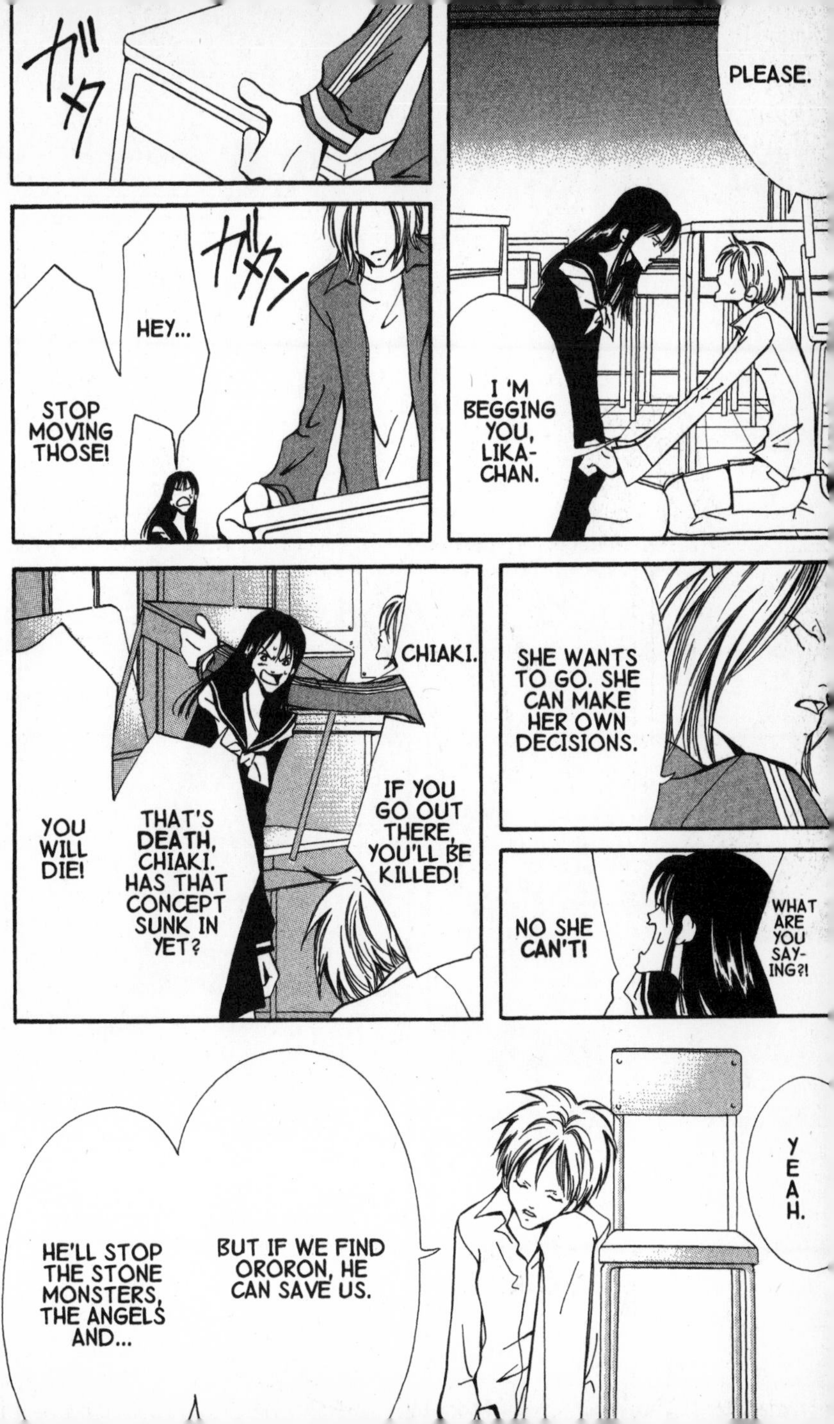
PLEASE.
I'M BEGGING YOU, LIKA-CHAN.
ガタ
ガタン
HEY...
STOP MOVING THOSE!
SHE WANTS TO GO. SHE CAN MAKE HER OWN DECISIONS.
WHAT ARE YOU SAYING?!
NO SHE CAN'T!
CHIAKI.
IF YOU GO OUT THERE, YOU'LL BE KILLED!
THAT'S DEATH, CHIAKI. HAS THAT CONCEPT SUNK IN YET?
YOU WILL DIE!
YEAH.
BUT IF WE FIND ORORON, HE CAN SAVE US.
HE'LL STOP THE STONE MONSTERS, THE ANGELS AND...

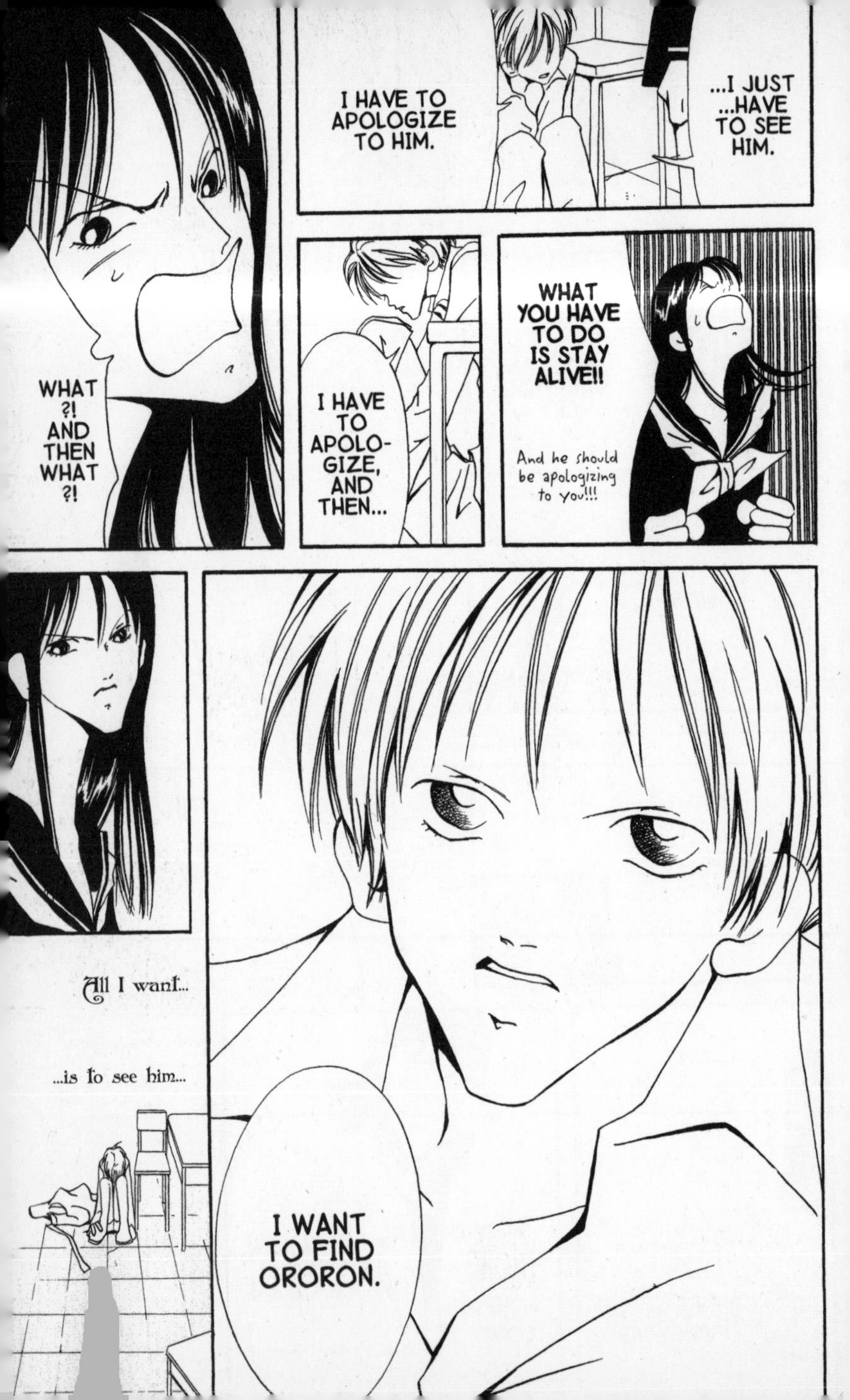
...I JUST ...HAVE TO SEE HIM.
I HAVE TO APOLOGIZE TO HIM.
WHAT YOU HAVE TO DO IS STAY ALIVE!!
And he should be apologizing to you!!!
I HAVE TO APOLOGIZE, AND THEN...
WHAT?! AND THEN WHAT?!
I WANT TO FIND ORORON.
All I want...
...is to see him...

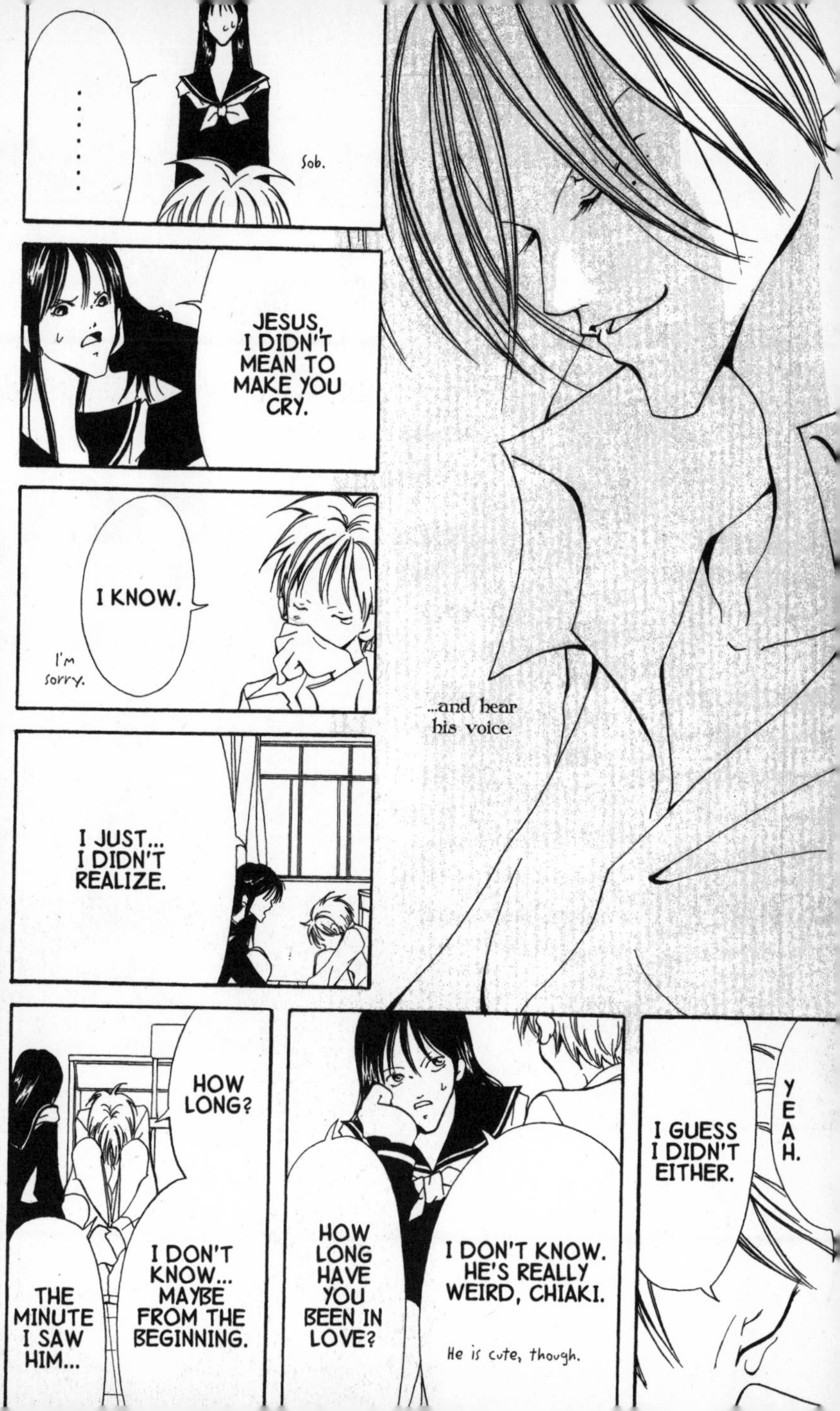
...and hear his voice.
......
Sob.
JESUS, I DIDN'T MEAN TO MAKE YOU CRY.
I KNOW.
I'm sorry.
I JUST... I DIDN'T REALIZE.
YEAH.
I GUESS I DIDN'T EITHER.
HOW LONG HAVE YOU BEEN IN LOVE?
I DON'T KNOW. HE'S REALLY WEIRD, CHIAKI.
He is cute, though.
HOW LONG?
I DON'T KNOW... MAYBE FROM THE BEGINNING.
THE MINUTE I SAW HIM...

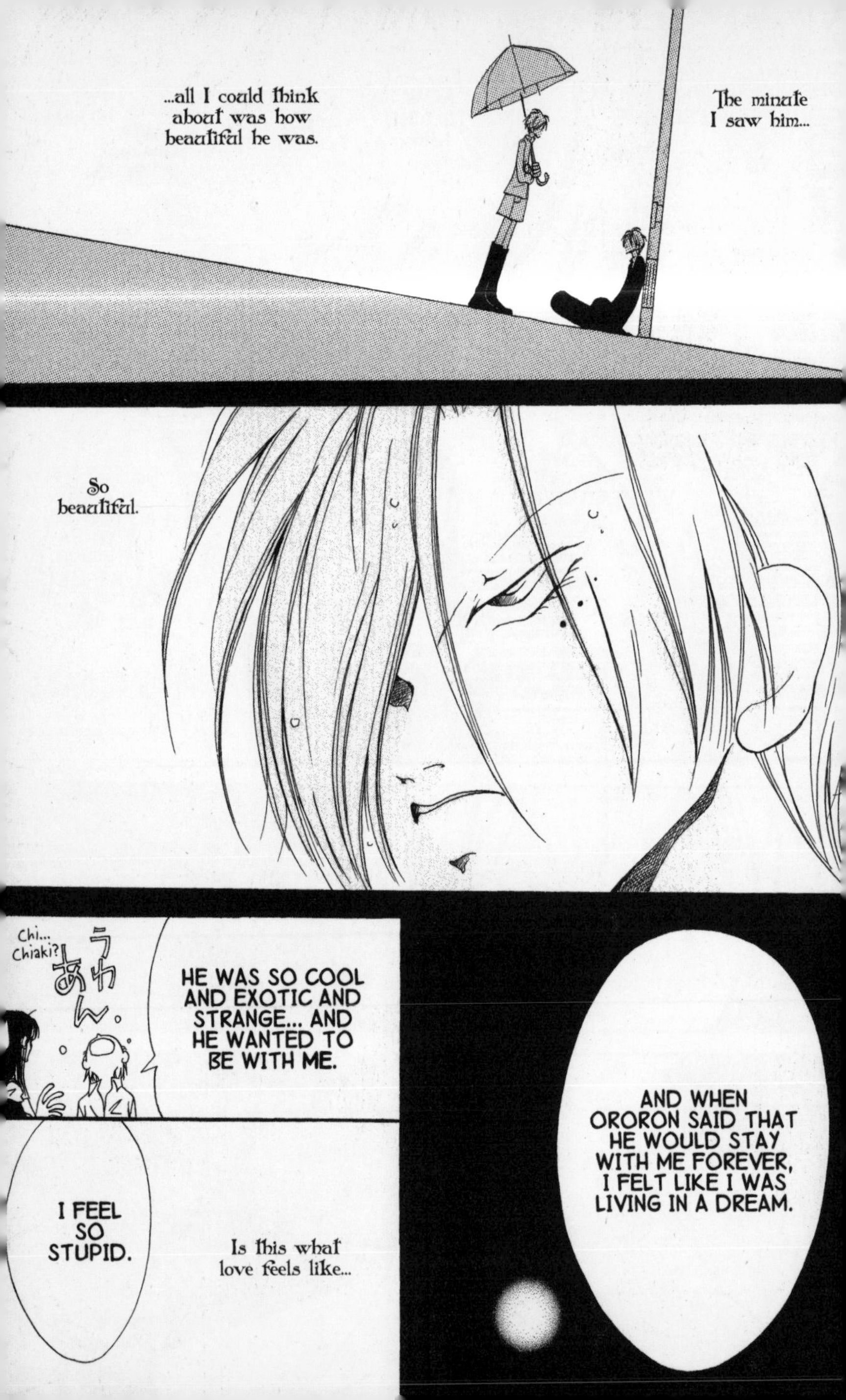
The minute I saw him...
...all I could think about was how beautiful he was.
So beautiful.
AND WHEN ORORON SAID THAT HE WOULD STAY WITH ME FOREVER, I FELT LIKE I WAS LIVING IN A DREAM.
HE WAS SO COOL AND EXOTIC AND STRANGE... AND HE WANTED TO BE WITH ME.
うわあん。
Chi... Chiaki?
Is this what love feels like...
I FEEL SO STUPID.

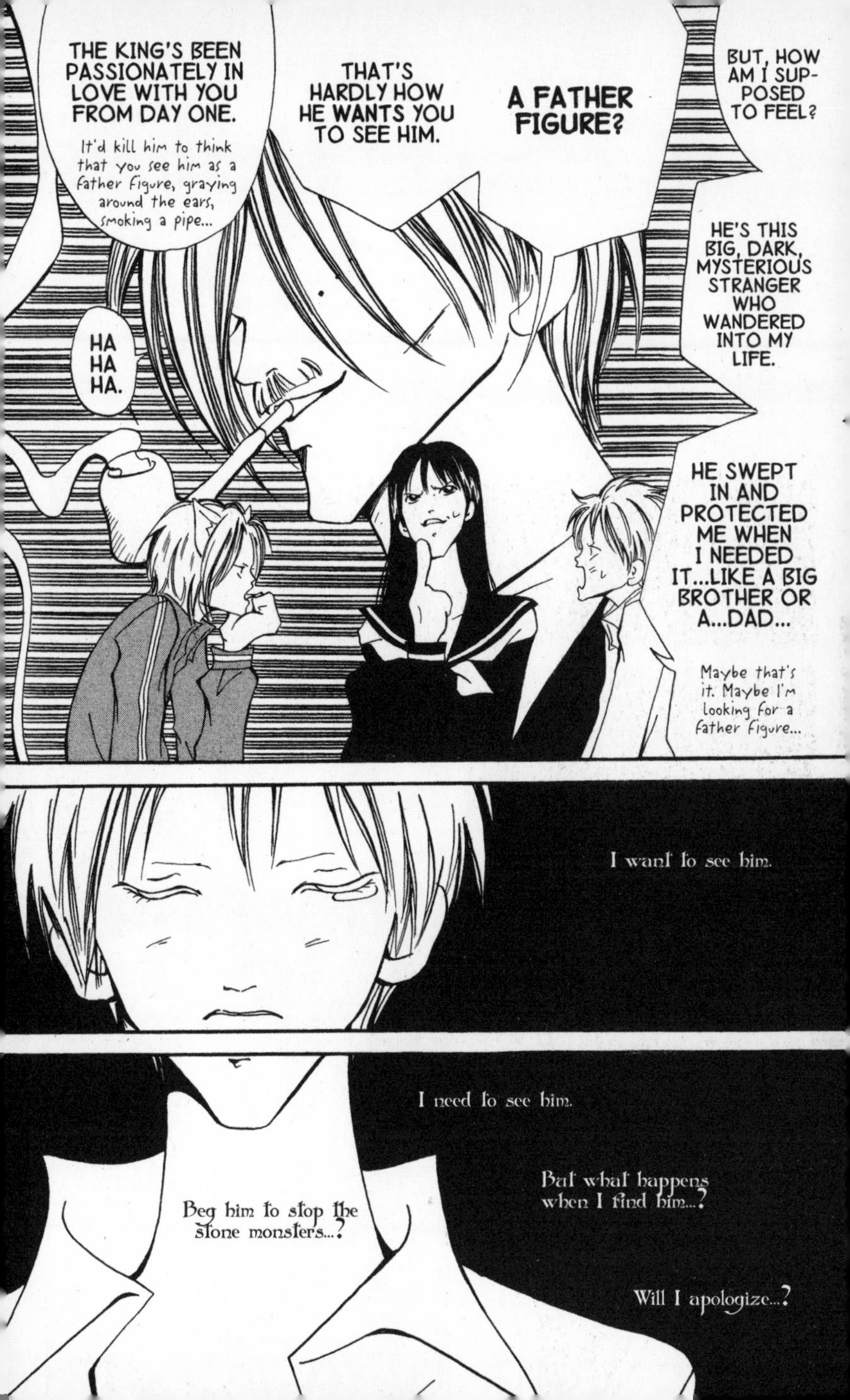
BUT, HOW AM I SUP-POSED TO FEEL?
HE'S THIS BIG, DARK, MYSTERIOUS STRANGER WHO WANDERED INTO MY LIFE.
HE SWEPT IN AND PROTECTED ME WHEN I NEEDED IT...LIKE A BIG BROTHER OR A...DAD...
Maybe that's it. Maybe I'm looking for a father figure...
A FATHER FIGURE?
THAT'S HARDLY HOW HE WANTS YOU TO SEE HIM.
THE KING'S BEEN PASSIONATELY IN LOVE WITH YOU FROM DAY ONE.
It'd kill him to think that you see him as a father figure, graying around the ears, smoking a pipe...
HA HA HA.
I want to see him.
I need to see him.
But what happens when I find him...?
Beg him to stop the stone monsters...?
Will I apologize...?

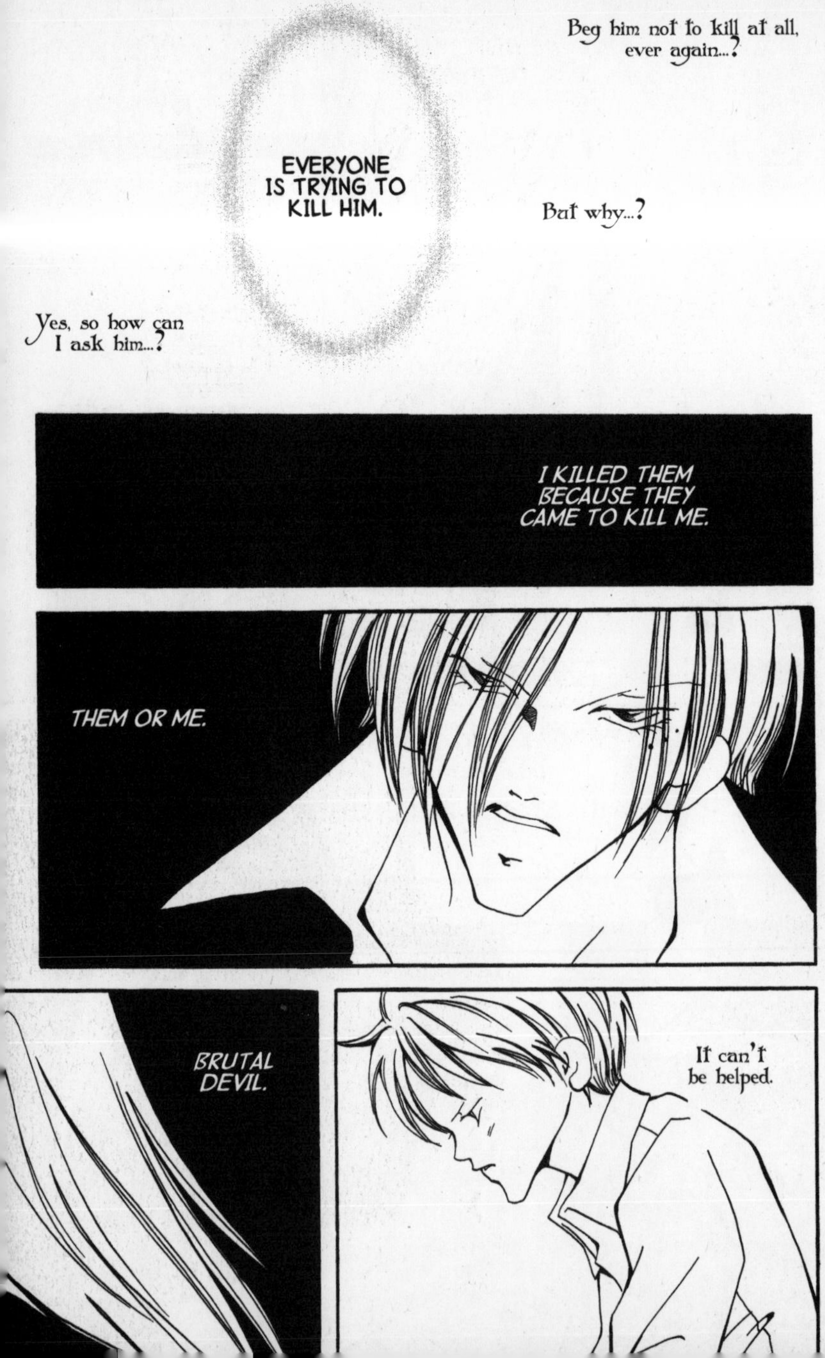
Beg him not to kill at all, ever again...?
But why...?
EVERYONE IS TRYING TO KILL HIM.
Yes, so how can I ask him...?
I KILLED THEM BECAUSE THEY CAME TO KILL ME.
THEM OR ME.
It can't be helped.
BRUTAL DEVIL.

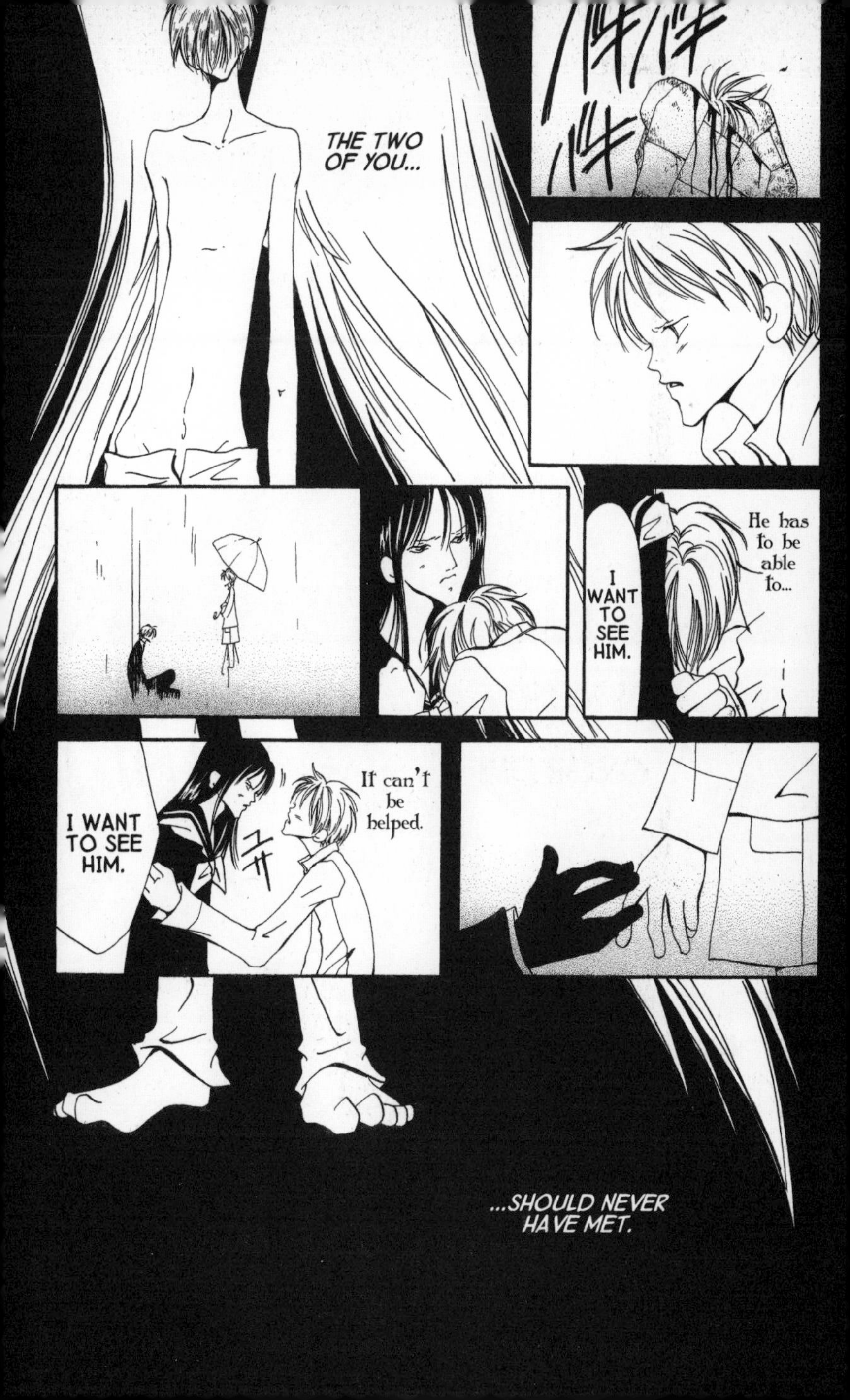

バキバキ
THE TWO OF YOU...
He has to be able to...
I WANT TO SEE HIM.
It can't be helped.
ユサ
I WANT TO SEE HIM.
...SHOULD NEVER HAVE MET.

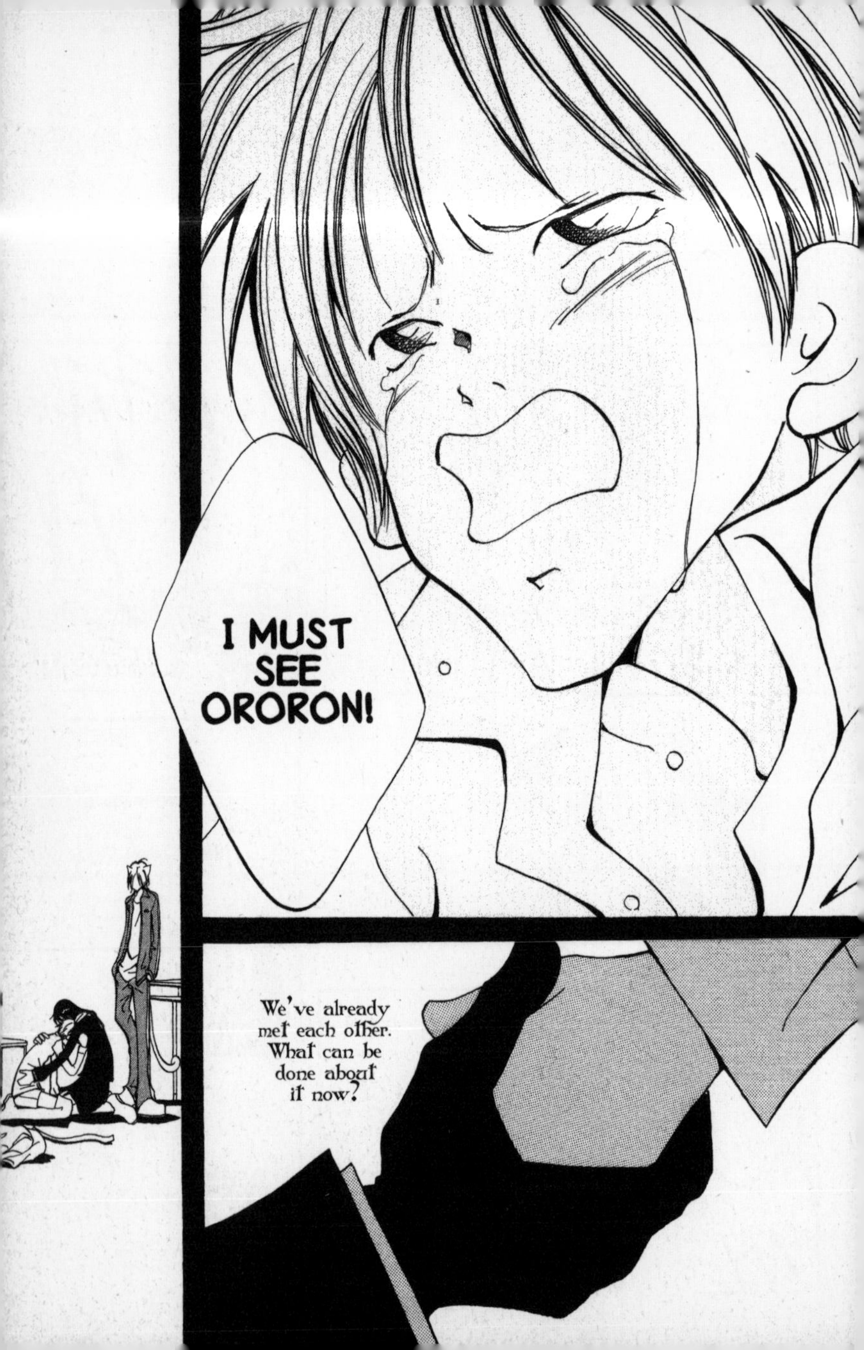
I MUST SEE ORORON!
We've already met each other. What can be done about it now?

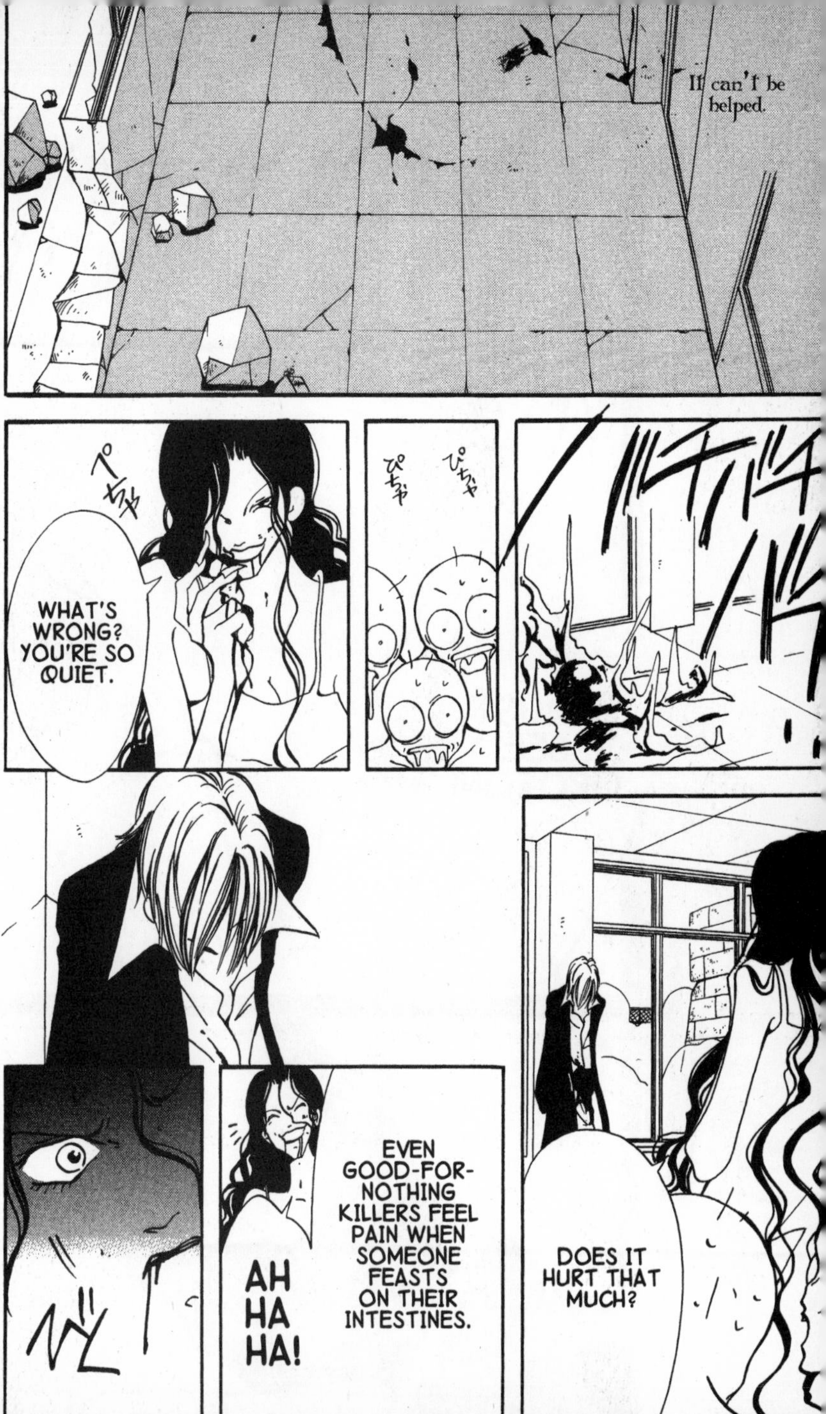
It can't be helped.
ぴちゃ
ぴちゃ
WHAT'S WRONG? YOU'RE SO QUIET.
DOES IT HURT THAT MUCH?
EVEN GOOD-FOR-NOTHING KILLERS FEEL PAIN WHEN SOMEONE FEASTS ON THEIR INTESTINES.
AH HA HA!

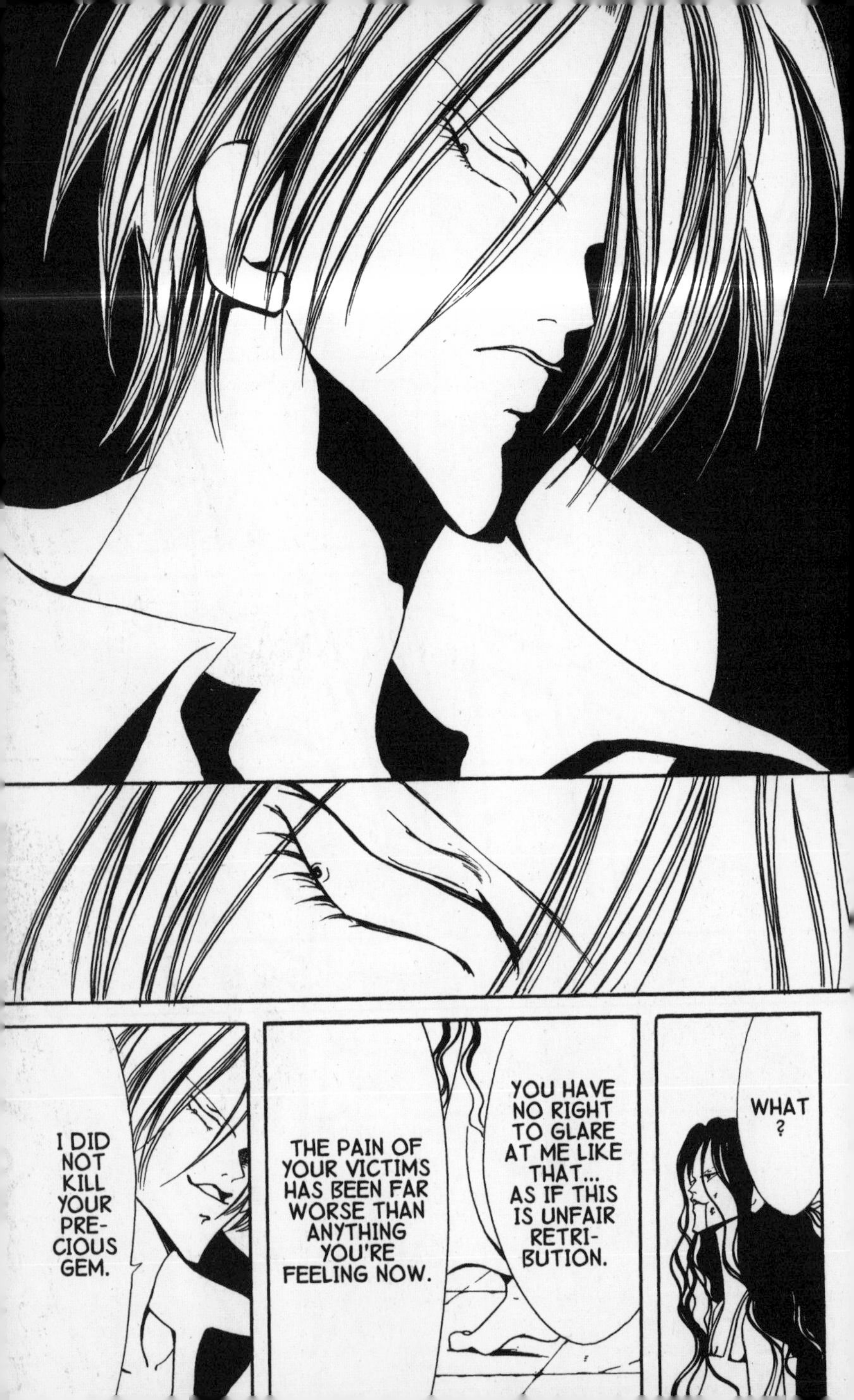
WHAT?
YOU HAVE NO RIGHT TO GLARE AT ME LIKE THAT... AS IF THIS IS UNFAIR RETRIBUTION.
THE PAIN OF YOUR VICTIMS HAS BEEN FAR WORSE THAN ANYTHING YOU'RE FEELING NOW.
I DID NOT KILL YOUR PRECIOUS GEM.

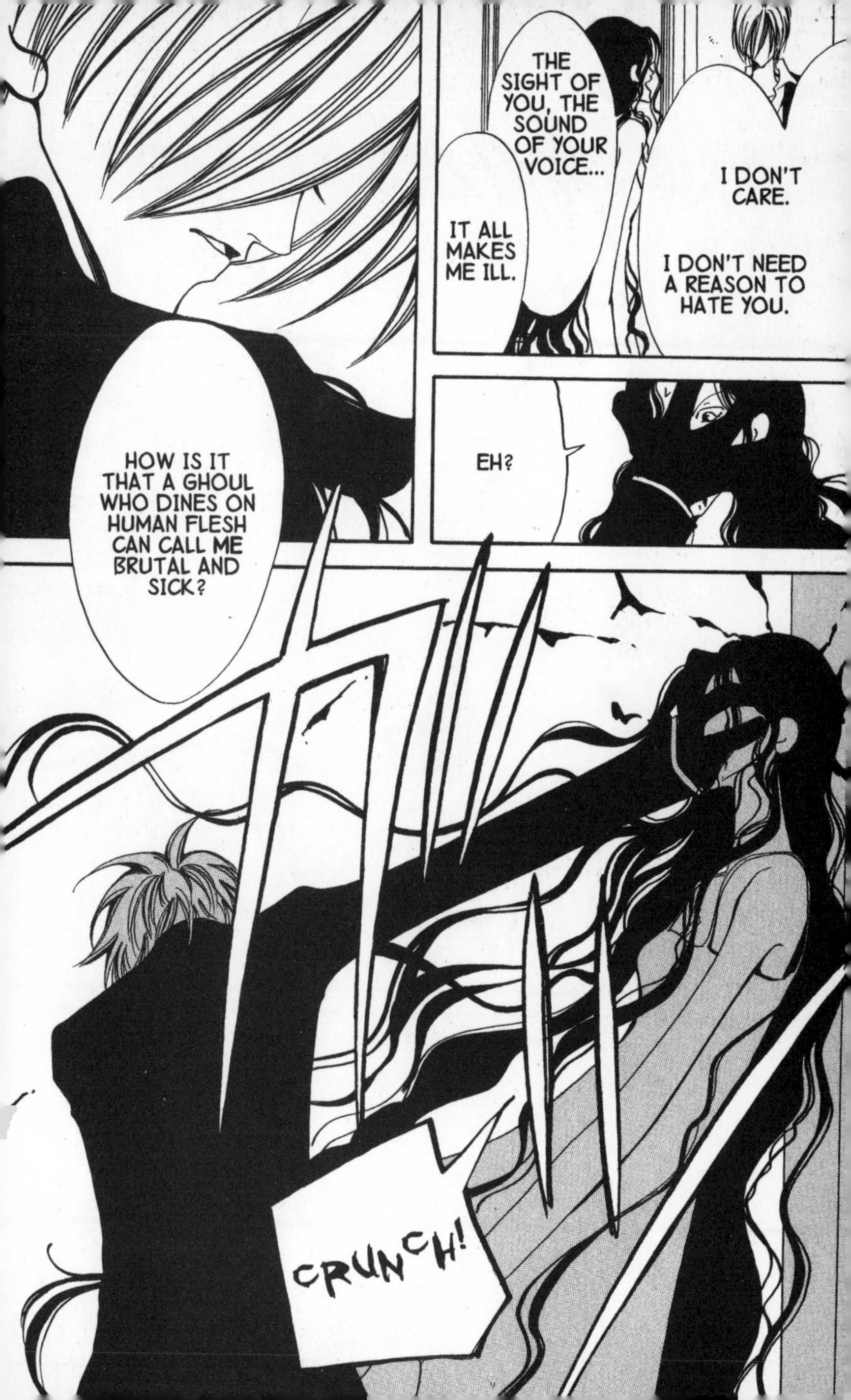
HOW IS IT THAT A GHOUL WHO DINES ON HUMAN FLESH CAN CALL ME BRUTAL AND SICK?
I DON'T CARE.
I DON'T NEED A REASON TO HATE YOU.
THE SIGHT OF YOU, THE SOUND OF YOUR VOICE...
IT ALL MAKES ME ILL.
EH?
CRUNCH!

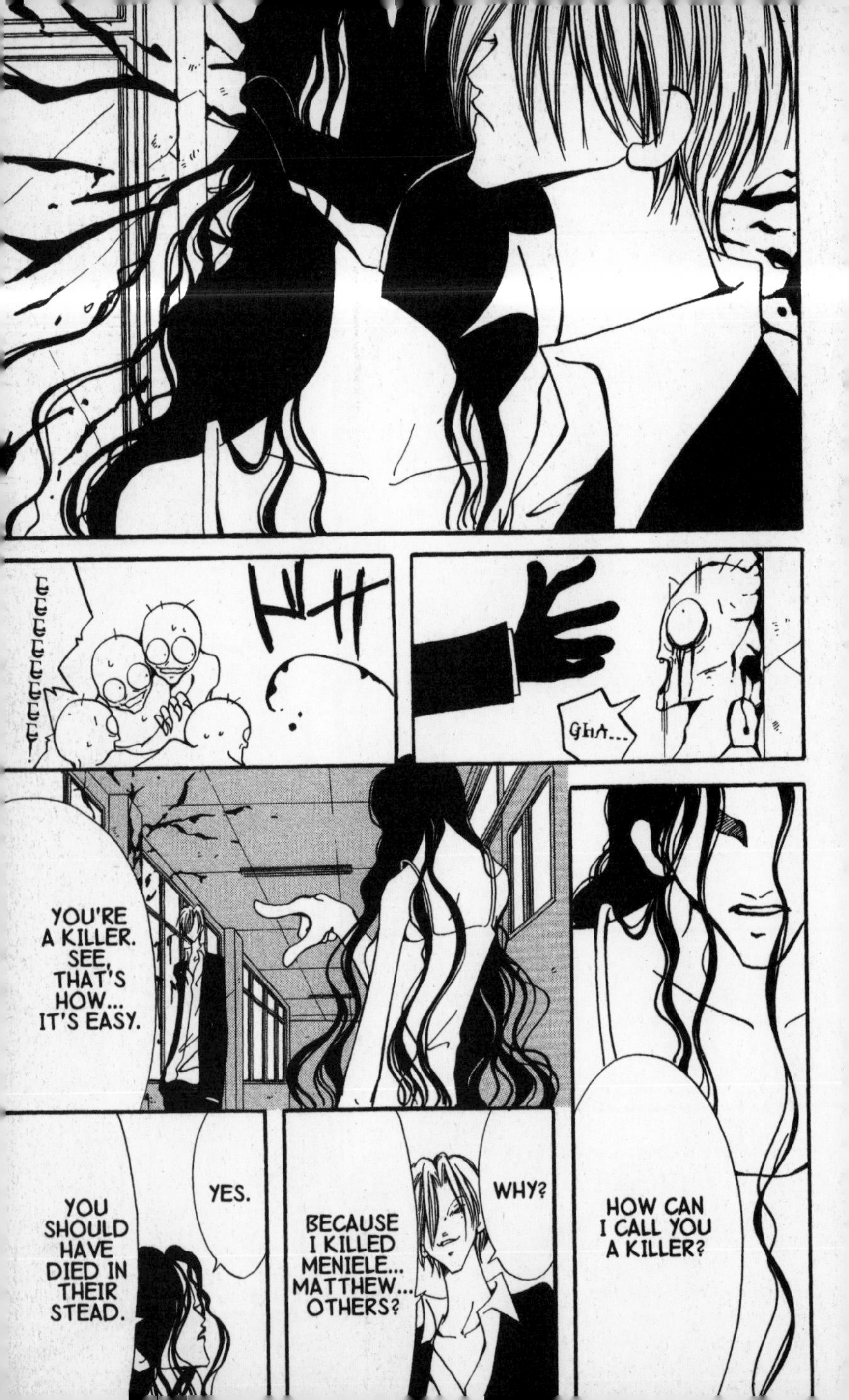
GHA...
HOW CAN I CALL YOU A KILLER?
YOU'RE A KILLER. SEE, THAT'S HOW... IT'S EASY.
WHY?
BECAUSE I KILLED MENIELE... MATTHEW... OTHERS?
YES.
YOU SHOULD HAVE DIED IN THEIR STEAD.

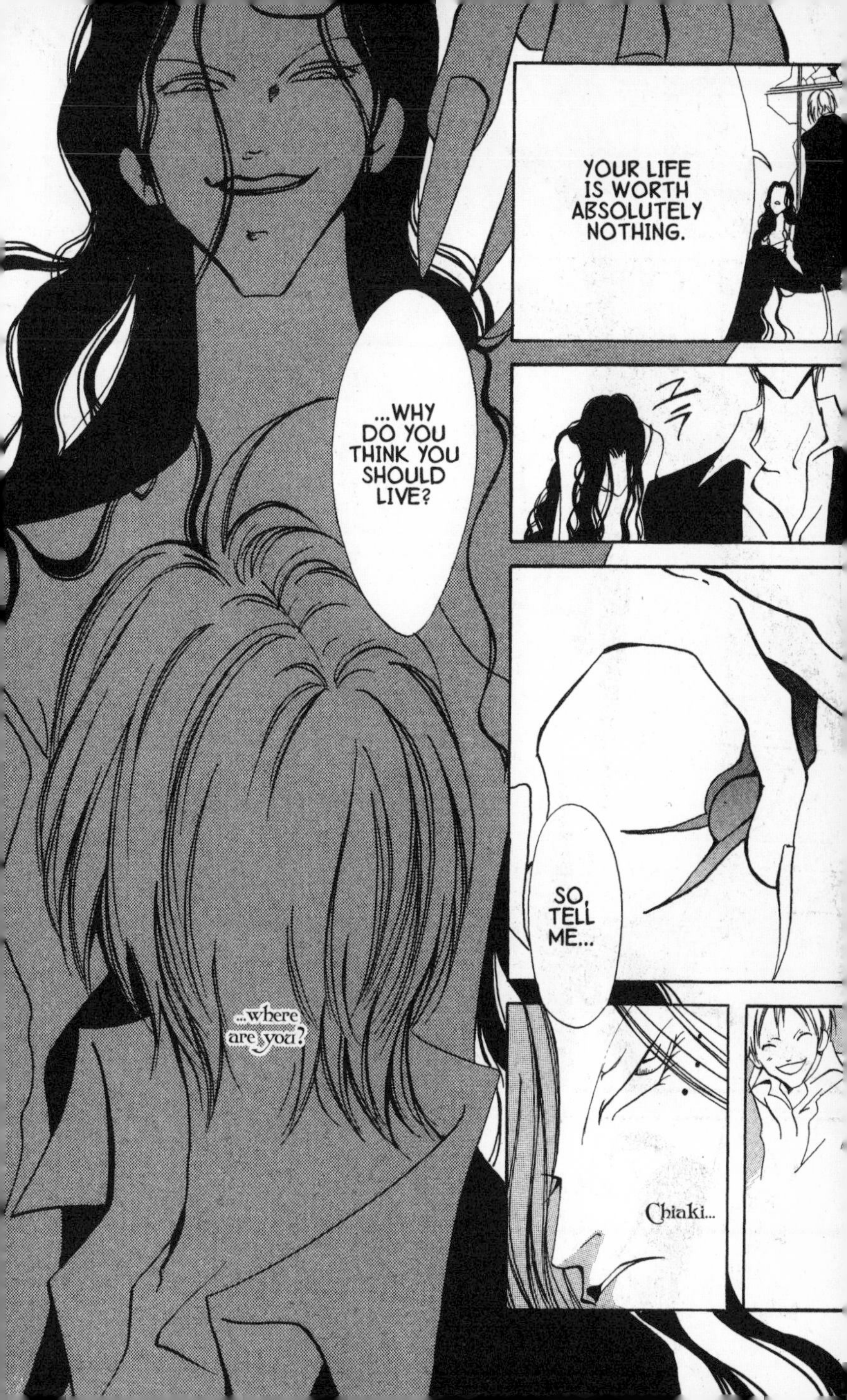
YOUR LIFE IS WORTH ABSOLUTELY NOTHING.
SO, TELL ME...
...WHY DO YOU THINK YOU SHOULD LIVE?
Chiaki...
...where are you?

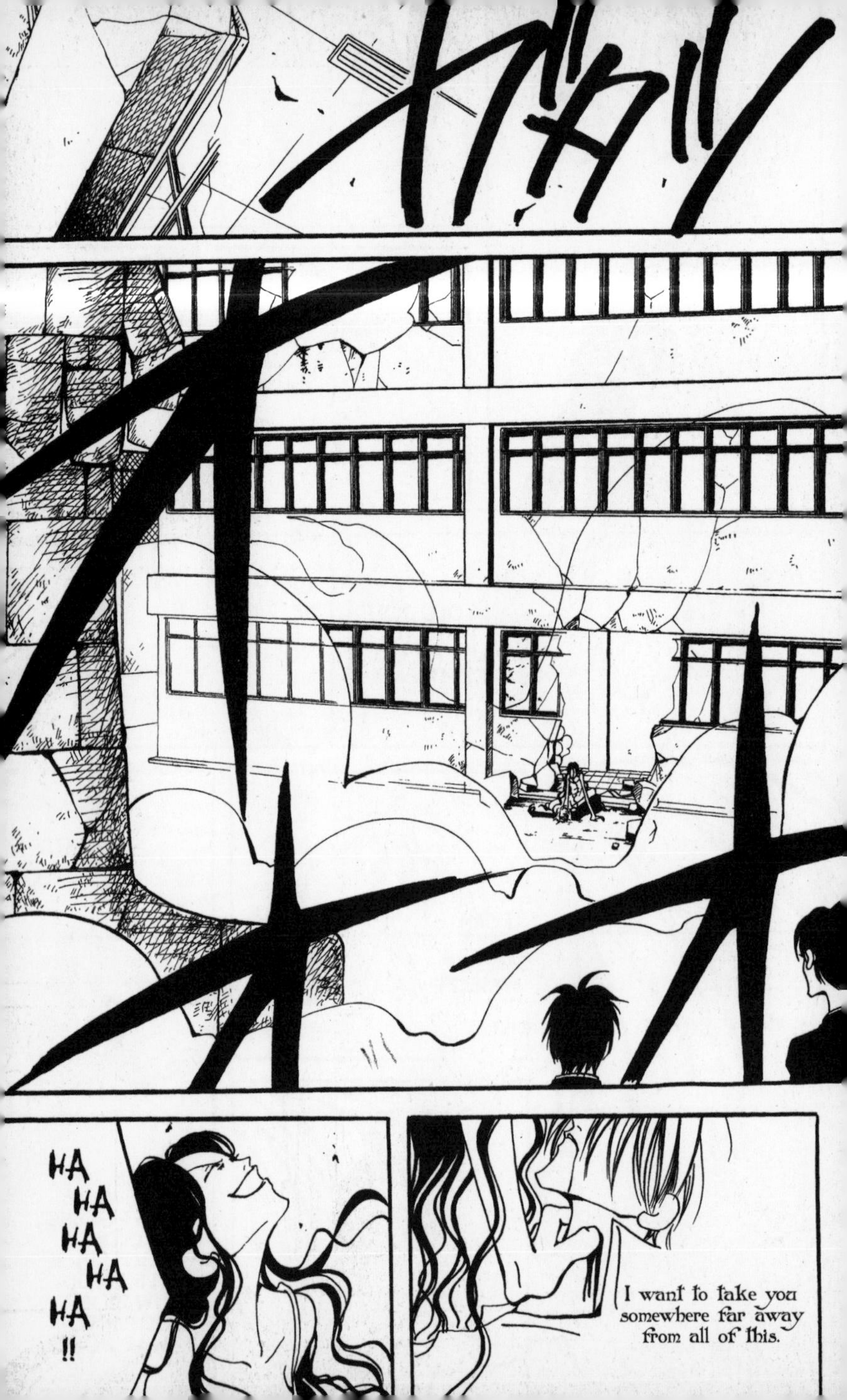
I want to take you somewhere far away from all of this.
HA HA HA HA HA!!

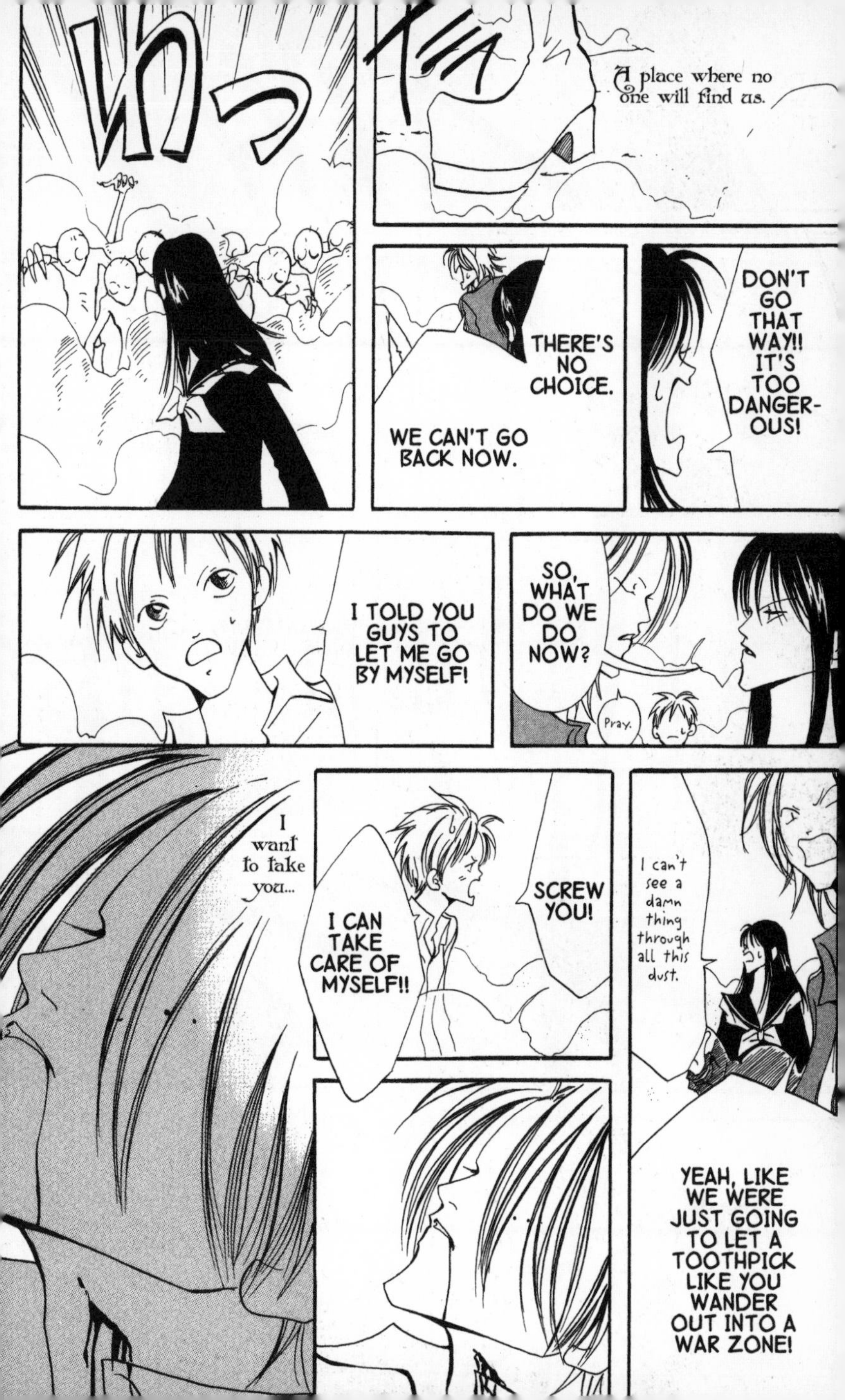
A place where no one will find us.
DON'T GO THAT WAY!! IT'S TOO DANGER-OUS!
THERE'S NO CHOICE.
WE CAN'T GO BACK NOW.
わっ
SO, WHAT DO WE DO NOW?
Pray.
I TOLD YOU GUYS TO LET ME GO BY MYSELF!
I can't see a damn thing through all this dust.
YEAH, LIKE WE WERE JUST GOING TO LET A TOOTHPICK LIKE YOU WANDER OUT INTO A WAR ZONE!
SCREW YOU!
I CAN TAKE CARE OF MYSELF!!
I want to take you...

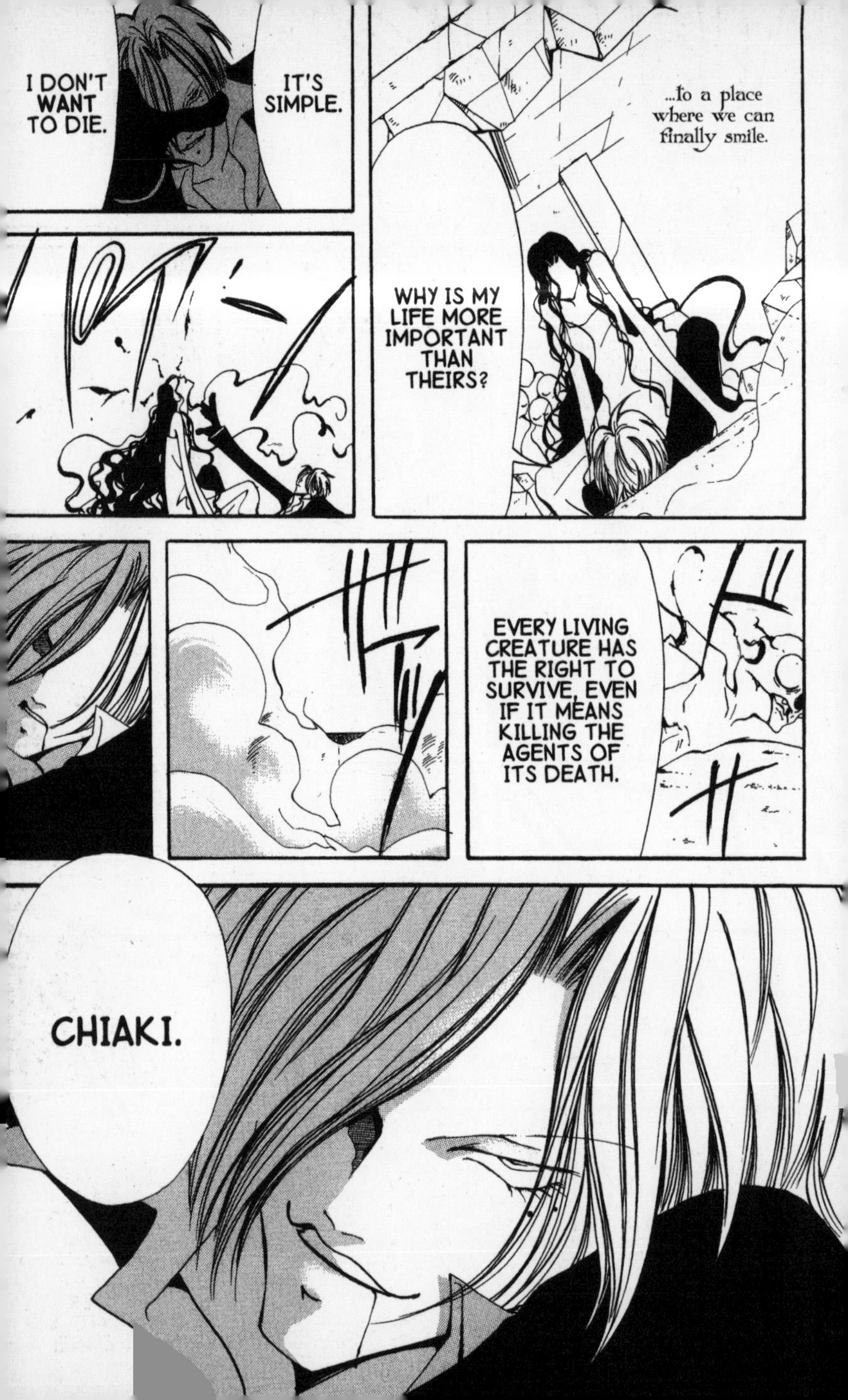
...to a place where we can finally smile.
WHY IS MY LIFE MORE IMPORTANT THAN THEIRS?
IT'S SIMPLE.
I DON'T WANT TO DIE.
EVERY LIVING CREATURE HAS THE RIGHT TO SURVIVE, EVEN IF IT MEANS KILLING THE AGENTS OF ITS DEATH.
CHIAKI.

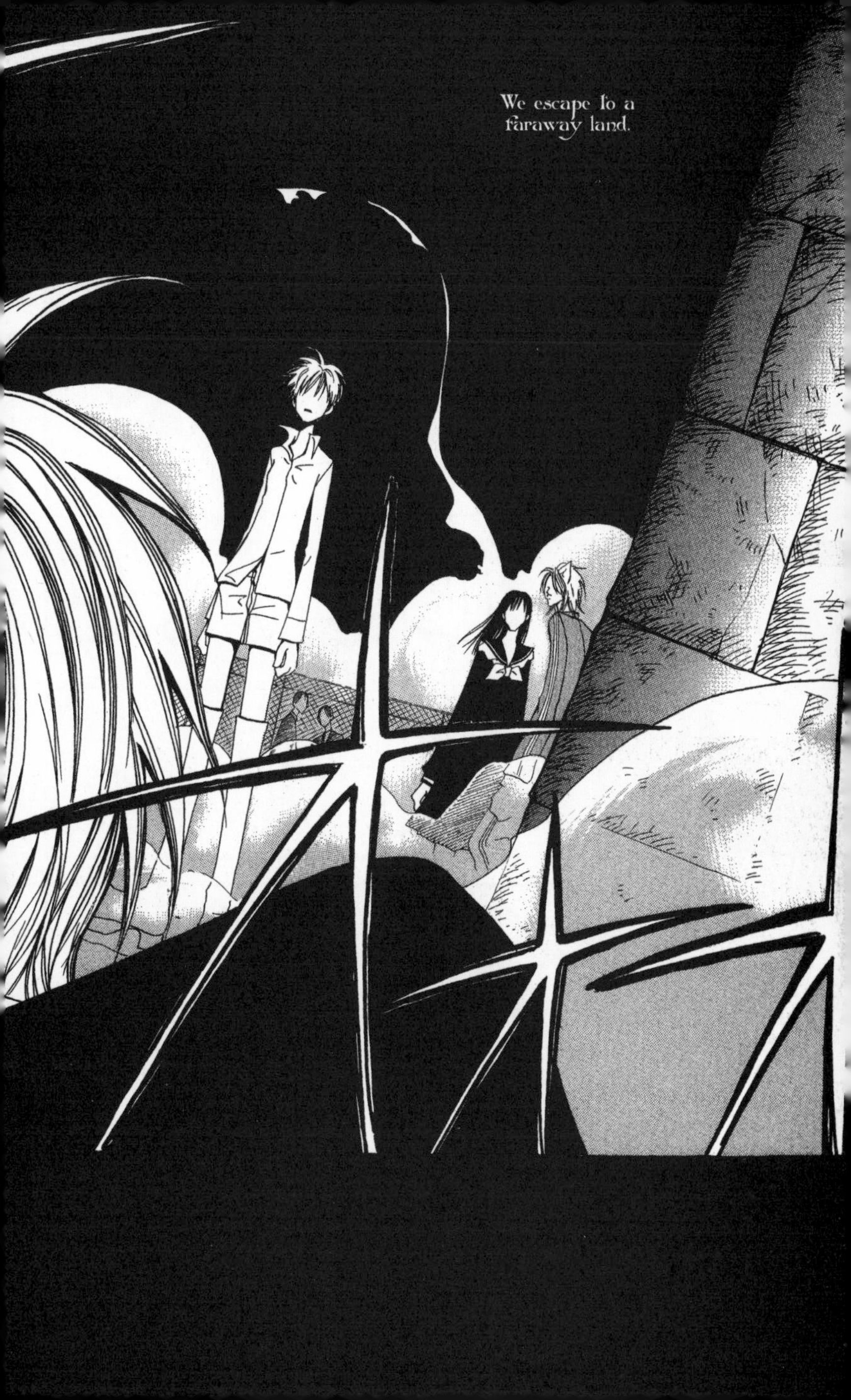
We escape to a faraway land.

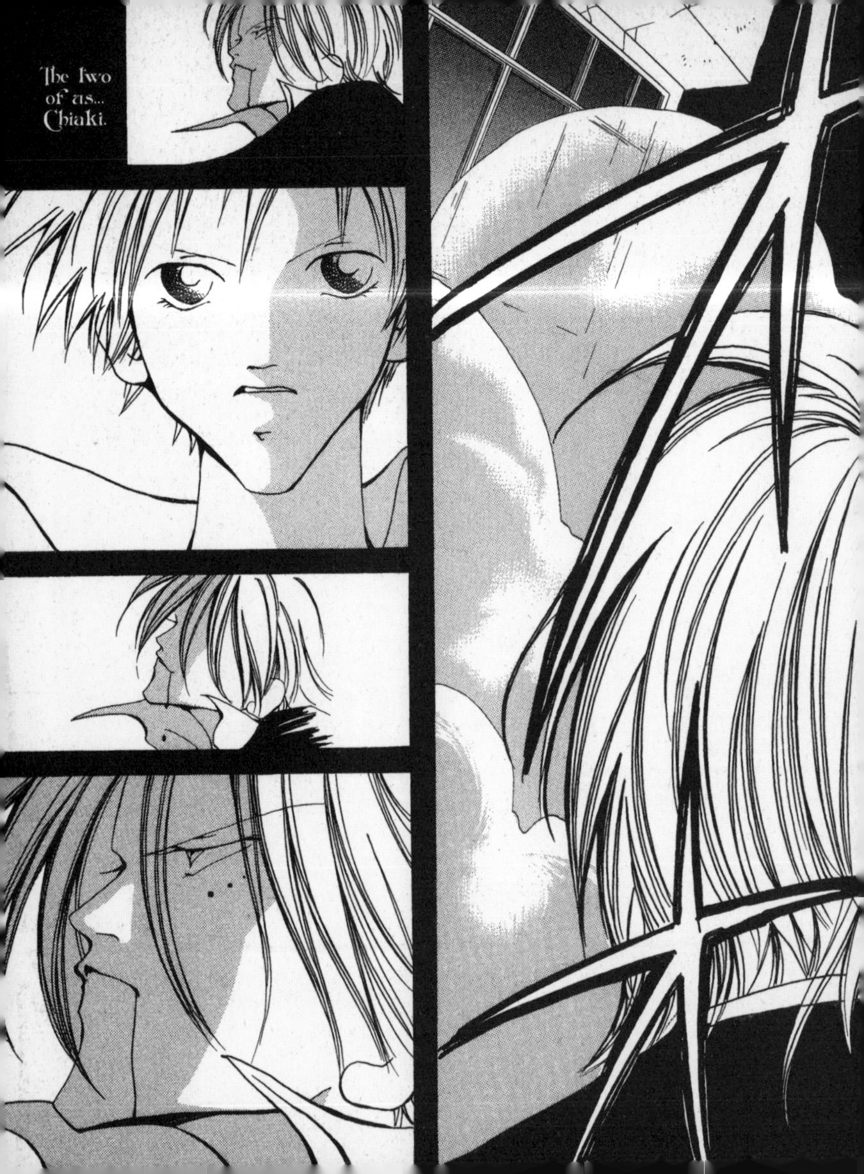
The two of us... Chiaki.

-09-

NIGHT

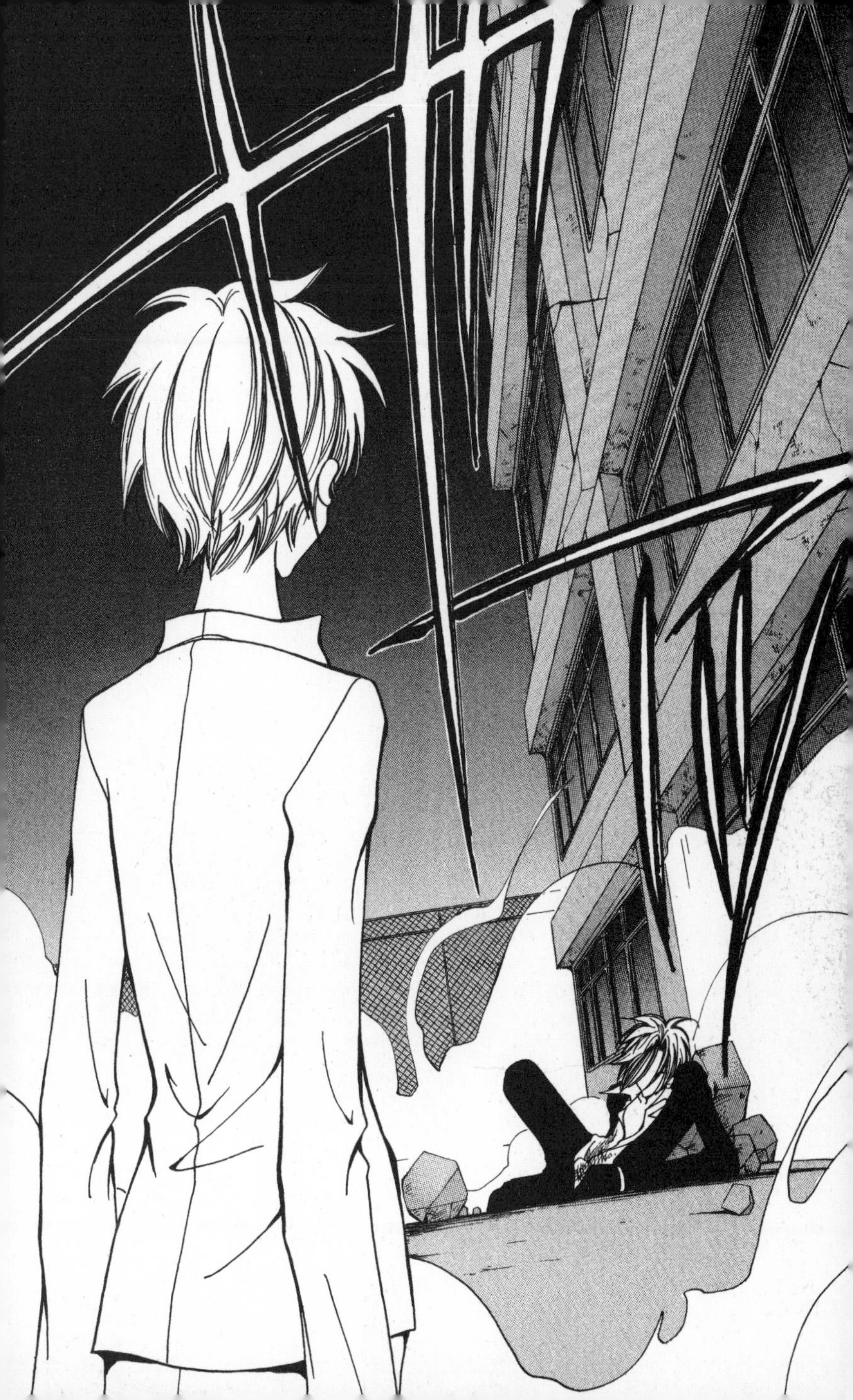

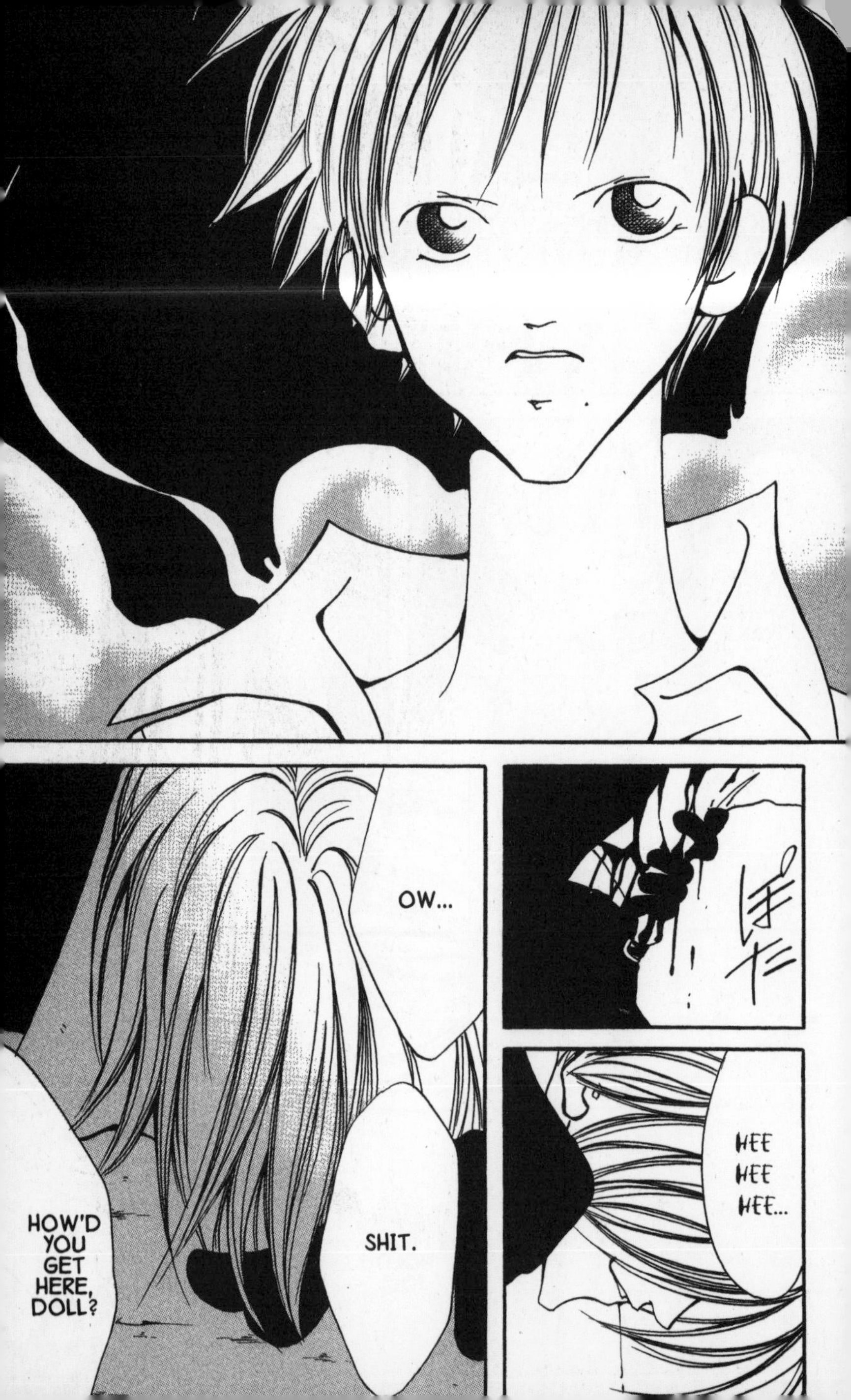
ぽた
HEE HEE HEE...
OW...
SHIT.
HOW'D YOU GET HERE, DOLL?

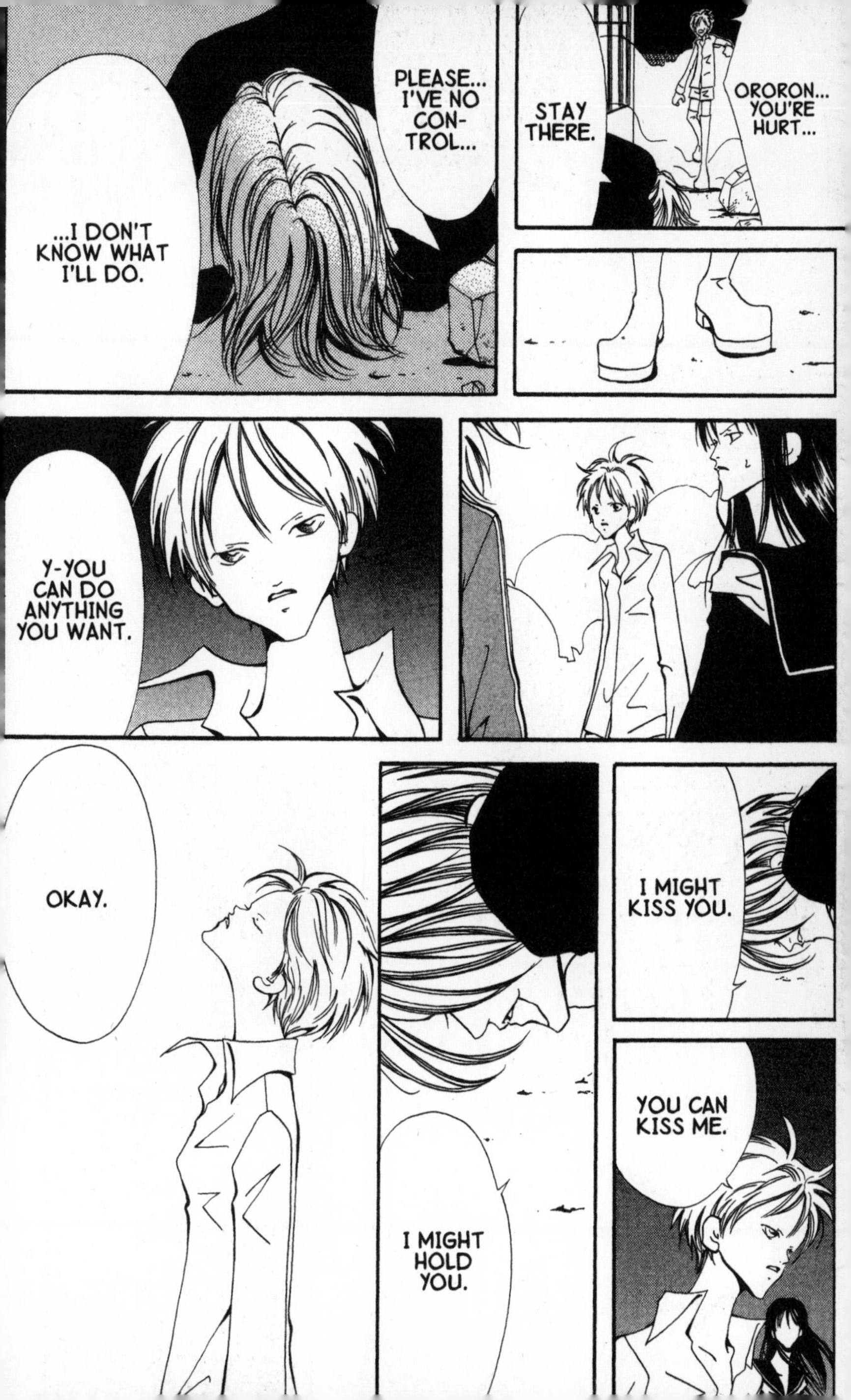
ORORON... YOU'RE HURT...
STAY THERE.
PLEASE... I'VE NO CON-TROL...
...I DON'T KNOW WHAT I'LL DO.
Y-YOU CAN DO ANYTHING YOU WANT.
I MIGHT KISS YOU.
YOU CAN KISS ME.
I MIGHT HOLD YOU.
OKAY.

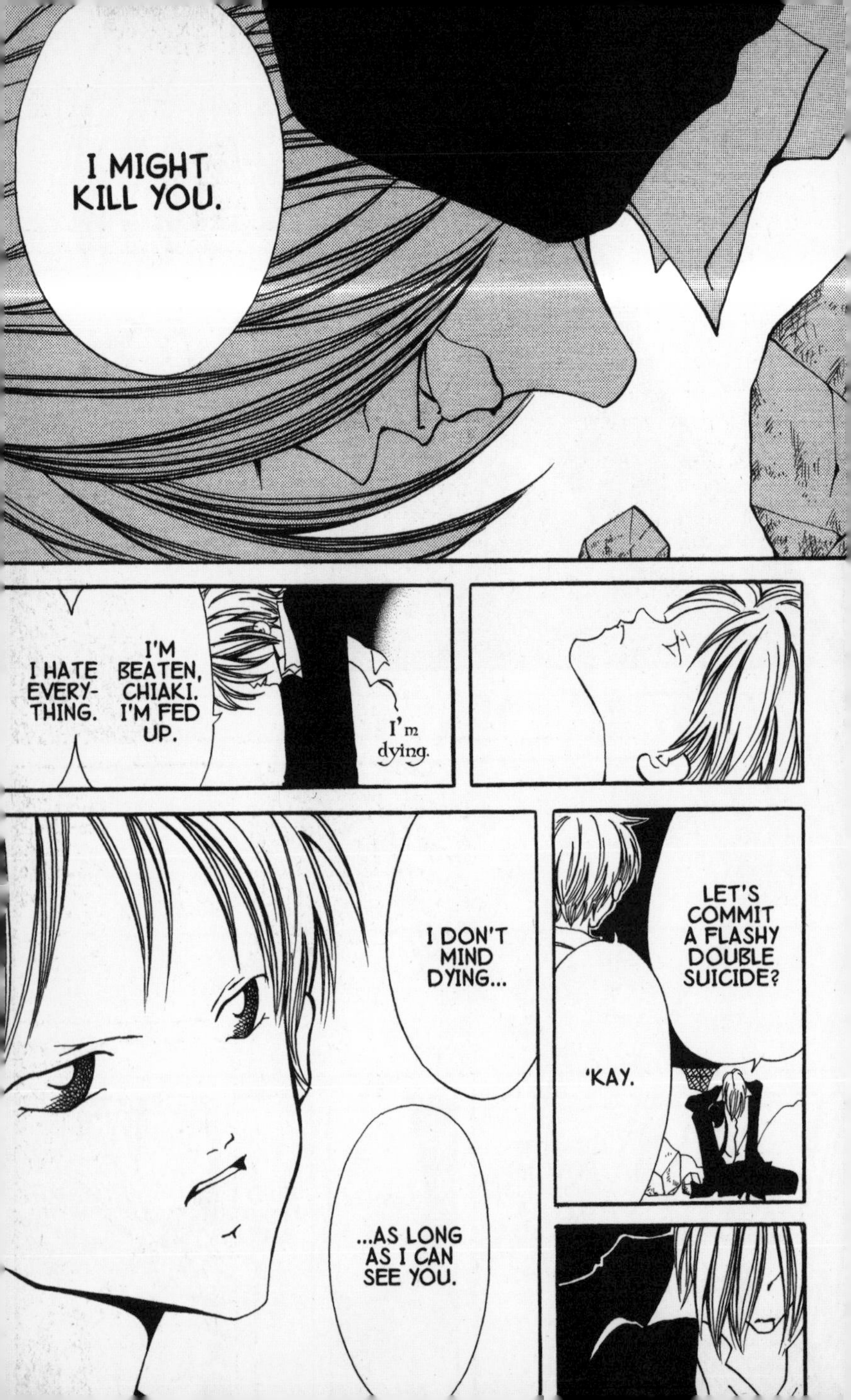
I MIGHT KILL YOU.
I'm dying.
I'M BEATEN, CHIAKI. I'M FED UP.
I HATE EVERYTHING.
LET'S COMMIT A FLASHY DOUBLE SUICIDE?
'KAY.
I DON'T MIND DYING...
...AS LONG AS I CAN SEE YOU.

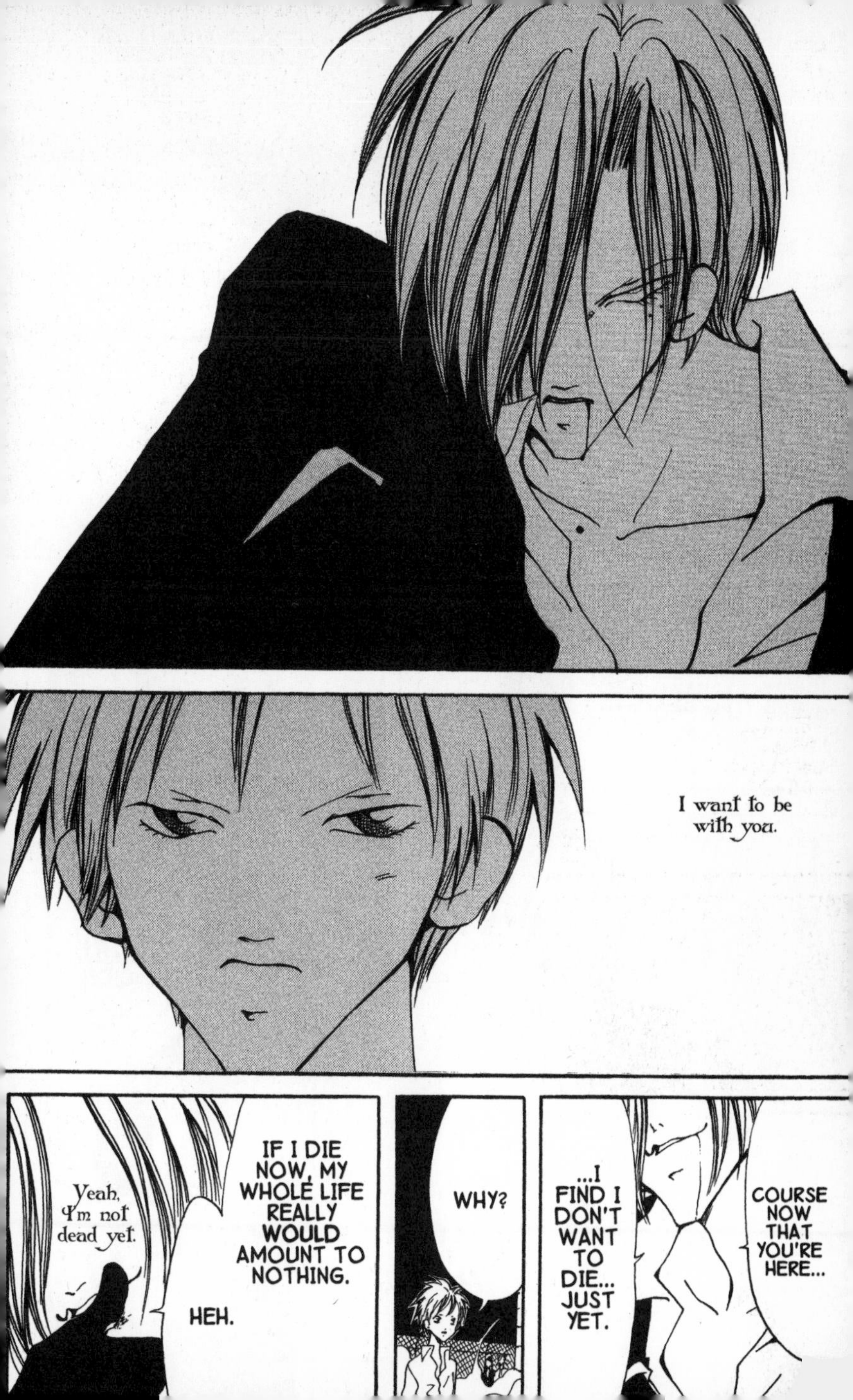
I want to be with you.
COURSE NOW THAT YOU'RE HERE...
...I FIND I DON'T WANT TO DIE... JUST YET.
WHY?
IF I DIE NOW, MY WHOLE LIFE REALLY WOULD AMOUNT TO NOTHING.
HEH.
Yeah, I'm not dead yet.

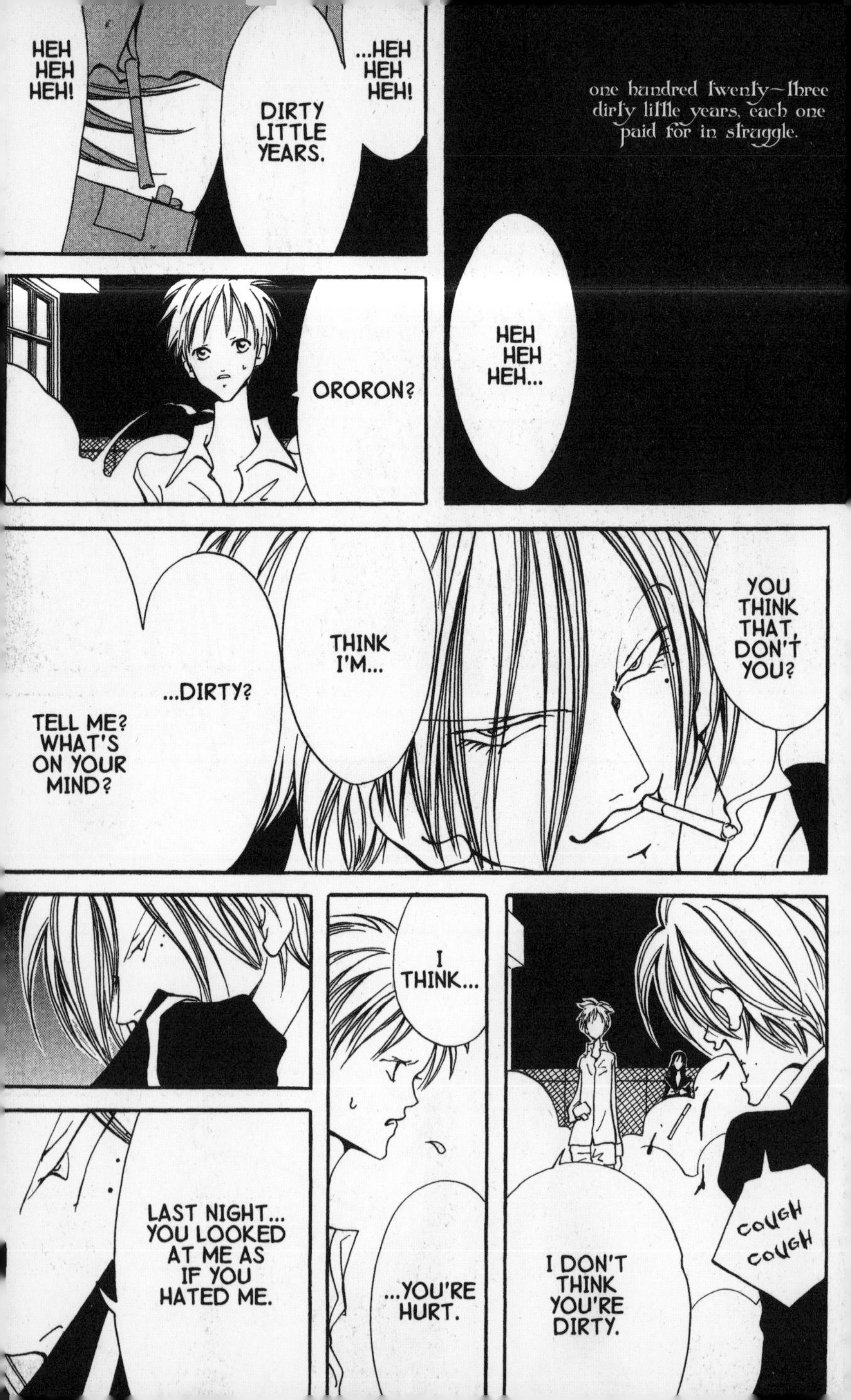
one hundred twenty-three dirty little years, each one paid for in struggle.
HEH HEH HEH...
...HEH HEH HEH!
DIRTY LITTLE YEARS.
HEH HEH HEH!
ORORON?
YOU THINK THAT, DON'T YOU?
THINK I'M...
...DIRTY?
TELL ME? WHAT'S ON YOUR MIND?
COUGH COUGH
I DON'T THINK YOU'RE DIRTY.
I THINK...
...YOU'RE HURT.
LAST NIGHT... YOU LOOKED AT ME AS IF YOU HATED ME.

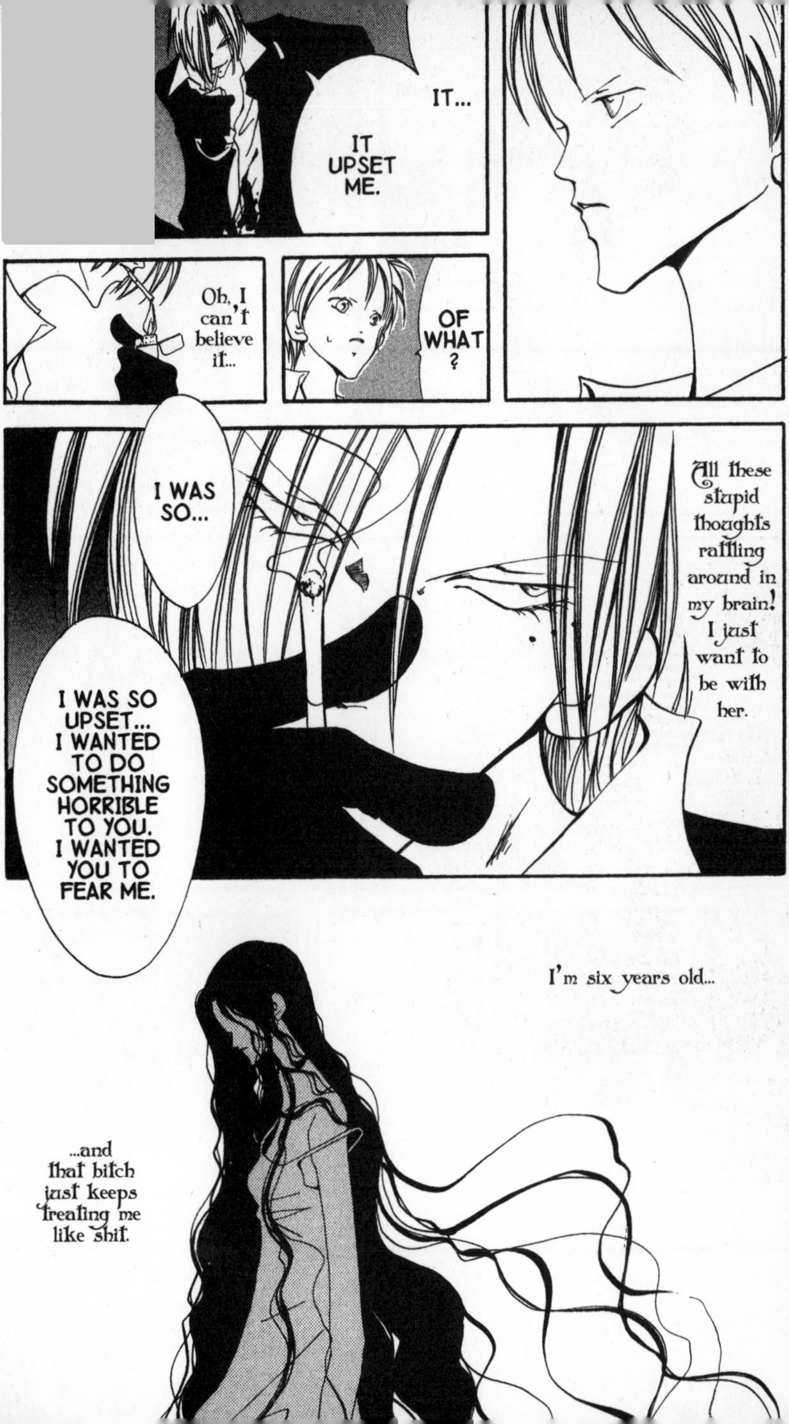
IT...
IT UPSET ME.
OF WHAT?
Oh, I can't believe it...
All these stupid thoughts rattling around in my brain! I just want to be with her.
I WAS SO...
I WAS SO UPSET... I WANTED TO DO SOMETHING HORRIBLE TO YOU. I WANTED YOU TO FEAR ME.
I'm six years old...
...and that bitch just keeps treating me like shit.

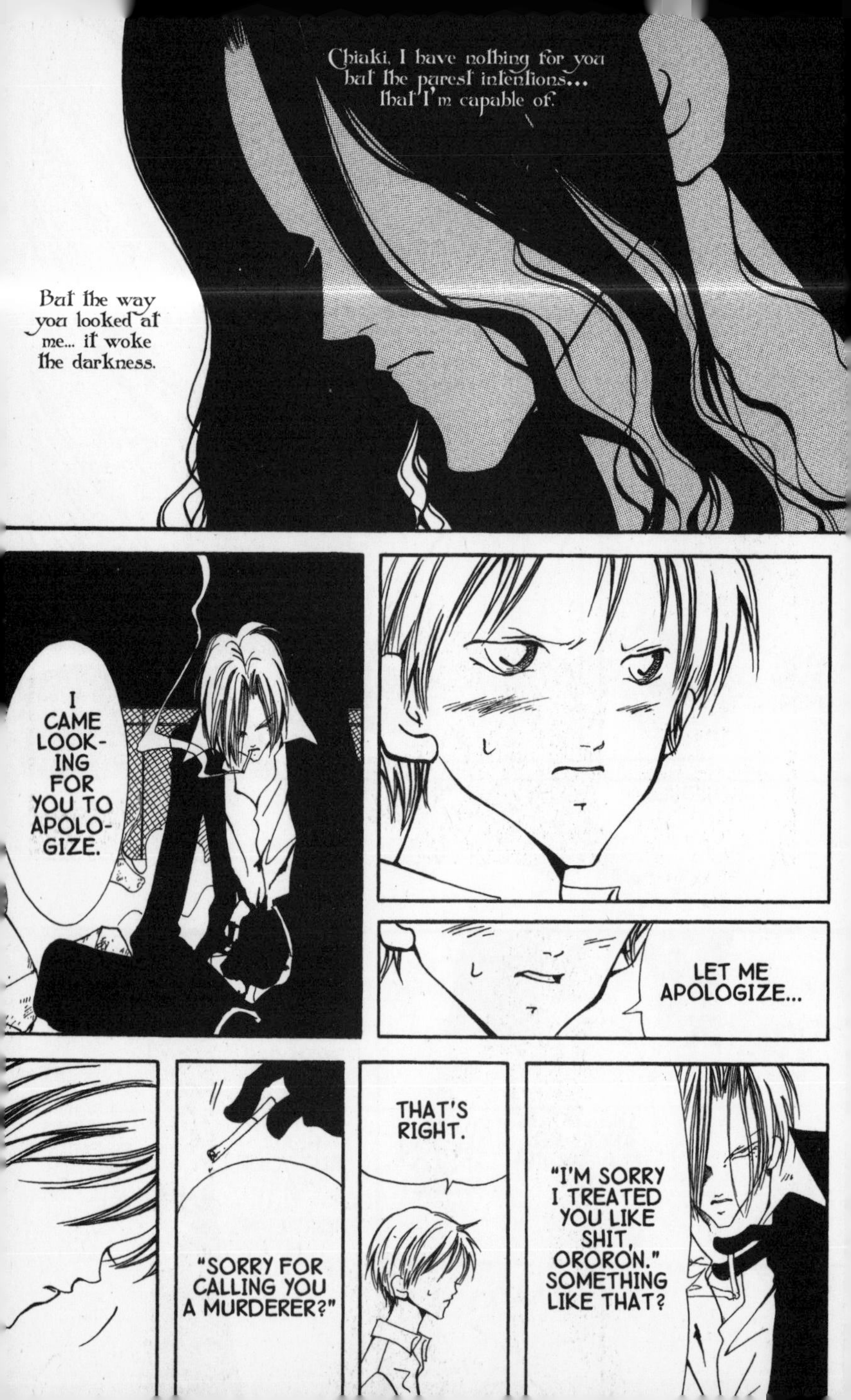
Chiaki, I have nothing for you but the purest intentions... that I'm capable of.
But the way you looked at me... it woke the darkness.
LET ME APOLOGIZE...
I CAME LOOKING FOR YOU TO APOLOGIZE.
"I'M SORRY I TREATED YOU LIKE SHIT, ORORON." SOMETHING LIKE THAT?
THAT'S RIGHT.
"SORRY FOR CALLING YOU A MURDERER?"

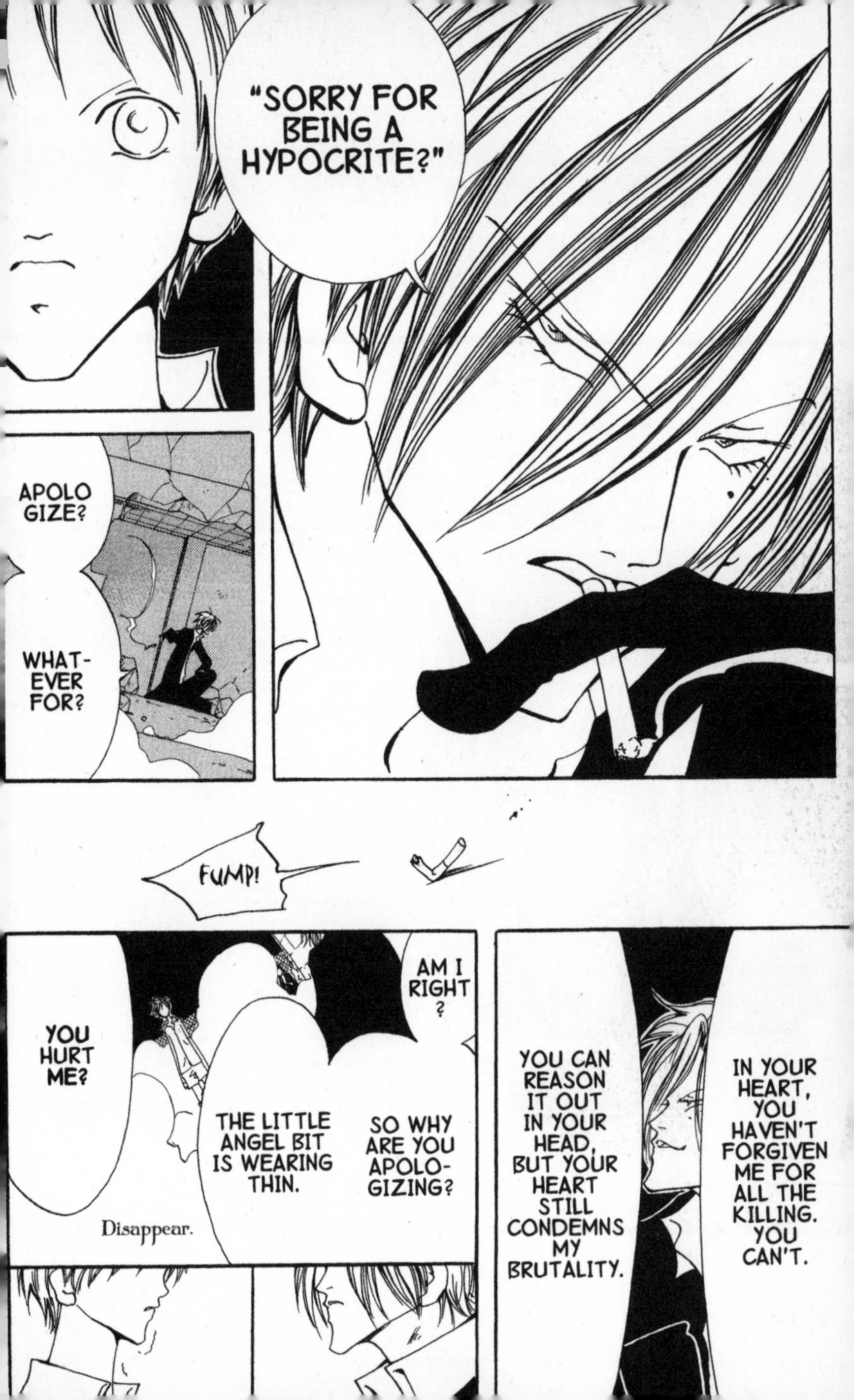
"SORRY FOR BEING A HYPOCRITE?"
APOLOGIZE?
WHATEVER FOR?
FUMP!
IN YOUR HEART, YOU HAVEN'T FORGIVEN ME FOR ALL THE KILLING. YOU CAN'T.
YOU CAN REASON IT OUT IN YOUR HEAD, BUT YOUR HEART STILL CONDEMNS MY BRUTALITY.
AM I RIGHT?
SO WHY ARE YOU APOLOGIZING?
THE LITTLE ANGEL BIT IS WEARING THIN.
YOU HURT ME?
Disappear.

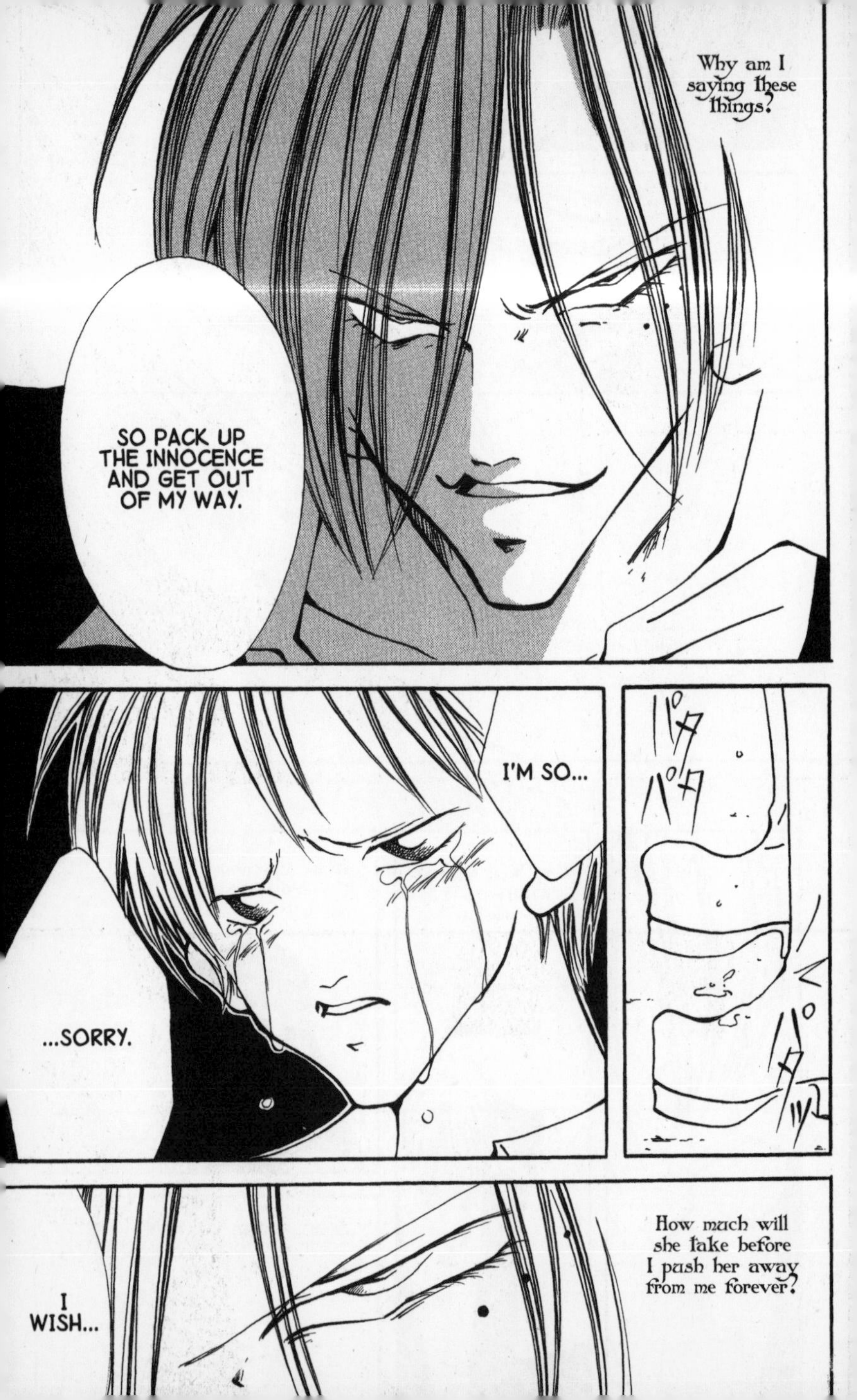
Why am I saying these things?
SO PACK UP THE INNOCENCE AND GET OUT OF MY WAY.
パタ
パタ
I'M SO...
...SORRY.
How much will she take before I push her away from me forever?
I WISH...

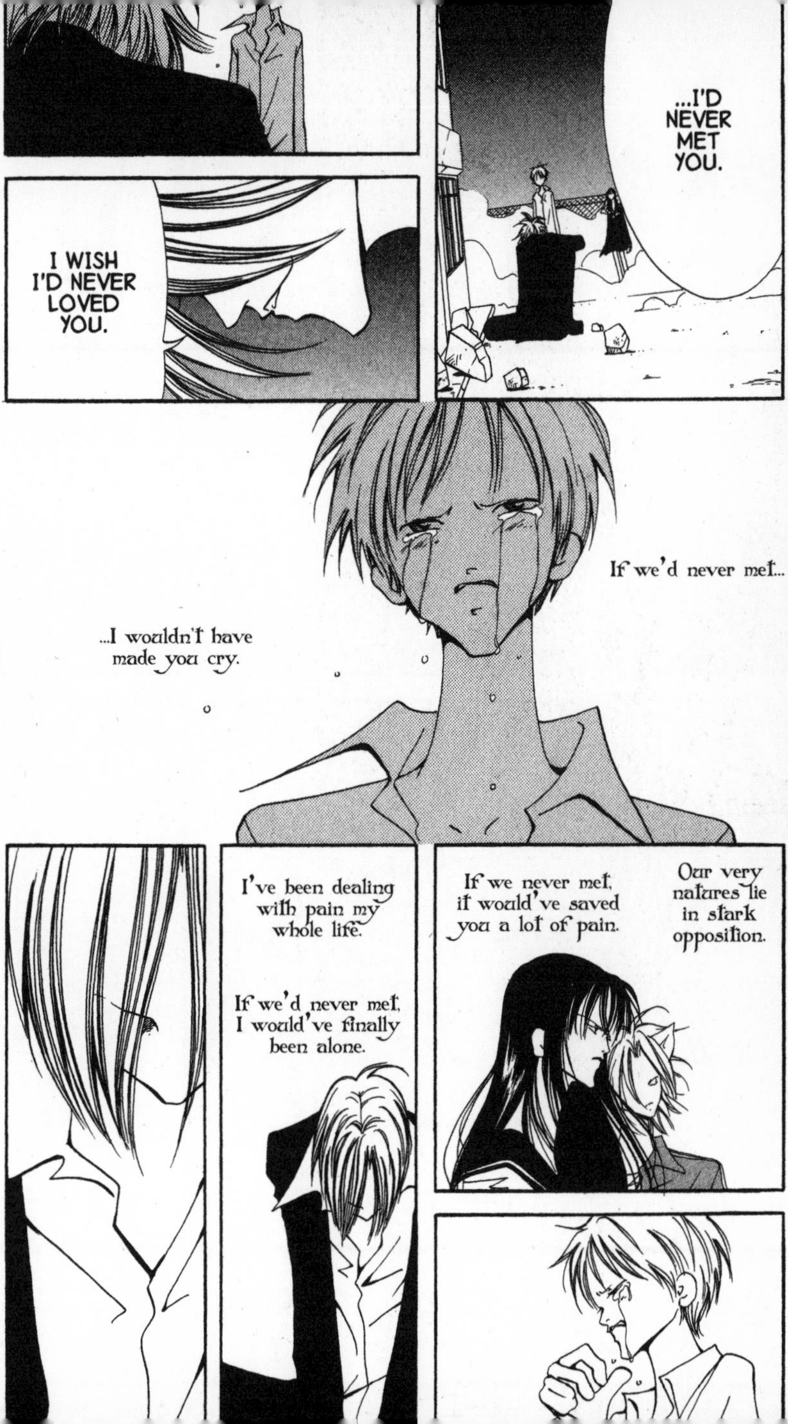
...I'D NEVER MET YOU.
I WISH I'D NEVER LOVED YOU.
If we'd never met...
...I wouldn't have made you cry.
Our very natures lie in stark opposition.
If we never met, it would've saved you a lot of pain.
I've been dealing with pain my whole life.
If we'd never met, I would've finally been alone.

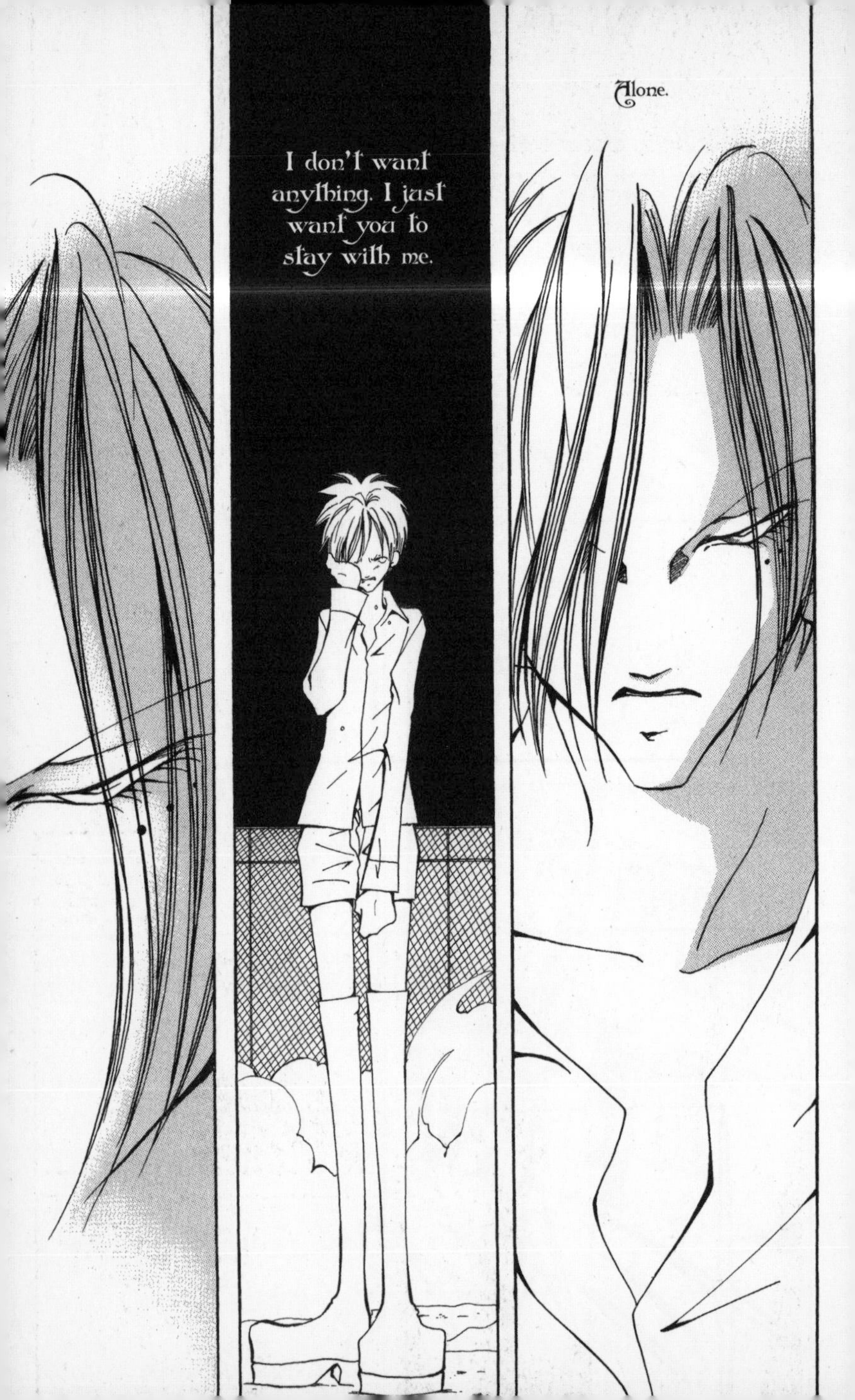
Alone.
I don't want anything. I just want you to stay with me.

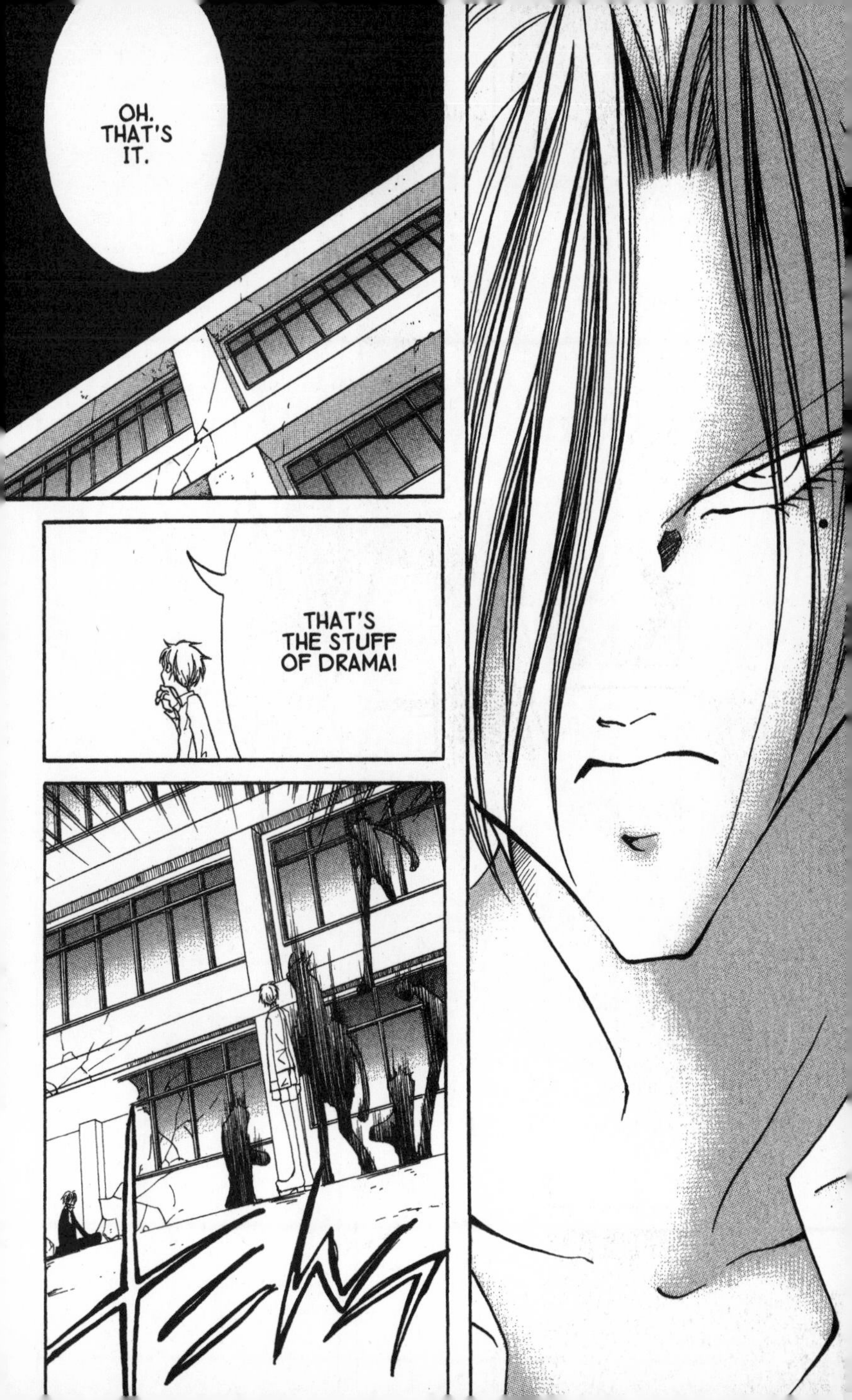
OH. THAT'S IT.
THAT'S THE STUFF OF DRAMA!

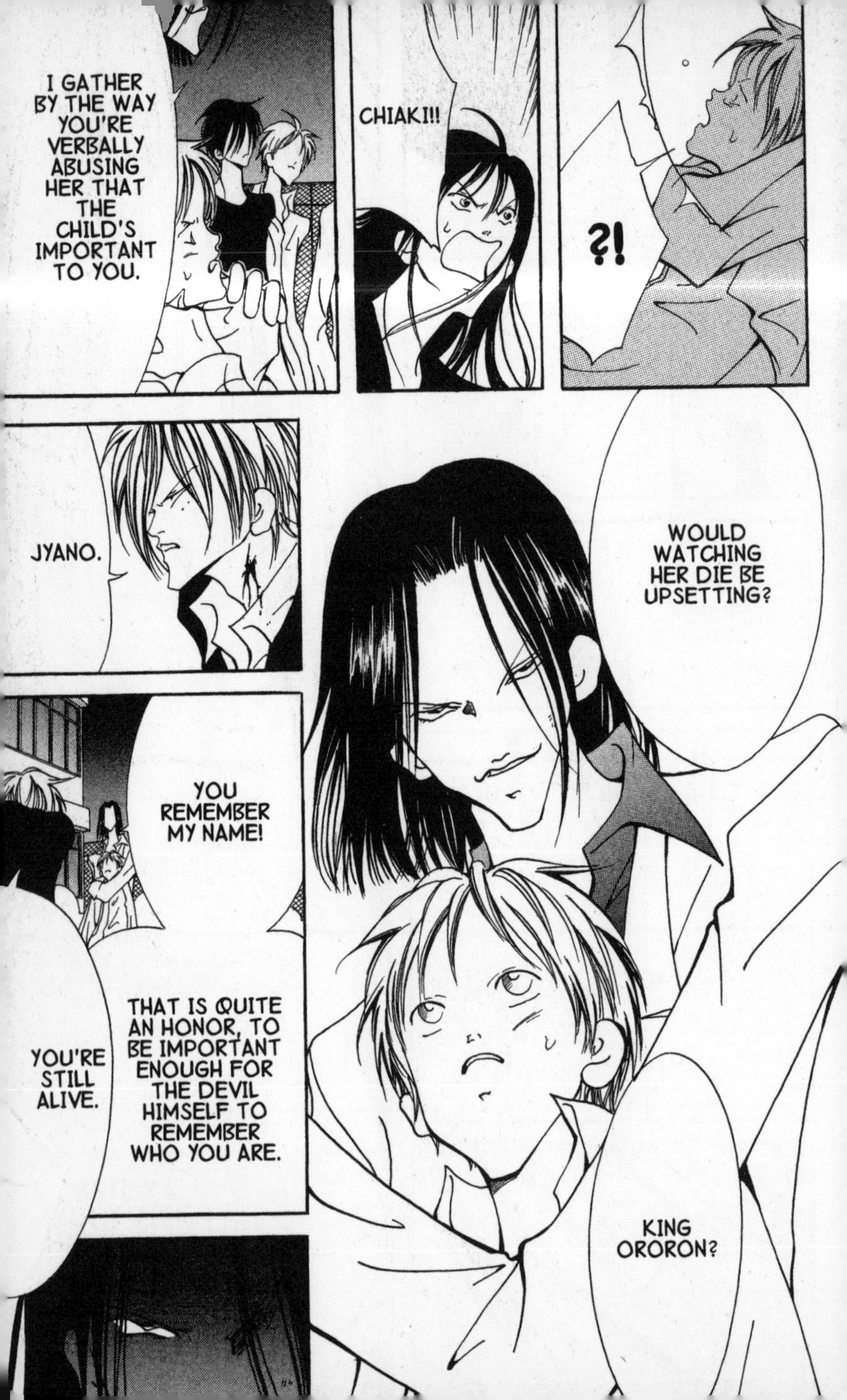
?!
CHIAKI!!
I GATHER BY THE WAY YOU'RE VERBALLY ABUSING HER THAT THE CHILD'S IMPORTANT TO YOU.
WOULD WATCHING HER DIE BE UPSETTING?
KING ORORON?
JYANO.
YOU REMEMBER MY NAME!
THAT IS QUITE AN HONOR, TO BE IMPORTANT ENOUGH FOR THE DEVIL HIMSELF TO REMEMBER WHO YOU ARE.
YOU'RE STILL ALIVE.

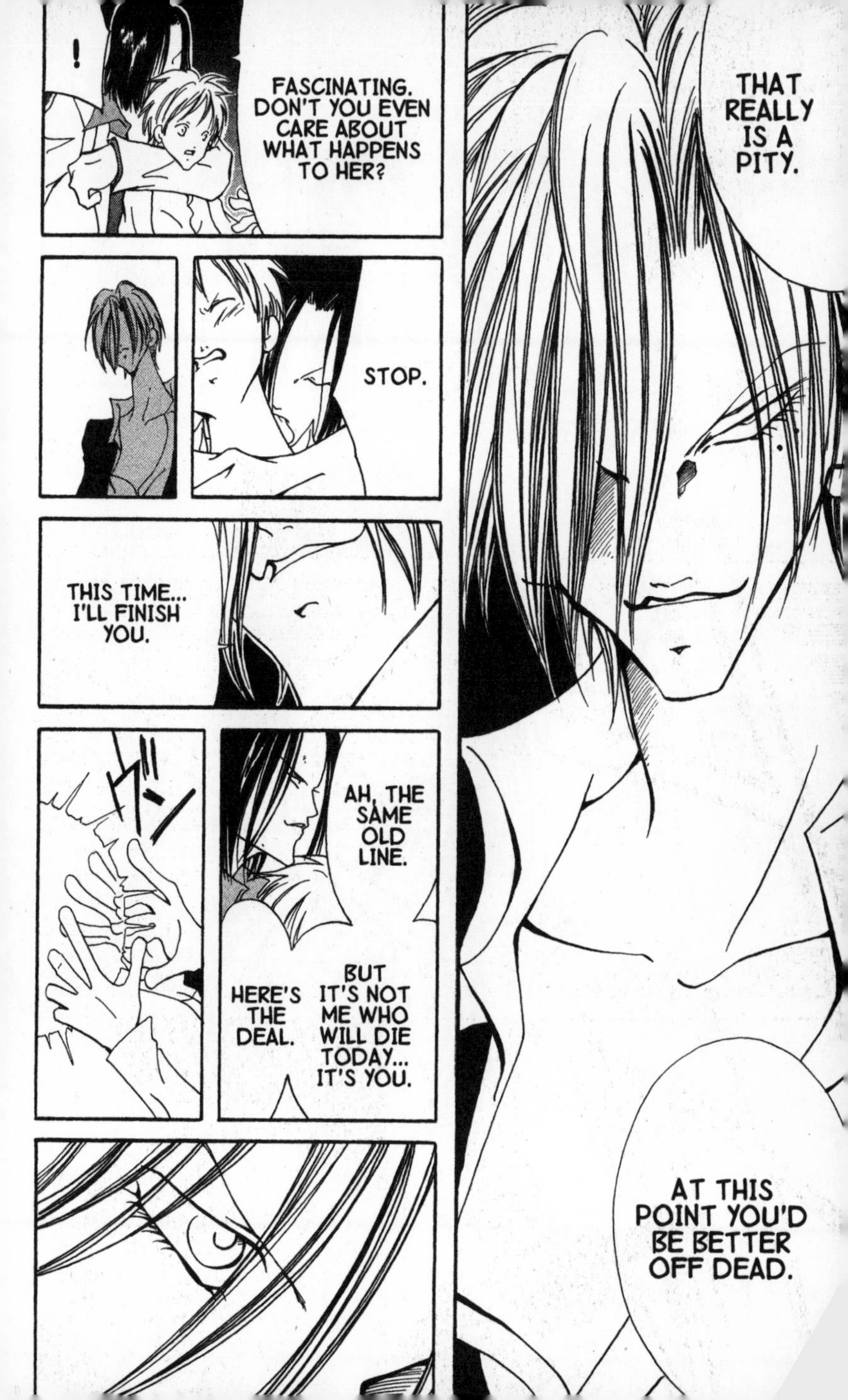
THAT REALLY IS A PITY.
AT THIS POINT YOU'D BE BETTER OFF DEAD.
FASCINATING. DON'T YOU EVEN CARE ABOUT WHAT HAPPENS TO HER?
!
STOP.
THIS TIME... I'LL FINISH YOU.
AH, THE SAME OLD LINE.
BUT IT'S NOT ME WHO WILL DIE TODAY... IT'S YOU.
HERE'S THE DEAL.

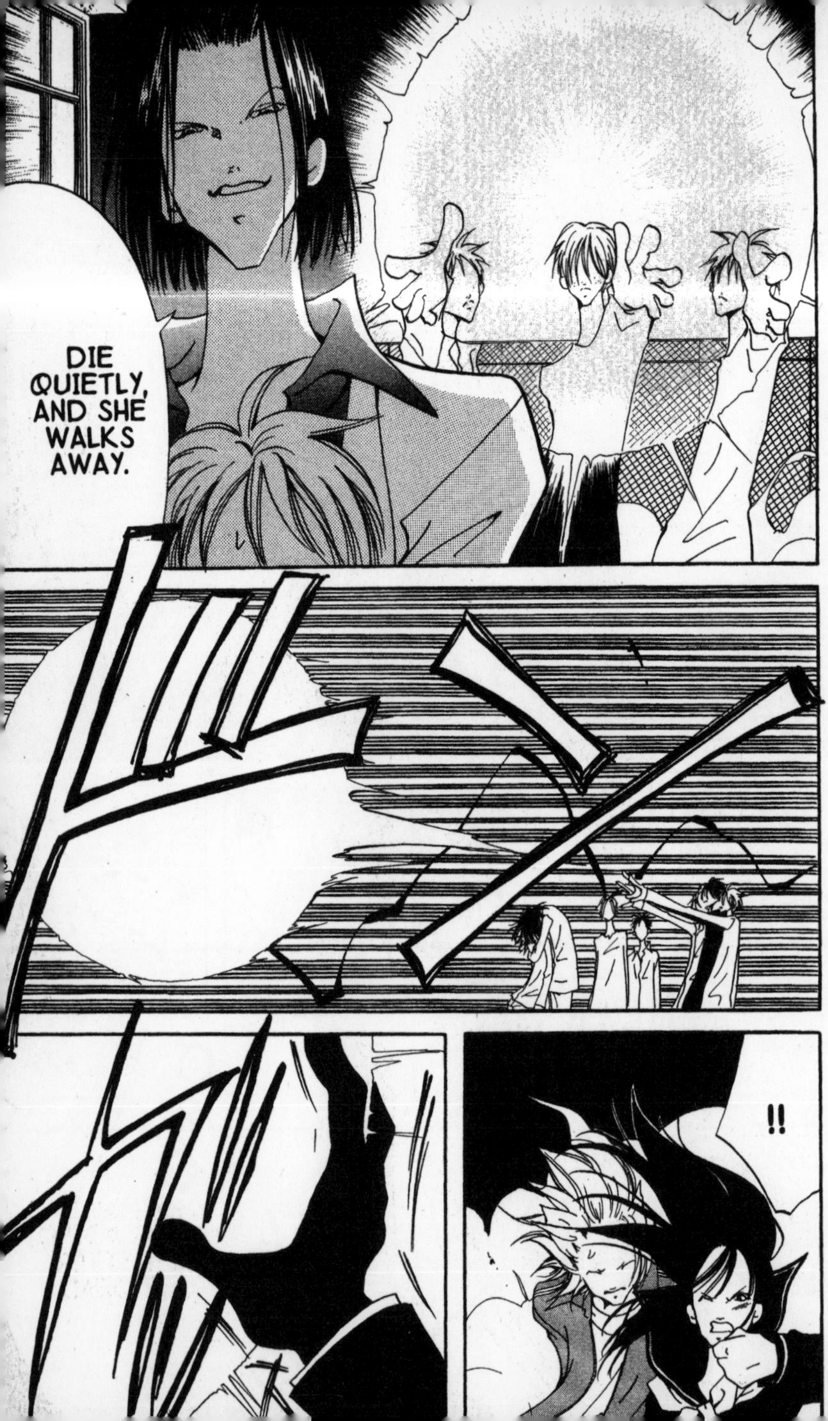
DIE QUIETLY, AND SHE WALKS AWAY.
!!

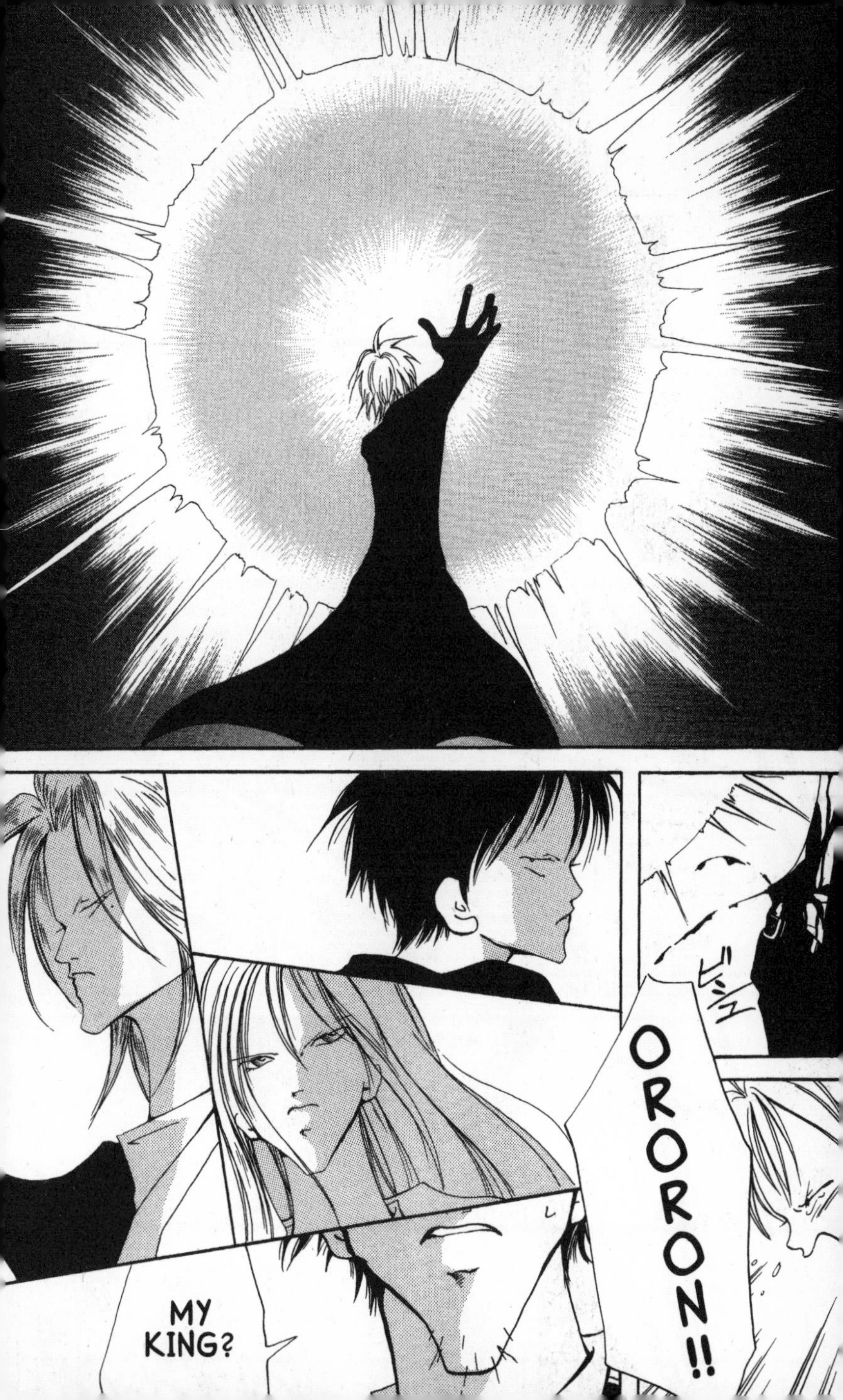
ビシュ
ORORON!!
MY KING?

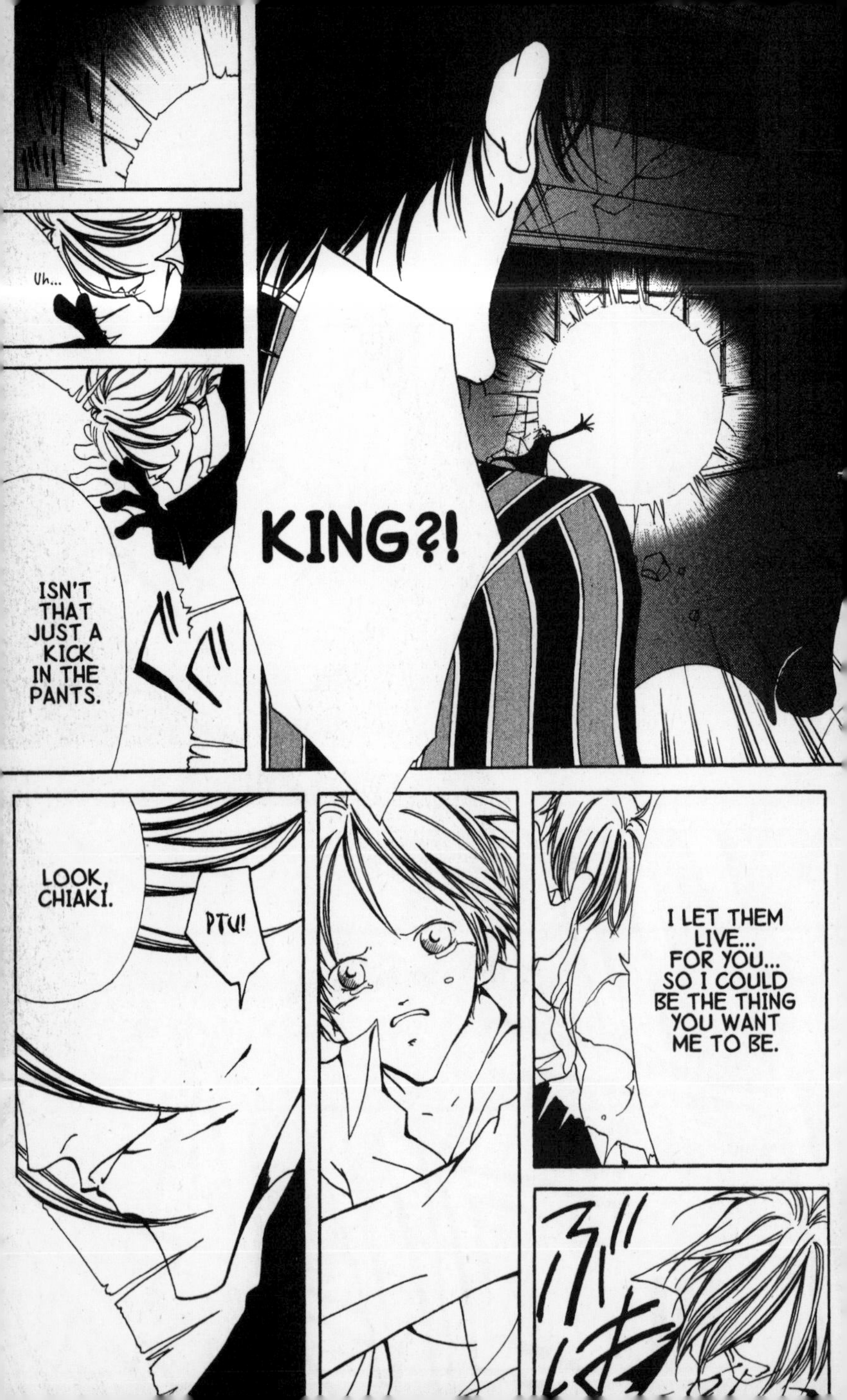
KING?!
Uh...
ISN'T THAT JUST A KICK IN THE PANTS.
I LET THEM LIVE... FOR YOU... SO I COULD BE THE THING YOU WANT ME TO BE.
ぶは
LOOK, CHIAKI.
PTU!

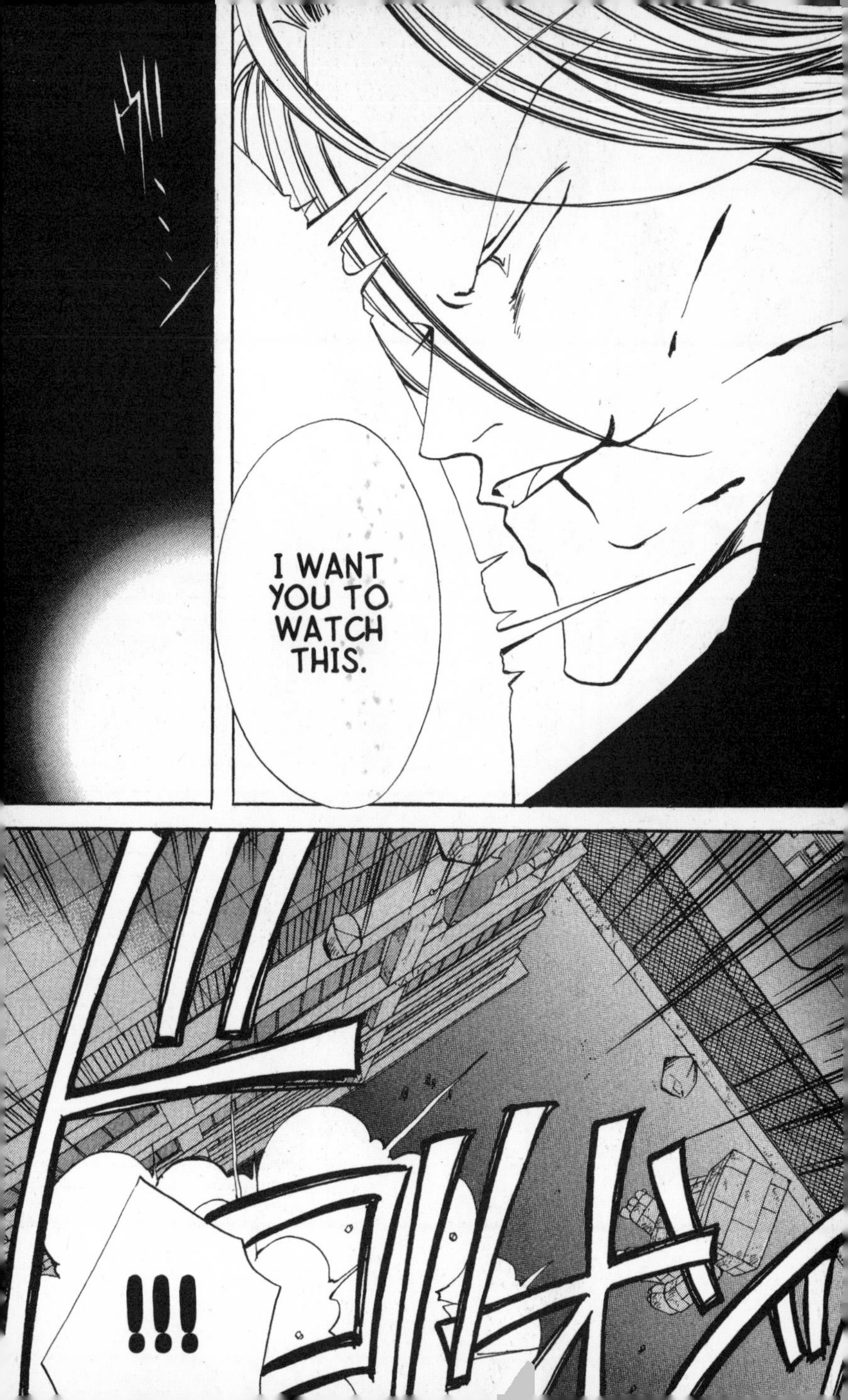
I WANT YOU TO WATCH THIS.
!!!

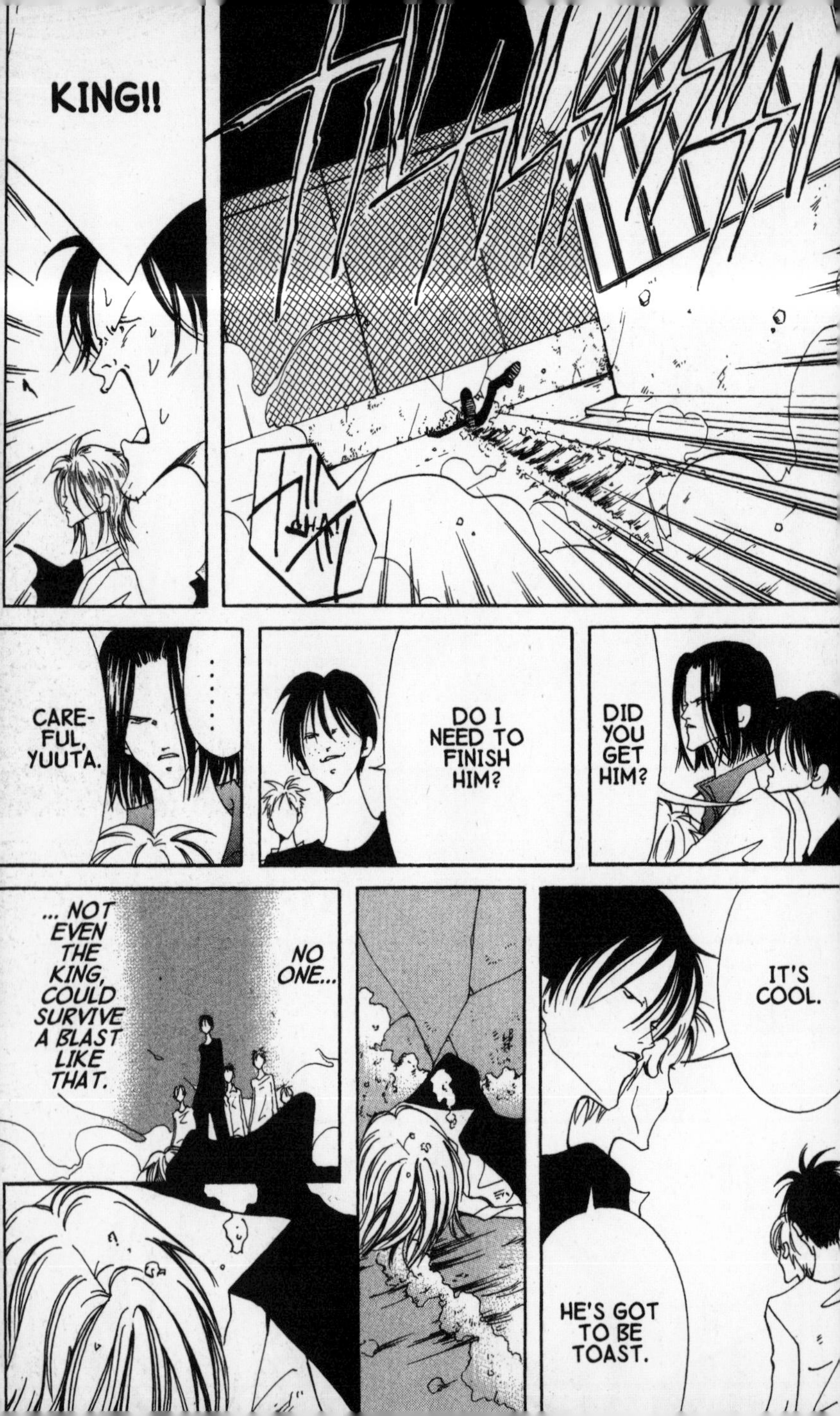
KING!!
DID YOU GET HIM?
DO I NEED TO FINISH HIM?
......
CARE-FUL, YUUTA.
IT'S COOL.
HE'S GOT TO BE TOAST.
NO ONE...
... NOT EVEN THE KING, COULD SURVIVE A BLAST LIKE THAT.

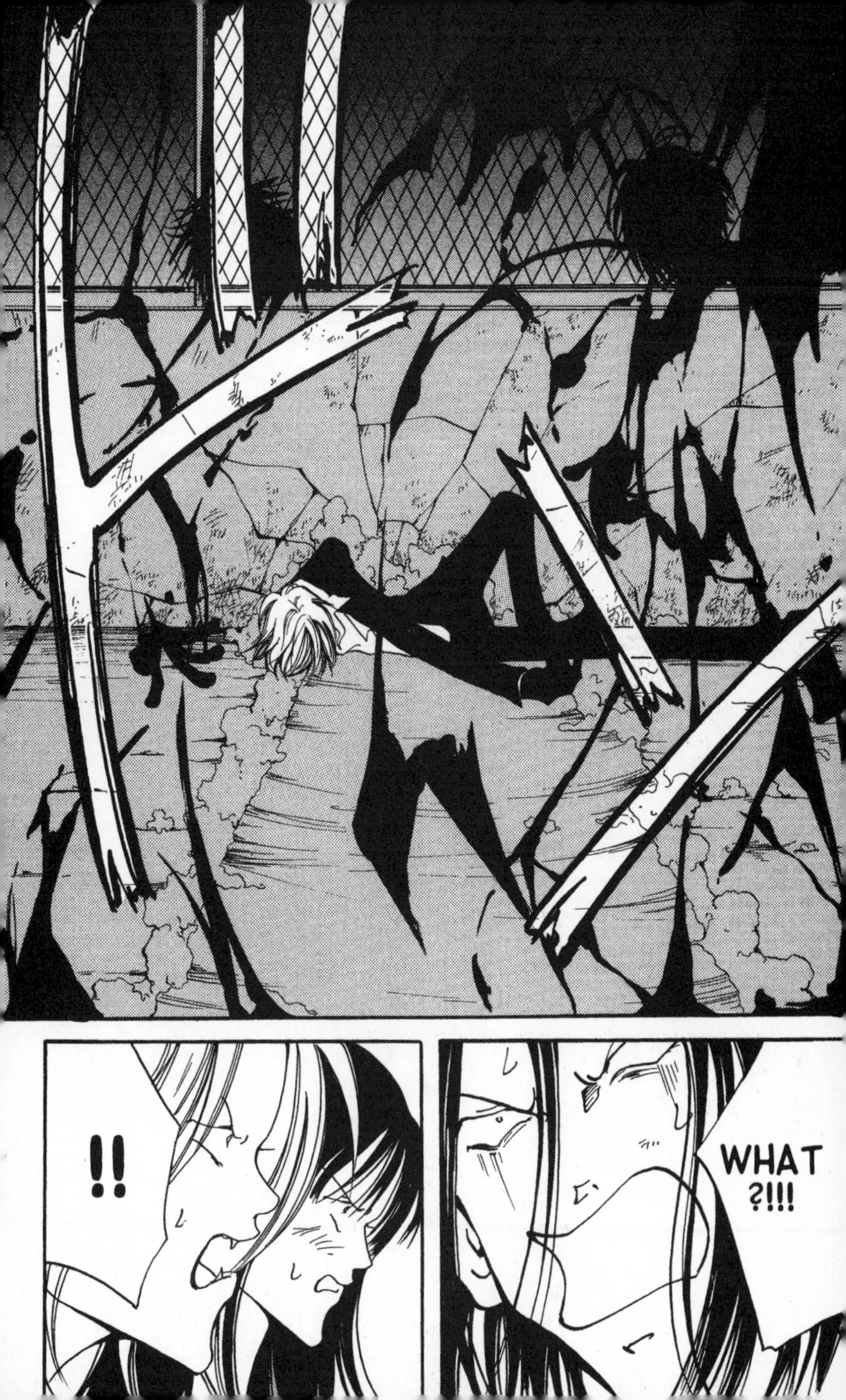
WHAT ?!!!
!!

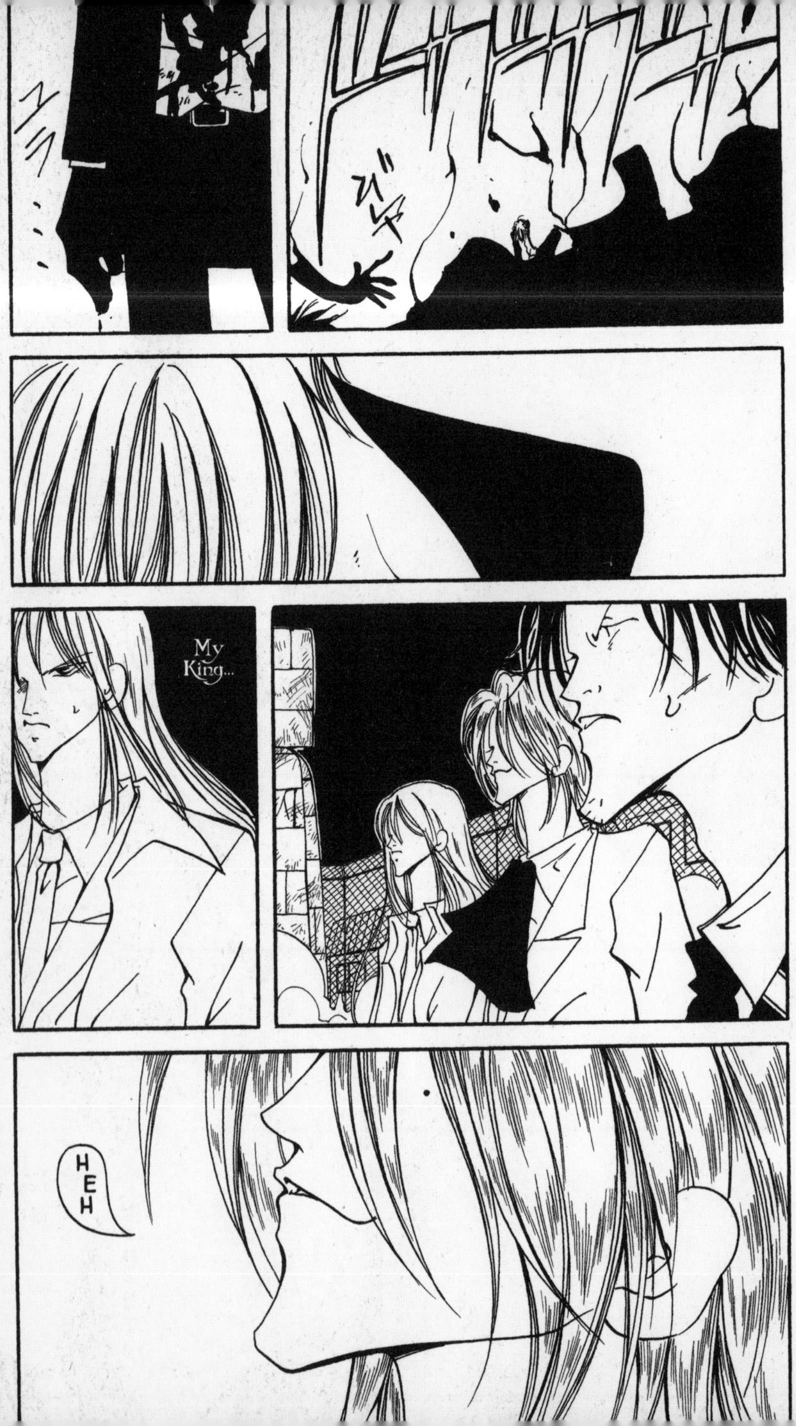
びしゃ
ユラ…
My King...
HEH

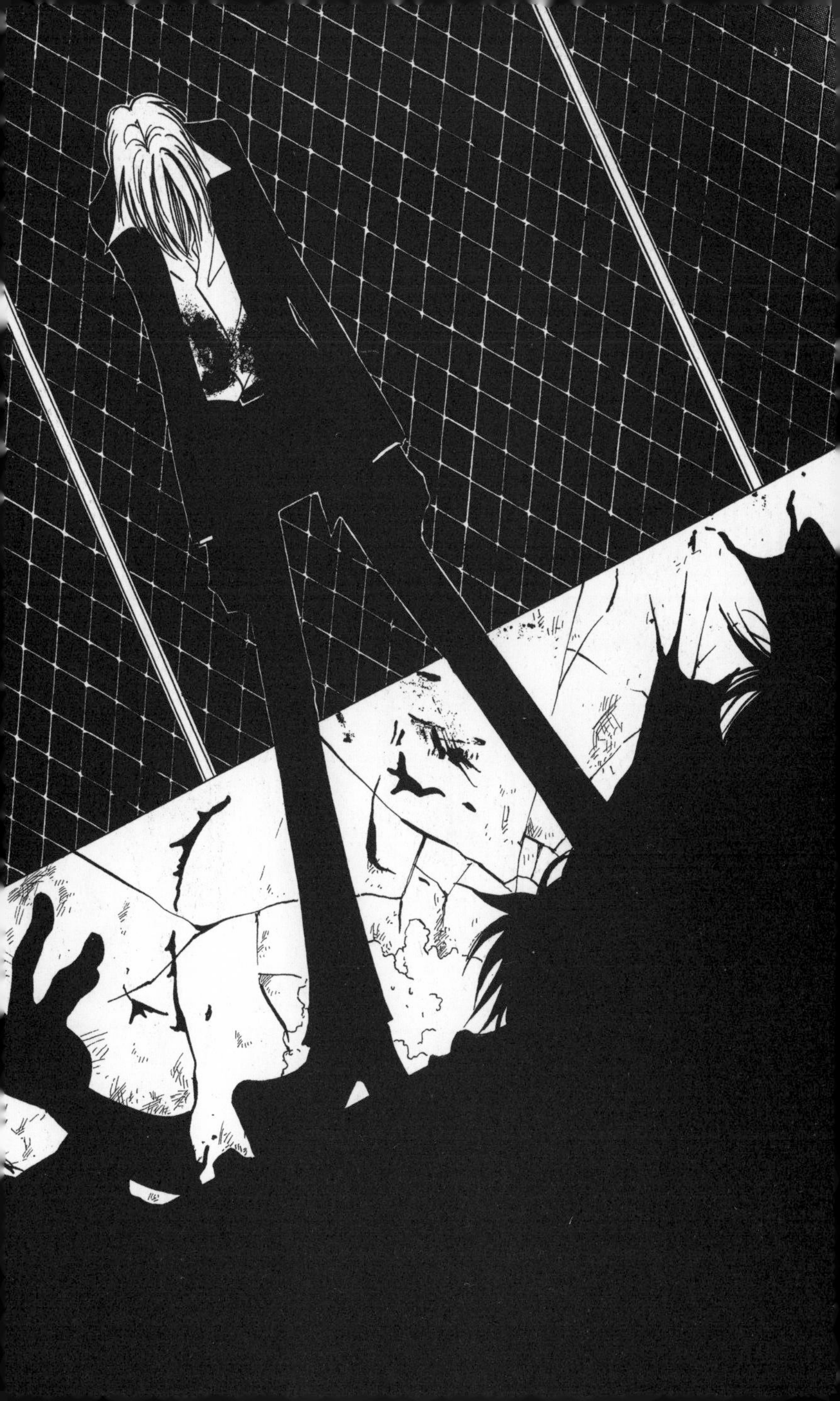

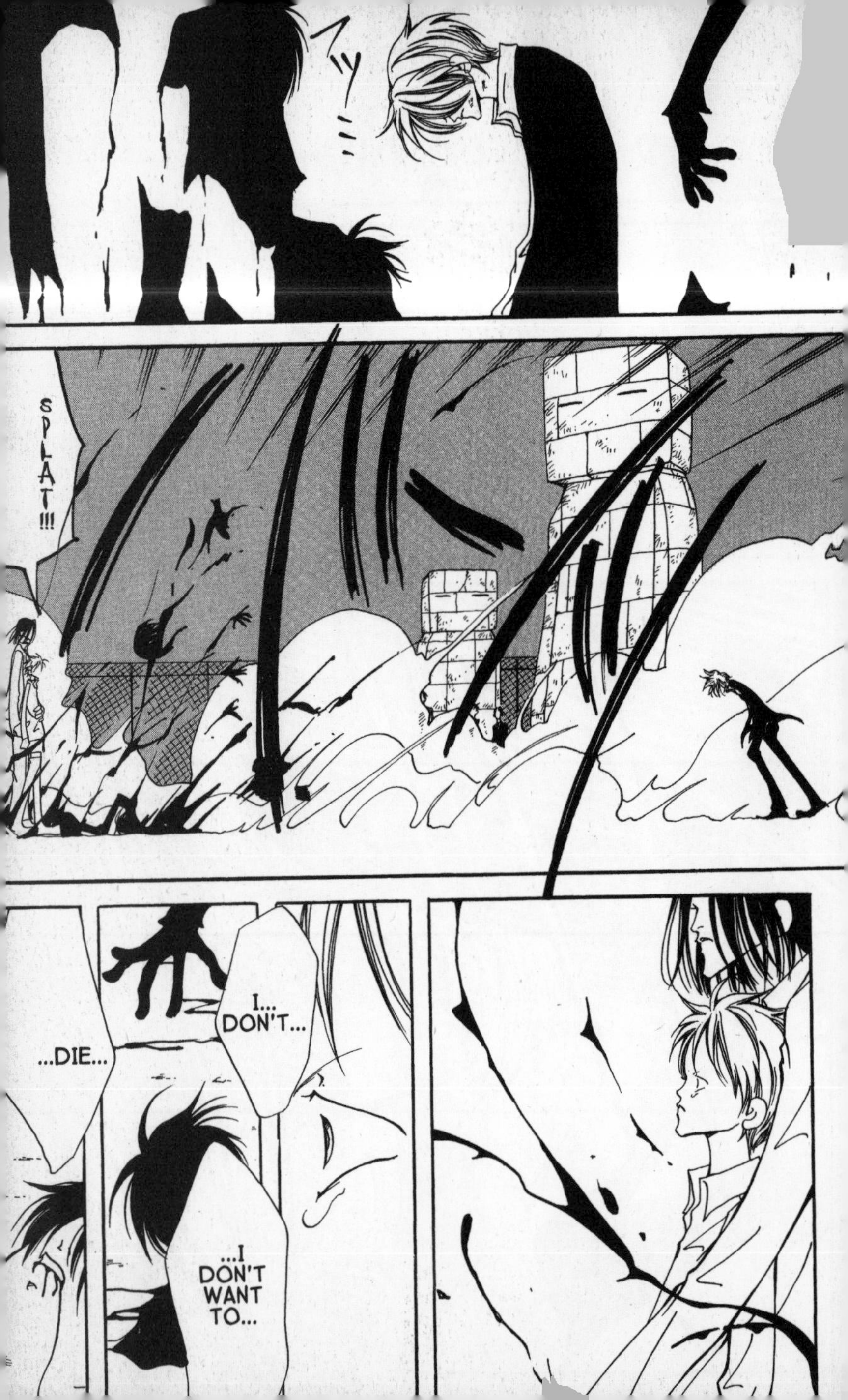
SPLAT!!!
I... DON'T...
...DIE...
...I DON'T WANT TO...

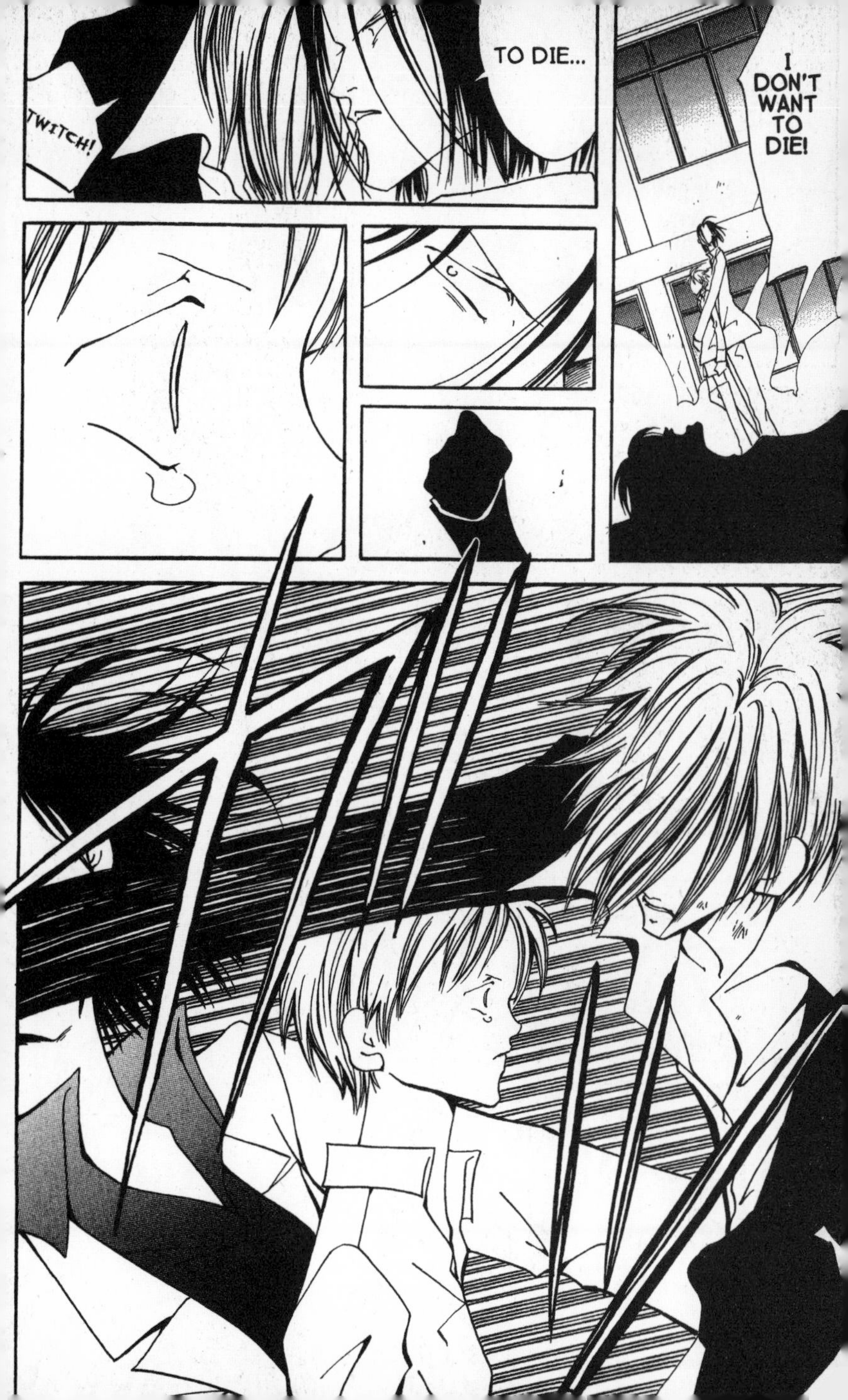
I DON'T WANT TO DIE!
TO DIE...
TWITCH!

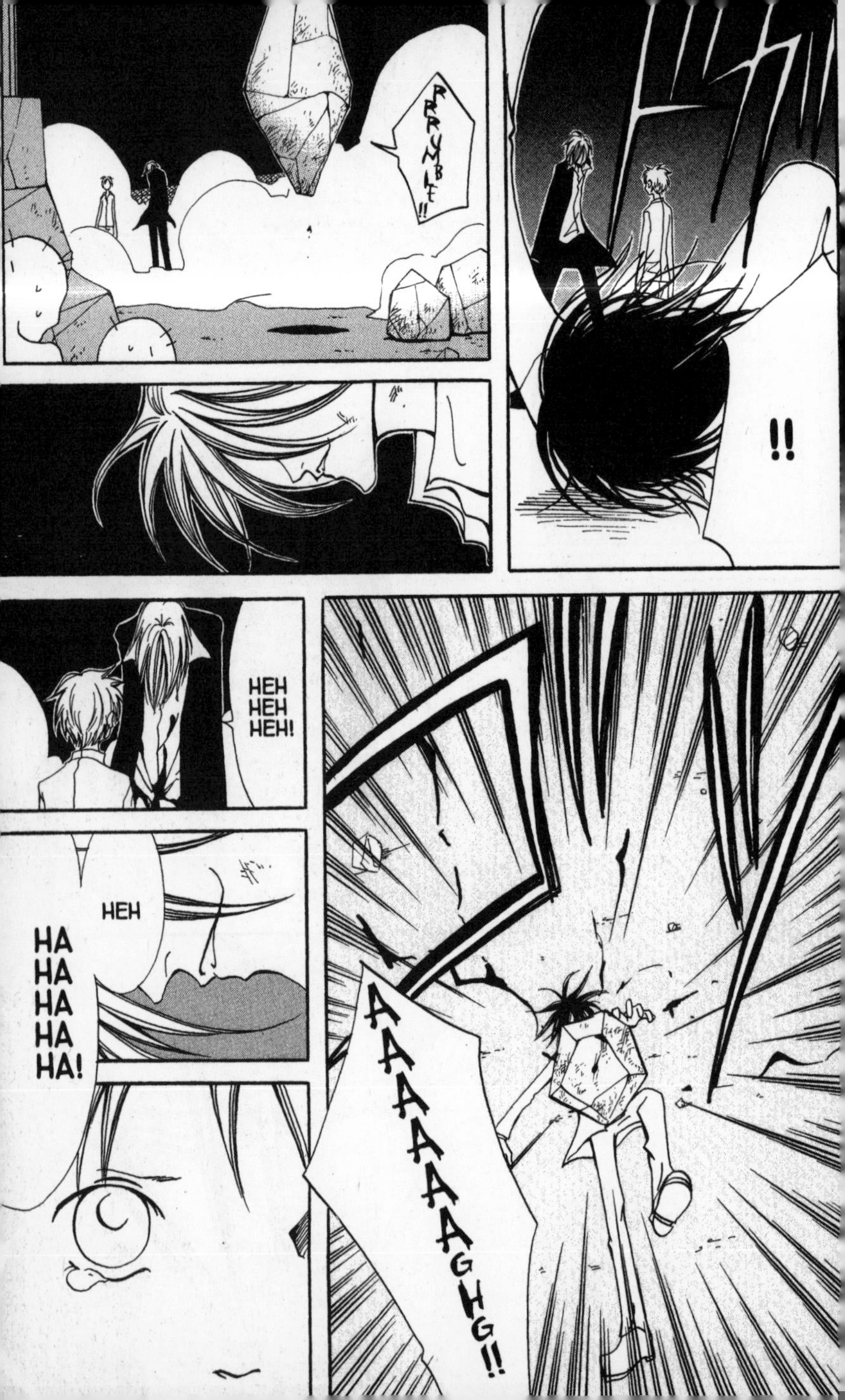
!!
RRRUMBLE!!
AAAAAAAGHG!!
HEH HEH HEH!
HEH
HA HA HA HA HA!

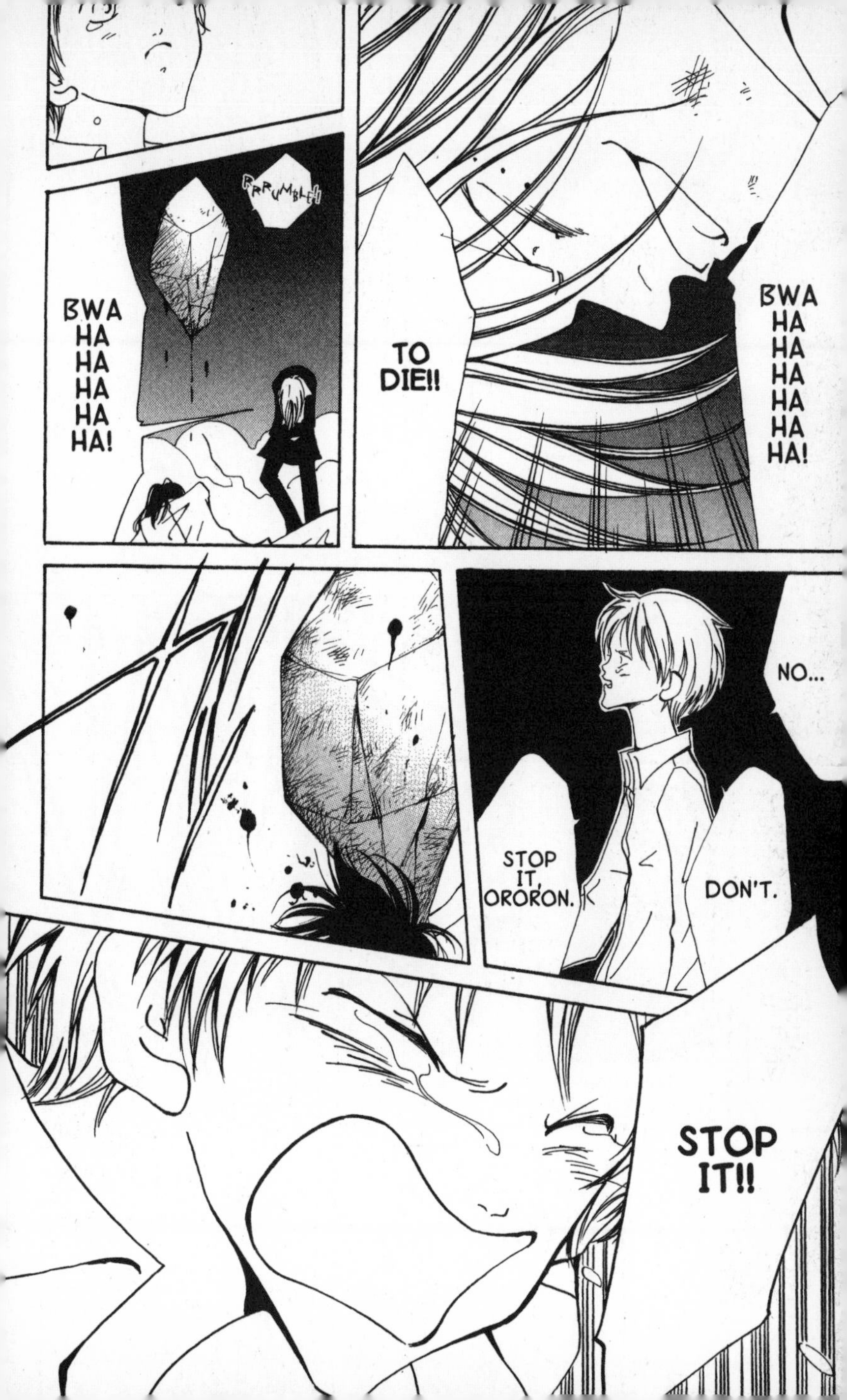
BWA HA HA HA HA HA HA HA!
TO DIE!!
PRRUMBLE!!
BWA HA HA HA HA HA!
NO...
DON'T.
STOP IT, ORORON.
STOP IT!!

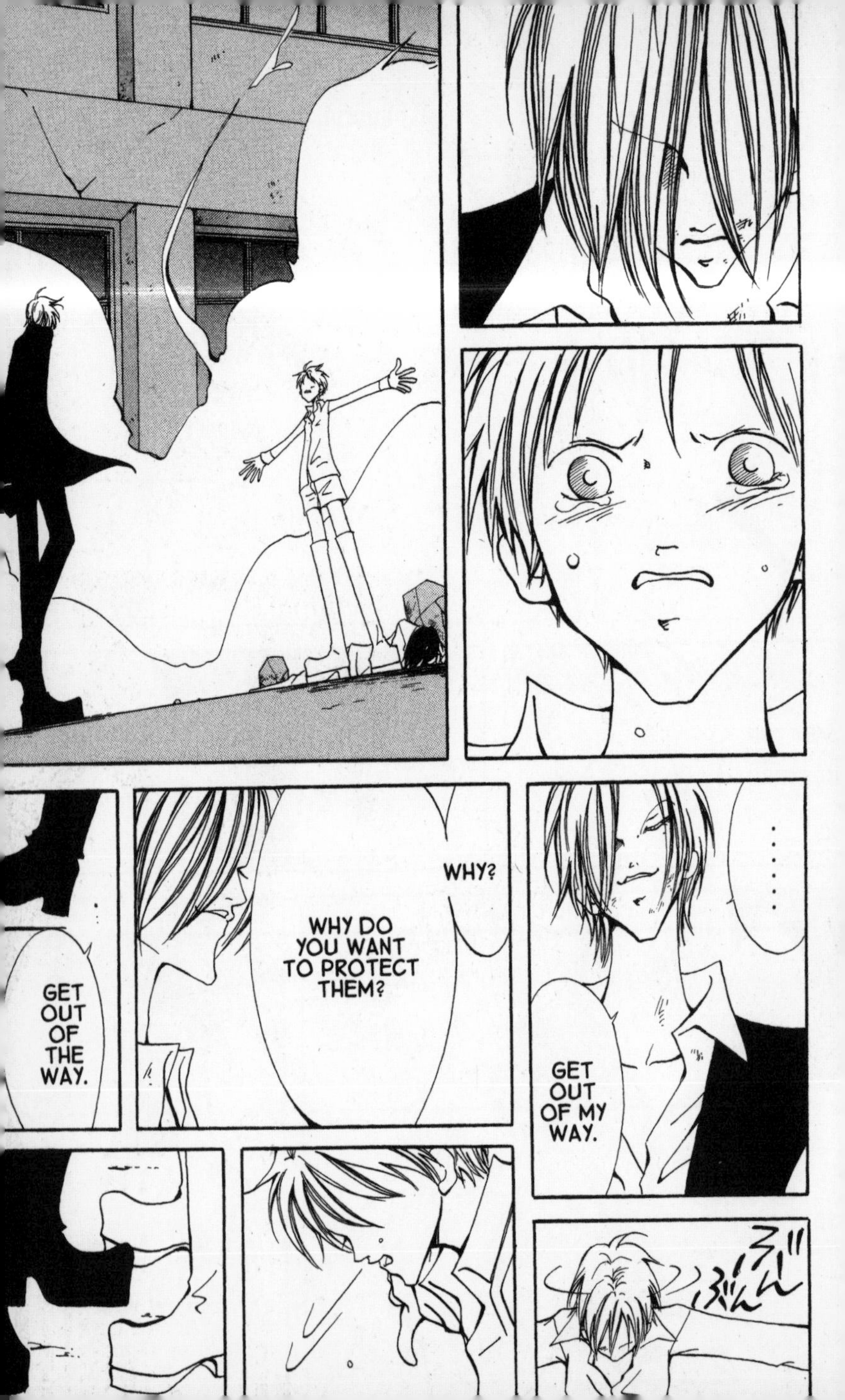
......
GET OUT OF MY WAY.
WHY?
WHY DO YOU WANT TO PROTECT THEM?
...
GET OUT OF THE WAY.
ぶんぶん

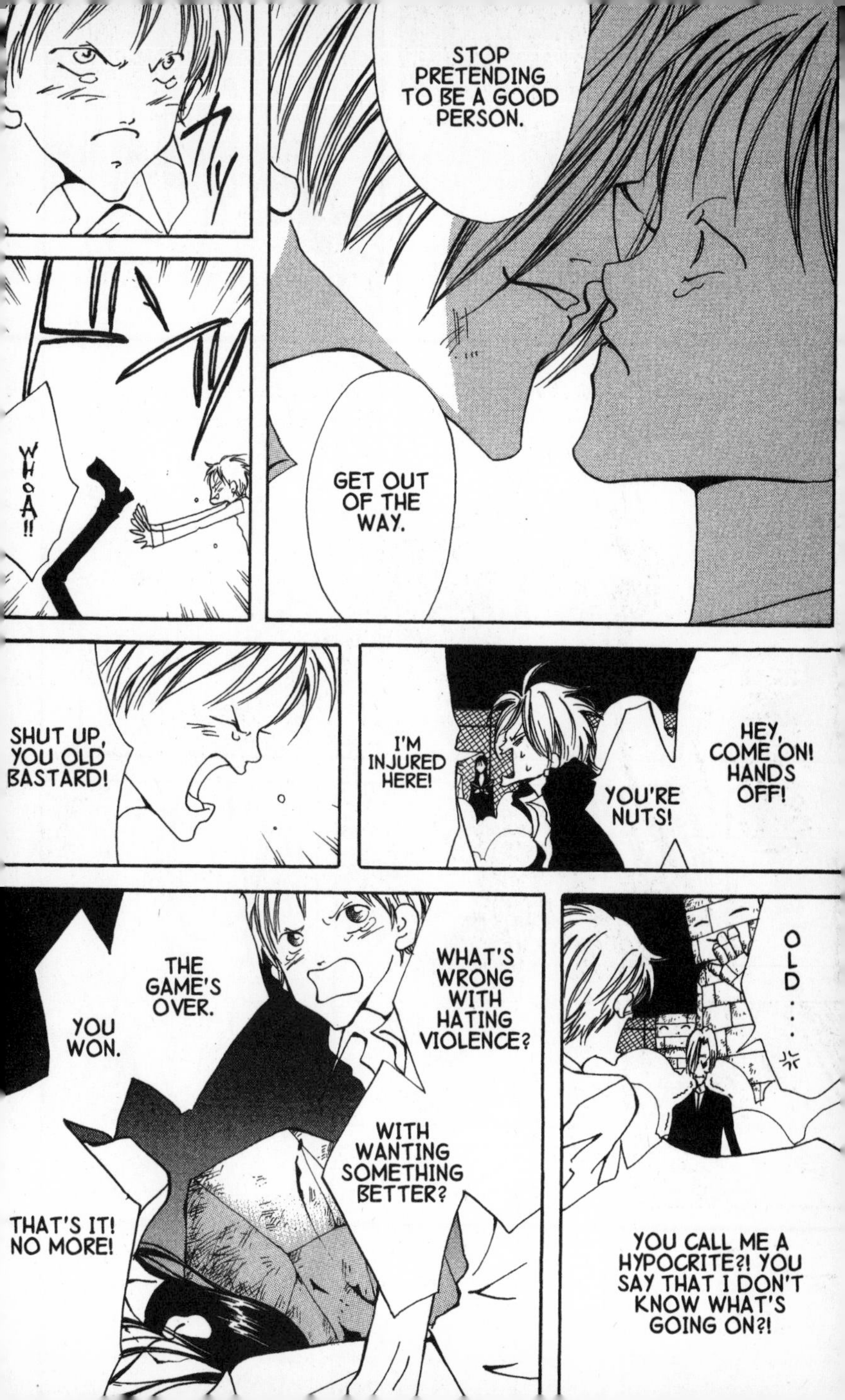
STOP PRETENDING TO BE A GOOD PERSON.
GET OUT OF THE WAY.
WHOA!!
HEY, COME ON! HANDS OFF!
YOU'RE NUTS!
I'M INJURED HERE!
SHUT UP, YOU OLD BASTARD!
OLD...
YOU CALL ME A HYPOCRITE?! YOU SAY THAT I DON'T KNOW WHAT'S GOING ON?!
WHAT'S WRONG WITH HATING VIOLENCE?
WITH WANTING SOMETHING BETTER?
THE GAME'S OVER.
YOU WON.
THAT'S IT! NO MORE!

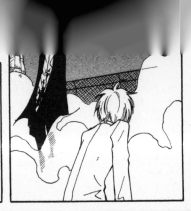

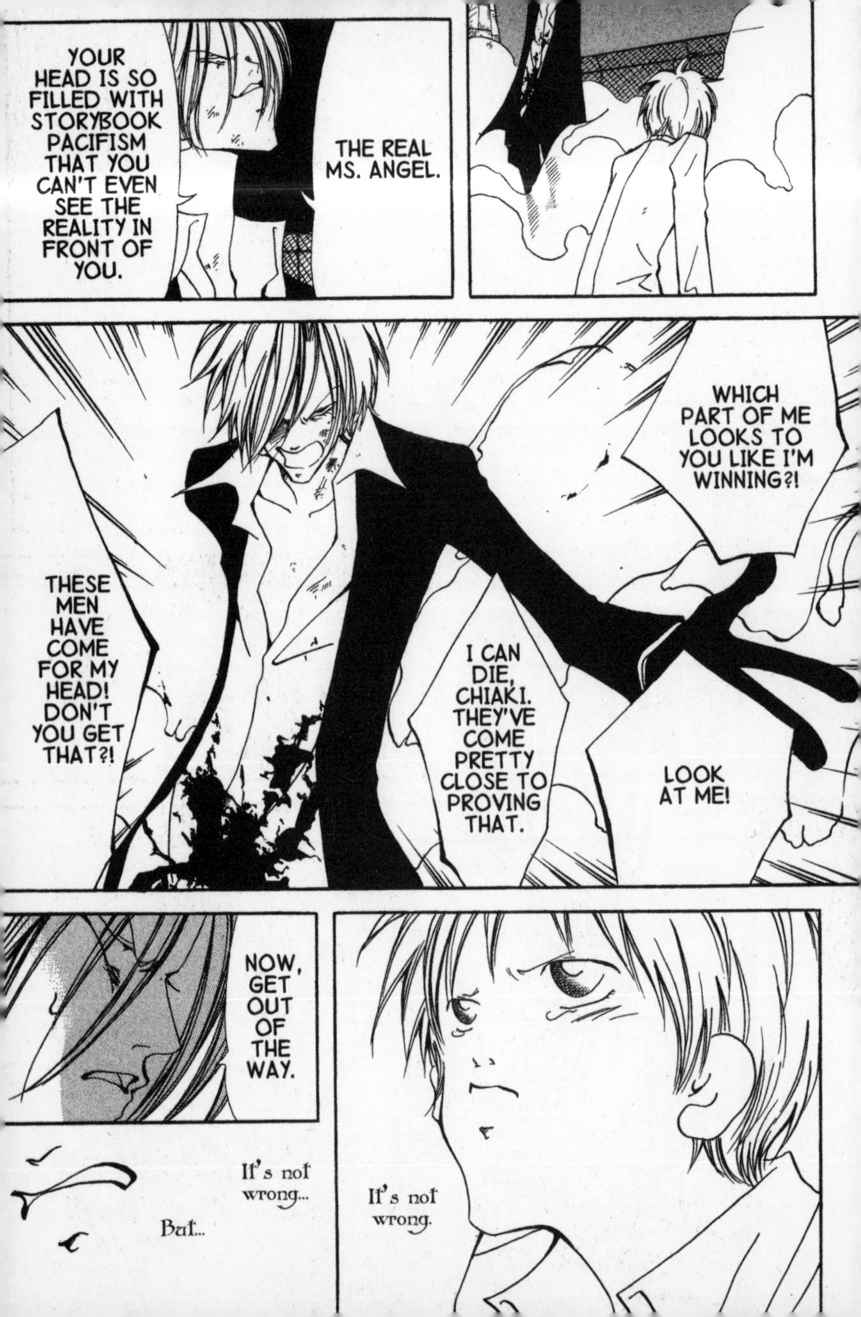
THE REAL MS. ANGEL.
YOUR HEAD IS SO FILLED WITH STORYBOOK PACIFISM THAT YOU CAN'T EVEN SEE THE REALITY IN FRONT OF YOU.
WHICH PART OF ME LOOKS TO YOU LIKE I'M WINNING?!
LOOK AT ME!
I CAN DIE, CHIAKI. THEY'VE COME PRETTY CLOSE TO PROVING THAT.
THESE MEN HAVE COME FOR MY HEAD! DON'T YOU GET THAT?!
It's not wrong.
NOW, GET OUT OF THE WAY.
It's not wrong...
But...

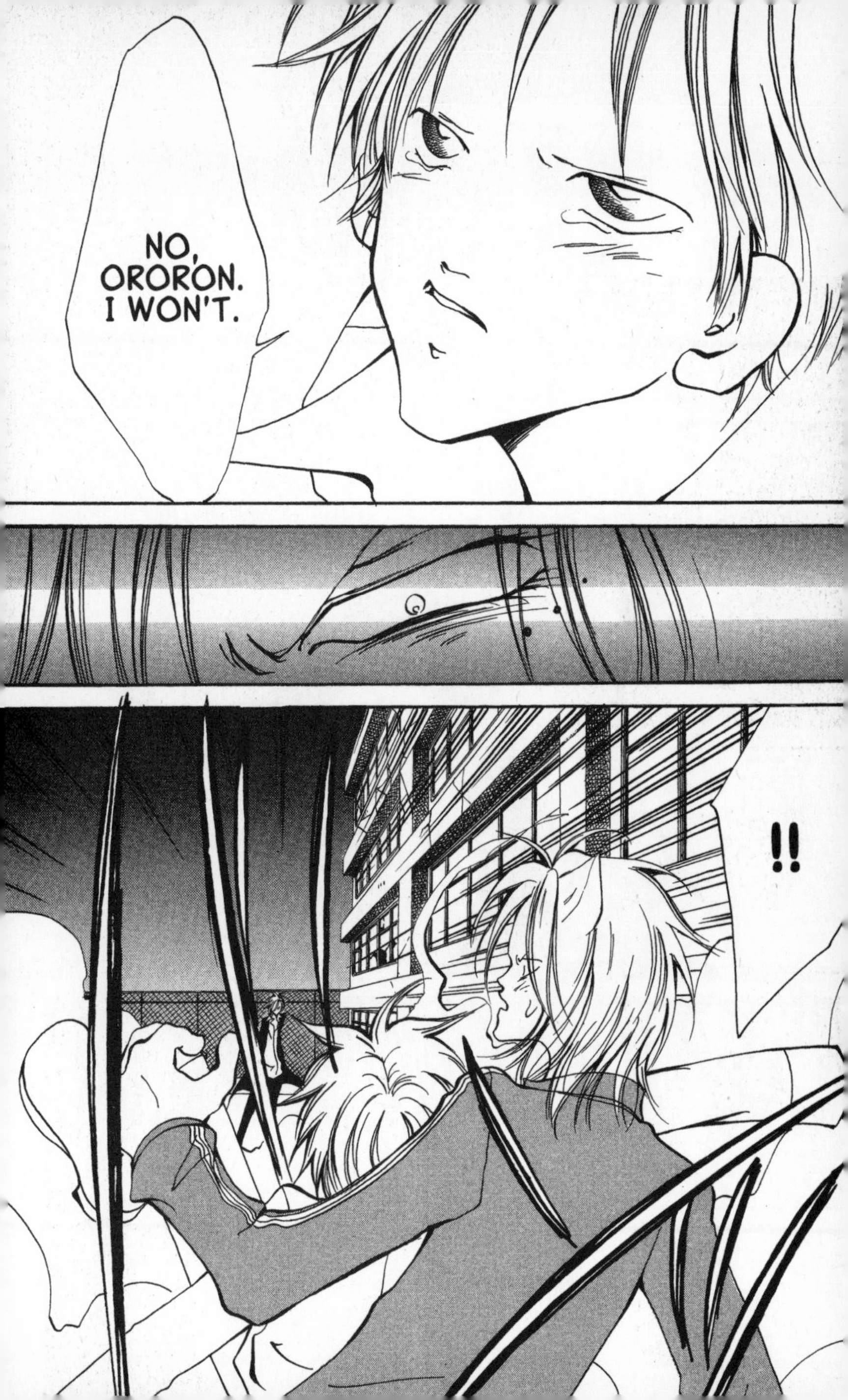
NO, ORORON. I WON'T.
!!

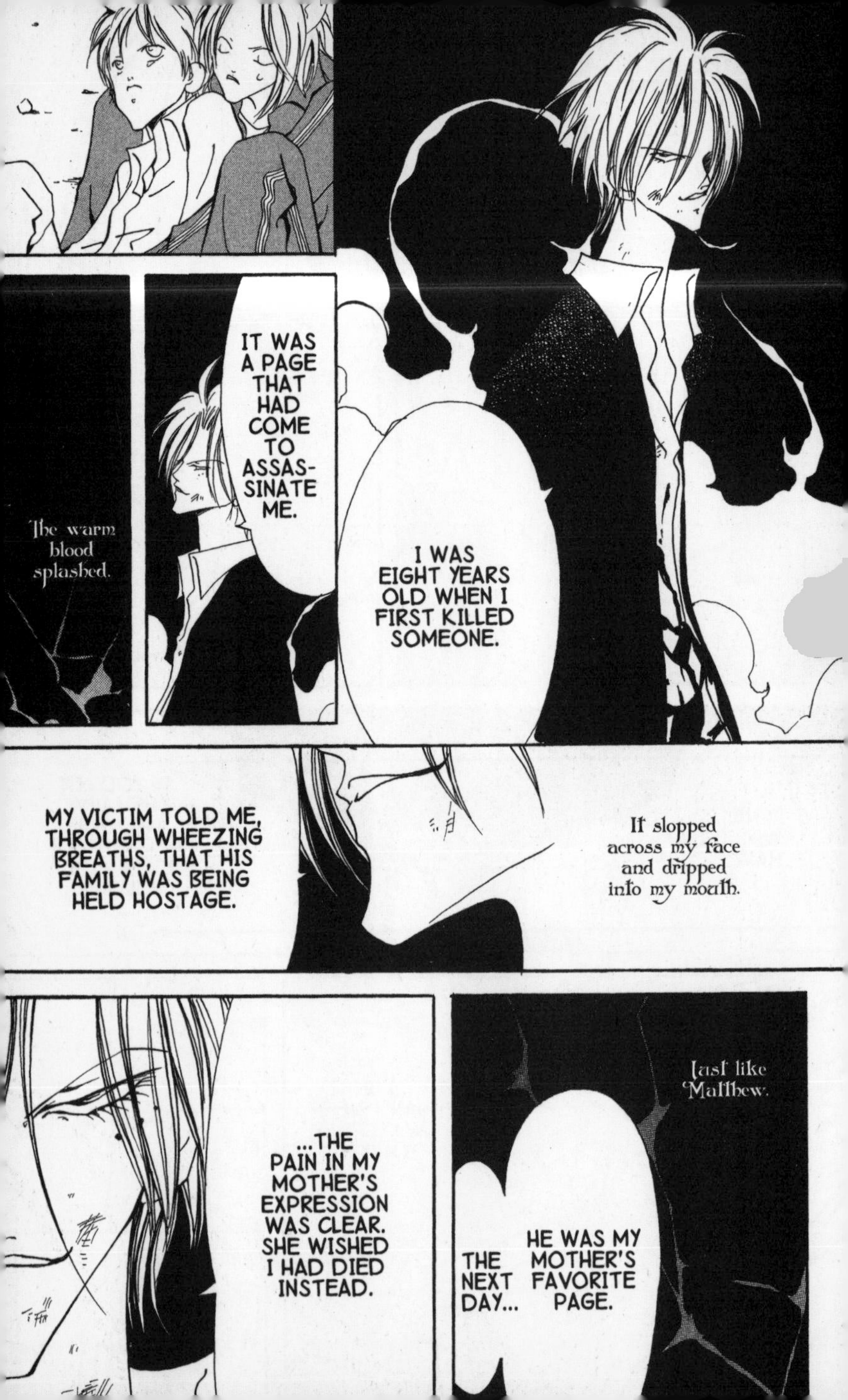
I WAS EIGHT YEARS OLD WHEN I FIRST KILLED SOMEONE.
IT WAS A PAGE THAT HAD COME TO ASSAS-SINATE ME.
The warm blood splashed.
It slopped across my face and dripped into my mouth.
MY VICTIM TOLD ME, THROUGH WHEEZING BREATHS, THAT HIS FAMILY WAS BEING HELD HOSTAGE.
Just like Matthew.
HE WAS MY MOTHER'S FAVORITE PAGE.
THE NEXT DAY...
...THE PAIN IN MY MOTHER'S EXPRESSION WAS CLEAR. SHE WISHED I HAD DIED INSTEAD.

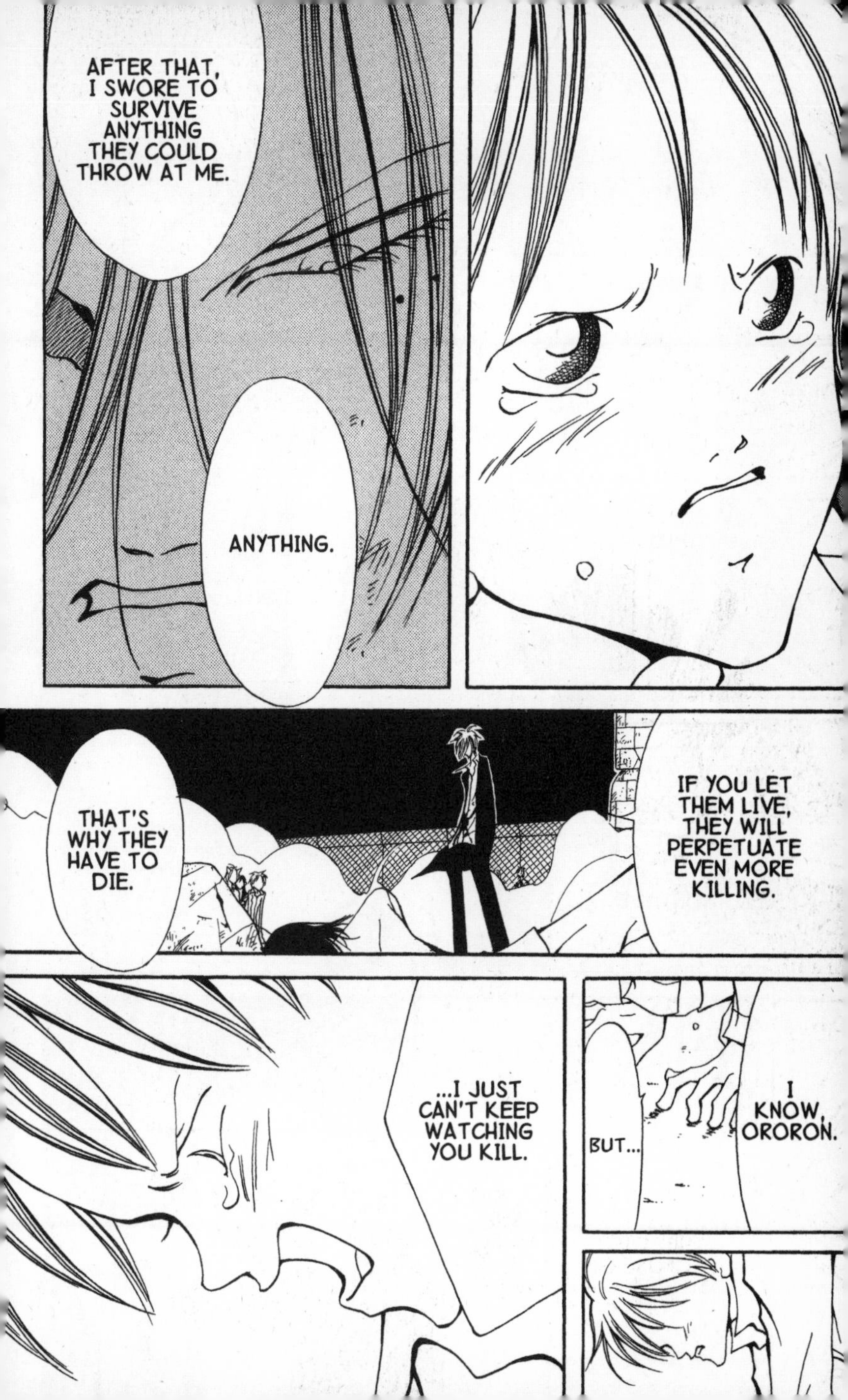
AFTER THAT, I SWORE TO SURVIVE ANYTHING THEY COULD THROW AT ME.
ANYTHING.
IF YOU LET THEM LIVE, THEY WILL PERPETUATE EVEN MORE KILLING.
THAT'S WHY THEY HAVE TO DIE.
I KNOW, ORORON.
BUT...
...I JUST CAN'T KEEP WATCHING YOU KILL.

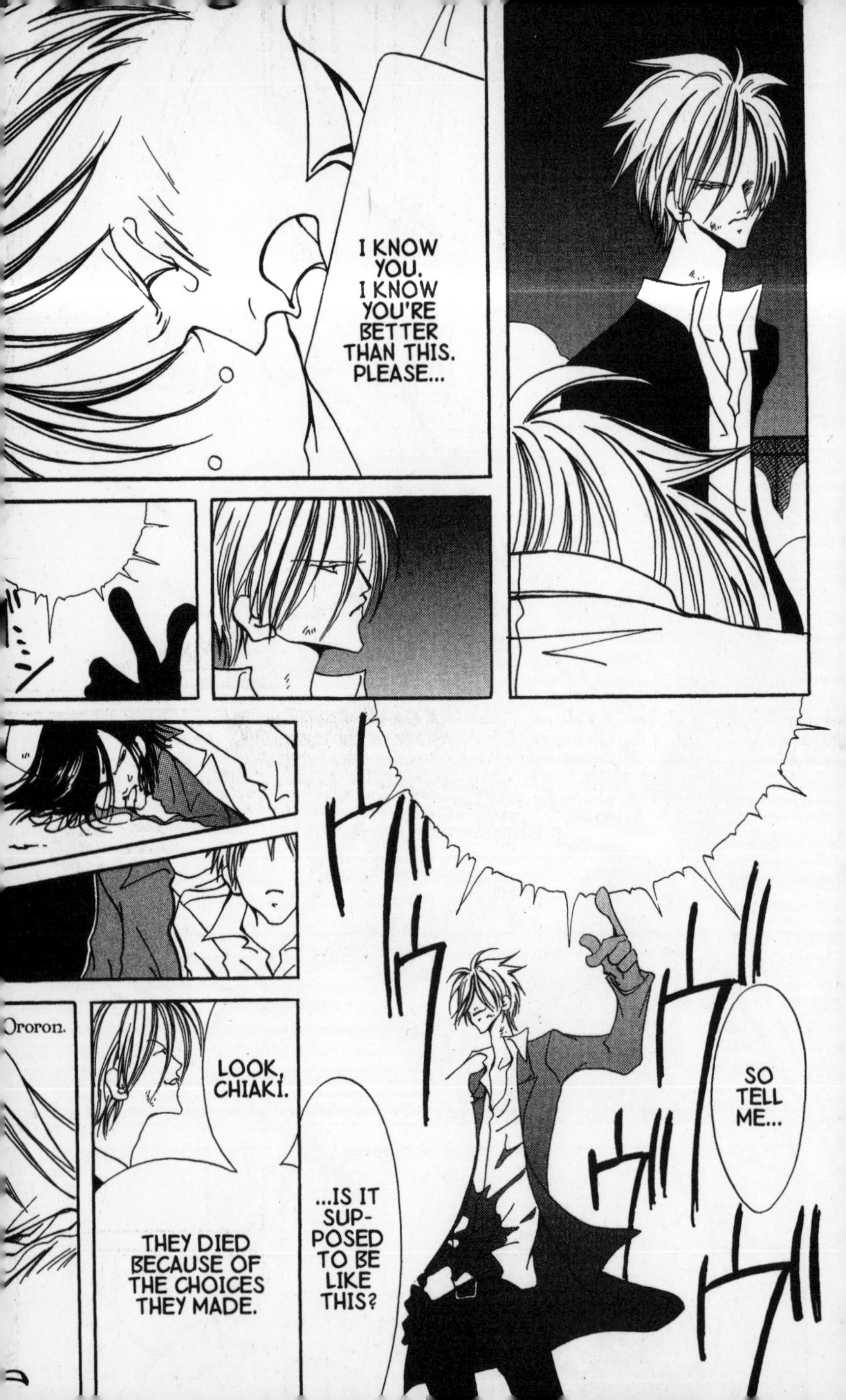

I KNOW YOU. I KNOW YOU'RE BETTER THAN THIS. PLEASE...
SO TELL ME...
...IS IT SUPPOSED TO BE LIKE THIS?
Ororon.
LOOK, CHIAKI.
THEY DIED BECAUSE OF THE CHOICES THEY MADE.

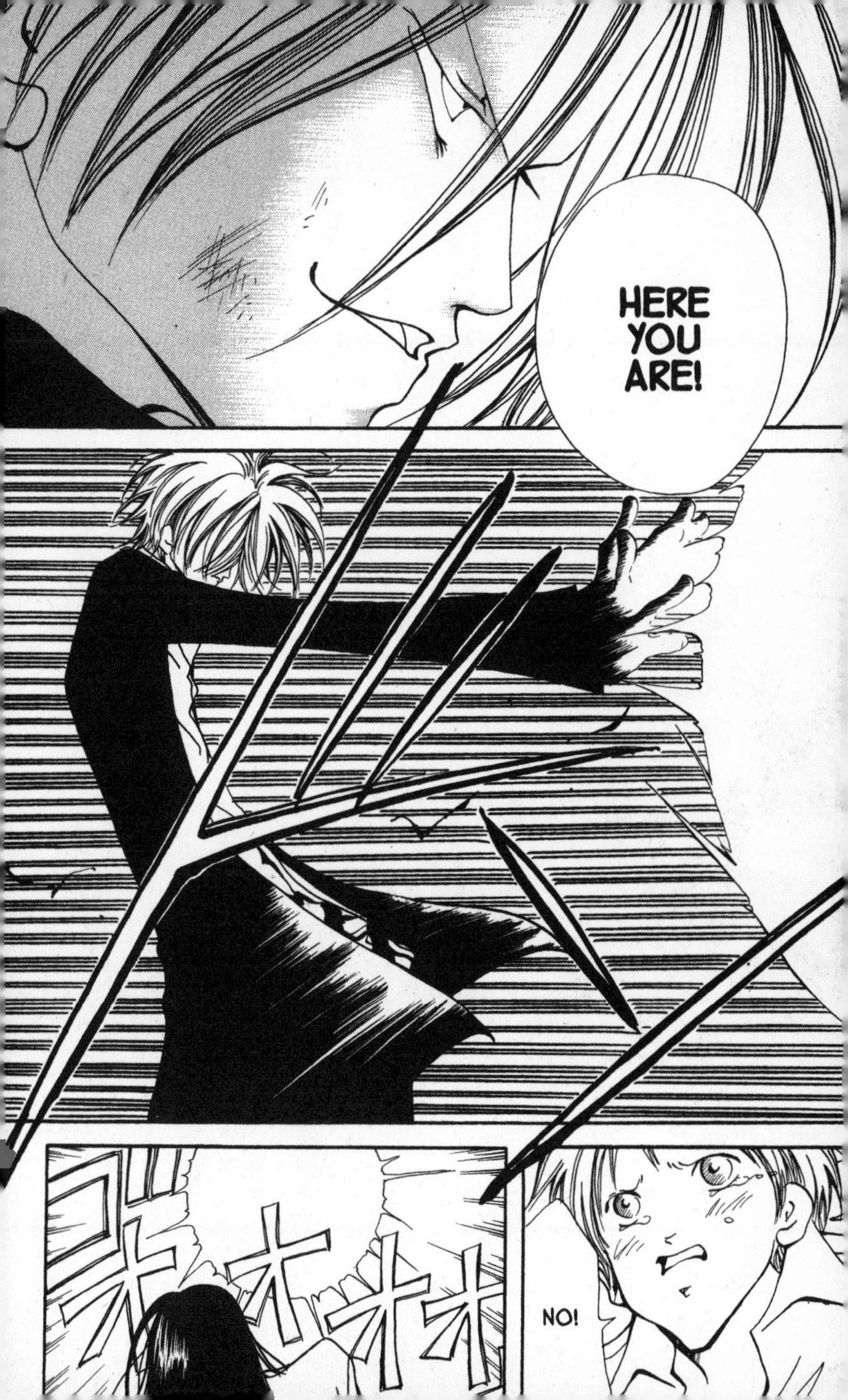
HERE YOU ARE!
NO!

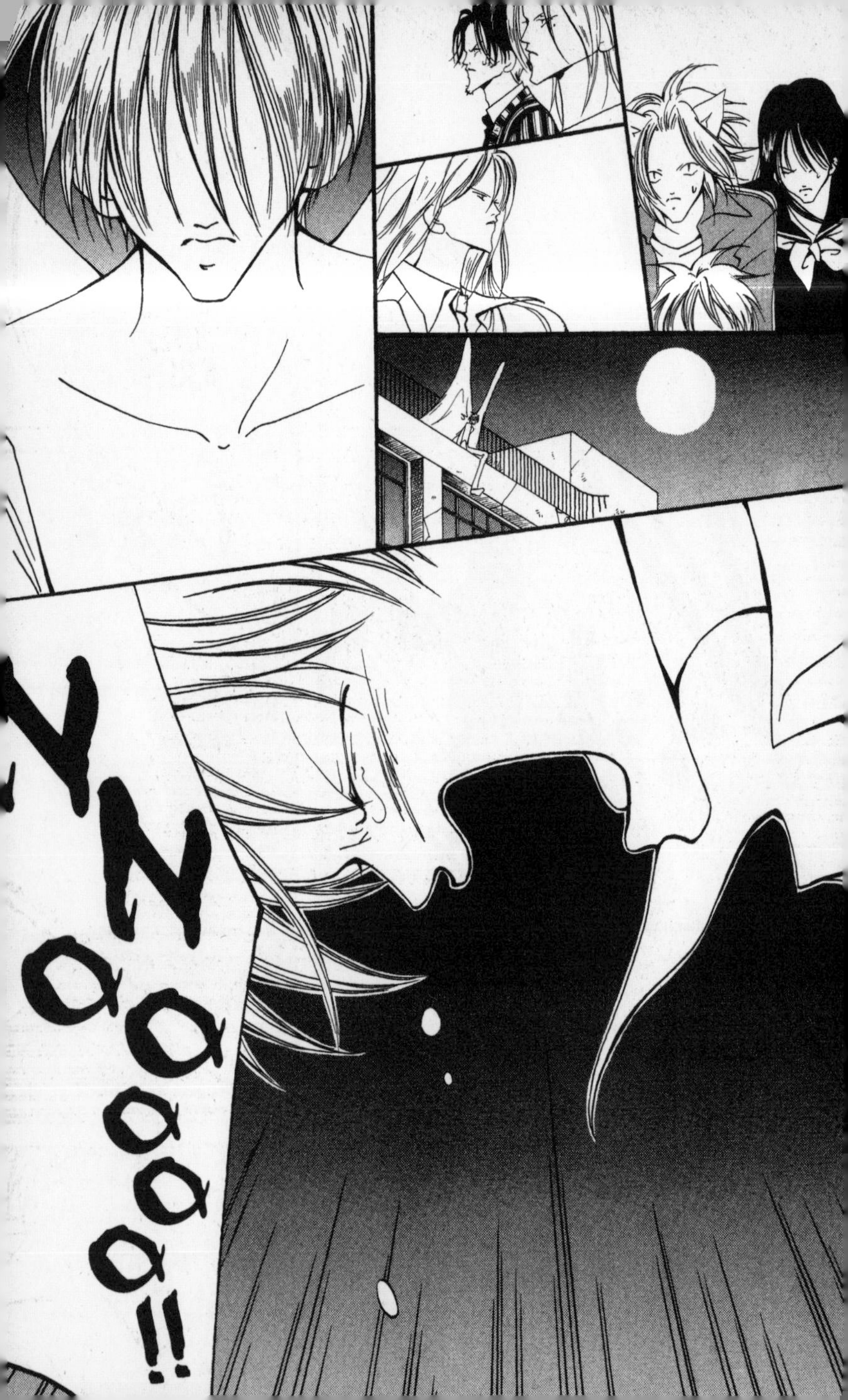
ZNaaaaa!!

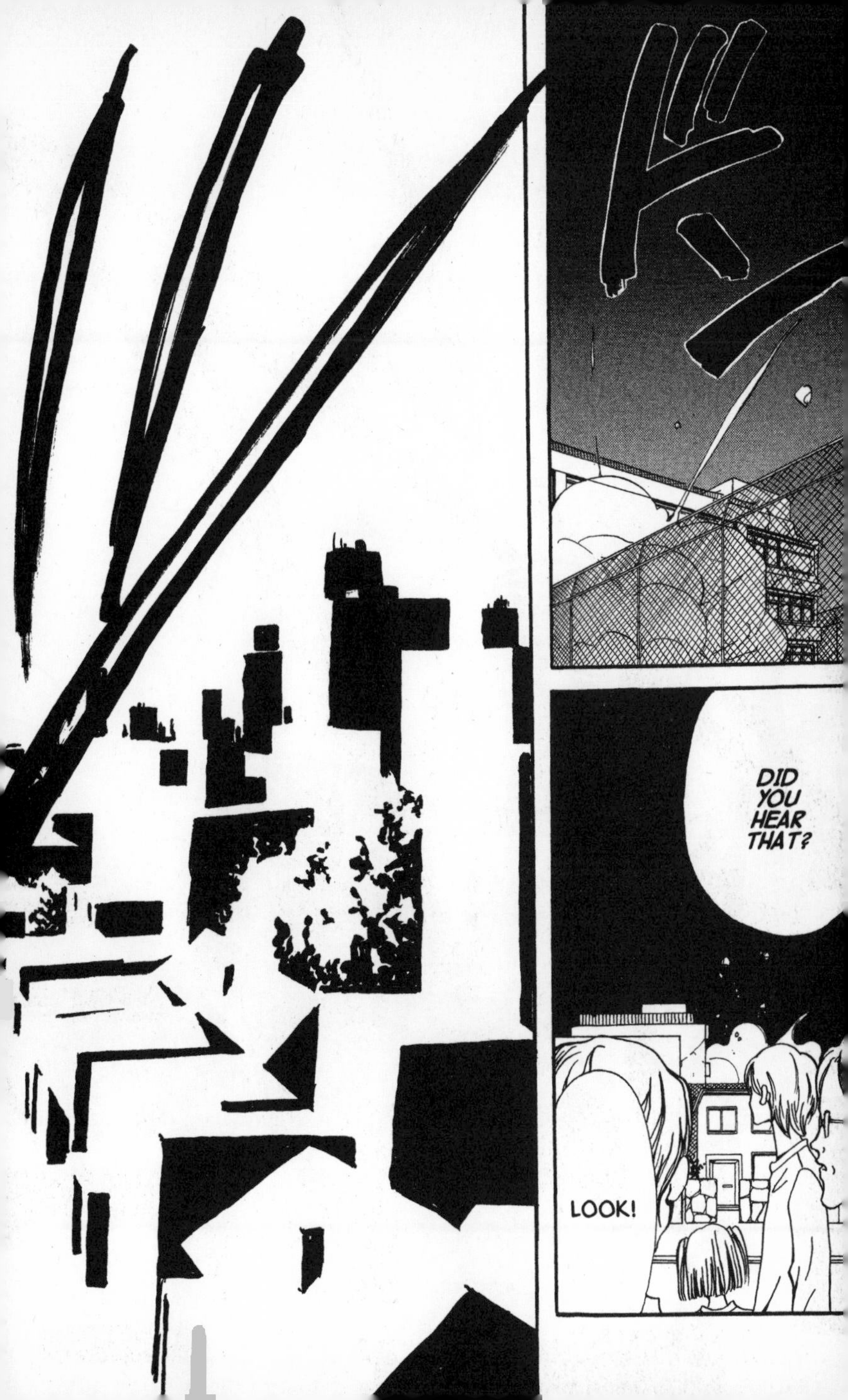
DID YOU HEAR THAT?
LOOK!

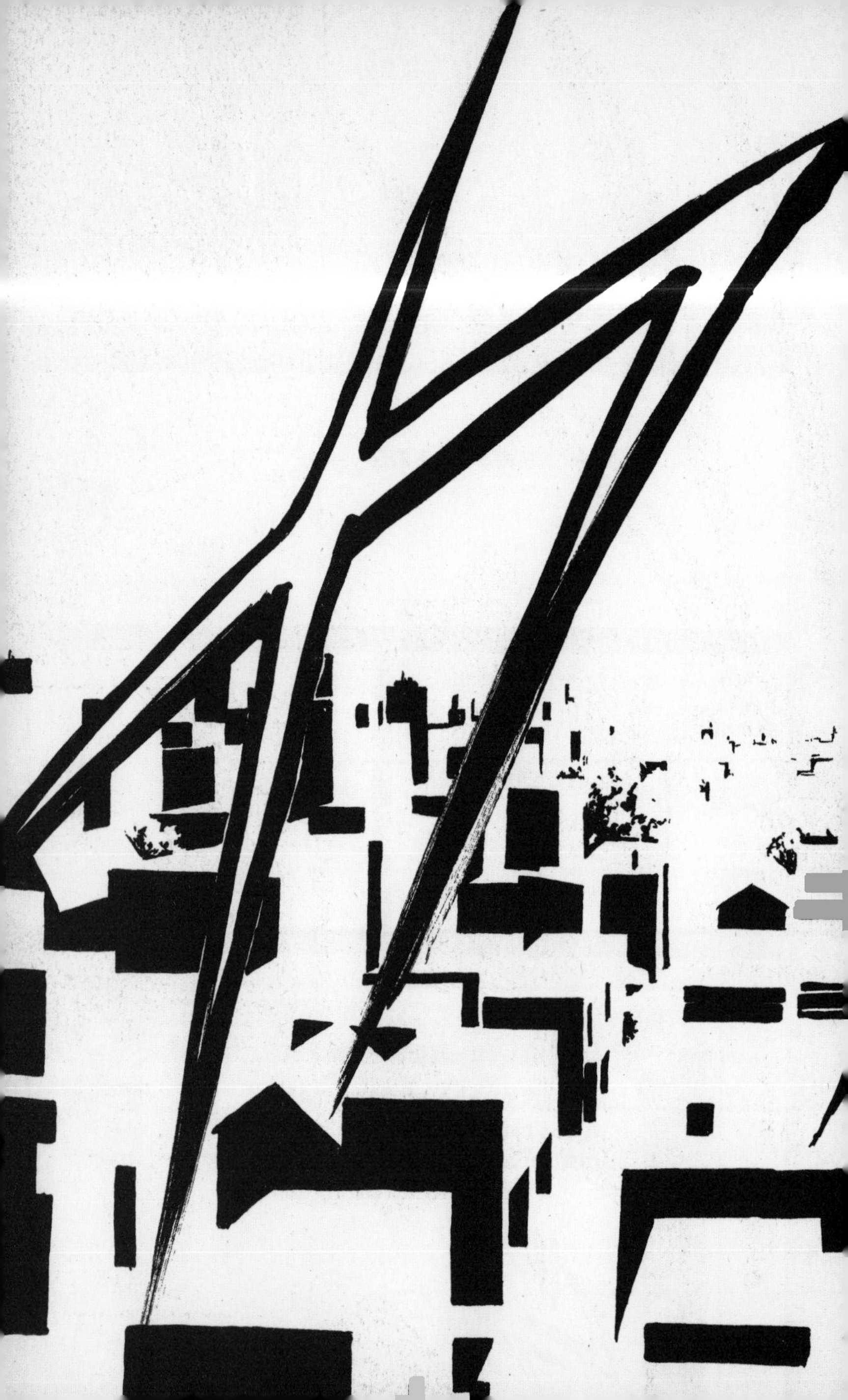

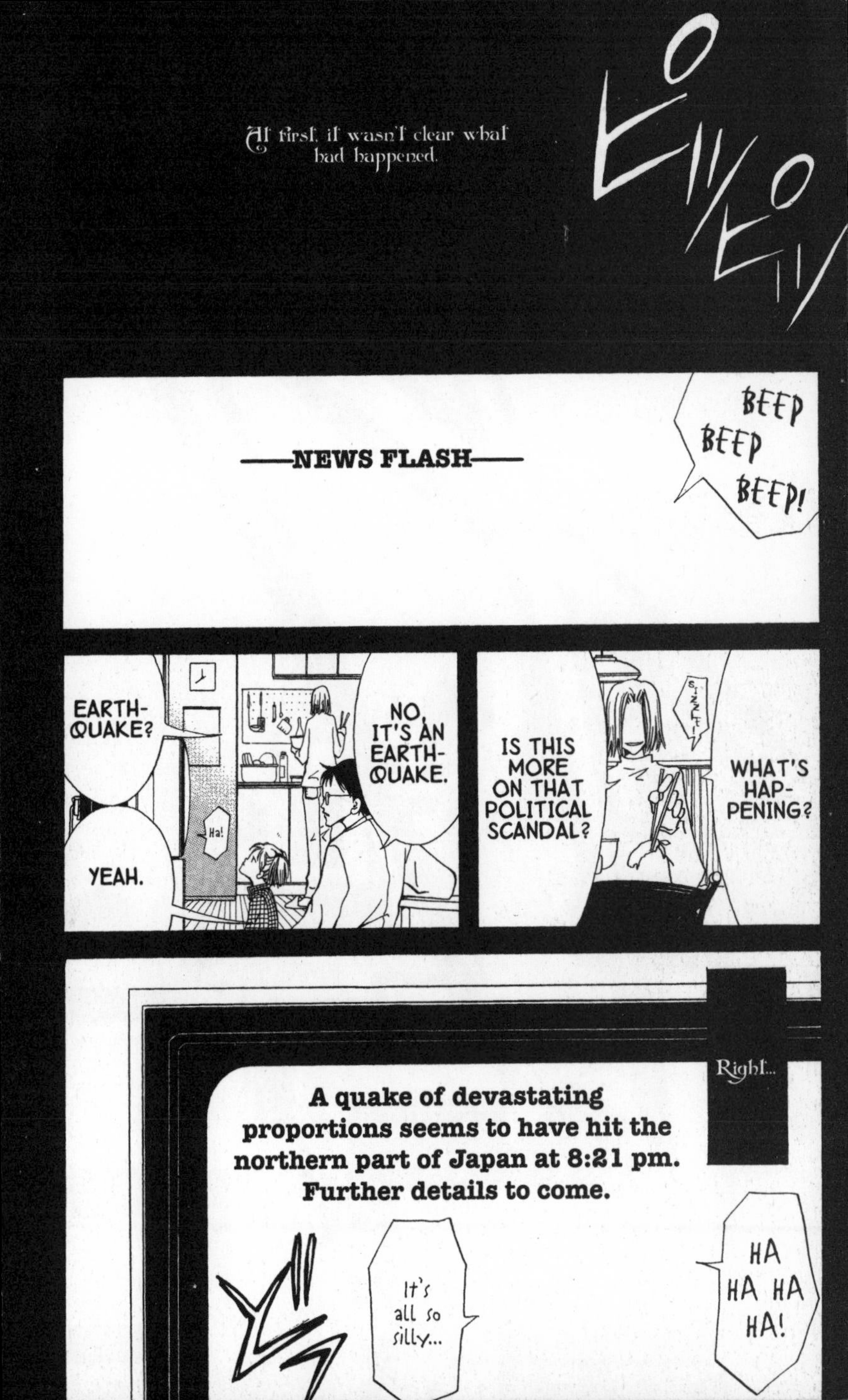
ピッ ピッ
At first, it wasn't clear what had happened.
BEEP BEEP BEEP!
——NEWS FLASH——
WHAT'S HAPPENING?
SIZZLE
IS THIS MORE ON THAT POLITICAL SCANDAL?
NO, IT'S AN EARTHQUAKE.
EARTHQUAKE?
Ha!
YEAH.
Right...
A quake of devastating proportions seems to have hit the northern part of Japan at 8:21 pm. Further details to come.
HA HA HA HA!
It's all so silly...

e of devastating
seems to have hit t
of Japan at 8:21 p
details to come.

At first, no one knew.

-10-

Ticket to Paradise

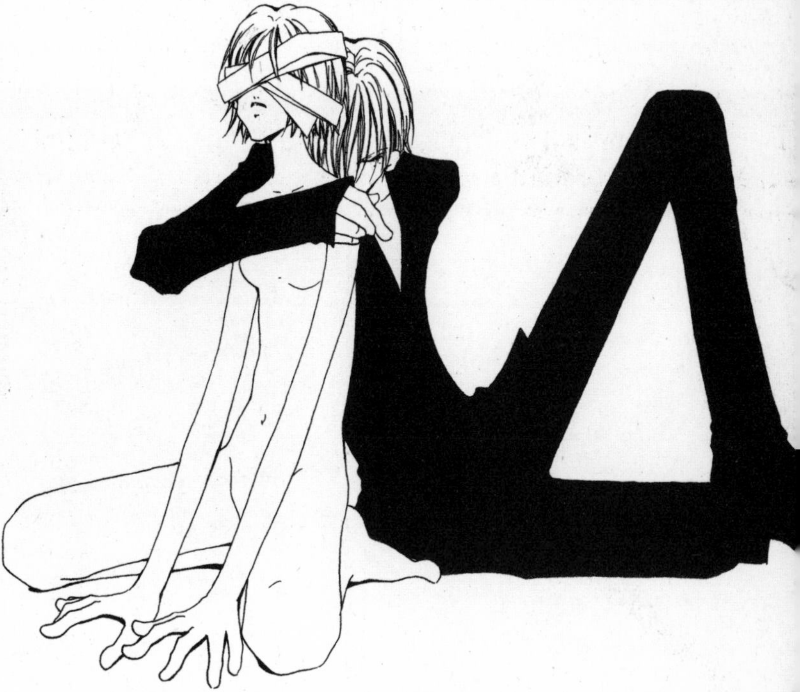

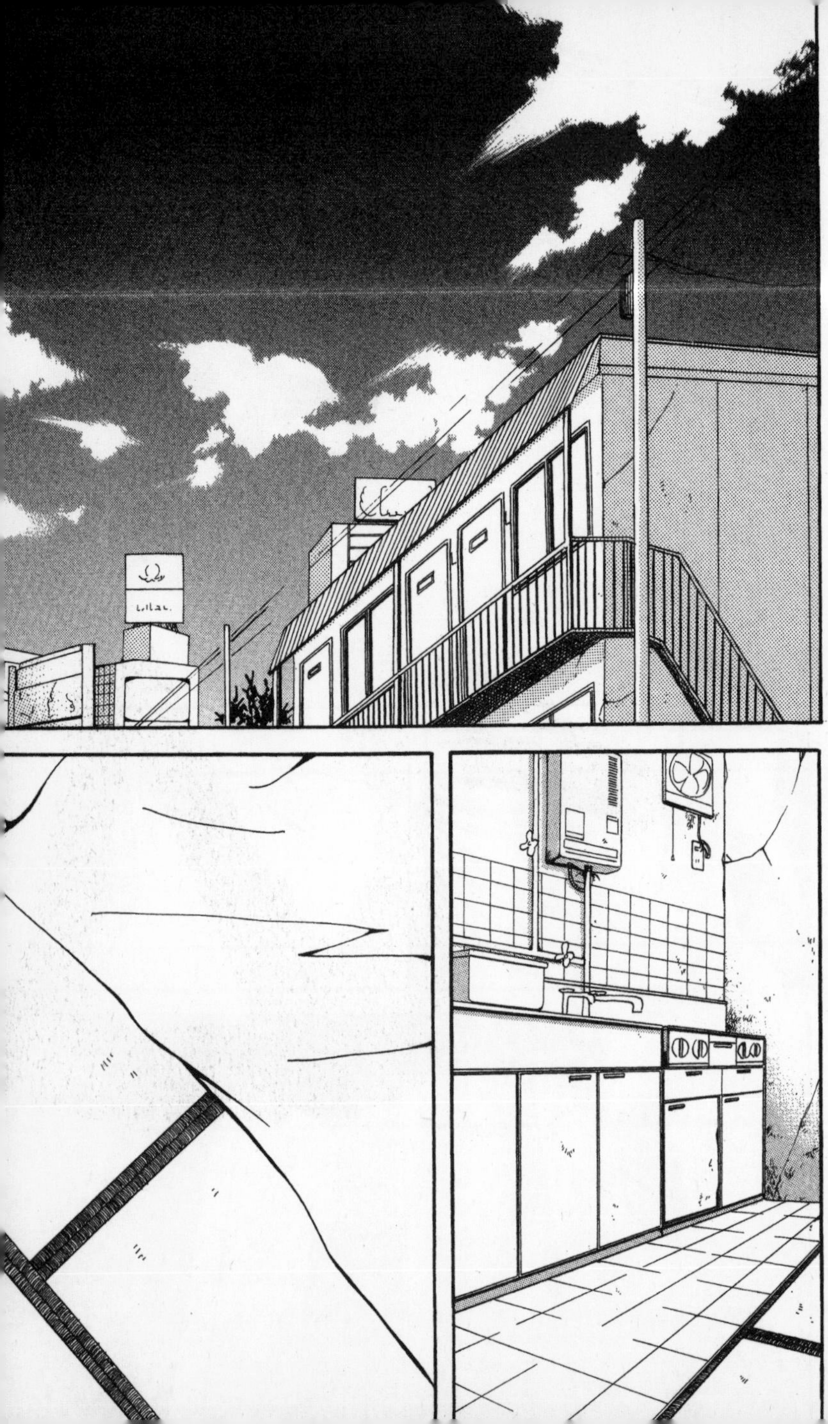

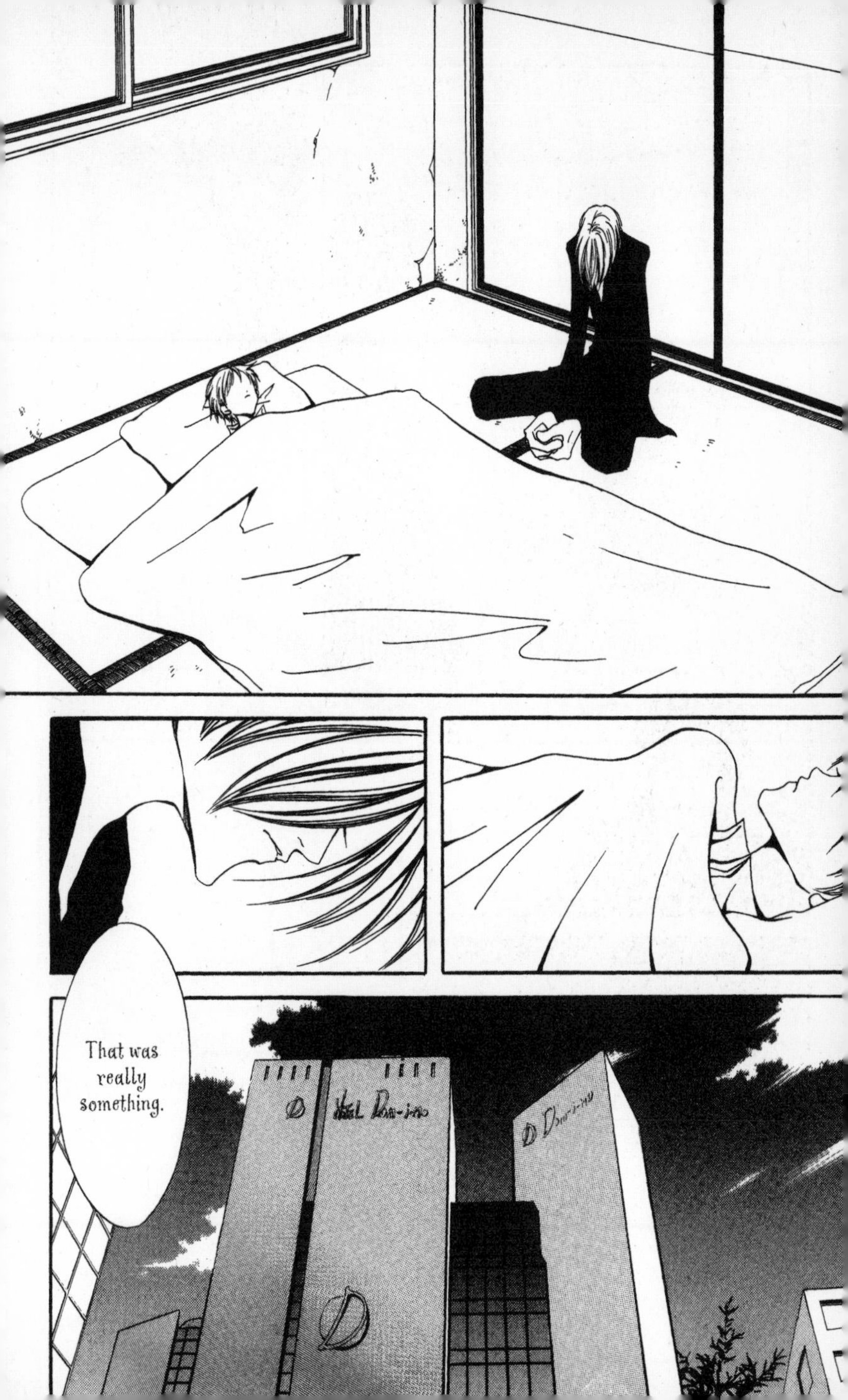
That was really something.

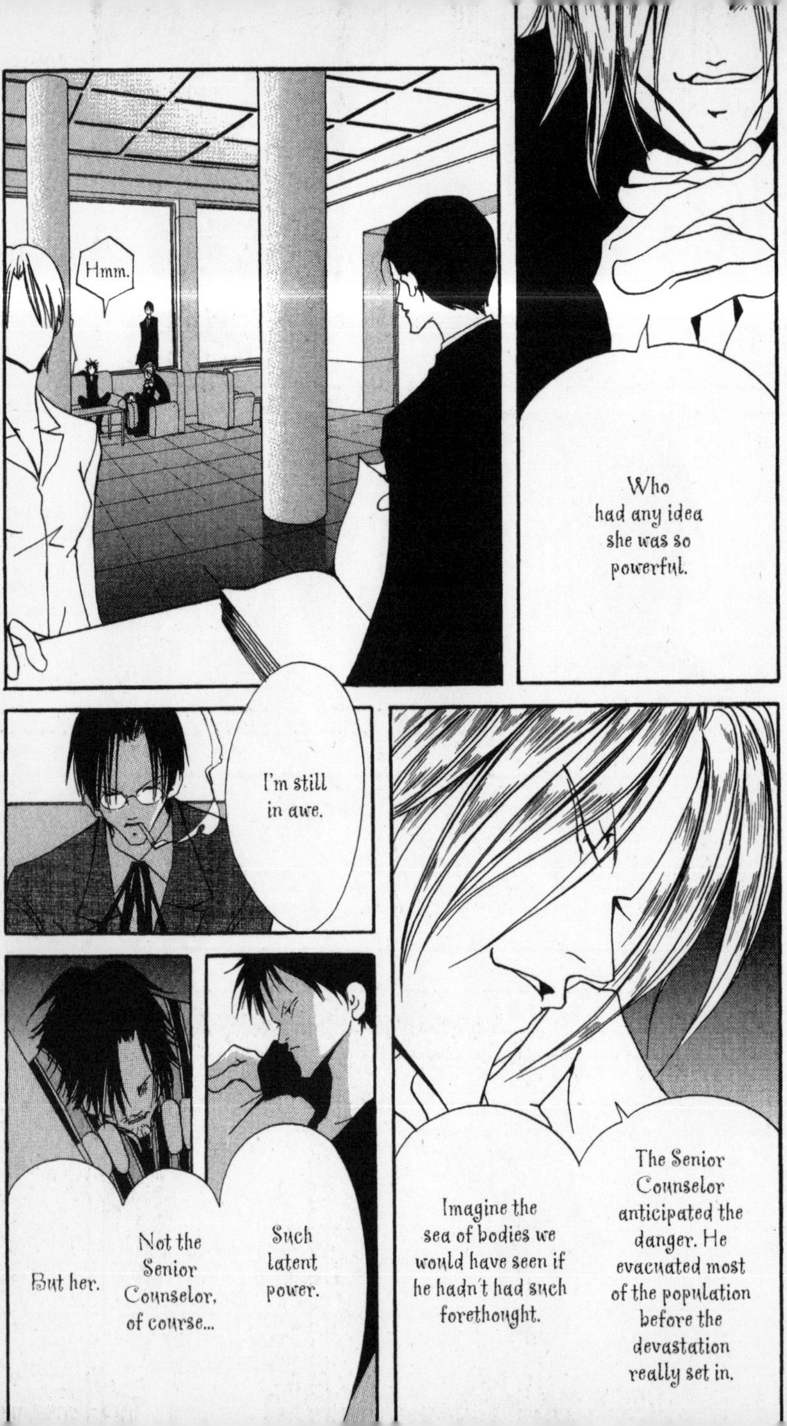

Who had any idea she was so powerful.
Hmm.
The Senior Counselor anticipated the danger. He evacuated most of the population before the devastation really set in.
Imagine the sea of bodies we would have seen if he hadn't had such forethought.
I'm still in awe.
Such latent power.
Not the Senior Counselor, of course...
But her.

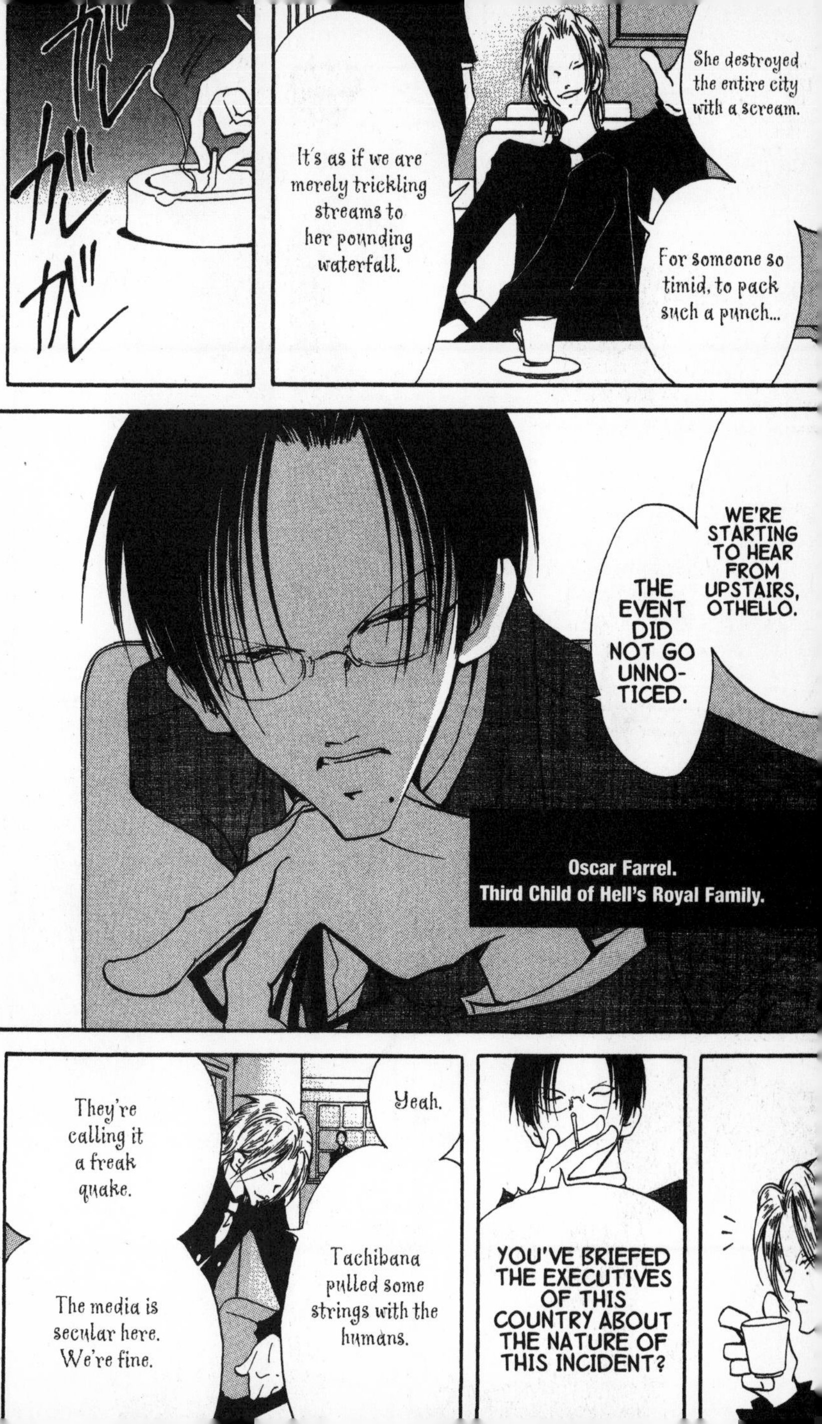
She destroyed the entire city with a scream.
For someone so timid, to pack such a punch...
It's as if we are merely trickling streams to her pounding waterfall.
WE'RE STARTING TO HEAR FROM UPSTAIRS, OTHELLO.
THE EVENT DID NOT GO UNNO-TICED.
Oscar Farrel.
Third Child of Hell's Royal Family.
YOU'VE BRIEFED THE EXECUTIVES OF THIS COUNTRY ABOUT THE NATURE OF THIS INCIDENT?
Yeah.
Tachibana pulled some strings with the humans.
They're calling it a freak quake.
The media is secular here. We're fine.

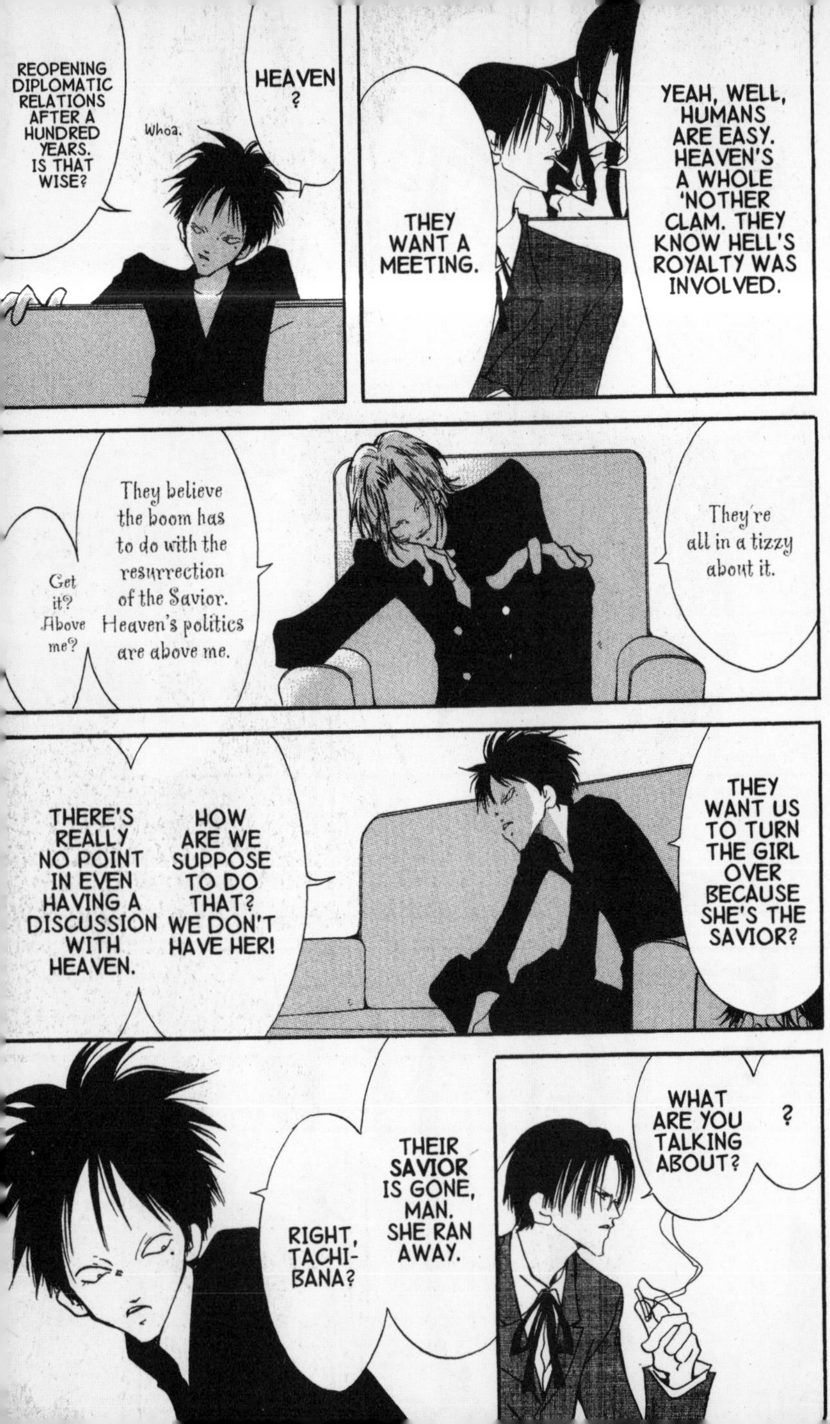
YEAH, WELL, HUMANS ARE EASY. HEAVEN'S A WHOLE 'NOTHER CLAM. THEY KNOW HELL'S ROYALTY WAS INVOLVED.
THEY WANT A MEETING.
HEAVEN?
Whoa.
REOPENING DIPLOMATIC RELATIONS AFTER A HUNDRED YEARS. IS THAT WISE?
They're all in a tizzy about it.
They believe the boom has to do with the resurrection of the Savior. Heaven's politics are above me.
Get it? Above me?
THEY WANT US TO TURN THE GIRL OVER BECAUSE SHE'S THE SAVIOR?
HOW ARE WE SUPPOSE TO DO THAT? WE DON'T HAVE HER!
THERE'S REALLY NO POINT IN EVEN HAVING A DISCUSSION WITH HEAVEN.
WHAT ARE YOU TALKING ABOUT?
?
THEIR SAVIOR IS GONE, MAN. SHE RAN AWAY.
RIGHT, TACHIBANA?

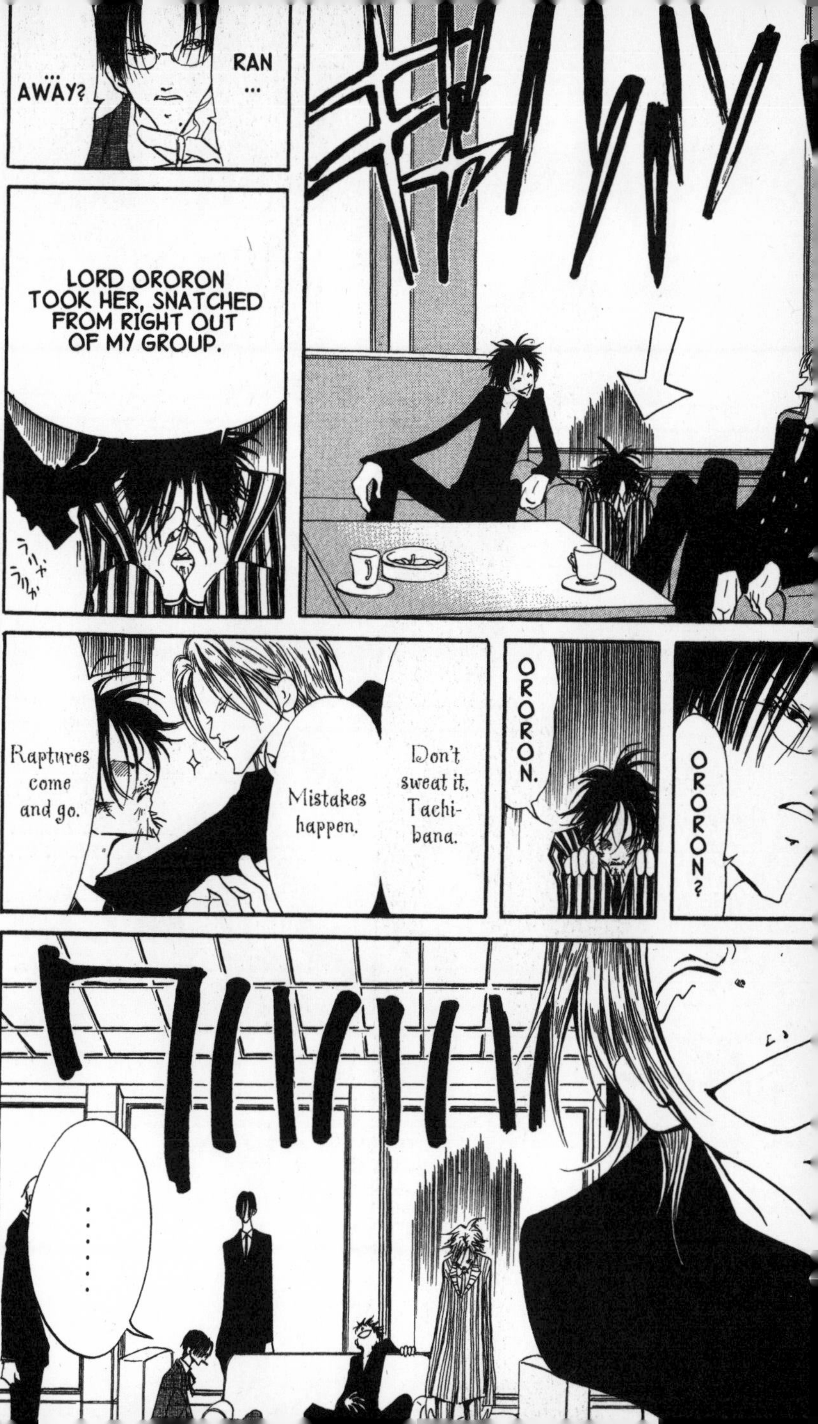
RAN ...
... AWAY?
LORD ORORON TOOK HER, SNATCHED FROM RIGHT OUT OF MY GROUP.
ORORON?
ORORON.
Don't sweat it, Tachibana.
Mistakes happen.
Raptures come and go.
......

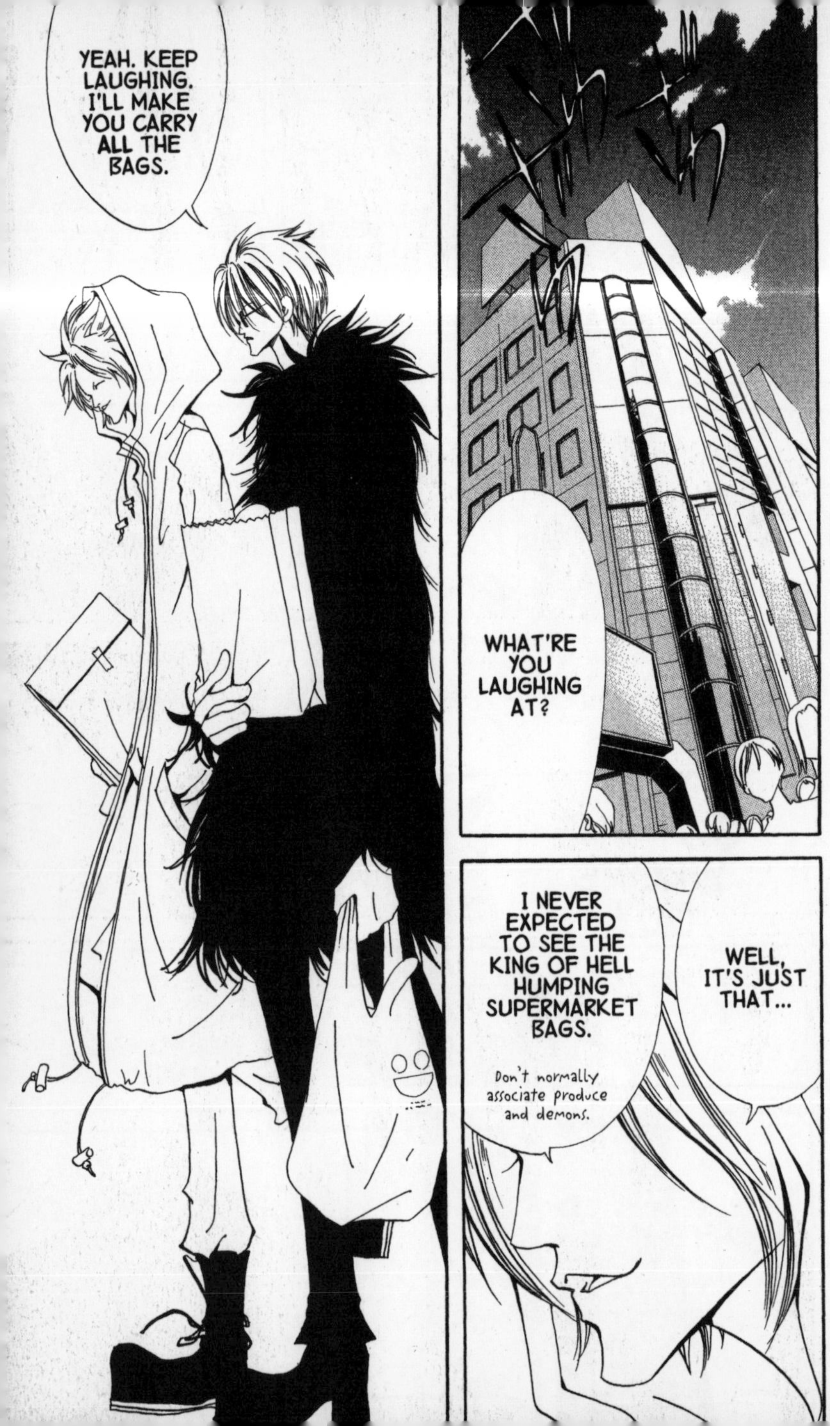
WHAT'RE YOU LAUGHING AT?
WELL, IT'S JUST THAT...
I NEVER EXPECTED TO SEE THE KING OF HELL HUMPING SUPERMARKET BAGS.
Don't normally associate produce and demons.
YEAH. KEEP LAUGHING. I'LL MAKE YOU CARRY ALL THE BAGS.

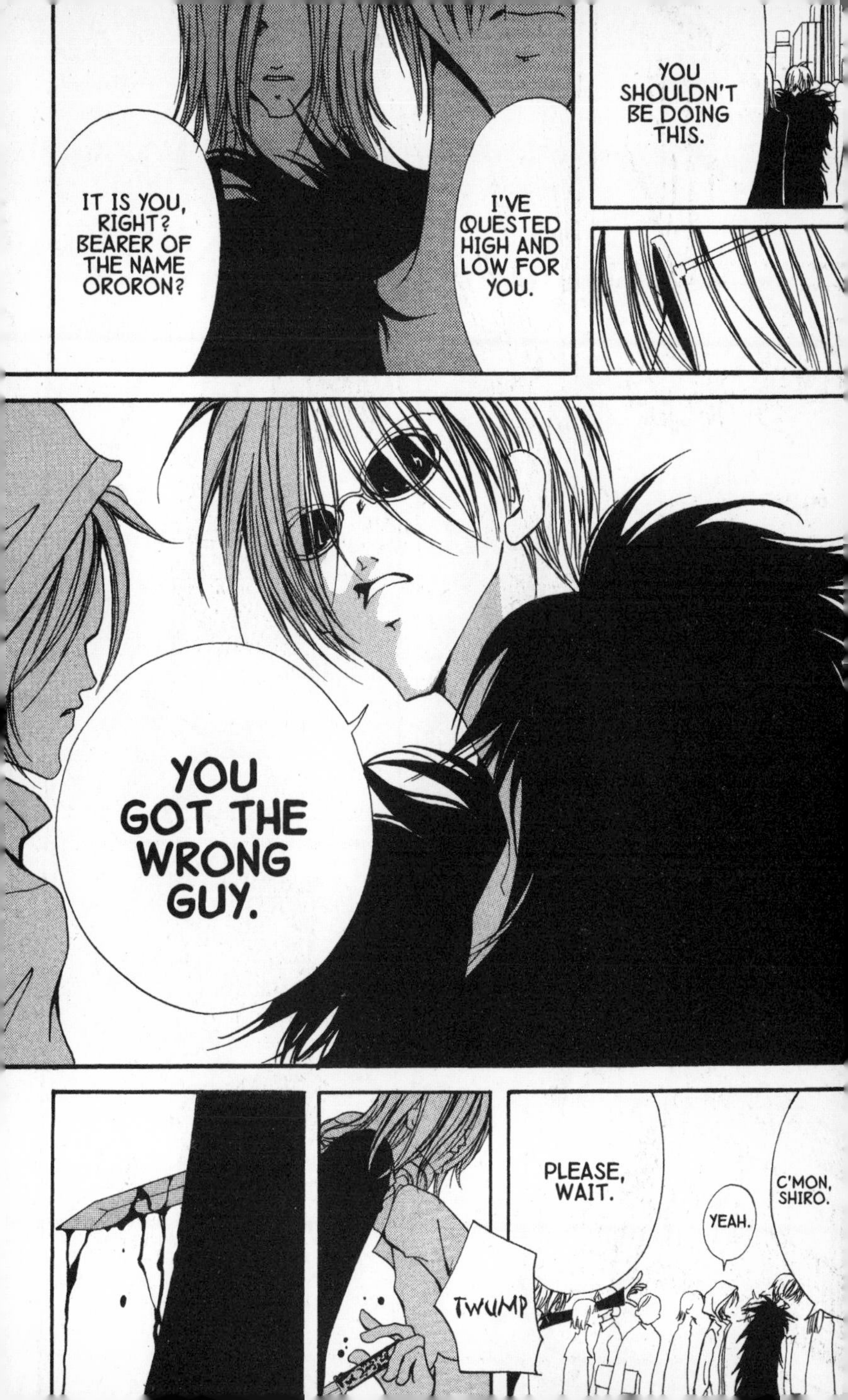
YOU SHOULDN'T BE DOING THIS.
I'VE QUESTED HIGH AND LOW FOR YOU.
IT IS YOU, RIGHT? BEARER OF THE NAME ORORON?
YOU GOT THE WRONG GUY.
C'MON, SHIRO.
YEAH.
PLEASE, WAIT.
TWUMP

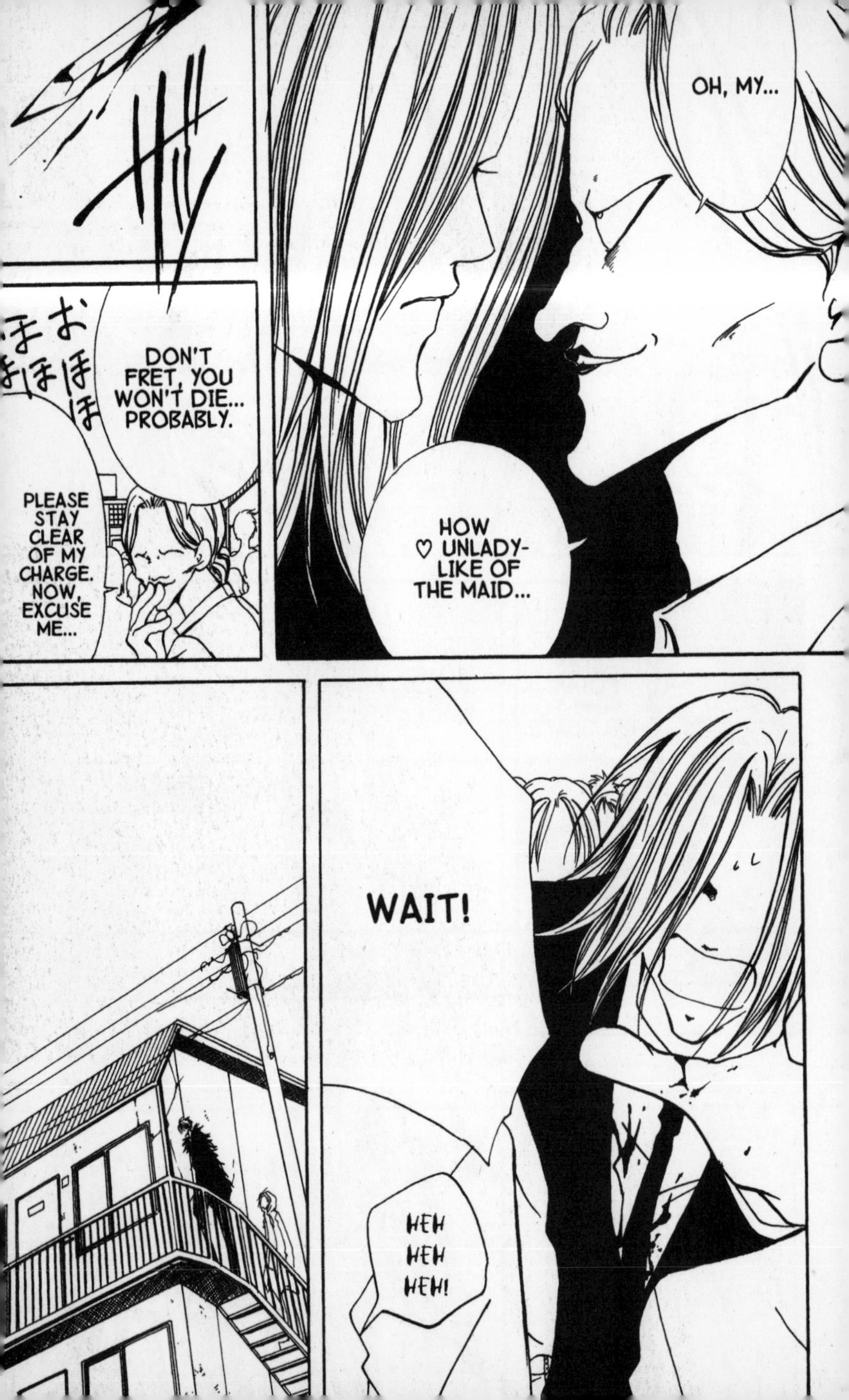
OH, MY...
HOW ♡ UNLADY-LIKE OF THE MAID...
DON'T FRET, YOU WON'T DIE... PROBABLY.
PLEASE STAY CLEAR OF MY CHARGE. NOW, EXCUSE ME...
WAIT!
HEH HEH HEH!

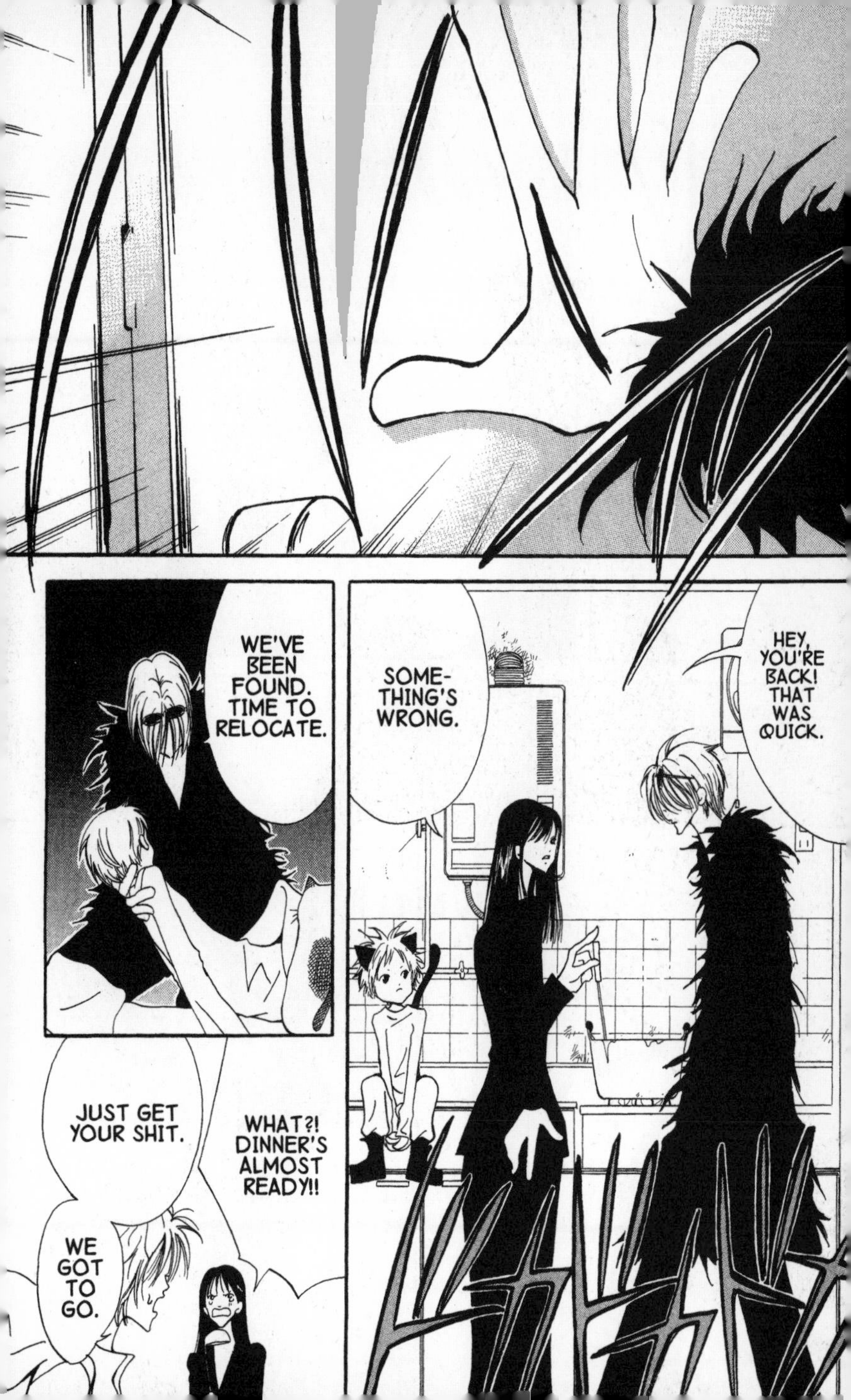
HEY, YOU'RE BACK! THAT WAS QUICK.
SOME-THING'S WRONG.
WE'VE BEEN FOUND. TIME TO RELOCATE.
WHAT?! DINNER'S ALMOST READY!!
JUST GET YOUR SHIT.
WE GOT TO GO.

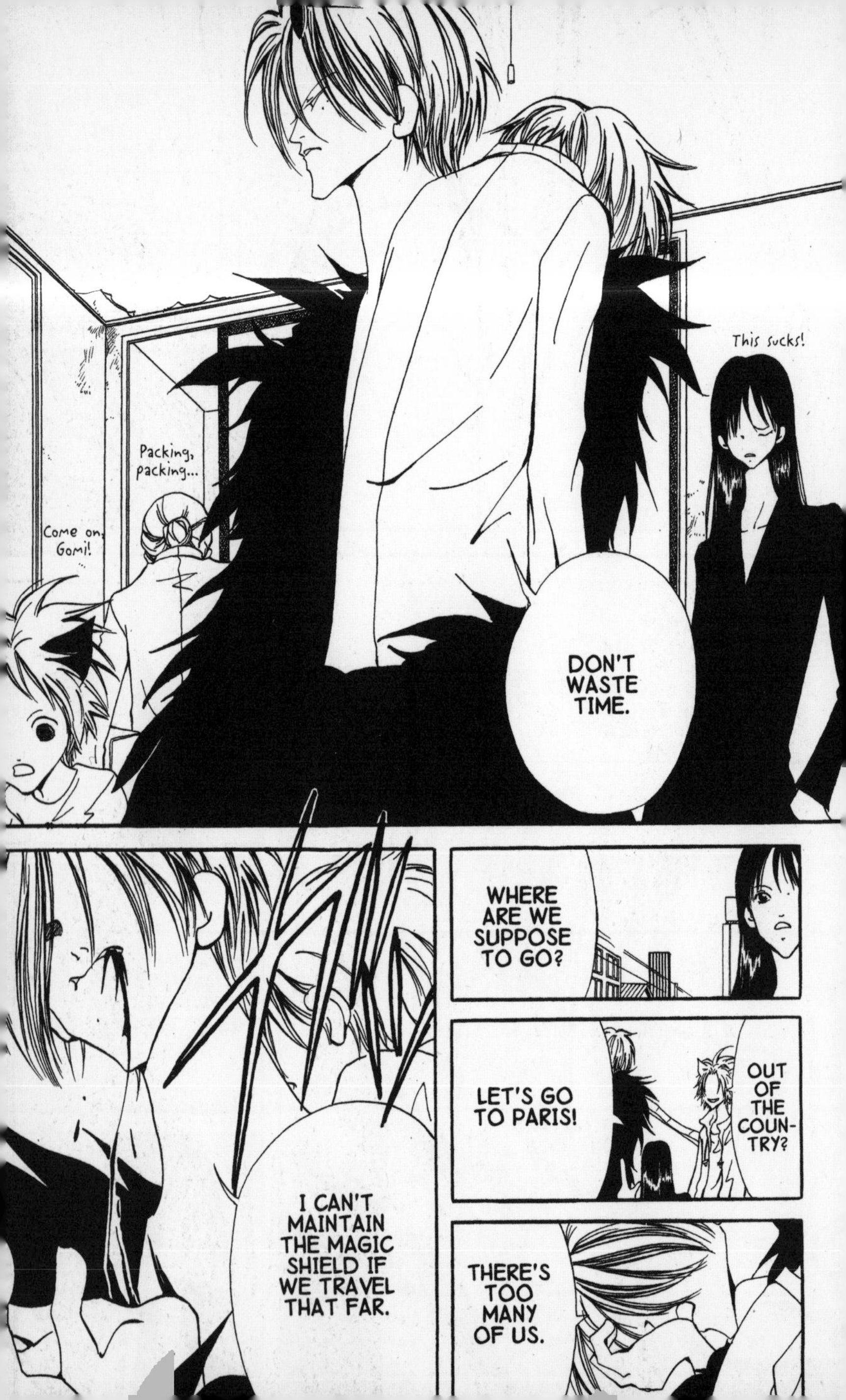
This sucks!
DON'T WASTE TIME.
Packing, packing...
Come on, Gomi!
WHERE ARE WE SUPPOSE TO GO?
OUT OF THE COUNTRY?
LET'S GO TO PARIS!
THERE'S TOO MANY OF US.
I CAN'T MAINTAIN THE MAGIC SHIELD IF WE TRAVEL THAT FAR.

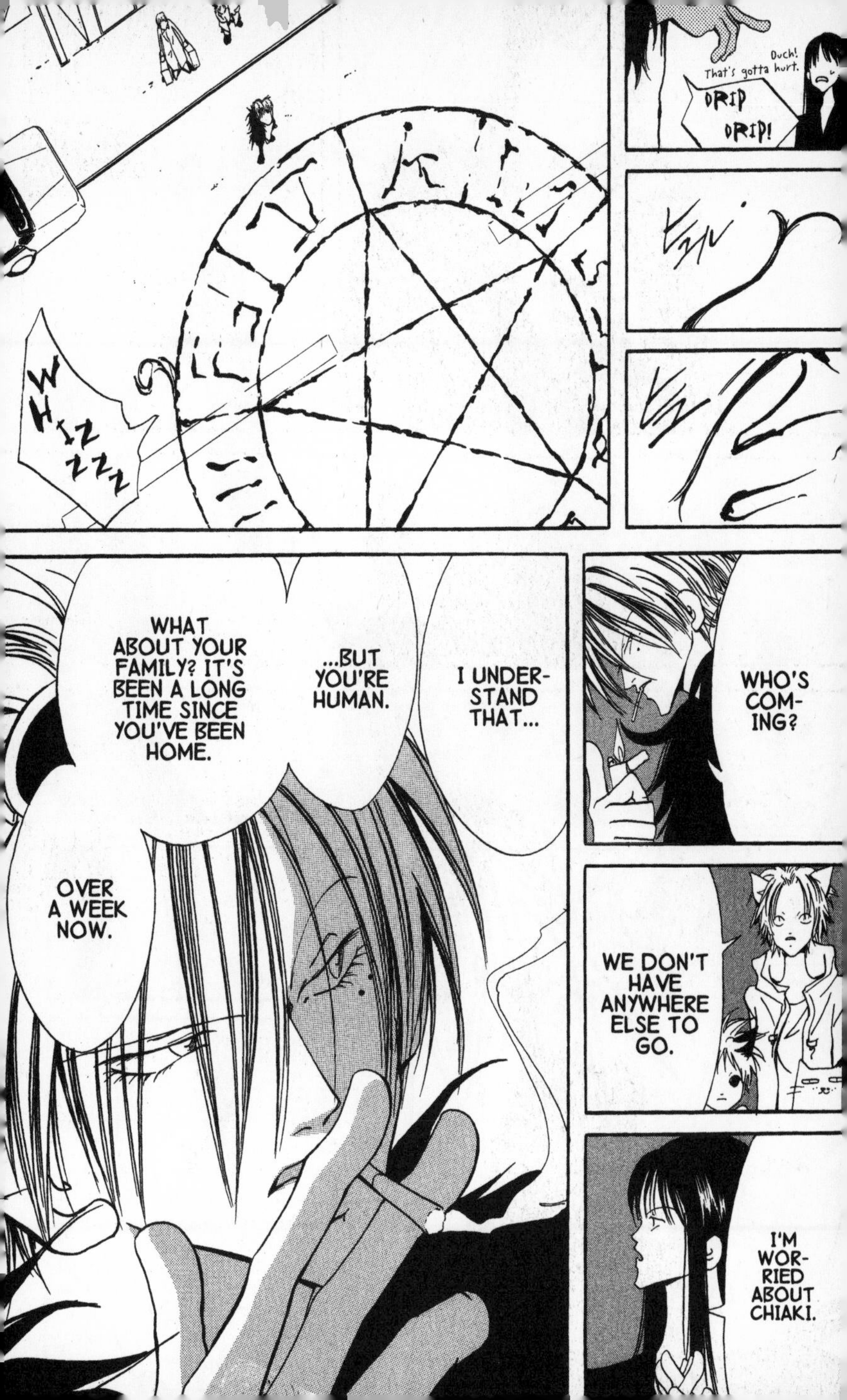

Ouch! That's gotta hurt.
DRIP DRIP!
ヒュル
ヒュ
WHIZZZZ
WHO'S COMING?
WE DON'T HAVE ANYWHERE ELSE TO GO.
I'M WORRIED ABOUT CHIAKI.
I UNDERSTAND THAT...
...BUT YOU'RE HUMAN.
WHAT ABOUT YOUR FAMILY? IT'S BEEN A LONG TIME SINCE YOU'VE BEEN HOME.
OVER A WEEK NOW.

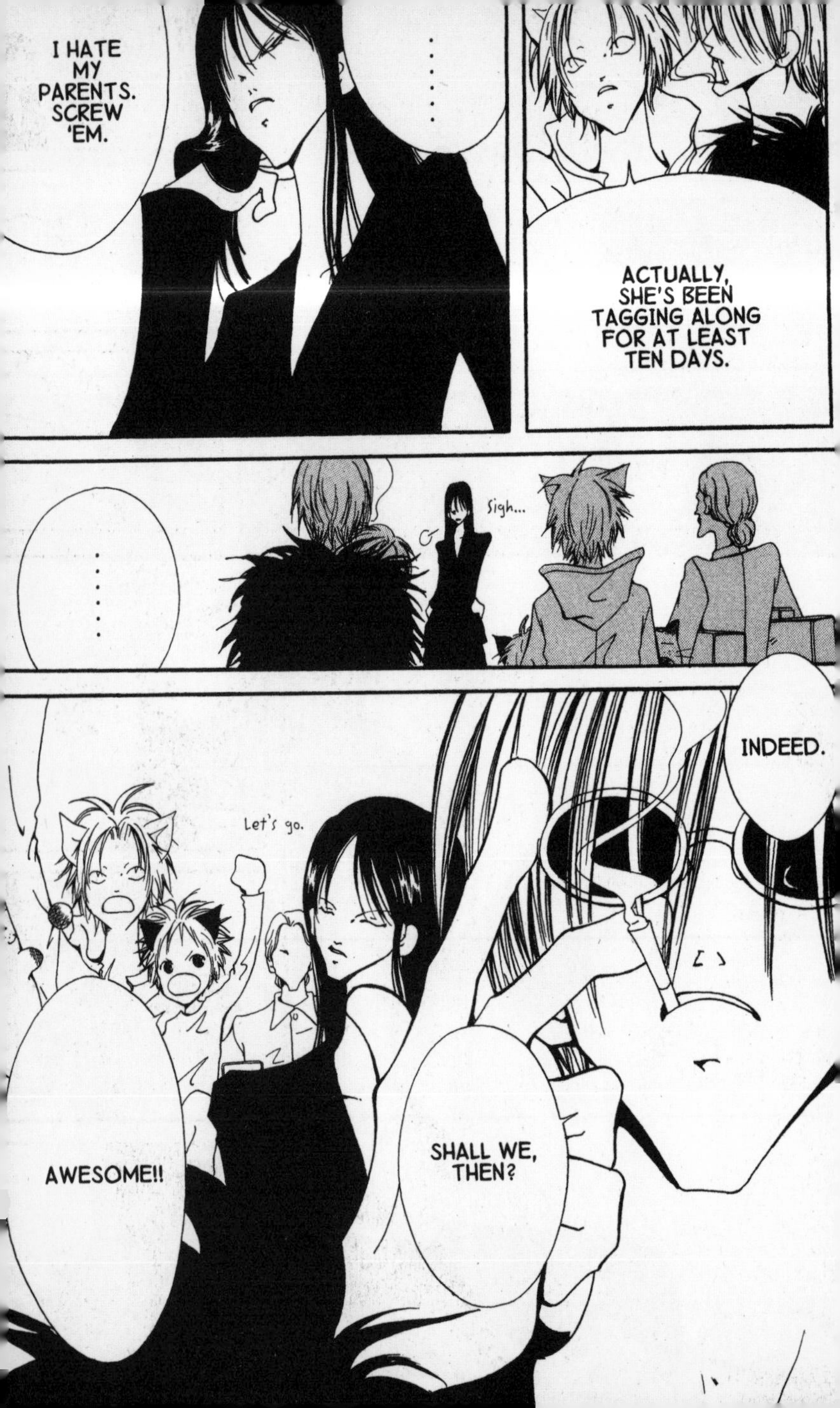
ACTUALLY, SHE'S BEEN TAGGING ALONG FOR AT LEAST TEN DAYS.
......
I HATE MY PARENTS. SCREW 'EM.
Sigh...
......
INDEED.
SHALL WE, THEN?
Let's go.
AWESOME!!

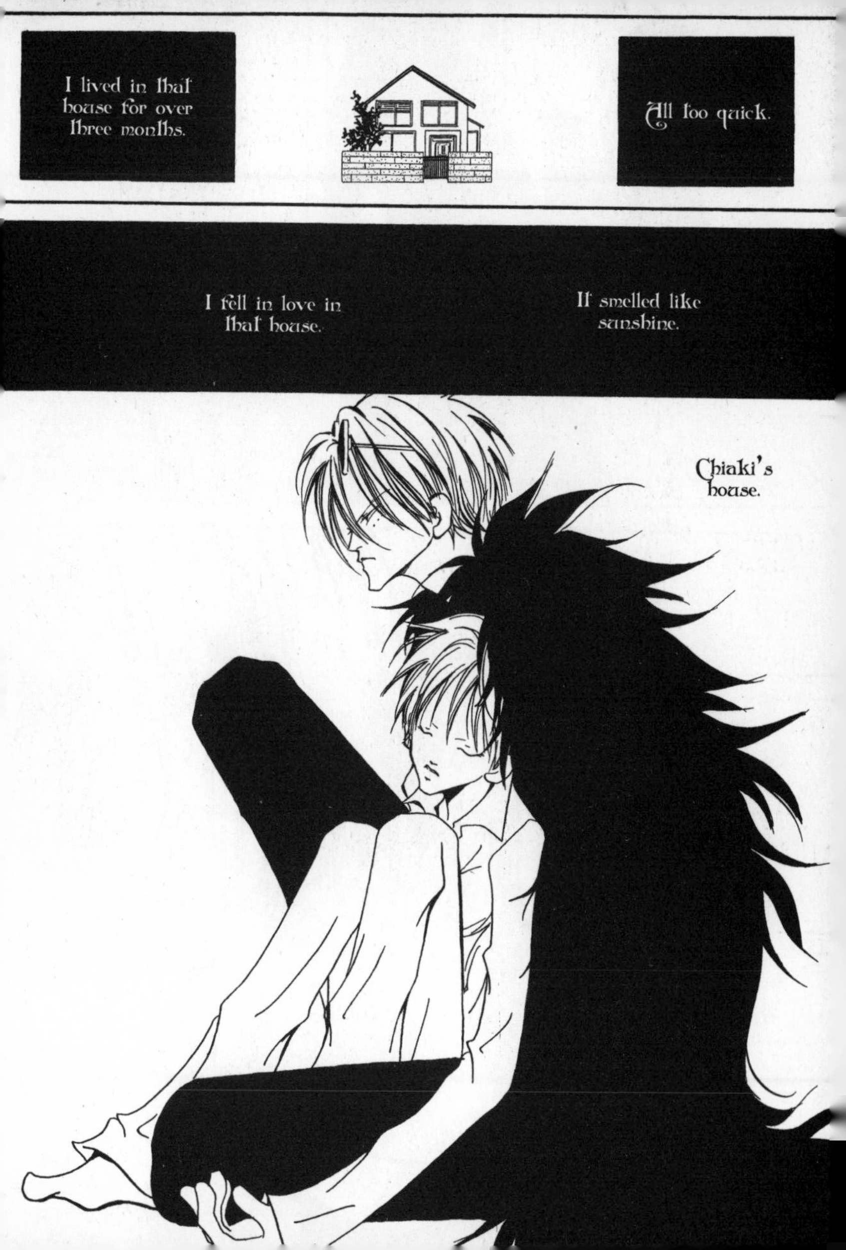
All too quick.
I lived in that house for over three months.
It smelled like sunshine.
I fell in love in that house.
Chiaki's house.

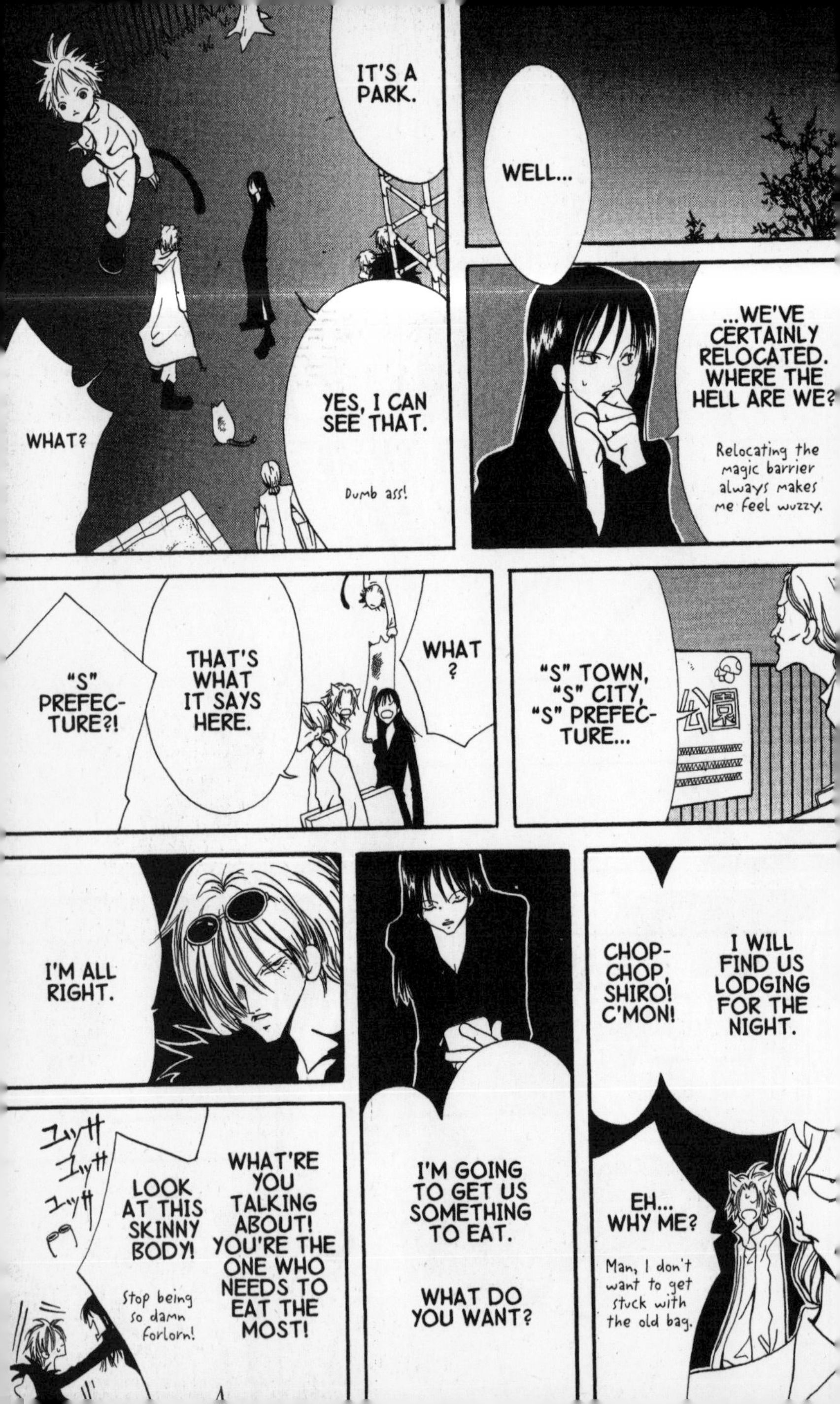
WELL...
...WE'VE CERTAINLY RELOCATED. WHERE THE HELL ARE WE?
Relocating the magic barrier always makes me feel wuzzy.
IT'S A PARK.
YES, I CAN SEE THAT.
Dumb ass!
WHAT?
"S" TOWN, "S" CITY, "S" PREFECTURE...
WHAT?
THAT'S WHAT IT SAYS HERE.
"S" PREFECTURE?!
I WILL FIND US LODGING FOR THE NIGHT.
CHOP-CHOP, SHIRO! C'MON!
EH... WHY ME?
Man, I don't want to get stuck with the old bag.
I'M GOING TO GET US SOMETHING TO EAT.
WHAT DO YOU WANT?
I'M ALL RIGHT.
WHAT'RE YOU TALKING ABOUT! YOU'RE THE ONE WHO NEEDS TO EAT THE MOST!
LOOK AT THIS SKINNY BODY!
Stop being so damn forlorn!
ユッサ
ユッサ
ユッサ

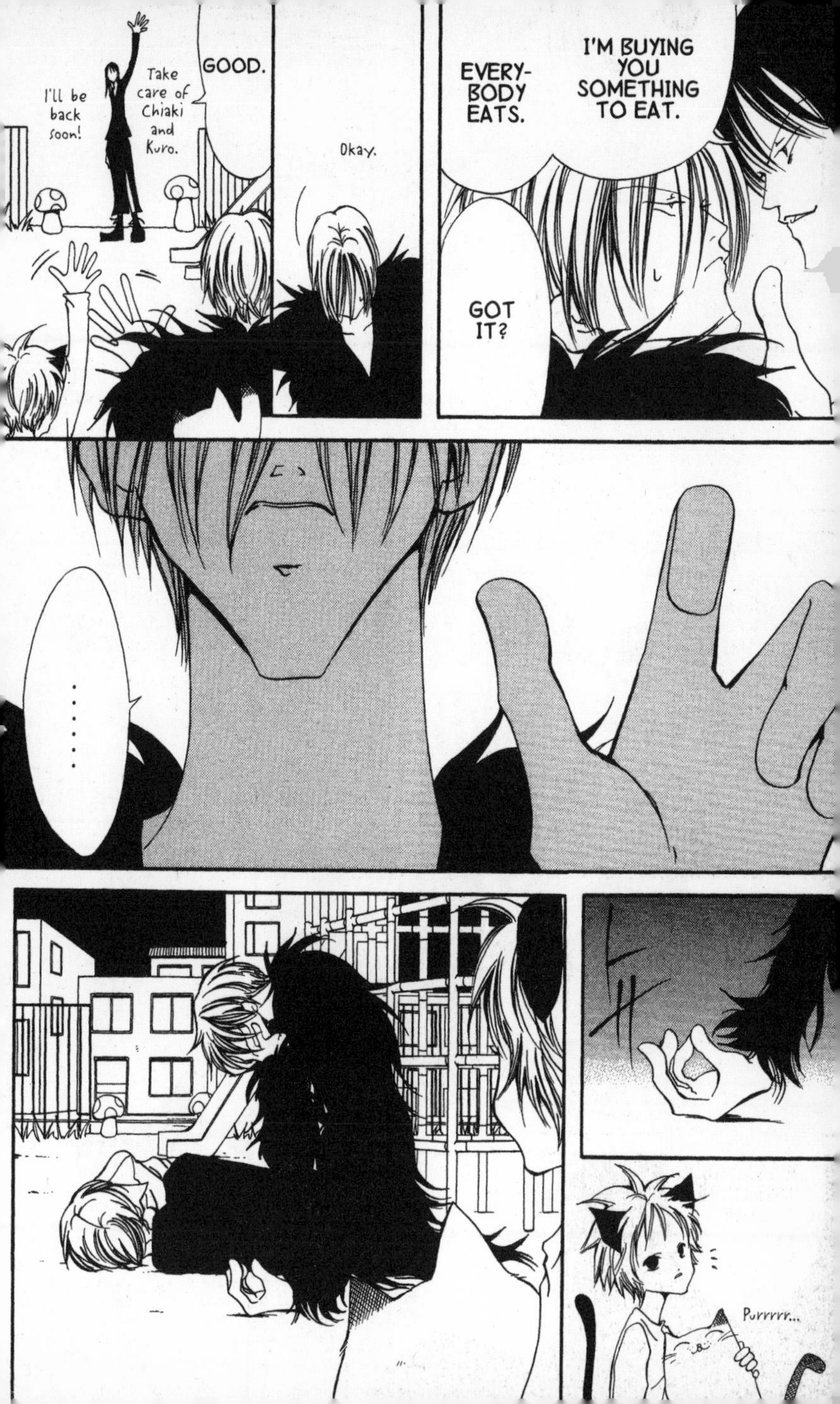
I'M BUYING YOU SOMETHING TO EAT.
EVERY-BODY EATS.
GOT IT?
Okay.
GOOD.
Take care of Chiaki and Kuro.
I'll be back soon!
......
Purrrrr...

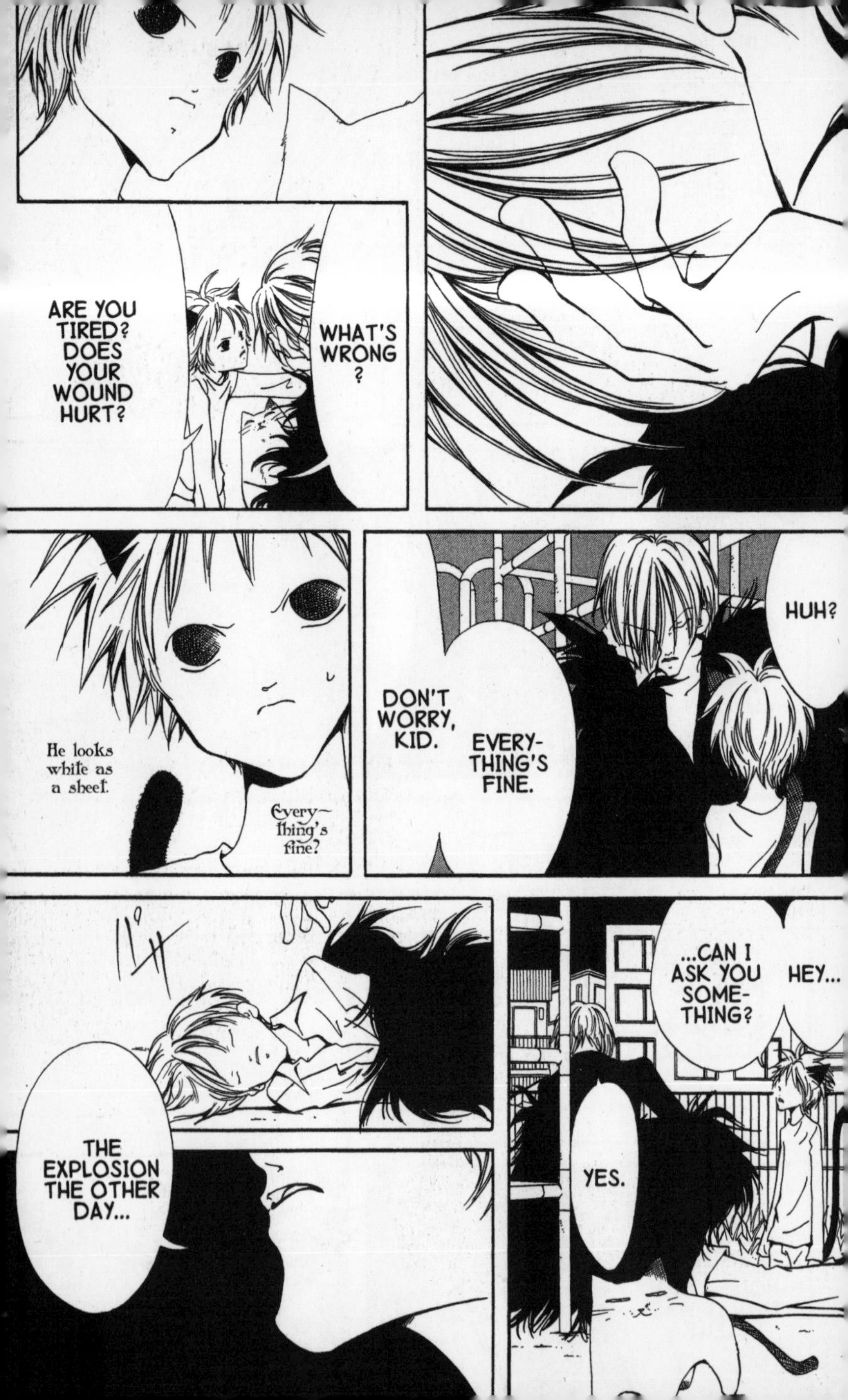
WHAT'S WRONG?
ARE YOU TIRED? DOES YOUR WOUND HURT?
HUH?
DON'T WORRY, KID.
EVERY-THING'S FINE.
He looks white as a sheet.
Every-thing's fine?
HEY...
...CAN I ASK YOU SOME-THING?
YES.
パッ
THE EXPLOSION THE OTHER DAY...

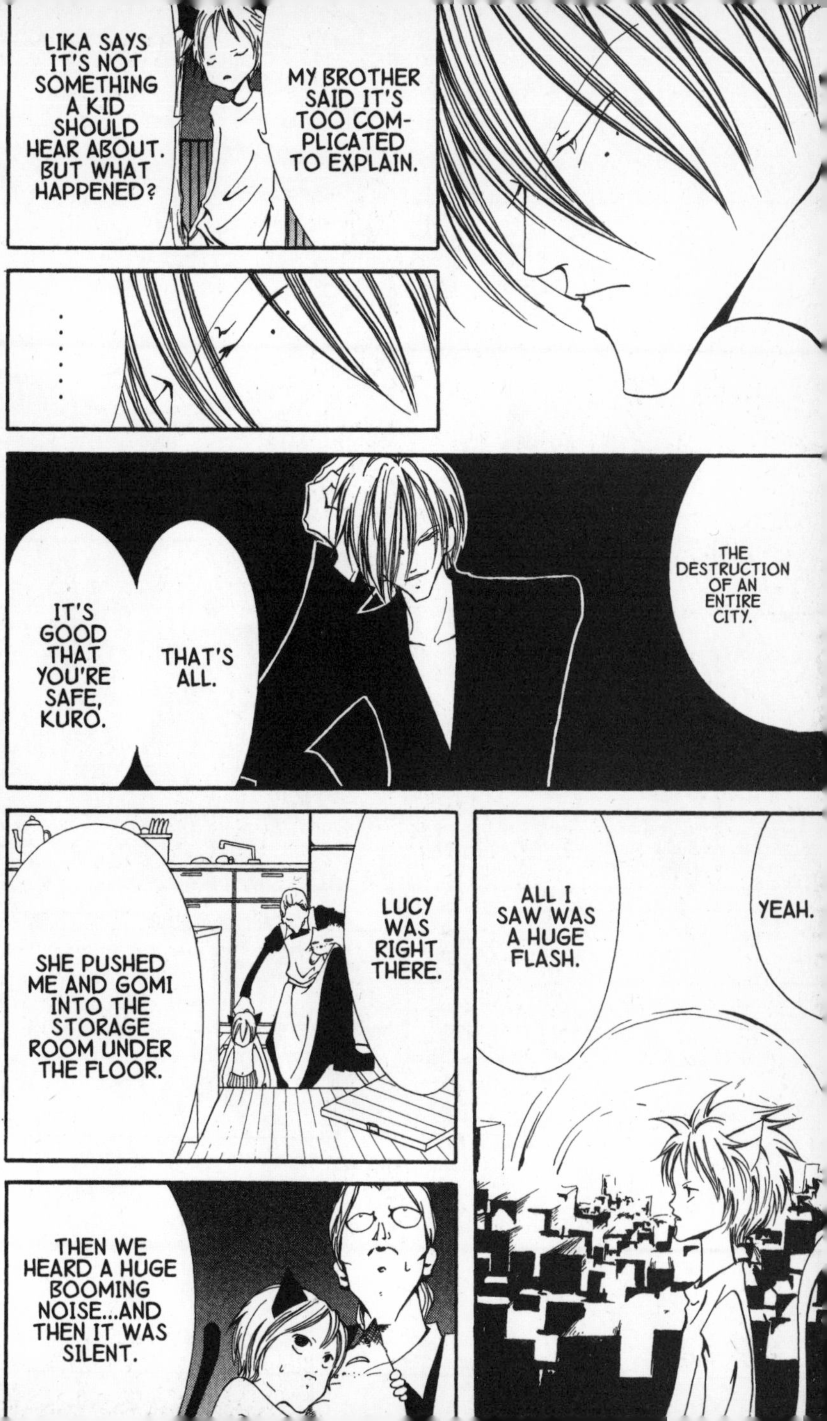
MY BROTHER SAID IT'S TOO COMPLICATED TO EXPLAIN.
LIKA SAYS IT'S NOT SOMETHING A KID SHOULD HEAR ABOUT. BUT WHAT HAPPENED?
......
THE DESTRUCTION OF AN ENTIRE CITY.
THAT'S ALL.
IT'S GOOD THAT YOU'RE SAFE, KURO.
YEAH.
ALL I SAW WAS A HUGE FLASH.
LUCY WAS RIGHT THERE.
SHE PUSHED ME AND GOMI INTO THE STORAGE ROOM UNDER THE FLOOR.
THEN WE HEARD A HUGE BOOMING NOISE...AND THEN IT WAS SILENT.

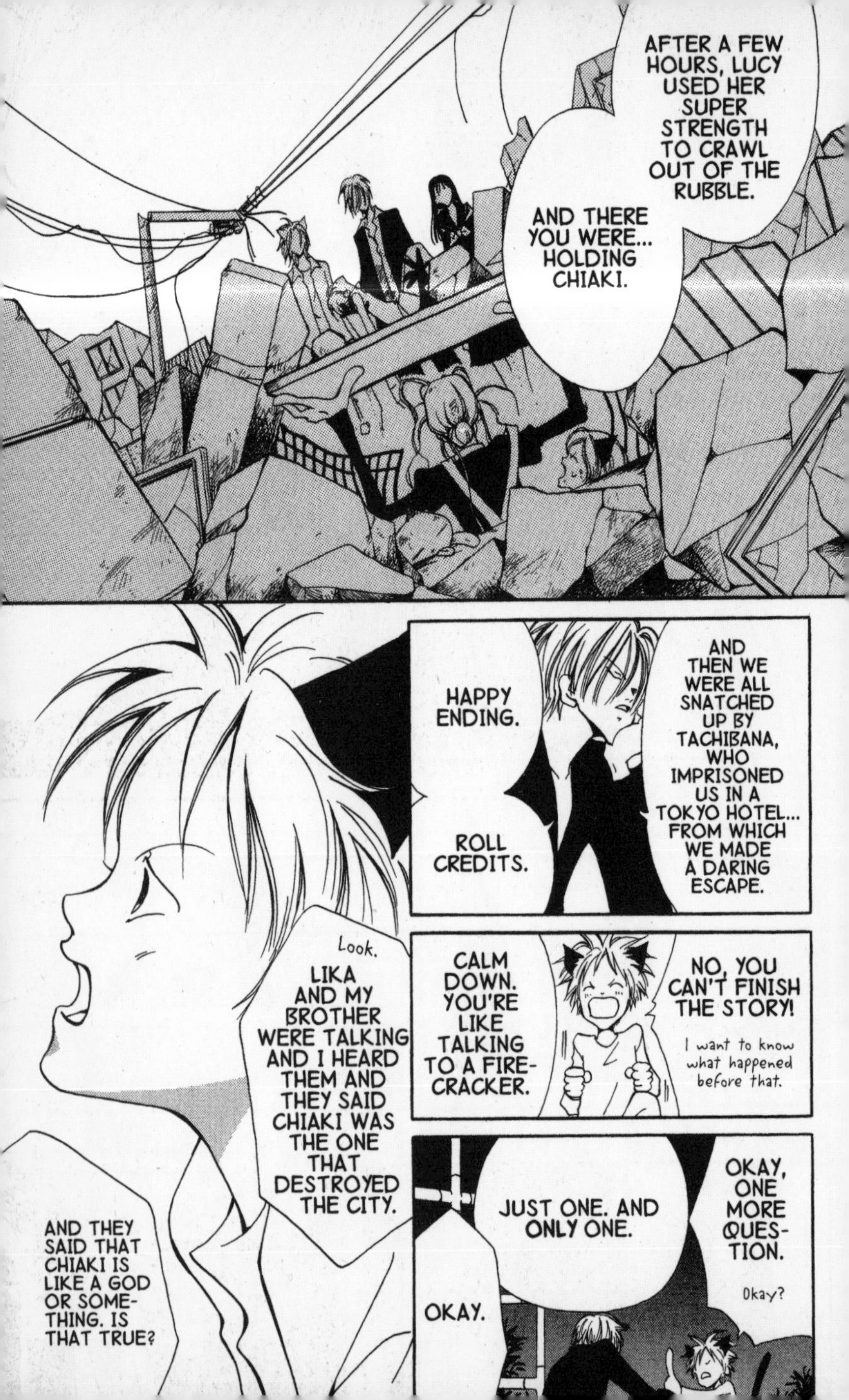
AFTER A FEW HOURS, LUCY USED HER SUPER STRENGTH TO CRAWL OUT OF THE RUBBLE.
AND THERE YOU WERE... HOLDING CHIAKI.
AND THEN WE WERE ALL SNATCHED UP BY TACHIBANA, WHO IMPRISONED US IN A TOKYO HOTEL... FROM WHICH WE MADE A DARING ESCAPE.
HAPPY ENDING.
ROLL CREDITS.
NO, YOU CAN'T FINISH THE STORY!
I want to know what happened before that.
CALM DOWN. YOU'RE LIKE TALKING TO A FIRE-CRACKER.
OKAY, ONE MORE QUES-TION.
Okay?
JUST ONE. AND ONLY ONE.
OKAY.
Look.
LIKA AND MY BROTHER WERE TALKING AND I HEARD THEM AND THEY SAID CHIAKI WAS THE ONE THAT DESTROYED THE CITY.
AND THEY SAID THAT CHIAKI IS LIKE A GOD OR SOME-THING. IS THAT TRUE?

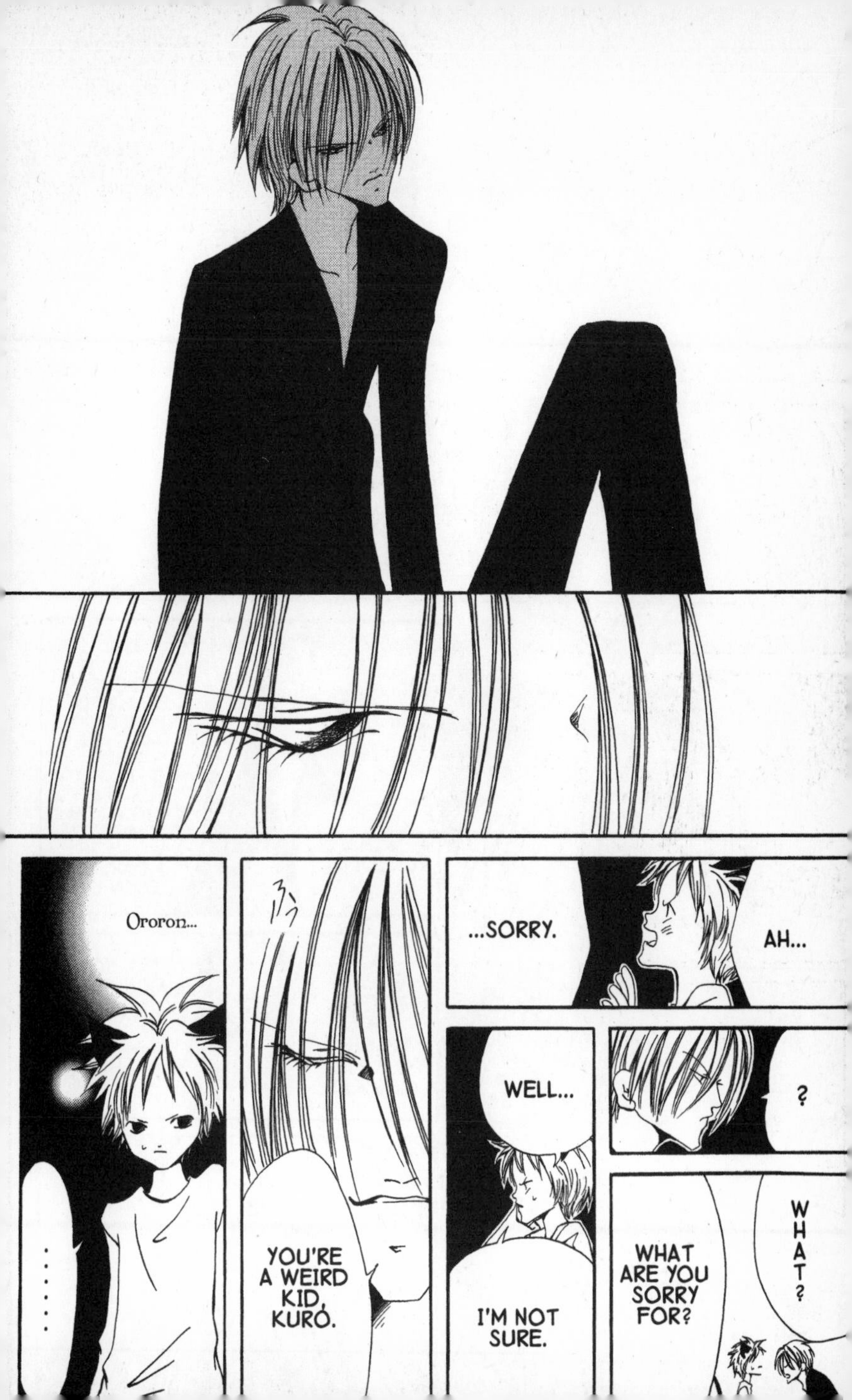
AH...
...SORRY.
?
WHAT?
WHAT ARE YOU SORRY FOR?
WELL...
I'M NOT SURE.
ふっ
YOU'RE A WEIRD KID, KURO.
Ororon...
......

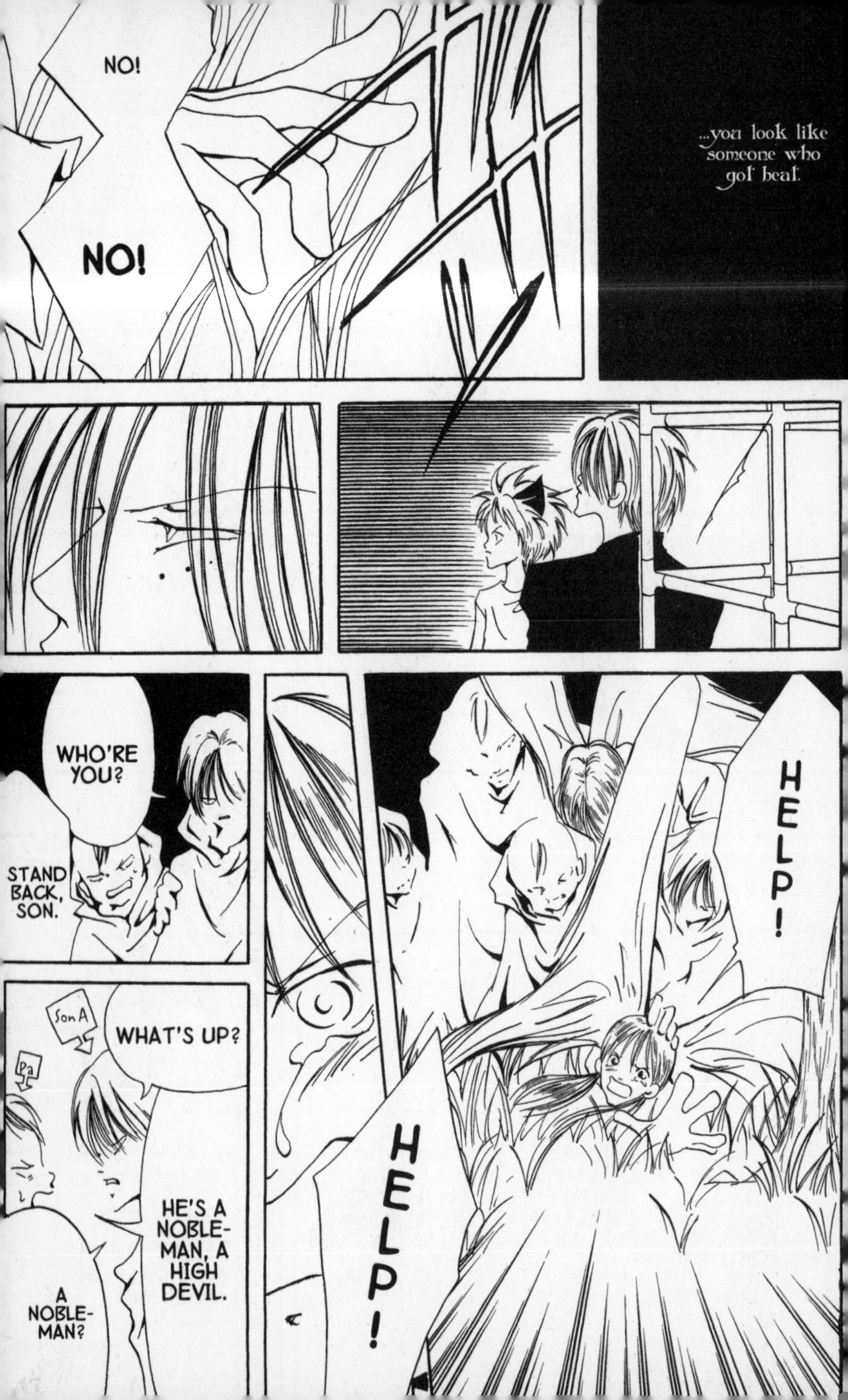
...you look like someone who got beat.
NO!
NO!
HELP!
HELP!
WHO'RE YOU?
STAND BACK, SON.
Son A
Pa
WHAT'S UP?
HE'S A NOBLE-MAN, A HIGH DEVIL.
A NOBLE-MAN?

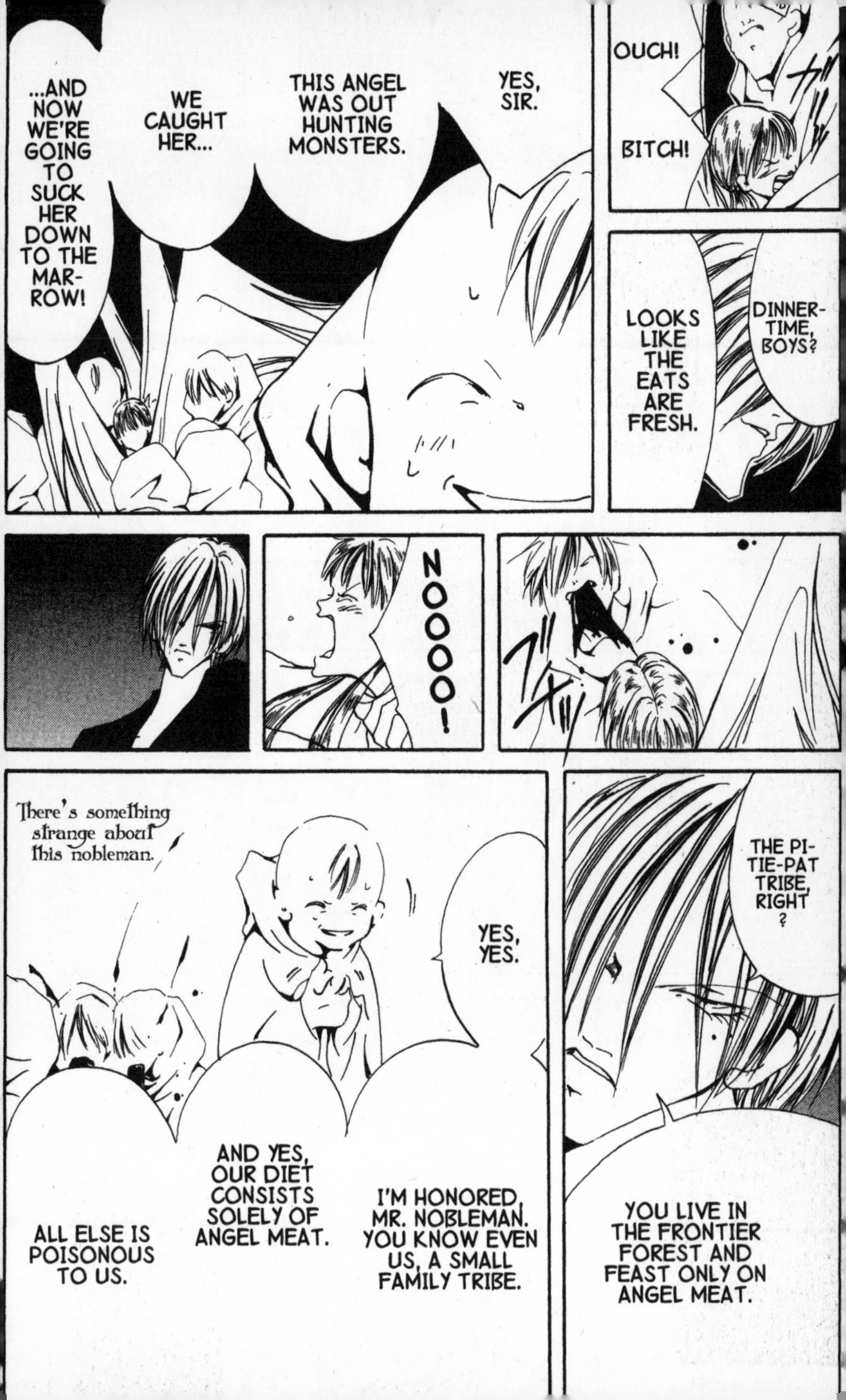
OUCH!
BITCH!
DINNER-TIME, BOYS?
LOOKS LIKE THE EATS ARE FRESH.
YES, SIR.
THIS ANGEL WAS OUT HUNTING MONSTERS.
WE CAUGHT HER...
...AND NOW WE'RE GOING TO SUCK HER DOWN TO THE MAR-ROW!
NOOOOO!
THE PI-TIE-PAT TRIBE, RIGHT?
YOU LIVE IN THE FRONTIER FOREST AND FEAST ONLY ON ANGEL MEAT.
YES, YES.
I'M HONORED, MR. NOBLEMAN. YOU KNOW EVEN US, A SMALL FAMILY TRIBE.
AND YES, OUR DIET CONSISTS SOLELY OF ANGEL MEAT.
ALL ELSE IS POISONOUS TO US.
There's something strange about this nobleman.

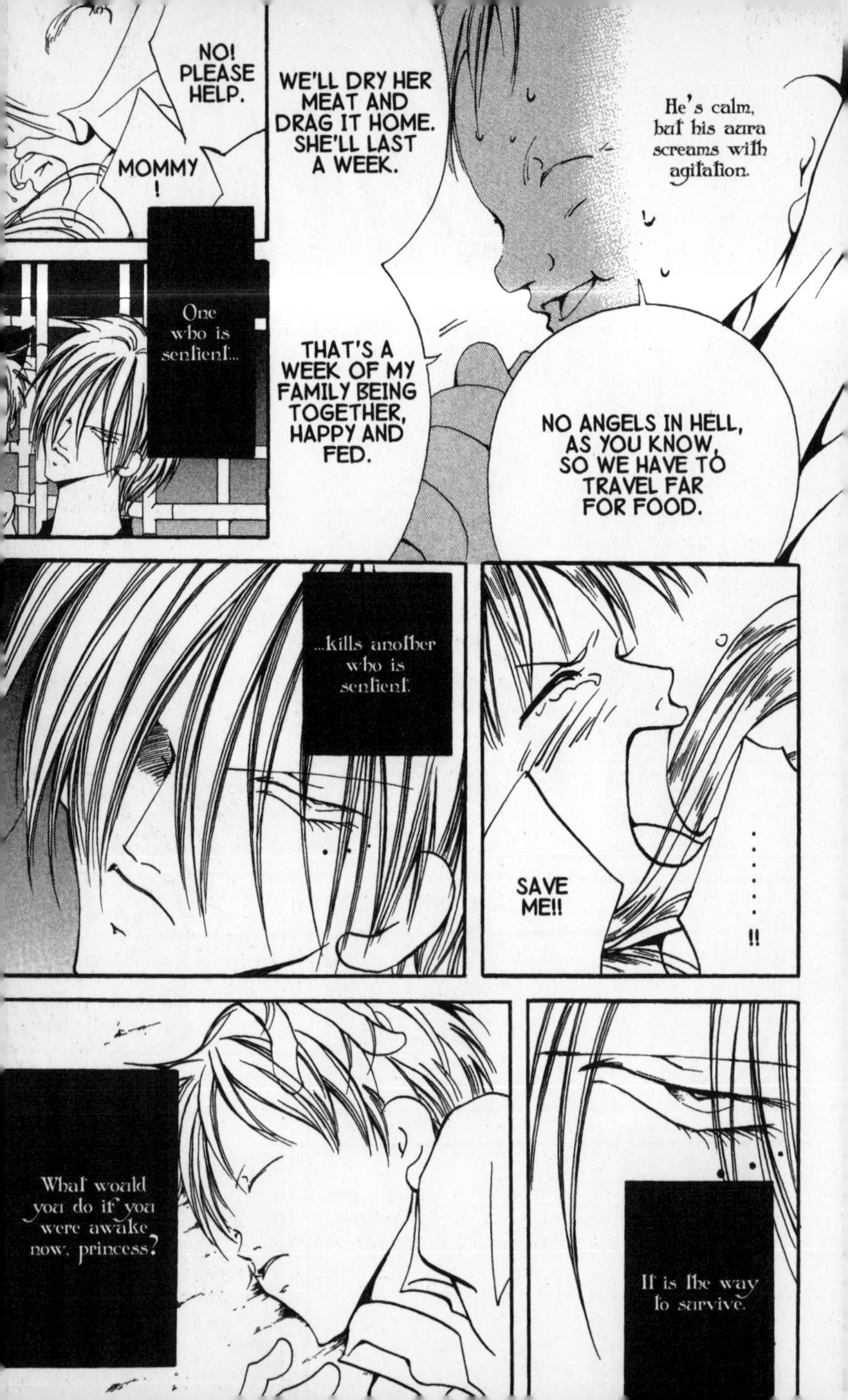
He's calm, but his aura screams with agitation.
WE'LL DRY HER MEAT AND DRAG IT HOME. SHE'LL LAST A WEEK.
NO ANGELS IN HELL, AS YOU KNOW, SO WE HAVE TO TRAVEL FAR FOR FOOD.
THAT'S A WEEK OF MY FAMILY BEING TOGETHER, HAPPY AND FED.
NO! PLEASE HELP.
MOMMY!
One who is sentient...
......!!
SAVE ME!!
...kills another who is sentient.
It is the way to survive.
What would you do if you were awake now, princess?

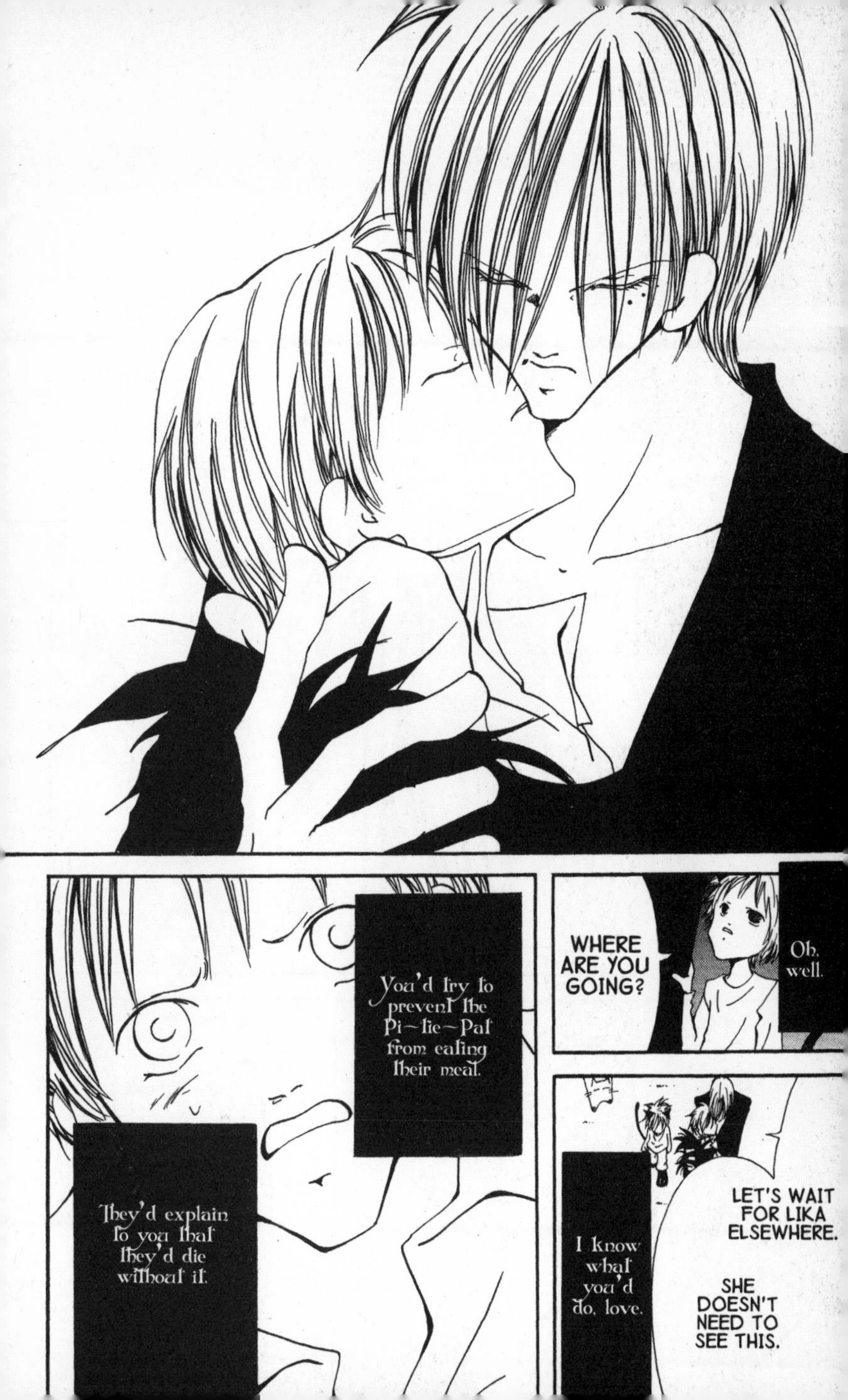
Oh, well.
WHERE ARE YOU GOING?
LET'S WAIT FOR LIKA ELSEWHERE.
SHE DOESN'T NEED TO SEE THIS.
I know what you'd do, love.
You'd try to prevent the Pi~tie~Pat from eating their meat.
They'd explain to you that they'd die without it.

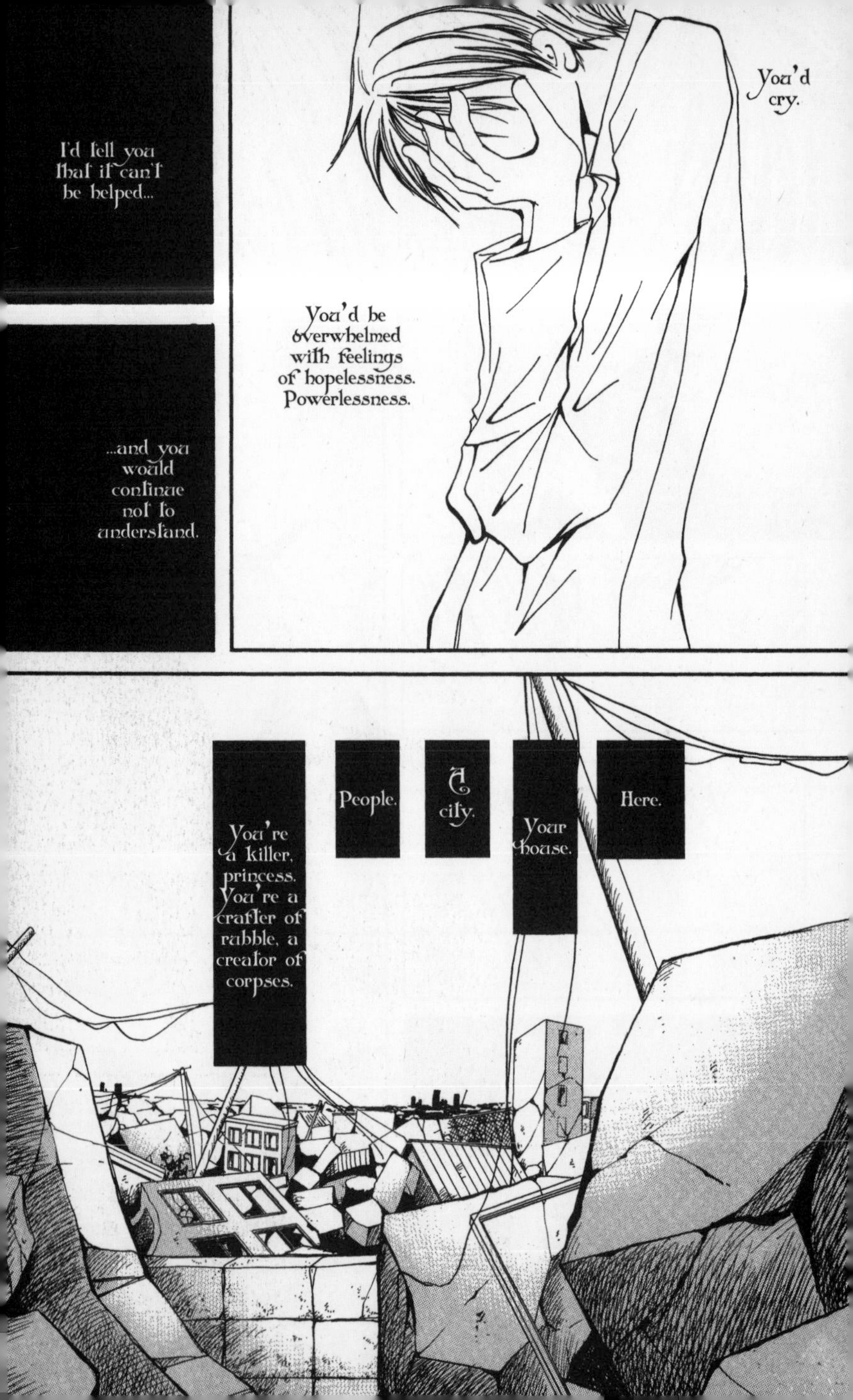
You'd cry.
You'd be overwhelmed with feelings of hopelessness. Powerlessness.
I'd tell you that it can't be helped...
...and you would continue not to understand.
Here.
Your house.
A city.
People.
You're a killer, princess. You're a crafter of rubble, a creator of corpses.

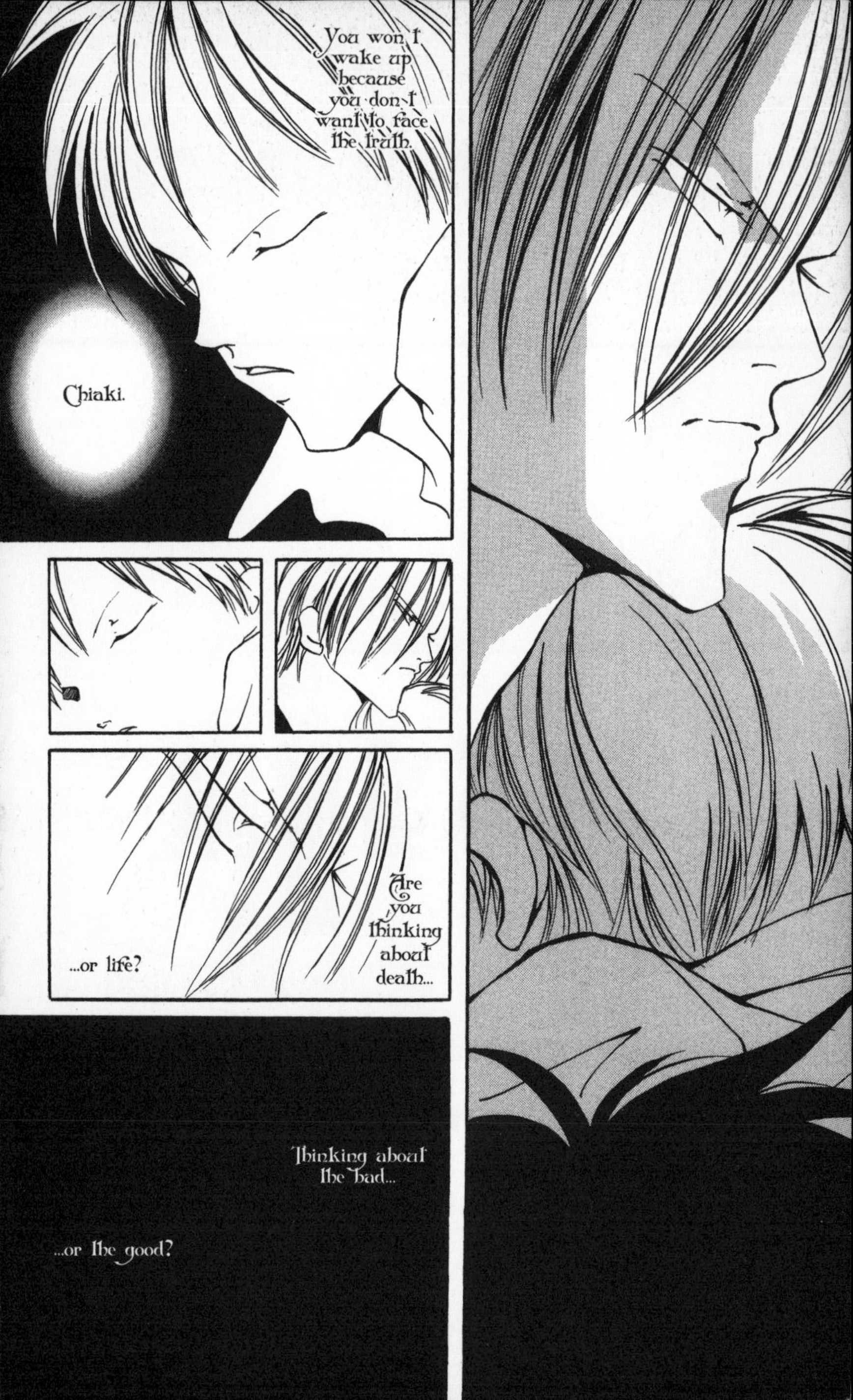
You won't wake up because you don't want to face the truth.
Chiaki.
Are you thinking about death...
...or life?
Thinking about the bad...
...or the good?

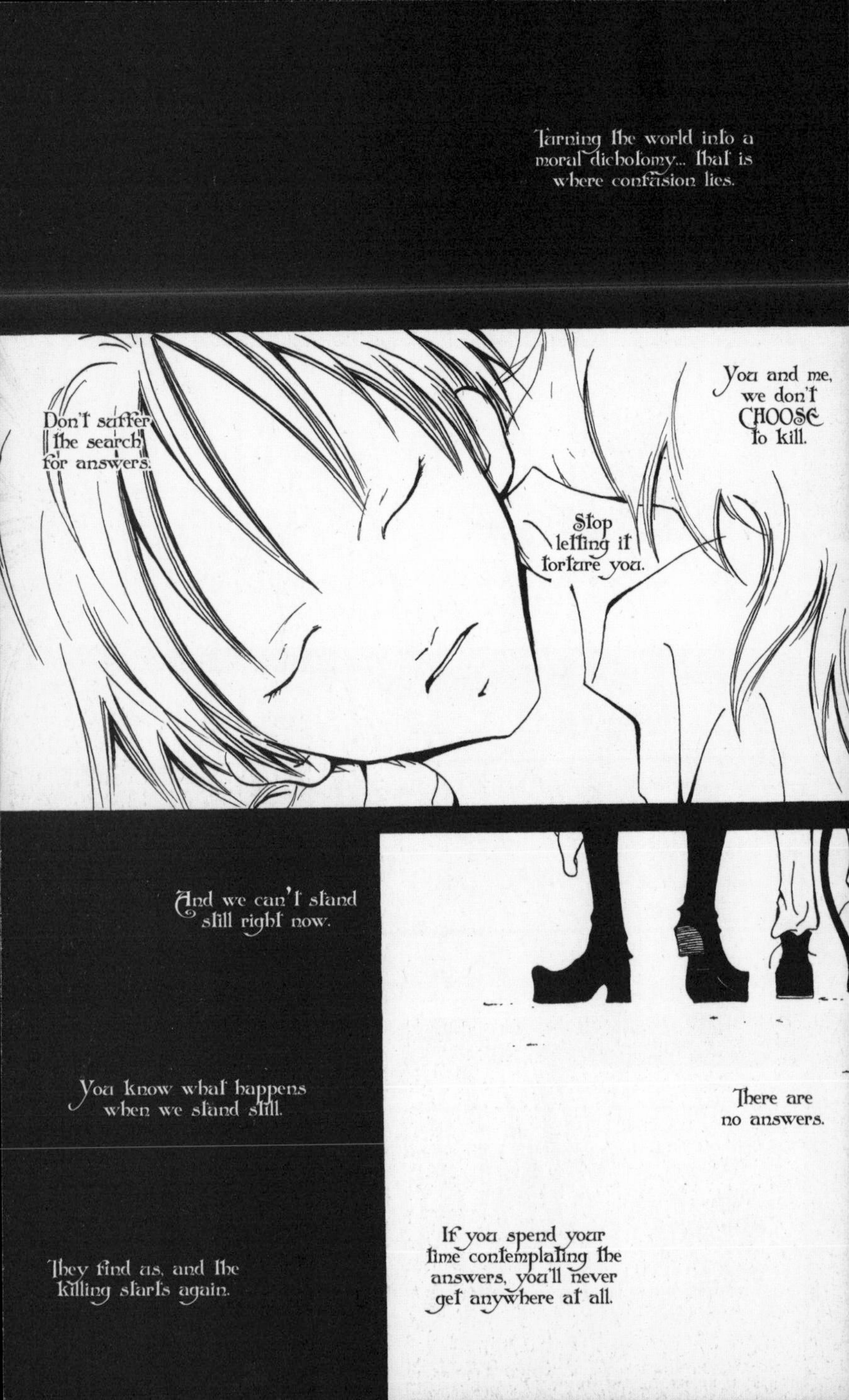
Turning the world into a moral dichotomy... that is where confusion lies.
You and me, we don't CHOOSE to kill.
Stop letting it torture you.
Don't suffer the search for answers.
There are no answers.
If you spend your time contemplating the answers, you'll never get anywhere at all.
And we can't stand still right now.
You know what happens when we stand still.
They find us, and the killing starts again.

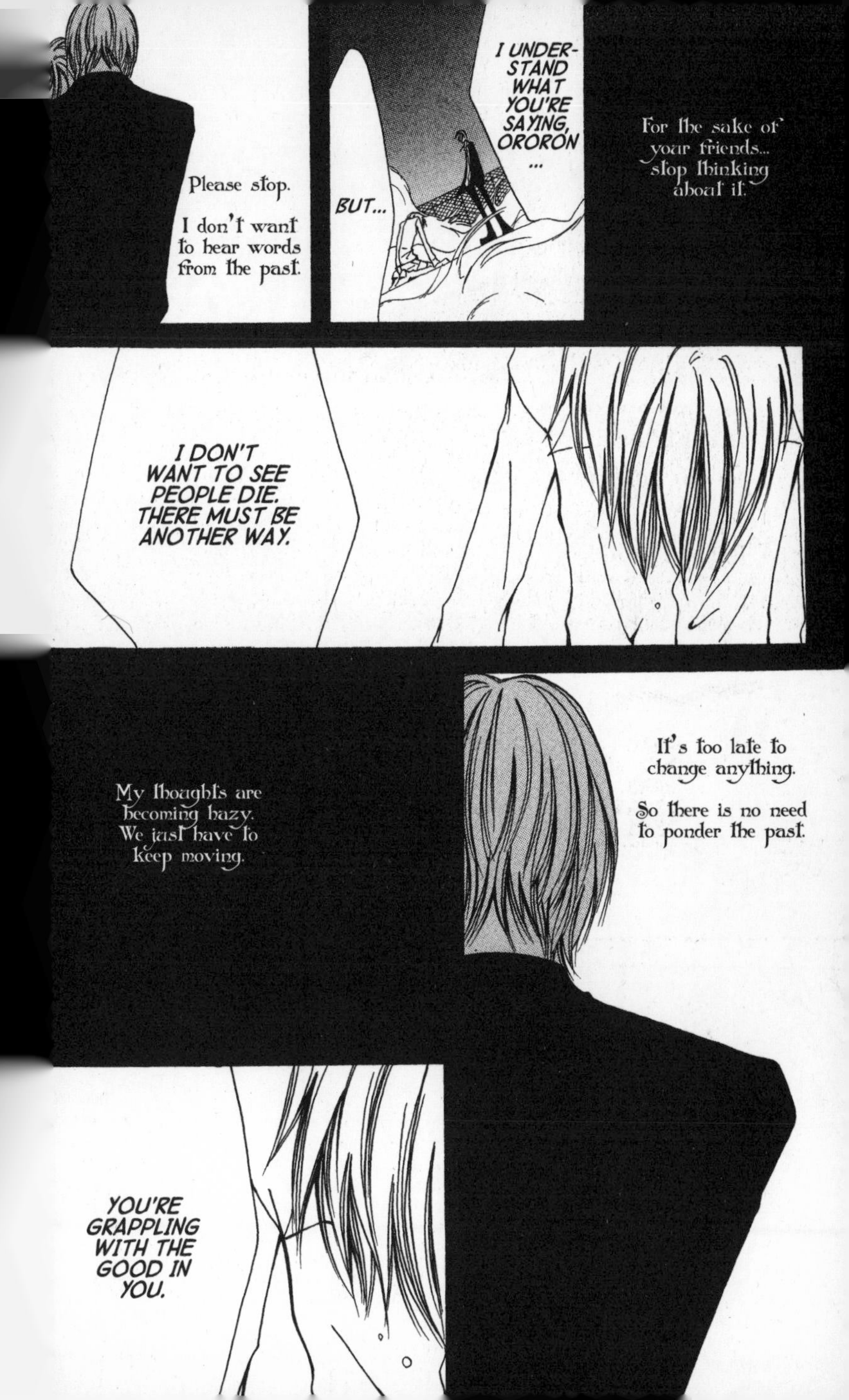
For the sake of your friends... stop thinking about it.
I UNDER-STAND WHAT YOU'RE SAYING, ORORON ...
BUT...
Please stop.
I don't want to hear words from the past.
I DON'T WANT TO SEE PEOPLE DIE. THERE MUST BE ANOTHER WAY.
It's too late to change anything.
So there is no need to ponder the past.
My thoughts are becoming hazy. We just have to keep moving.
YOU'RE GRAPPLING WITH THE GOOD IN YOU.

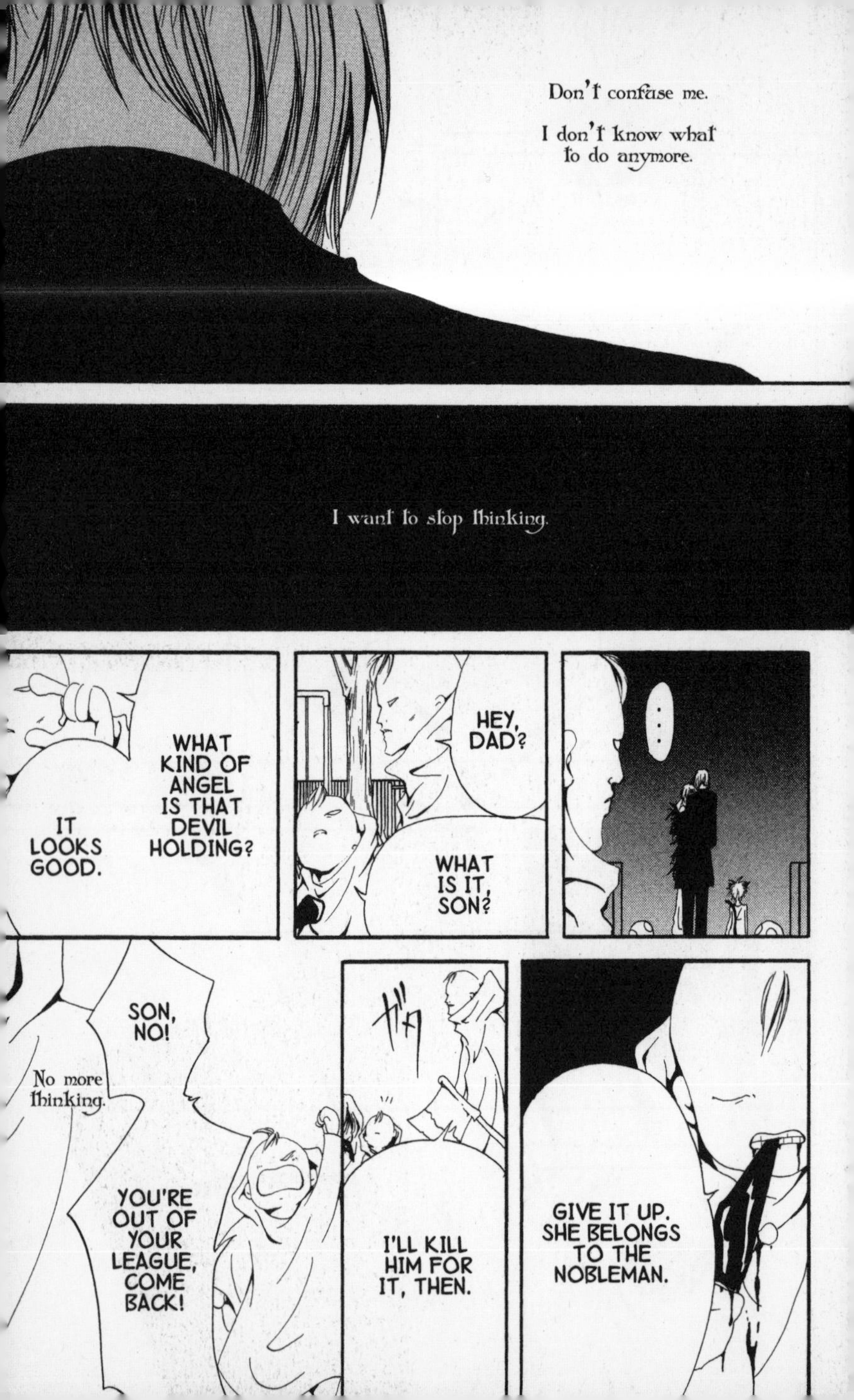
Don't confuse me.
I don't know what to do anymore.
I want to stop thinking.
...
HEY, DAD?
WHAT IS IT, SON?
WHAT KIND OF ANGEL IS THAT DEVIL HOLDING?
IT LOOKS GOOD.
GIVE IT UP. SHE BELONGS TO THE NOBLEMAN.
I'LL KILL HIM FOR IT, THEN.
SON, NO!
YOU'RE OUT OF YOUR LEAGUE, COME BACK!
No more thinking.

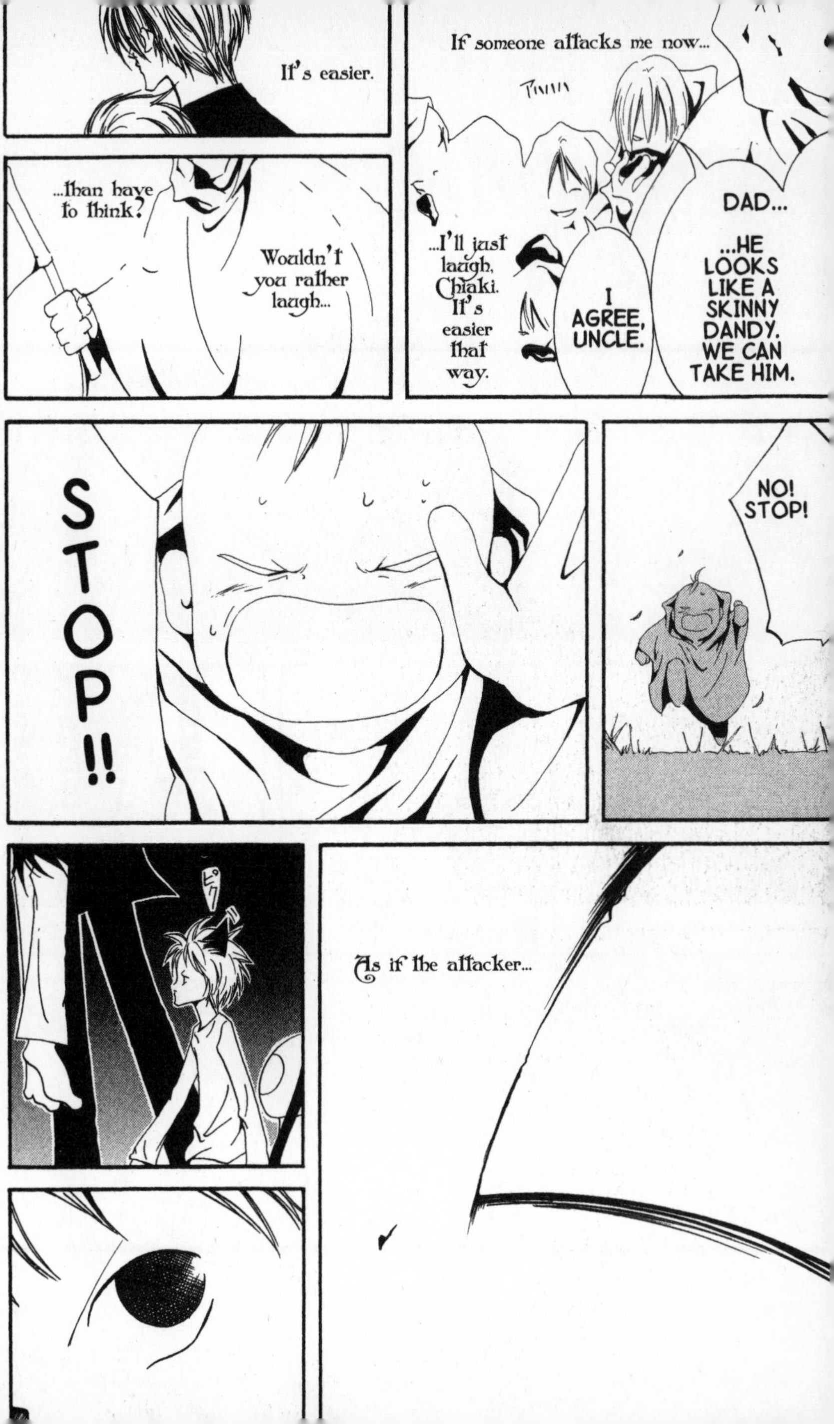
If someone attacks me now...
DAD...
...HE LOOKS LIKE A SKINNY DANDY. WE CAN TAKE HIM.
...I'll just laugh, Chiaki. It's easier that way.
I AGREE, UNCLE.
It's easier.
Wouldn't you rather laugh...
...than have to think?
NO! STOP!
STOP!!
As if the attacker...

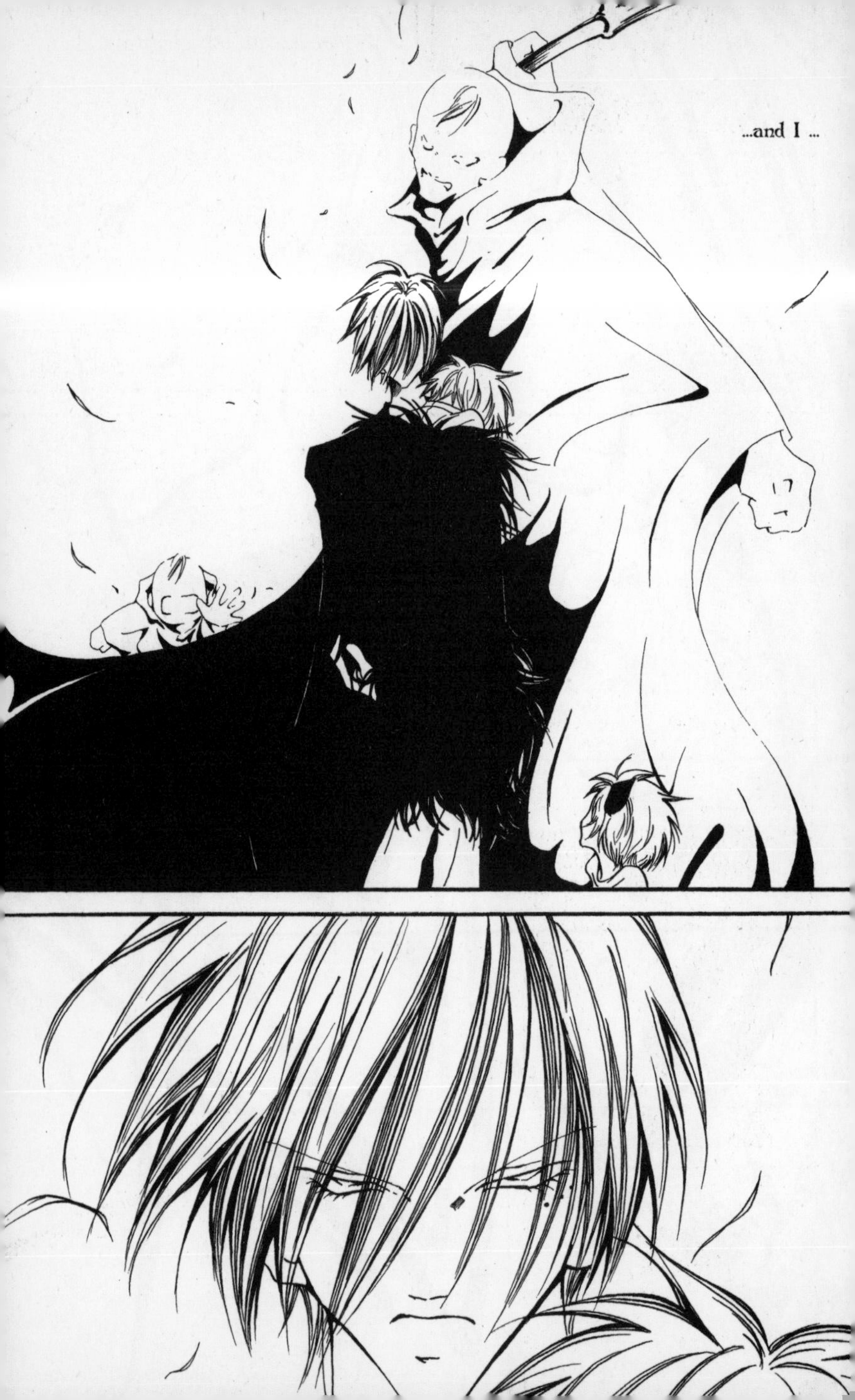
...and I ...

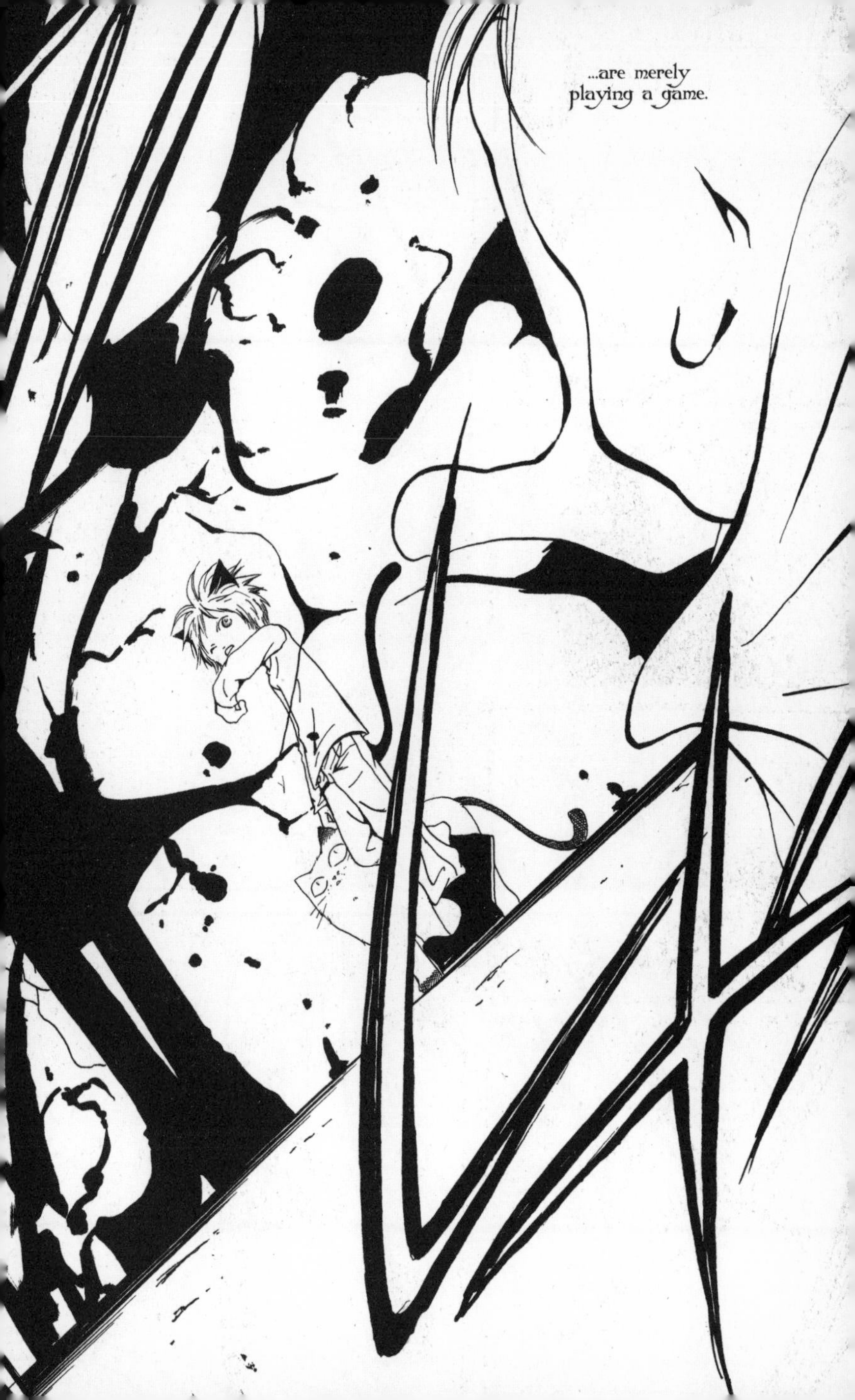
...are merely
playing a game.

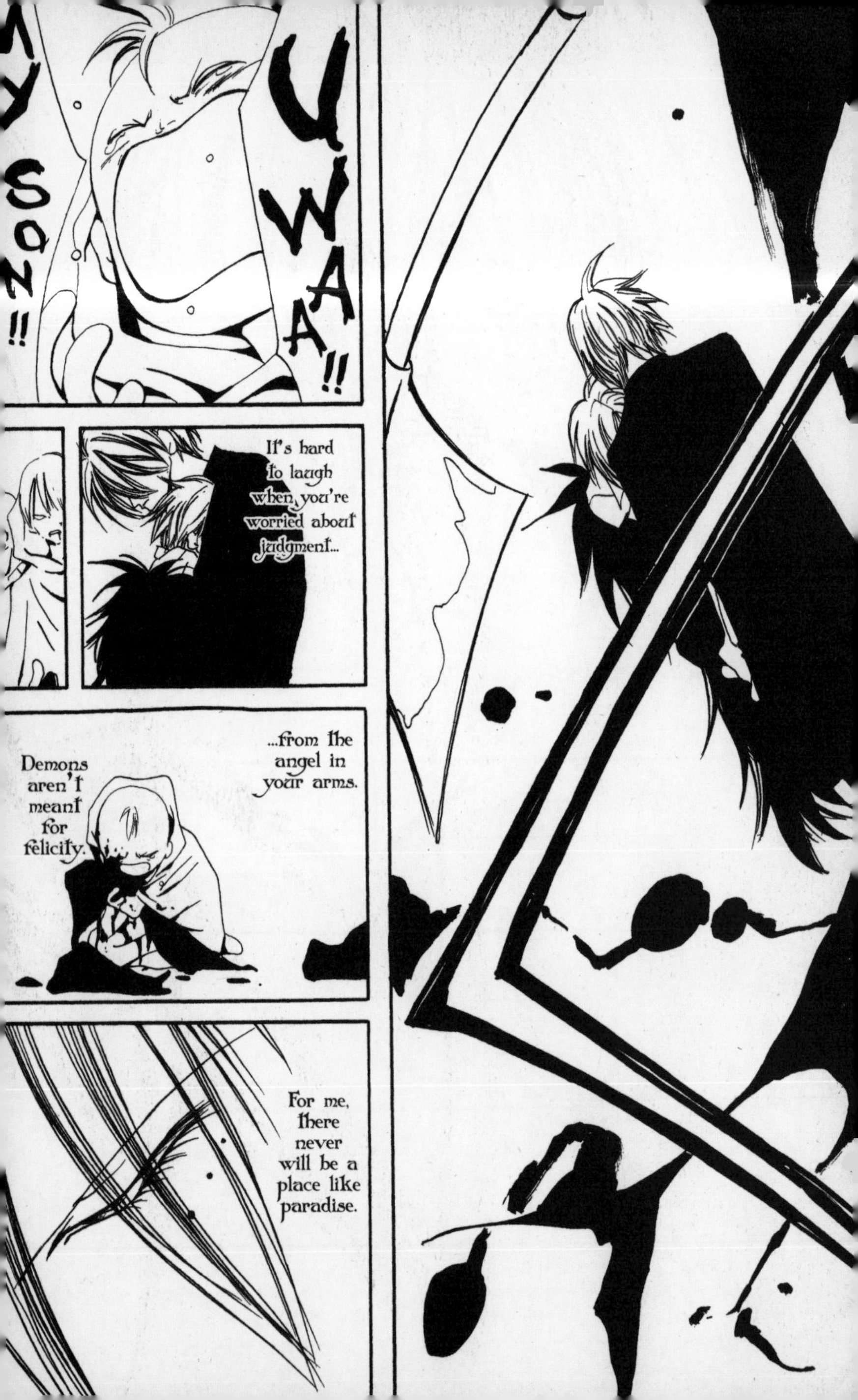
UWAA!!
MY SON!!
It's hard to laugh when you're worried about judgment...
...from the angel in your arms.
Demons aren't meant for felicity.
For me, there never will be a place like paradise.

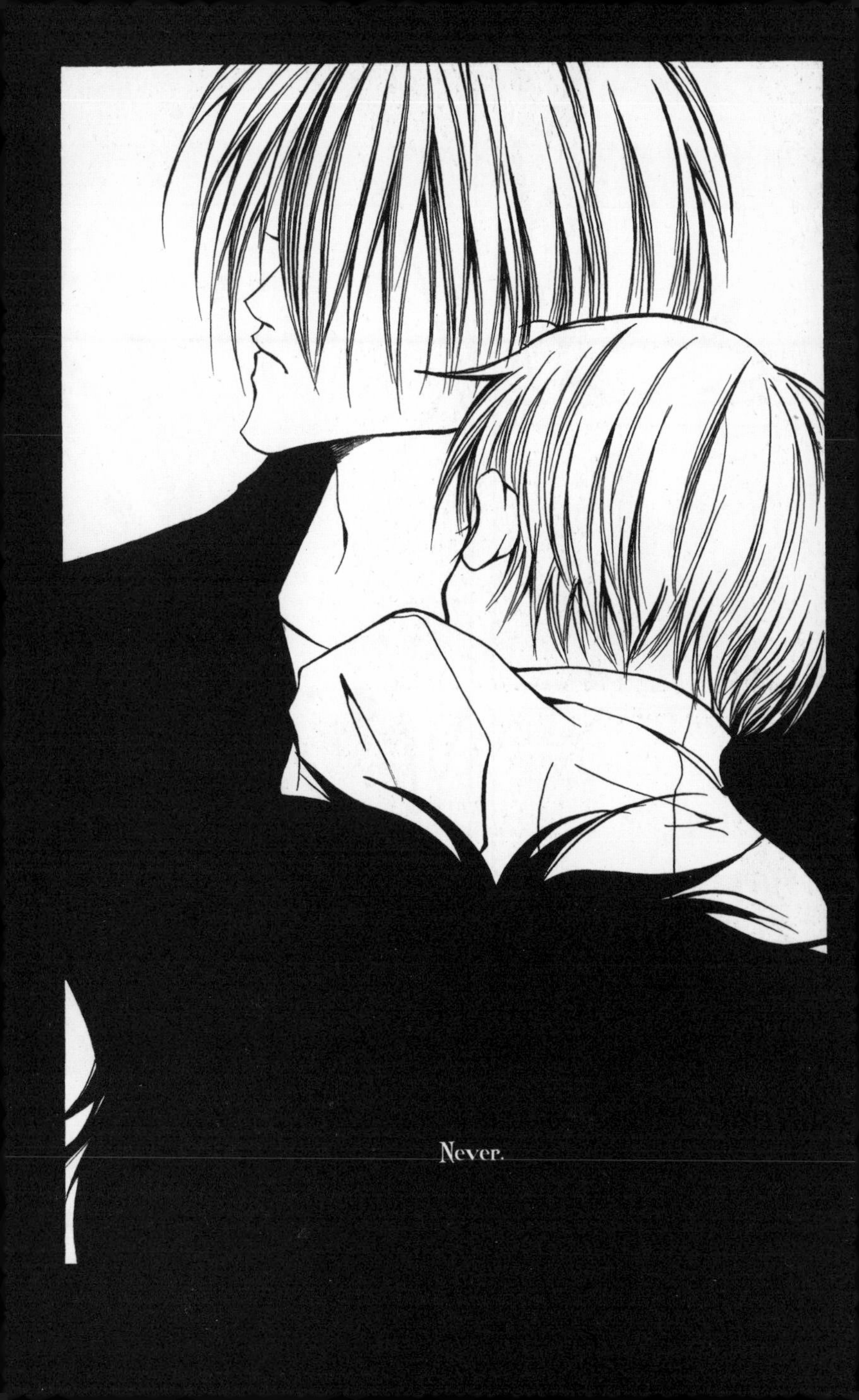
Never.

Oh, I forgot
to tell you.
Everyone died.

Your
friends,
I mean.

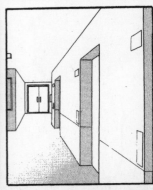

Are
you
mad?

CHEW
CHEW!

GULP!

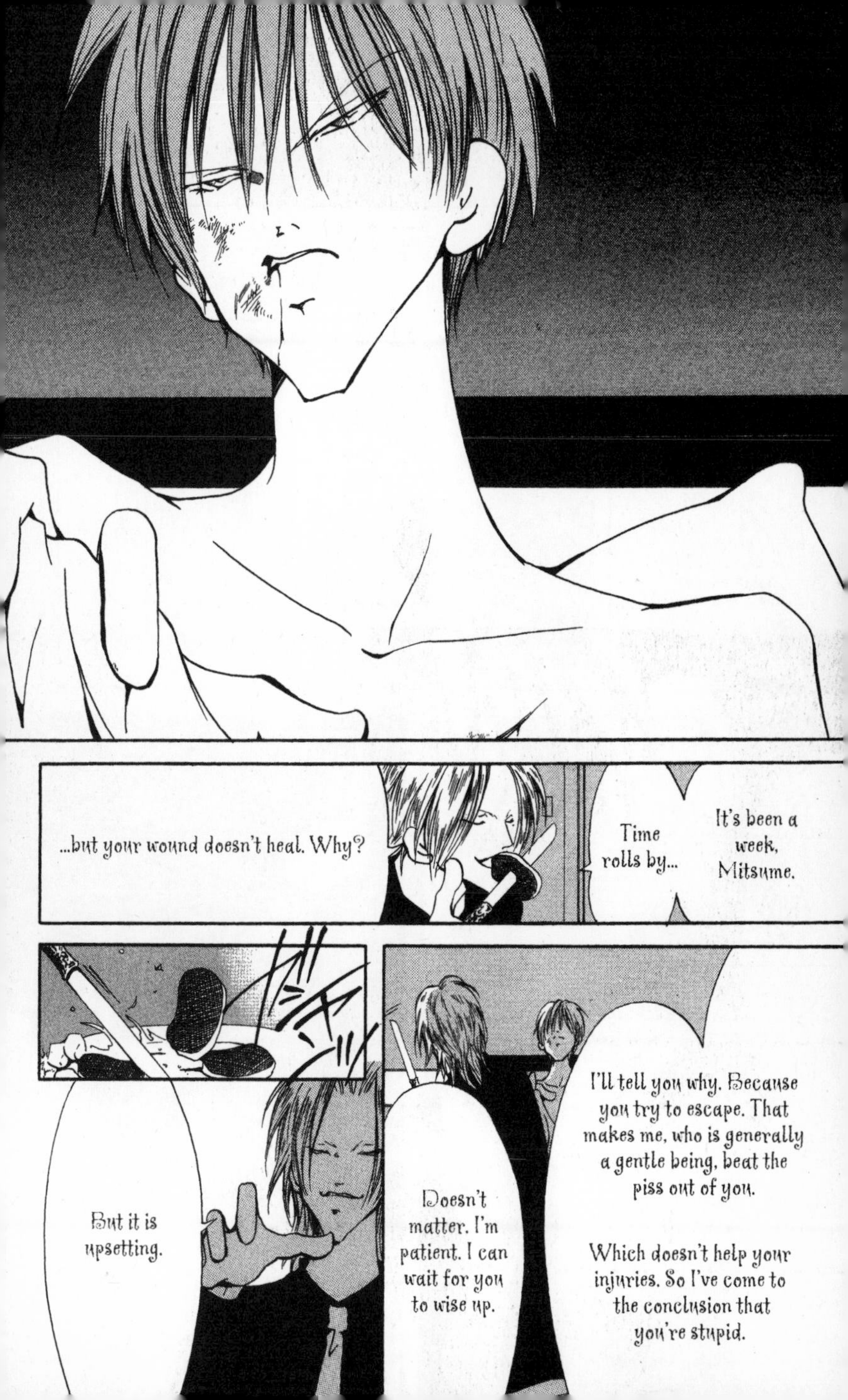
It's been a week, Mitsume.
Time rolls by...
...but your wound doesn't heal. Why?
I'll tell you why. Because you try to escape. That makes me, who is generally a gentle being, beat the piss out of you.
Which doesn't help your injuries. So I've come to the conclusion that you're stupid.
Doesn't matter. I'm patient. I can wait for you to wise up.
But it is upsetting.

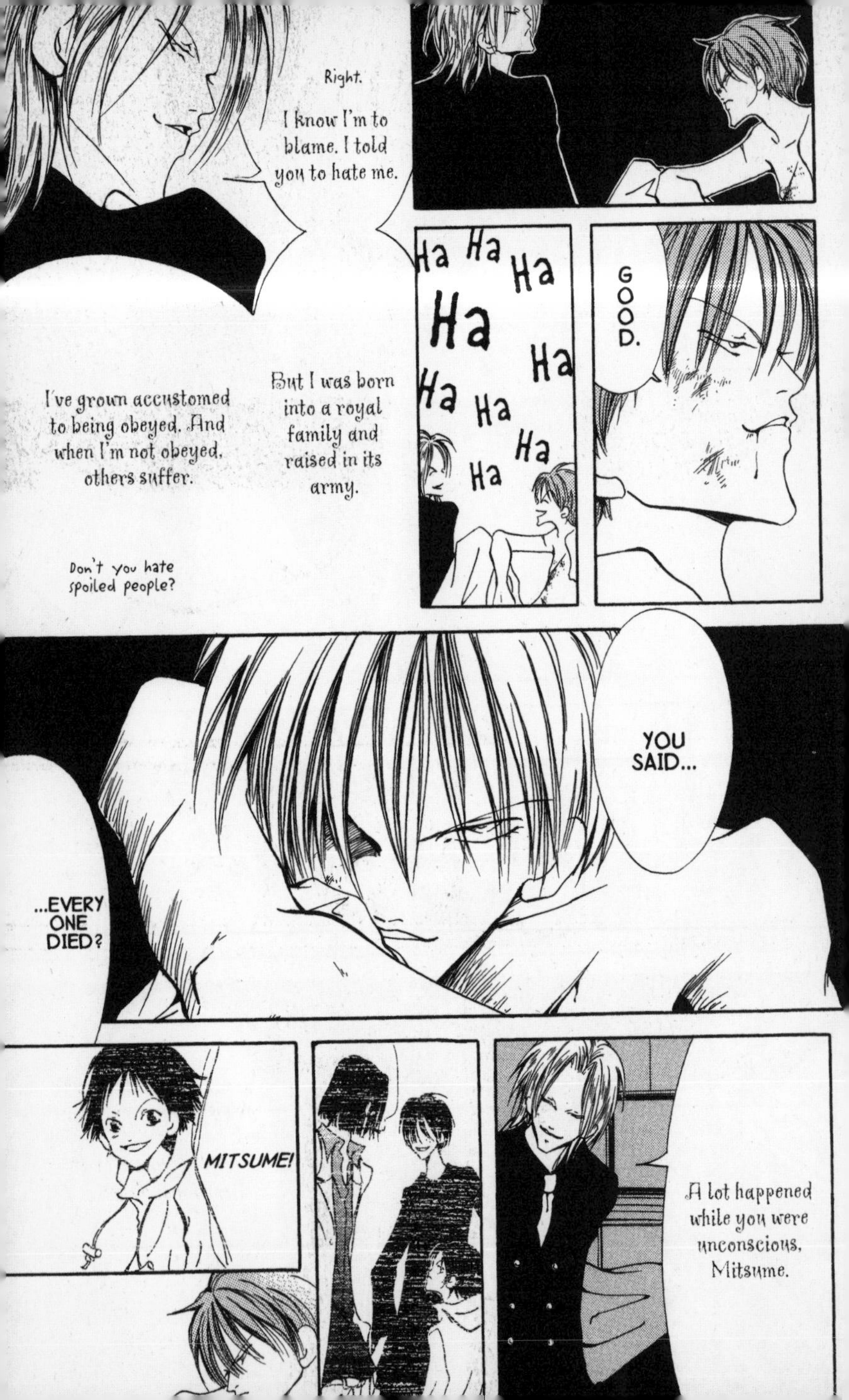

Right.
I know I'm to blame. I told you to hate me.
But I was born into a royal family and raised in its army.
I've grown accustomed to being obeyed. And when I'm not obeyed, others suffer.
Don't you hate spoiled people?
GOOD.
Ha Ha Ha Ha Ha Ha Ha Ha Ha
YOU SAID...
...EVERY ONE DIED?
A lot happened while you were unconscious, Mitsume.
MITSUME!

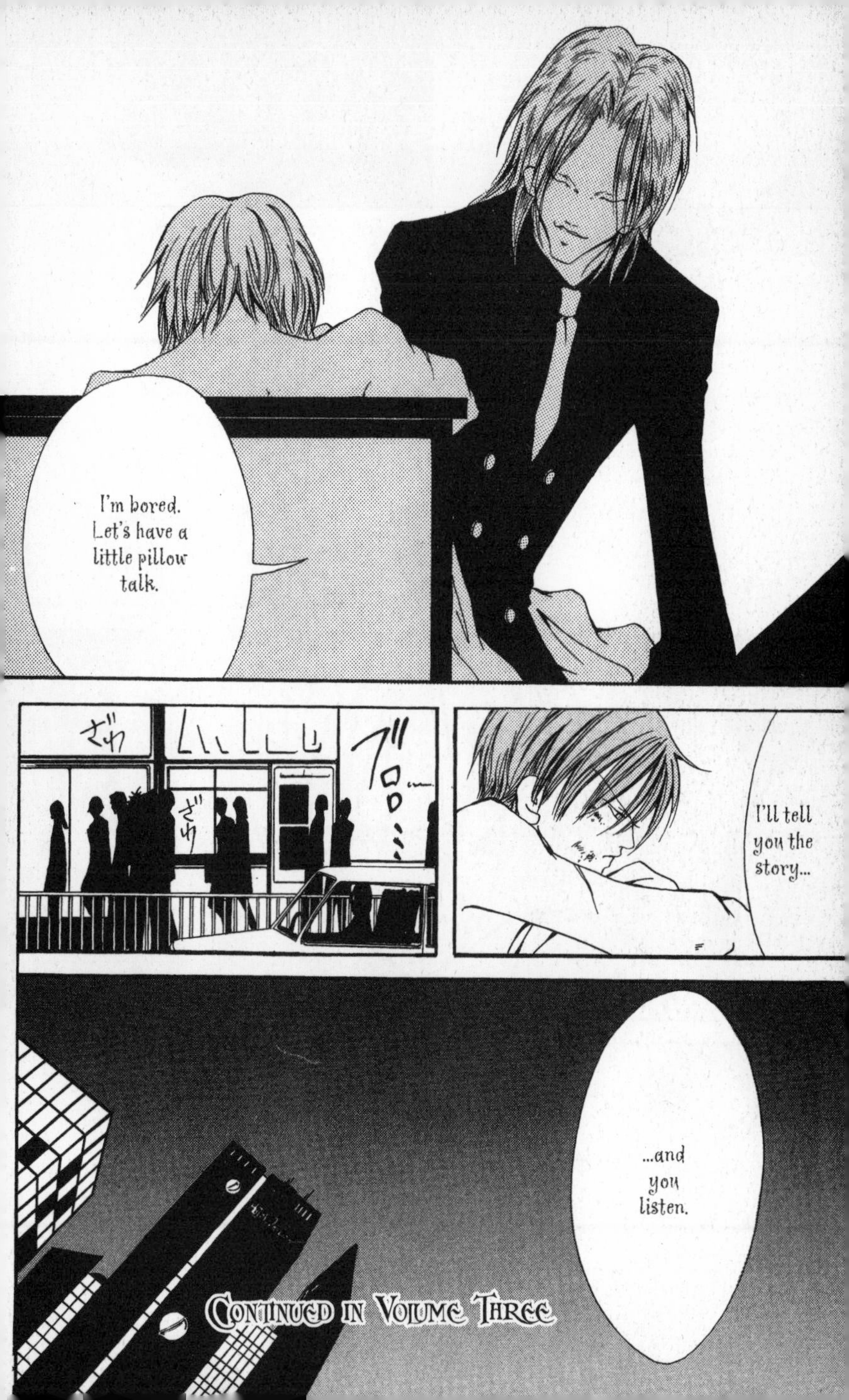
I'm bored. Let's have a little pillow talk.
I'll tell you the story...
ざわ
ブロロ…
ざわ
...and you listen.
Continued in Volume Three

IN THE NEXT INSTALLMENT OF THE
DEMON ORORON SAGA...

HER ATTEMPTS TO PREVENT THE DEATH OF A SINGLE
BOUNTY HUNTER AT THE HANDS OF ORORON CAUSED THE
DEATH OF SO MANY MORE. IS THERE SUCH A THING AS AN
ENTIRELY PEACEFUL WORLD...OR HAS FATE DICTATED THAT
SOME MUST DIE SO THAT OTHERS WILL LIVE?

WITH HER CITY IN RUINS AROUND HER, CHIAKI IS FACED
WITH THE REALITY OF HER OWN DEVASTATING POWERS.

ALSO AVAILABLE FROM TOKYOPOP®

PITA-TEN
PLANET LADDER
PLANETES
PRIEST
PRINCESS AI
PSYCHIC ACADEMY
QUEEN'S KNIGHT, THE
RAGNAROK
RAVE MASTER
REALITY CHECK
REBIRTH
REBOUND
REMOTE
RISING STARS OF MANGA
SABER MARIONETTE J
SAILOR MOON
SAINT TAIL
SAIYUKI
SAMURAI DEEPER KYO
SAMURAI GIRL REAL BOUT HIGH SCHOOL
SCRYED
SEIKAI TRILOGY, THE
SGT. FROG
SHAOLIN SISTERS
SHIRAHIME-SYO: SNOW GODDESS TALES
SHUTTERBOX
SKULL MAN, THE
SNOW DROP
SORCERER HUNTERS
STONE
SUIKODEN III
SUKI
THREADS OF TIME
TOKYO BABYLON
TOKYO MEW MEW
TOKYO TRIBES
TRAMPS LIKE US
UNDER THE GLASS MOON
VAMPIRE GAME
VISION OF ESCAFLOWNE, THE
WARRIORS OF TAO
WILD ACT
WISH
WORLD OF HARTZ
X-DAY
ZODIAC P.I.

NOVELS

CLAMP SCHOOL PARANORMAL INVESTIGATORS
KARMA CLUB
SAILOR MOON
SLAYERS

ART BOOKS

ART OF CARDCAPTOR SAKURA
ART OF MAGIC KNIGHT RAYEARTH, THE
PEACH: MIWA UEDA ILLUSTRATIONS

ANIME GUIDES

COWBOY BEBOP
GUNDAM TECHNICAL MANUALS
SAILOR MOON SCOUT GUIDES

TOKYOPOP KIDS

STRAY SHEEP

CINE-MANGA™

ALADDIN
CARDCAPTORS
DUEL MASTERS
FAIRLY ODDPARENTS, THE
FAMILY GUY
FINDING NEMO
G.I. JOE SPY TROOPS
GREATEST STARS OF THE NBA
JACKIE CHAN ADVENTURES
JIMMY NEUTRON: BOY GENIUS, THE ADVENTURES OF
KIM POSSIBLE
LILO & STITCH: THE SERIES
LIZZIE MCGUIRE
LIZZIE MCGUIRE MOVIE, THE
MALCOLM IN THE MIDDLE
POWER RANGERS: DINO THUNDER
POWER RANGERS: NINJA STORM
PRINCESS DIARIES 2
RAVE MASTER
SHREK 2
SIMPLE LIFE, THE
SPONGEBOB SQUAREPANTS
SPY KIDS 2
SPY KIDS 3-D: GAME OVER
THAT'S SO RAVEN
TOTALLY SPIES
TRANSFORMERS: ARMADA
TRANSFORMERS: ENERGON
VAN HELSING

**For more
information visit
www.TOKYOPOP.com**

03.30.04T

ALSO AVAILABLE FROM ◎TOKYOPOP®

MANGA

.HACK//LEGEND OF THE TWILIGHT
@LARGE
ABENOBASHI: MAGICAL SHOPPING ARCADE
A.I. LOVE YOU
AI YORI AOSHI
ANGELIC LAYER
ARM OF KANNON
BABY BIRTH
BATTLE ROYALE
BATTLE VIXENS
BRAIN POWERED
BRIGADOON
B'TX
CANDIDATE FOR GODDESS, THE
CARDCAPTOR SAKURA
CARDCAPTOR SAKURA - MASTER OF THE CLOW
CHOBITS
CHRONICLES OF THE CURSED SWORD
CLAMP SCHOOL DETECTIVES
CLOVER
COMIC PARTY
CONFIDENTIAL CONFESSIONS
CORRECTOR YUI
COWBOY BEBOP
COWBOY BEBOP: SHOOTING STAR
CRAZY LOVE STORY
CRESCENT MOON
CROSS
CULDCEPT
CYBORG 009
D•N•ANGEL
DEMON DIARY
DEMON ORORON, THE
DEUS VITAE
DIABOLO
DIGIMON
DIGIMON TAMERS
DIGIMON ZERO TWO
DOLL
DRAGON HUNTER
DRAGON KNIGHTS
DRAGON VOICE
DREAM SAGA
DUKLYON: CLAMP SCHOOL DEFENDERS
EERIE QUEERIE!
ERICA SAKURAZAWA: COLLECTED WORKS
ET CETERA
ETERNITY
EVIL'S RETURN
FAERIES' LANDING
FAKE
FLCL
FLOWER OF THE DEEP SLEEP
FORBIDDEN DANCE
FRUITS BASKET
G GUNDAM

GATEKEEPERS
GETBACKERS
GIRL GOT GAME
GIRLS' EDUCATIONAL CHARTER
GRAVITATION
GTO
GUNDAM BLUE DESTINY
GUNDAM SEED ASTRAY
GUNDAM WING
GUNDAM WING: BATTLEFIELD OF PACIFISTS
GUNDAM WING: ENDLESS WALTZ
GUNDAM WING: THE LAST OUTPOST (G-UNIT)
GUYS' GUIDE TO GIRLS
HANDS OFF!
HAPPY MANIA
HARLEM BEAT
HONEY MUSTARD
I.N.V.U.
IMMORTAL RAIN
INITIAL D
INSTANT TEEN: JUST ADD NUTS
ISLAND
JING: KING OF BANDITS
JING: KING OF BANDITS - TWILIGHT TALES
JULINE
KARE KANO
KILL ME, KISS ME
KINDAICHI CASE FILES, THE
KING OF HELL
KODOCHA: SANA'S STAGE
LAMENT OF THE LAMB
LEGAL DRUG
LEGEND OF CHUN HYANG, THE
LES BIJOUX
LOVE HINA
LUPIN III
LUPIN III: WORLD'S MOST WANTED
MAGIC KNIGHT RAYEARTH I
MAGIC KNIGHT RAYEARTH II
MAHOROMATIC: AUTOMATIC MAIDEN
MAN OF MANY FACES
MARMALADE BOY
MARS
MARS: HORSE WITH NO NAME
MINK
MIRACLE GIRLS
MIYUKI-CHAN IN WONDERLAND
MODEL
MY LOVE
NECK AND NECK
ONE
ONE I LOVE, THE
PARADISE KISS
PARASYTE
PASSION FRUIT
PEACH GIRL
PEACH GIRL: CHANGE OF HEART
PET SHOP OF HORRORS

03.30.04T